SHAKESPEARE'S DARK LADY

Amelia Bassano Lanier:
The Woman Behind
Shakespeare's Plays?

JOHN HUDSON

AMBERLEY

This book is dedicated to the Dark Lady Players

First published 2014

Amberley Publishing
The Hill, Stroud
Gloucestershire, GL5 4EP

www.amberley-books.com

British Library Cataloguing in Publication Data.
A catalogue record for this book is available from the British Library.

ISBN 978 1 4456 2160 9 (hardback)
ISBN 978 1 4456 2166 1 (ebook)

Typeset in 10pt on 12pt Sabon.
Typesetting and Origination by Amberley Publishing.
Printed in the UK.

Praise for *Shakespeare's Dark Lady*

'[Amelia Bassano Lanier] is an amazing character and well worth the study.'
Mark Rylance.

'Controversial and provocative, this well-researched and wide-ranging book represents a legitimate new area for scholarship.'
Dr Catherine M. S. Alexander, Fellow, The Shakespeare Institute, was formerly Secretary of the International Shakespeare Association. She is co-editor with Stanley Wells of *Shakespeare & Race* and *Shakespeare & Sexuality*, editor of *The Cambridge Companion to Shakespeare's Last Plays*, and editor of the Cambridge Shakespeare Library.

'John Hudson's perseverance to tell Amelia's extraordinary story speaks to his commitment to secure her rightful place in theatrical and literary history as well as speaks to his passion to explore and reveal Shakespearean text in its *true* context. Once we see Amelia through John Hudson's eyes, we can never again read "Shakespeare" without seeing Amelia's hand and heart in the plays.'
Professor Ellen Faith Brodie, Director of Theatre at Eastern Connecticut State University.

'This research is absolutely fascinating and supported by a huge amount of documentary evidence.'
Dr William Green was formerly Professor of English Queen's College, CUNY, and is past President of the International Federation for Theatre Research, and Secretary of the American Society for Theatre Research. He is co-editor of *Elizabethan Drama*.

'The circumstances of Amelia's life, the knowledge she could have picked up from them, and aspects of her own writings all fit numerous features of the plays well.'
Dr David Lasocki is a music historian, who previously taught at Indiana University and is the co-author with Roger Prior of the biography *The Bassanos*.

'The case for Amelia Bassano Lanier is as plausible as Shakespeare's.'
Michael Posner, 'Rethinking Shakespeare', *The Queen's Quarterly*, Summer 2008.

'What an amazing story! This meticulous and thoughtful research is groundbreaking. Its "radical reading" suggests that "William Shakespeare" was actually the *nom de plume* of a woman living in Queen Elizabeth's Court. We have to re-think everything we know about Shakespeare.'
Dr Jane Gabin has written two books restoring the reputations of forgotten women writers.

'Marvelous and revolutionary. I read it with awe and reverence and a feeling of real excitement in my guts.'
Vicky McMahon, Lecturer, Drama Department, University of Winnipeg.

'Your scholarship, research and willingness to put it on the line and on its feet makes your efforts rare and totally worthy of applause – it is valuable and exciting.'
Dr Jack Wann is Professor Emeritus and former Chair of Theatre at Northwestern State University. He teaches Shakespeare at the American Academy of Dramatic Arts.

'Through his ample research and scholarly probing of the canon, John Hudson has unearthed fascinating evidence that the poet Amelia Bassano Lanier had a hand in crafting what we know as Shakespeare's plays.'
Professor Andrew B. Harris was formerly Chair of Theatre at Columbia University. He is a playwright and theatre historian.

'These insights could open new and breathtaking performance avenues for professional companies and a multitude of possibilities for academic researchers.'
Professor Kelly Morgan was formerly Chair of Theatre at Case Western Reserve University and is the founder of the Mint Theatre Company.

'Hudson's historical sleuthing and careful speculation make the Lanier theory at least as plausible as most of the others … Well-researched, fascinating and thought-provoking.'
Kirkus Reviews

I always feel something Italian, something Jewish about Shakespeare ... perhaps Englishmen admire him because of that, because it's so unlike them.

Jorge Luis Borges

CONTENTS

Map of Elizabethan London Showing the Theatres

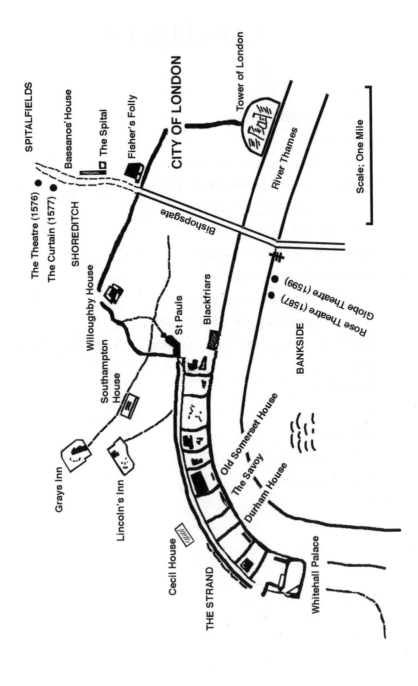

SPITALFIELDS

The Theatre (1576)
The Curtain (1577)
SHOREDITCH

Bassanos' House
The Spital
Fisher's Folly

Willoughby House

Southampton House

Grays Inn

Lincoln's Inn

Cecil House

THE STRAND

St Pauls

Blackfriars

Old Somerset House
The Savoy
Durham House

Whitehall Palace

Bishopsgate

CITY OF LONDON

Tower of London

River Thames

Rose Theatre (1587)
Globe Theatre (1599)

BANKSIDE

Scale: One Mile

Foreword by Michael Posner

I stumbled upon the fertile mind of John Hudson quite by accident four years ago – in an article in an online magazine devoted to Jewish cultural issues. Immediately intrigued, I tracked him down, conducted a phone conversation about his work, and later pitched the story to my editors at the *Globe and Mail* in Toronto.

Despite a kind of reflex scepticism about his core theory – that history's greatest exemplar of English literature was not in fact 'the sweet swan of Avon' but Amelia Bassano, a virtually unknown Marrano Jewess living in East London – they gave me the go-ahead. I guess the idea was so outré that it had humour value.

I confess that I had some sympathy for their viewpoint. After all, while a cottage industry devoted to proving that Shakespeare was not Shakespeare has grown up in recent years – offering up such alternative candidates as Mary Sidney, William Stanley, John Florio, Christopher Marlowe, Sir Francis Bacon, Edward de Vere (the Earl of Oxford) and dozens more – there was a broad consensus at one time that such thinking was at once deeply heretical and seriously misguided.

The anti-Stratfordian discussion thus percolated at the dim margins of literary thought. It was not widely assessed in university lecture halls and, when journalists found something about Shakespeare interesting enough to write about, it typically dealt with some new portrait of the man that had turned up or some new or speculative aspect of his biography.

For the vast Shakespeare community at large – the worlds of academe, publishing, the theatre, tourism, merchandising (a multimillion-dollar annual industry) – there simply was no Shakespeare authorship question to debate. People who thought otherwise must therefore be either half-cocked conspiracy theorists or literary snobs – somehow incapable of believing that a mere country lad from the Midlands with a grade six education could be capable of writing the plays.

That bias has shifted dramatically, nourished in part by the Internet – websites devoted to promoting or assailing the claims of various 'Shakespeare' candidates, a spate of new books, and some new, compelling scholarship. The debate, now fully joined, is at once lively and entertaining.

But even today, I cannot say that John Hudson's remarkable advocacy of the Bassano candidacy is a slam dunk. I believe he would concede the point. His theory is, of course, provocative. It is tantalising. It is highly suggestive. And it is certainly plausible, as plausible, I submit, as any other. But what remains true for

Shakespeare and all the other candidates is also true for Amelia Bassano. For now, there is no definitive smoking gun.

However, what I can say, having spent the last few years diving deeper into the authorship quagmire, is that the likelihood of William Shaksper (as he was known in Stratford) being responsible for the 37 plays, 154 sonnets, and other works of poetry seems increasingly unsustainable. What we can infer about the author from the content of the plays themselves, and from his mastery of dozens of fields of knowledge and several languages, bears no similarity to what we know about the life of the man who was Shakespeare.

And the few certifiable facts that we have about the life of that Shakespeare – his pettiness, his litigiousness, his consuming interest in money and property – seem entirely at odds with the capacious humanist reflected in the authorship of the canon. All the candidacies eventually require a leap of faith, including the Bard's. The so-called biographies that purport to buttress the Stratfordian claim are full of conditional sentences constructed along the lines of 'he surely must have ... it seems likely that ... one can safely assume that ... the probability is ...' Indeed, if you set all the documented facts of his life beside the work he is alleged to have produced, and presented them to a visitor from another planet, a very quizzical eyebrow would doubtless be raised. 'This came from that? You must be kidding. *Ce n'est pas possible.*'

Into this charged arena now comes a suggestion that seems, on its face, no less preposterous. Amelia Bassano Lanier. A woman. A secret Jew. The 'dark lady' of the sonnets. Writing plays that invoke not only the Hebrew language and Jewish holy books, but elaborate, coded allegories that speak to the horrors that Rome visited upon Jewish communities in the Holy Land 1,500 years earlier.

Again, I don't know whether Hudson is right. I do know that when you have finished reading this book, his brilliance will stay with you. And you will never think of William Shakespeare in quite the same way ever again.

Michael Posner, Toronto, August 2013

Introduction

'Shakespeare was superhuman.' That is how the exasperated biographer Samuel Schoenbaum explained how the man from Stratford had managed to write the plays that appeared under his name, without access to any of the skills and knowledge that would normally be required.

It places Shakespeare firmly in the territory of the supernatural, the magical, and the mythic, as a kind of divine figure, a secular deity born in Stratford-upon-Avon. It is time to abandon such bizarre fantasies. Scholarship has uncovered the hands of many playwrights as co-authors on nearly a third of these play scripts – including the hands of Nashe, Fletcher, Wilkins, Kyd, Marlowe, Middleton and Peele. Nonetheless, the identity of the primary author has increasingly and insistently been called into question. A recent survey shows that in the Midlands almost half the adult population no longer accepts that Mr Shakespeare was the main author of these plays. Overall, about a third of the UK population believe that *none* of the usual candidates wrote the plays and that the real primary author still has to be found.[1]

In retrospect it seems that the Shakespearean plays appeared at an unfortunate time. The complex intellectual world view of the Renaissance was ending, and realism, which had begun to emerge by the seventeenth century, insisted that a play should be performed on a proscenium arch stage, as if these were real people, with real emotions, in a slice of life. By the early twentieth century, modernism focused on the surfaces of things as if the surface constituted the primary reality and things could be judged by their looks alone. Seen from these perspectives, Shakespeare's plays appeared simple but financially successful products, and were credited to a straightforward, but financially shrewd, man of the theatre.

Only more recently, with the advent of postmodernism, are we recovering an understanding that works of art, like other aspects of our world, are not 'reality' but complex constructions and simulations, fictional narratives and deceptive appearances, created and performed for particular ideological purposes. Even some of today's best-known epic artworks appear to be one story on the surface, but underneath were intended by the authors as something else entirely. *Battlestar Galactica* was originally intended by its creator, Glen Larson, as a satire of the *Book of Mormon*. The *Harry Potter* series is a straightforward pro-Christian allegory. *Star Trek* was created by Gene Roddenberry in the 1960s as a sociopolitical commentary on the Vietnam War and America's imperial intervention overseas.

So as we delve beneath the surface, and Shakespeare's plays are revealed as the extraordinary constructions that they are – using allegorical and rhetorical techniques from Elizabethan court culture – those hidden layers of meaning, once revealed, demonstrate that the old simple model of the author no longer works. Thus it becomes urgent to rethink our assumptions not just about what these plays are, but about who created them and why.

The Shakespeare story is strange even on its face. Nearly forty plays written in London between 1589 and 1611 do not sink into obscurity or the province of scholars like almost all other sixteenth- or seventeenth-century English plays, but begin to shape the whole of Western culture in a way matched only by the Bible – and even, if Harold Bloom is to be taken at his word, shape our conception of what it means to be human. But the story is more bizarre even than that.

As James Shapiro has traced in his book *Contested Will*, beginning in the eighteenth century an entire cult of 'Bardolatry' develops that treats Shakespeare as almost divine.

It starts in contemporary records, when Ben Jonson claimed metaphorically that Shakespeare came 'like Mercury to charme' the age, and another commendatory verse referred to 'Shakespeare, that nimble *Mercury* thy braine'. Gradually, however, metaphors gave way to more concrete worship of 'the god of our idolatry', as the great Shakespearean actor David Garrick put it in 1769, repurposing the poet's own words.

Yet nobody understands how he can have written the plays. Indeed, it is one of the most remarkable things about Shakespeare scholarship that there is almost nothing about quite how he pulled off this extraordinary feat, but this only serves, in the traditional narrative, to make his achievement more amazing. Perhaps he was directly inspired by God, by 'divine afflatus', as the eighteenth-century editor of Shakespeare, Nicholas Rowe, implied. The nineteenth-century Italian writer Ugo Foscolo called him 'the master of all superhuman geniuses'.[2] As his leading biographer Samuel Schoenbaum put it, in the same tradition, 'There is something incomprehensible about genius. Shakespeare was superhuman.' By the late nineteenth century the plays were being referred to as a 'secular Bible'. There was even a group that formed churches to worship Shakespeare, created hymns to sing to Shakespeare, and renamed one of the days of the week in Shakespeare's honour, along with other great names in the secular humanist canon. In 1799 George Romney depicted Shakespeare's birth as a kind of secular Nativity scene, in which baby William took the place of baby Jesus and Mother Nature is poised to pour her knowledge into him.

Today, 400 years after these plays were written, Shakespeare has become a global multibillion-dollar business. It employs many thousands of Shakespeare professors. Millions of students a year in China are studying *The Merchant of Venice*, and Shakespeare is being studied in primary and secondary schools by half the world's population. A dozen replicas of the open-air Globe Theatre have been built around the world. There are serious debates about whether the age of five is too young to introduce children to Shakespeare. Tens of thousands of people wait in line for three days to get free tickets to Shakespeare in the Park in Manhattan. The Globe Theatre plans to tour its version of *Hamlet* to every single country on the planet. Many productions are not viewed live on stage at all but as an adaptation on a screen, and using technologies that impact the audience perception in extraordinary ways.

Nonetheless, in a world in which we have historically taken many things on trust – that our tap water is drinkable, that our banks are run honestly, or that smoking tobacco makes us sexier – Shakespeare has functioned as a trustworthy icon, whose portrait is even used to brand credit cards. By 2011, according to a survey, Shakespeare had become the single cultural symbol of which those in Britain were most proud,[3] even ahead of the National Trust and the Union Jack. Mark Rylance even claims that Shakespeare has become 'a fundamental part of the English or British psyche'.[4] Just about everyone regards these plays as one of the high points of Western culture – perhaps the highest point – and many thousands of productions are put on around the world.

This is surprising for many reasons. For one thing, in the seventeenth century there seemed nothing special about Shakespeare's plays (other than their publication in a folio). Often when they were performed it was in dramatically shortened versions, sometimes with different endings and with added characters and spectacle. Some of them would not be performed as written for another century. Then, as Jonathan Bate has observed, there was hostile criticism. George Bernard Shaw declared that there was no writer whom he despised as much as Shakespeare. In 1906, Tolstoy wrote an entire hostile essay, which George Orwell summarised as follows: 'Shakespeare is a trivial, shallow writer, with no coherent philosophy, no thoughts or ideas worth bothering about.' Orwell himself agreed that 'Shakespeare is not a thinker … he usually stole his plots from other people … often introducing absurdities and inconsistencies'. Curiously these critical views have only supported the Stratfordian position that the plays were written by a rural lad from Stratford-upon-Avon who could not be expected to write anything better.

But there is a problem. Two problems, actually. First, with every passing day and every additional article that presses the question of what the primary author of these plays would have had to know to write them (and, indeed, the weakness of the refutations offered), Shakespeare becomes a less and less credible candidate for the authorship. And, in a relatively recent development in Shakespeare scholarship, with every day we are learning more about the underlying hidden intellectual content of the plays, in the form of anti-Christian allegories and Jewish materials – which make it equally unlikely that Shakespeare, apparently an orthodox Christian, whether Catholic or Protestant, wrote them.

As for the problem of Shakespeare's knowledge – it has been made much more visible by Roland Emmerich's movie *Anonymous*, an enjoyable but deeply flawed 2011 thriller based on the notion that the Earl of Oxford wrote Shakespeare's plays. Initially the Shakespearean plays were published anonymously. Then they began to appear with the name 'Shakespeare' on the cover. Undoubtedly the actor William Shakespeare was a member of the company that performed the plays, and handed the copies of them to the members of the acting company, who believed that he wrote them. But that does not mean he *actually* did write them. Not only were plays then, like screenplays today, often written by half a dozen individuals whose names were not attached to them, there was also an existing practice of 'underhand brokery' in which actors occasionally fronted plays that they did not write. As over 17,000 pseudonymous literary works make clear, the name on the cover is not necessarily that of the true author. Moreover, although a number of the plays were clearly written collaboratively, that collaboration was structured like no other, as traditional scholars have discovered – so that Mr Shakespeare did not have to be in the same room writing with Fletcher, or Peele, or Middleton. The relevant manuscripts appear to have been passed back and forth.

Now to the second problem, the evidence of Shakespeare's allegory, a common Renaissance technique by which the writer says one thing on the surface but indicates that there is also an underlying story – or more than one – to be uncovered. When these plays were written 400 years ago, upper levels of society were deeply educated in the classics, in Roman and Tudor history, rhetoric, the Bible, in theology and the law, and were familiar with contemporary literature. They would have easily recognised a classical allusion, for instance, to the work of Suetonius, the Roman historian, or a phrase from a psalm. Unlike Shaw or Tolstoy or Orwell, they would have understood something of Shakespeare's allegories. Indeed, they would have been looking for them, in a world where the government's censors were usually in the audience and, metaphorically speaking, the government's torturer a step or two behind them. Each play consists of multiple layers of these allegories, which make up entire plots that exist below the surface. The reason why the secret service had 'state decipherers' sitting in the Elizabethan theatre was precisely because the government knew that playwrights (or 'stage-wrights' as Ben Jonson also called them), were creating materials that challenged an audience to engage in the process of deciphering or 'pick locking' the scene.

In the Renaissance nobody treated characters in plays as if they were 'real'. They were literary abstractions there to serve the purpose of the playwright. The Elizabethan world was one in which, to read a pageant, a play, an entertainment or a portrait correctly, one required 'a mind well versed in late renaissance allegory' to comprehend all the 'riddling emblematics that became all the rage in late Elizabethan England'.[5] But even if the mindsets of audience members were attuned to the role of the 'wiser sort' in discerning allegories, despite the excellent memories of many Elizabethans they would have found it extremely difficult to solve the allegories by simply hearing a couple of afternoon performances.

Today, however, modern audiences know next to nothing about any of this. Shakespeare is now a global product and is performed and read around the world in cultures that have next to no relationship to those audiences for which the plays were first created. For instance, today, thanks to Stanislavski and realism, a focus on the psychology of the characters, and a tendency to treat them as if they are simply representations of individuals, has become the dominant one in modern theatre. The best of those productions are dazzling and brilliantly acted, such as those of the London Globe Theatre, and construct a powerful and seductive surface presentation. Whereas Elizabethan audiences went to 'hear' a play, modern audiences go to 'see' a play: it is a visual rather than an auditory experience.[6] This is especially true for television and movie versions where camera techniques highlight the realism. The result is that an audience has no idea that any other layers of meaning beneath that surface even exist. This is in part due to modern stage and directing techniques, customised costuming, having actors memorise their lines and having the kind of rehearsal period that can be supported by long runs. It has no relation to the 'metatheatrical' Elizabethan stage,[7] on which actors spoke Renaissance English (known as Original Pronunciation), and where there was little rehearsal, where women were played by boys, where actors read their lines from cue scripts, and where a play received typically two or three performances. (At nine days, Middleton's play *Game at Chess*, at the Globe, had the longest run of any show in Tudor or Stuart London.)

Whereas a scholar working on a major edition of a Shakespearean play may require a decade of research or more, a director of a play in the theatre today rarely has more than a few months paid preparation, and the cast typically only a rehearsal period of a few weeks. So, with the exception of a few companies like the Dark Lady Players and Pig Iron, there is simply no time to go into the text very deeply. In any case, the surface text – namely the conflated one created by editors of popular editions – is all that most theatre critics, and most audiences, have any interest in.

In other words, the very way that theatres today perform Shakespeare's plays, as good modernists burnishing the surface story, discourages anyone from looking past that surface to the underlying allegorical meanings that the author intended to be discerned. Theatres that put on the plays in the open air, using 'original practices', or with actors wearing original seventeenth-century lace and reproduction Elizabethan underwear, are just as guilty as those that put on modern versions. Reproducing the material circumstances of how a Shakespearean play was originally performed doesn't change the fact that modern audiences have twenty-first-century world views and terms of reference. To produce Shakespeare's plays today is an exercise in communicating across different cultures: even the jokes that were funny 400 years ago aren't always funny any longer.

While Shakespeare scholarship has done much to uncover some of the deep meanings in the plays, these findings are buried in obscure journals largely inaccessible to an audience and ignored by stage directors. This split in the Shakespeare industry between research and performance would not be found in any commercial business. It takes generally around forty years for a few insights in the world of scholarship to move into performance, and sometimes up to a century.

Yet there is absolutely no reason – other than the critical reasons of organisational inertia, economics, and lack of demand – why academic research should not be translated into stage performance in a matter of months. Perhaps that research simply has not had sufficiently profound implications for performance for anyone to care. Not until now.

It is crucial that we restore Shakespeare's allegories to their original prominence, and it is equally critical that we ignore the temporary fashions of modern stage production and consider Shakespeare's works within the literary frameworks prevalent at the time in which they were written. This is the only context that makes sense; anything else is anachronistic, and will lead us astray. Unfortunately this is not, however, a fashionable point of view in English literature departments. There, one of the latest trends is 'presentism', in which a Shakespearean play is considered purely in terms of what it means to us in the present day, and the historical context is disregarded because in a postmodern world all that supposedly matters is the continuous 'now'.[8]

The Authorship Controversy

The claim that Shakespeare was not the author of the Shakespearean canon has a long history – if not always, admittedly, a distinguished one. It became clear very early that the known biography of the man from Stratford fits very poorly with the specialist areas of knowledge manifested in the plays. Indeed, by the late 1590s, a couple of contemporaries were speculating about the author of the works. The first unequivocal record goes back to Edward Ravenscroft, a seventeenth-century dramatist who claimed in 1687 that 'some[one] anciently conversant with the stage' told him that *Titus Andronicus* had been brought to Shakespeare by a 'private author to be acted'.[9] In 1728, one Captain Goulding claimed that Shakespeare had the assistance of a 'historian' in writing the plays. Similarly, the *Chambers's Edinburgh Journal* of 1852 suggested that Shakespeare 'kept a poet'.[10]

While the academy fiercely supported (and continues to support) Shakespeare as the primary author, a string of independent researchers proposed that the plays had been written by Sir Francis Bacon (theory proposed in 1856), Queen Elizabeth (1857), Sir Walter Raleigh (1877), Christopher Marlowe (1895), or the Earl of Oxford (1920). All of this research has been rightly dismissed by the academy: it is badly argued and factually inaccurate. But the fact that these candidates did not write the plays does not mean that Mr Shakespeare did. Certainly, it may have made it easier for mainstream scholars to cast alternative-author theorists as cranks. But it has done nothing to help them produce more evidence *for* Shakespeare rather than against these other candidates, nor to make convincing arguments as to why many people – among them Charles Dickens, Ralph Waldo Emerson, Mark Twain, Orson Welles, Henry and William James, and Walt Whitman – have declined to believe that William Shakespeare wrote the plays attributed to him. And it does nothing to answer the critical 'access problem', the question of how Shakespeare obtained access to the areas of knowledge demonstrated in these plays.

Perhaps it is not entirely surprisingly that before turning to Shakespeare I had spent much of my professional life working on an analogous problem: creating new paradigms and new industry models in high-tech industries. In other words, I was treating knowledge as created through a social and organisational process. I later began my studies at the Shakespeare Institute at the University of Birmingham, where I wrote a thesis on an experimental allegorical staging of *A Midsummer Night's Dream*. I then returned to New York as Artistic Director of the Dark Lady Players, one of the world's most experimental Shakespeare companies, to try and find a way of taking the insights buried in Shakespearean scholarship and giving them a wider audience through small-scale proof-of-concept demonstration productions.

In this regard I would like to make clear that, while I present a radical reading of Shakespeare's plays in the course of making a case for a particular alternative author, I am often leaning on and extending the work of other Shakespeare scholars. In building on their work, I have leaned on the truism that the only way to urge a group of people who are committed to an existing view of the world to change that view is to oblige them to think about their assumptions. They have to think, that is, to think about their thinking, if they are to be open enough to see the world in new ways. That is what this book is about. It assumes that an open dialogue, based on facts, is the way to establish truth and that just because something is accepted wisdom does not necessarily make it correct. There will be those deeply conservative traditionalists who will insist – due to their own personal biases – that Shakespeare must be white, male and Christian. For those who live in this kind of alternative reality, in an intellectual world sealed off from the factual evidence, this work is unlikely to be persuasive.

Yet, as we shall see, despite their being tamed by so many years of familiarity, the plays are extremely strange and make considerable use of very peculiar areas of unusual knowledge. None of the potential candidates that have been put forward could have written them. So we need to take a fresh look at the evidence and be open to looking in corners that have been neglected in our search for the new candidate. As I hope to show, it is as if our collective Western worldview has prevented us from seeing something that is right in our face, but that has been dismissed without proper consideration.

However, although doubts have been expressed about Mr Shakespeare's authorship for a long time, those doubts have not persuaded the Shakespeare establishment to change their tune. Most professors of English literature continue to believe that the plays were written by William Shakespeare.[11] Yet, as the experience of other industries makes painfully clear, existing experts are quite often wrong, and their models and theories fail to fit the data. This is because their perception of the data is shaped by various biases – social and political processes, inherited cognitive illusions, and explicit financial rewards. These biases include a 'confirmation bias' that skews the information scholars are willing to consider, and 'path dependency' in which an existing approach precludes experts from considering alternatives, because they live within a self-reinforcing information loop. For many years, research on 'groupthink' has documented how this works in homogeneous groups, editing out disparate views and ultimately creating views that are dysfunctional and incorrect. Greater scrutiny is only just beginning to uncover biases and the extent of errors in academic publications generally. It is time for the same scrutiny to be brought to bear on academic research on Shakespeare, where – as in many other instances today – scholars exist in hermetically sealed ideological bubbles which prevent them from encountering anything that might challenge their orthodox opinions.

As Henry James wrote to a friend in 1903, 'I am "a sort of" haunted by the conviction that the divine William is the biggest and most successful fraud ever practiced on a patient world.' Unfortunately, like most entrenched industries, the Shakespeare industry seems to resemble the old cult of Bardolatry, rather than taking a rational approach to investigating evidence. In part, a commitment to the status quo makes it easier to get grants and lucrative positions: announcing that you don't believe Shakespeare wrote Shakespeare will not only fail to secure grants, it will make you unwelcome in English departments. Dr Ros Barber, for instance, recently described the subject as 'completely taboo' since if she wanted to do serious research on the subject it was made clear to her that '[she] would not be allowed to research it at a British university at all'.[12]

Nonetheless, a rational approach to the evidence is necessary. As always, the answers depend on the questions one chooses to ask. To solve the authorship puzzle, the first thing required is the openness to see something hitherto almost unseen, or rejected. In art criticism, as recently as half a century ago, judgements about the authenticity or the attribution of a painting were often made by appealing to experts' opinions. They were not only invariably biased, but also made their judgement based on subjective experience rather than upon data in an assessment that could be independently replicated – for example taking into account such highly technical factors as the age and composition of the paint, the origin of brush hairs left in the paint, the date of the canvas and so on.

In art criticism at least, this is fortunately no longer the case. Yet with a few exceptions, literary criticism today is in this regard frequently stuck where art criticism was in the 1950s. If it is now accepted that no expert can simply look at a painting in order to determine that it is a genuine Pollock or Rembrandt, similarly, it should also be accepted that nobody, however expert, can simply look at a piece of verse and determine immediately whether or not it was created by the writer of the Shakespearean plays – a writer who used a great many different compositional styles. Indeed, there are many examples of people who have tried to make such judgements and who have been proved wrong. These include the editors of the 1663 Folio, who added in various extra plays, at least five of which are now thought not to be by the Shakespearean author, and also T. S. Eliot, who wrote in 1927 that it seemed incredible that Shakespeare had any hand in *Titus Andronicus* at all. Judgments based upon prejudice or an impression of style are wholly insufficient to answer such a complex question accurately. Nor are applications of computer-based techniques which are limited to stylistic issues sufficient. Instead it needs to be answered based on a large number of highly technical grounds including compositional elements, structures, philology, use of sources, rare words, and precise comparisons to equivalent samples – some of the criteria employed into this book.

The main reason that *Salve Deus*, Amelia Lanier's poetry collection, has not been widely appreciated to be by the same writer as the Shakespearean plays is that critics have jumped to make simplistic stylistic judgements, rather than engaging in detailed and time-consuming technical analysis (see Appendix 1). Solving the authorship puzzle also means, as we shall see, letting go of some of our political, racist and sexist assumptions. It means opening up to the possibility that the primary author was a radical, feminist, dark-skinned Jewish woman – Lanier (see Appendix 2) was the first woman in England to publish a volume of original poetry, and was claimed first by A. L. Rowse in the 1970s as the so-called 'dark lady' of the sonnets (see Appendix 3). Entrenched structures of anti-Semitism, racism and sexism immediately confront such a proposition.

It is also the case that few people are well equipped to enter the conversation because of the specific skills it requires. Even if people possess the technical skills they may not be able to reflect critically on the methodological issues involved. And even if they can do both, then the forums easily available to them, such as the academic journals, have gatekeepers who favour discussions of technical issues rather than considering broad and interdisciplinary perspectives. The mass media also lacks the capacity for handling such nuanced and complex material. Conservative institutions have curatorial and financial interests that favour entrenched existing knowledge rather than new paradigms. Indeed the conservatism in the Academy favours a process of incremental growth in knowledge, and anything that transgresses this norm simply does not fit their evaluation processes. Academics may occasionally stray into such speculative territory in private after-dinner conversation, but not in the execution of their formal professional responsibilities. Normal academic frames of reception are not capacious enough to digest an entire new model. As for other stakeholders – such as theatres – they are not equipped to conduct such an evaluation, and do not to see it as their function to do so, but rather follow whatever lead is set by the Academy.

It is sometimes said that Shakespeare is a kind of Rorschach inkblot, on to which one can project anything, and in which evidence can be found for any position. Three points need to be made in response. First, although lack of knowledge has prevented many practitioners from applying it, it has become increasingly obvious that a historicist approach – one that takes into account the historical context in which literary works were created – is preferred.

At the time these plays were crafted, plays and literary works were written in order to convey coherent systems of meaning intended by their authors, challenging local audiences, who shared the author's world view, to discover them. Indeed, the dominance over a long period of Practical Criticism and New Criticism, both of which lacked a historicist approach, is one of the reasons why the Shakespearean plays have not been fully understood. They were attractive doctrines, because very few Shakespeare scholars had (or have) the necessary training in the Bible, in the classics and in Roman history that make up the very core of the Elizabethan world view. This is why, even in recent years, only a tiny number of Shakespeare scholars have paid any attention to the religious content of the plays at all. Lacking the training to see it, some have denied that such content even exists. According to the 'presentist' world view of English departments that strive to be relevant to contemporary life, unless something is having an obvious impact on people today, it might as well not be there at all.

Then there is the matter of bias. Whereas the leadership of the Oxfordian movement, for instance, includes a descendant of the 17th Earl of Oxford hoping to show the achievements of his ancestor, and whereas the Stratfordian movement has long been led by officials of the Shakespeare Birthplace Trust defending their tourist traffic, I had no vested interests in beginning this investigation. I am not a descendant of Amelia Bassano Lanier. Nor am I a Jewish woman of colour. I did not investigate the data in pursuit of a predetermined outcome or to defend an entrenched position. Amelia was a little-known poet who emerged out of this analysis, and even the portrait that I have suggested may be of her requires much more research (see Appendix 4).

Without better documentation we can aim not at the certainty of truth but merely at identifying the most probable candidate. This led physics professor Peter Sturrock to create a do-it-yourself book, *AKA Shakespeare: A Scientific Approach to the Authorship Question*, in which twenty-five areas of evidence are outlined and the reader is asked to estimate the level of probability of each. It is strange that Shakespeare scholars make such excessive claims for the certainty of their orthodox case. Stanley Wells and Paul Edmondson's *Shakespeare Bites Back*, written in response to the Emmerich movie, is a polemic in support of the Stratford-upon-Avon tourist industry.

The same writers edited *Shakespeare Beyond Doubt: Evidence, Argument, Controversy*, which claims a certainty 'beyond doubt' that simply cannot be justified, as with any case that rests upon hearsay, inference and assessment of probabilities. For one thing, although the various contributors to this book refer to there being eighty different authorship candidates, and examine and dismiss quite a number of them, like other academics who claim to have surveyed this field they have a critical blind spot. They do not even mention Amelia Bassano Lanier as an authorship candidate, let alone objectively review the case for her. This is despite the fact that her case is summarised on the website of the Shakespearean

Authorship Trust; that the peer-reviewed article 'Amelia Bassano Lanier: A New Paradigm' appeared in a special issue of *The Oxfordian*, covering the major authorship candidates, in 2009; and that the announcement of her as a new authorship candidate was made at an open lecture at the Smithsonian some years before that as part of the Washington Shakespeare Festival. It is also despite major cover stories on the research – listed in the World Shakespeare Bibliography – by Michael Posner: 'Rethinking Shakespeare,' in *The Queen's Quarterly* (summer 2008) and 'Unmasking Shakespeare' in *Reform Judaism* (summer 2010), as well as an article 'Was Shakespeare a Woman?' in the Canadian paper *The Globe and Mail* (15 January 2010). Through a regrettable oversight Wells and Edmondson, and their contributors, completely ignored this evidence: this is 'groupthink' writ large.

The present book, on the other hand, contains the same kind of careful factual analysis done by competent management consultants advising a Fortune 500 company. The methodologies used are transparent and can be replicated. The details of the analysis are laid out for anyone to examine, and to refute if they wish. Finally the fact that people have drawn very different conclusions from the data does not mean that Shakespeare can be used *legitimately* to prove anything. It means that people have used the data to attempt to support different propositions – in this instance eighty different authorship cases – but most are extremely poorly argued.

By examining their arguments, their logic, their assumptions, and their treatment of the data, it becomes possible for the reader to reject the faulty cases, and to identify the one for which the arguments are sound and which has the greater probability of being correct. It is my hope that the reader will indeed take the time to review the evidence for all the major candidates – summarised in this book – and compare it to the case for Amelia, in order to draw their own conclusions, whatever those may be. My own comparisons are summarised in the Knowledge Map table in Chapter 10. Unlike other authorship theories, which are invariably rooted in some kind of conspiracy theory, the present approach assumes nothing more untoward than the normal literary processes of writing for the Elizabethan and Jacobean stage.

The stakes are high. If this work proves correct, then as *Library Journal* put it, in reviewing Jacobson's fictionalised presentation of the research, it 'could change the history of the written word forever'.[13] However, over the last few hundred years Shakespeare has been politicised, so it is essentially a territory for a power struggle about who gets to define their version of what Shakespeare is. That conflict starts in the entertainment industry, where different theatres are in competition to produce a version of Shakespeare that generates box office returns. The same political process has been responsible for turning the satirical cartoon in the First Folio – the only authentic record – into a whole range of romanticised paintings and engravings for which there is no historical evidence whatsoever. They are the distant precursor of modern North American representations of the Bard in the *Kill Shakespeare* comic books as a virile, sexualised action hero.[14]

Because of this 'mythologisation', and because the case of Amelia as an authorship candidate carries dimensions of sexism, racism and anti-Semitism, regrettably facts alone are not enough to make people change their minds. Indeed a focus on the facts is not the only possible view of the world. When Theseus and Hippolyta debate the nature of allegory in *A Midsummer Night's Dream*, the data-driven view that Theseus expresses is what Dante referred to as the Allegory of Poets, namely that the surfaces of stories are not real, and we need to look beneath the surface to discover objective reality. Hippolyta's view (in contrast with that of Theseus) reflects Dante's Allegory of the Theologians, namely that facts do not exist, reality is totally subjective and that a fantastic story, however wondrous, becomes reality if repeated enough times.[15]

As the playwright puts it, 'the story of the night told over' (5.1.23) will transfigure people's minds and become 'something of great constancy; / But howsoever, strange and admirable' (5.1.26–7). The conflict between these two epistemologies, between postmodernists and fundamentalists, lies at the heart of the social divisions in American, and possibly global, politics. As a member of the Bush administration, echoing Hippolyta, told the *New York Times* in 2004, 'we create our own reality' through multiple repetitions of the same stories. This is the same epistemological perspective that Stratfordians have traditionally adopted. Their 'rags to riches' story of the ordinary country lad who goes to the big city and, almost supernaturally, becomes transformed into the world's greatest playwright is indeed a fascinating – though not a data-driven and therefore not a true – story.

In this book, I, like Theseus, adopt the opposite, 'reality-based', approach – the idea that there is an objective factual reality and that it can be independently determined by judicious investigation. As an alternative to the extreme and, as we will see, rather bizarre ideological positions adopted both by Stratfordians and by Oxfordians, here instead I put forward a middle ground. In conducting my examination, I have employed three distinct kinds of data-driven approaches: the argument from biography, showing that Amelia was in all the right places at the right times to possess the knowledge and networks implied by the plays, including their concealed religious allegories; the argument from detailed technical characteristics of her poetry and its compatibility with the plays; and the competitive argument, showing that other candidates are not plausible.

We begin, however, by considering the background in Elizabethan London, the context in which the plays and poems were written, and the theatrics of everyday life at the Elizabethan court. This was far more theatrically sophisticated than anything shown in the public playhouses until the advent of Shakespeare's work, and is a major clue to the context that shaped the mind behind these plays. This book will range widely over a number of controversial areas. However my hope in doing so is that, in the words of Dr Catherine Alexander, this book will establish 'a legitimate new area for scholarship', which will be of interest to anyone interested in issues of religion, race and gender.

1

Elizabethan London:
City, Court and Theatre

In the next chapters we will examine the extraordinary knowledge possessed by the major author of the Shakespearean works and the extent to which this is matched by the man from Stratford and other claimants. We will then evaluate the fit of a new candidate, Amelia Bassano Lanier. However, to establish the background, it is important to reflect on the character of Elizabethan London as an early modern city – one in which the entire government and the court operated as a kind of theatre without walls, and in which courtiers were 'dissemblers', or actors, performing roles. We know that the early history plays in particular show special knowledge of both the court, and of Tudor family history. So the nature of court life is a good starting point, since Amelia Bassano's relationship with certain key individuals at court, including Lord Willoughby, Countess Susan Bertie, and Lord Hunsdon, gave her unusual insight into the stagecraft that permeated court affairs. Reflecting the sequence of illustrations in this book, we begin with a perspective on London itself, then focus on the government and the court, and then go even deeper to identify some key individuals.

Elizabethan London was a crowded, hectic city of about 200,000 inhabitants, compressed into a tiny area stretching along the river from the power centre of Westminster Abbey and Whitehall Palace in the west to St Paul's and the Tower of London in the east. The Strand was the city's luxury district of goldsmiths, jewellers and clockmakers, and this was where the greatest nobles had their mansions, with gardens running down to the river. The Thames was the main route through the centre of the city, populated by fleets of boats, including water taxis that would take you from one side to the other. This saved the need to use London Bridge, decorated as it was with dozens of black, boiled heads of traitors hanging on spears, which can be seen sticking out from the roof of the gatehouse in Claes Visscher's famous engraving. Facing St Pauls Cathedral was Bankside, South London's entertainment district, offering bear-baiting, numerous brothels and the Rose Theatre. The other popular entertainment district, Shoreditch, with its two purpose-built theatres, the Curtain and the Theatre (each with the capacity of a modern Broadway theatre), lay north of the City walls. These theatres were in some ways the predecessor of today's mass media – places in which plays by local companies, at least those that had passed the censors, could offer an alternative reality to the corporate state theatre of pageantry and church sermons.

Today, the nearest we can get to a street in pre-industrial London might be a bazaar in the more remote parts of Asia. The streets were stinking and slippery, with not only horse droppings underfoot but also the refuse of pigs and goats who wandered down the streets, and the contents of chamber pots, thrown out of the windows of nearby houses onto those below. The streets were packed with people, with carts, men on horses, large crowds of boys playing football, musicians, contortionists, acrobats, female impersonators, dwarfs, giants, men with talking chickens, people selling everything imaginable in tiny quantities, butchers slaughtering animals in the street, and stalls similar to those found today at country fairs. Every street swarmed with beggars, lunatics, pedlars and prostitutes, shouting, jostling and trying to get each other's attention. The theatrical pretences of court life were mirrored, in a less glamorous form, on the streets. In addition to commonplace inhabitants, the street was populated with 'Abraham men' who pretended to have mental illness, 'Whipjacks' who pretended to have lost everything at sea, 'Counterfeit Cranks' who feigned epilepsy, 'Walking Mortes' who pretended to be widows, and a whole rowdy rabble of amputees, 'conycatchers' and confidence tricksters. In Elizabethan London, a fabulously wealthy elite lived cheek by jowl with the desperately poor, who were kept in their place through a mixture of religion, propaganda, threats of torture and state theatrics.

Courtiers lived on a thousand promises and a hundred hopes. In his private diary, the *Commentarius Solutus*, Sir Francis Bacon records his manipulative plotting to make acquaintance with influential nobles, including what one should say to them, and how to 'insinuate' oneself into their privy concerns. Courtiers only succeeded in life by creating an appropriate presentation of self, which covered everything from allowing Her Majesty to win at cards to making declarations of love. At the pageant for the new Queen's Champion in 1590, the Earl of Essex wore black mourning clothes to symbolise his fall from the queen's favour. When another expert gamester, Sir George Carey, needed to return to London for private reasons, he diplomatically announced that he was motivated to return by his desire to see Her Majesty. Similarly Frances Carew, being advised by Raleigh that the queen believed he was longing to see her, was able to use this inside information to make an appropriately 'spontaneous' appearance.

As Puttenham wrote in *The Art of English Poesie*, the 'profession of a very courtier' was 'in plain terms to be able to dissemble'. For the courtier, 'in any matter of importance his wordes and his meaning very seldom meete', so the use of allegory, 'the figure of faire semblant', was essential. That was why this particular rhetorical form was even known as 'the courtier', because it enabled men to 'speake otherwise than we think'. Puttenham claims that without it, men cannot 'thrive and prosper' – 'not onlie every common courtier but also the gravest counsellor'. Similarly, when one of the characters in Lyly's *Sapho and Phao* naively asks, 'Why, do you think in Court any use to dissemble?' the reply is that it is necessary to live (see Appendix 6).

It is this climate of courtly stage management and calculated dissembling that is reproduced in the Shakespearean plays. Most notably in *Richard III*, the successful courtier is compared to an actor who will have 'enforced smiles' at his service like a 'deep tragedian', and woe to those who attempt to distinguish a man's true intentions from their 'outward show', which never 'jumpeth with the heart' (2.1.7–12). The entire play is a demonstration of Richard's success as a courtier by means of his successful dissembling, or acting. This is why he is able to wet his cheek with 'artificial tears', and why Henry VI acknowledges him as an actor like the famous Roman actor Roscius: 'what scene of death hath Roscius now to act' (*Henry VI, Part 3*, 5.6.10). His follower Lord Buckingham packs his own adherents into a crowd shouting for the new king, and in a blatantly stage-managed play-within-the-play, Richard contrives to appear supported by two clergy who are his 'props of virtue' (3.7.95), acting both as theatrical props as well as physical supports. Such behaviour by fictional courtiers in the Shakespearean plays ultimately draws on first-hand observation of the Elizabethan court, where the entire organisational culture assumed that the good courtier, like the good poet 'ought to dissemble his art'.[1]

From the very beginning of her reign the queen had commenced what was to be a forty-five-year exercise in propaganda. She had toured through London in her litter, and talked to the common people with 'goodly wit' – carefully going only to those locations where there were no 'troubles and disturbances'. This was no casual tour. A kind of reporter, who wrote a government pamphlet – *The Queen's Majesty's Passing Through the City of London to Westminster* – collected all her remarks. He wrote that the city had become a stage on which was displayed the wonderful spectacle of a noble-hearted princess. In fact, his report was largely fiction. In Cheapside, where the painters went on strike, he describes freshly painted signs praising the queen, which did not actually exist.

Other events were spectacles deliberately staged by the government as pieces of glittering stagecraft (see Appendix 6). After all, as the Frenchman Boiastuau put it, the art of governing was *The Theetor of the World*. Queen Elizabeth would freely tell people that 'we princes are set on stages in sight of all the world', and that she expected to be treated with full theatrical glamour. 'God hath written out for us and appointed all the parts we are to play', as Sir Walter Raleigh liked to observe. So this theatre without walls was simply best practice. As John Hayward wrote in his *Certain Yeres of Queen Elizabeth's Raigne* (1636), 'In pompous ceremonies a secret of government doth much consist, for that the people are naturally both taken and held with exterior show.' We can see some of this 'show' in Robert Peake's painting of Elizabeth being carried in procession by her courtiers, and it is even clear in the engraving of that painting done by George Vertue.

After the defeat of the Spanish Armada, the queen visited Tilbury. Referring to that visit, James Aske wrote his *Elizabetha Triumphans* in 1588, praising her for her visit to the troops. The government released a batch of propaganda of its own, including a letter supposedly from a Spanish well-wisher. Of course, it had actually been written by Secretary of State Lord Burghley in his own hand, describing how the people celebrated by bringing a 'great number of Banners, Streamers and Ensigns' into St Paul's Courtyard by the cathedral. Then some while later, in November, there was the actual formal celebration, which, as the great early travel writer Richard Hakluyt says, involved 'the Queen's Majesty imitating the ancient Romans;' she 'rode into London in triumph,' 'in robes of triumph' and 'in a triumphant chariot'. Not content with a real triumph, however, the court poets set about creating additional propaganda. One even published a collection of praises called *Triumphalia de Victories Elisabethae*, which was most notable for its accounts of a non-existent monument on the sea-shore and a non-existent water triumph in which the queen supposedly sailed up the Thames. The account must have made a huge impression on the gullible populace, as was the intention. As one contemporary account put it, the whole of the city of London was nothing more than 'a stage wherein was shewed the wonderful Spectacle of a noble hearted Princess'.[2]

Like the Caesars, Elizabeth practiced government as a kind of theatre without walls. Better to govern by spinning false webs of illusion to deceive and pacify, rather than risk rebellion. Was this why Lodowick Lloyd called her *Sidanen*, Welsh for the 'silken one'? Did he, too, recognise that she was a spider spinning her colossal web?

Part of that web was the royal theatre company The Queen's Men, founded by the head of the secret service, which performed plays commissioned by the government. Another part was the Church of England. The Church was a way of communicating to the people every Sunday through the pulpits of England – the distant predecessor of presidential radio broadcasts. That was why Elizabeth said clergymen did not need to be scholars – they merely had to be able to read aloud the government-produced sermons on subjects like 'obedience to rulers and magistrates', which were produced for their services.

At the centre of it all was the court itself, a fascinating world of courtiers that continues to be memorialised today in movies, television series and other media. To understand the life of Amelia Bassano, we need to situate her in this web of relationships at court, and we need also to examine the lives of the men and women she lived among, who profoundly influenced her education and her development.

The courtiers at Elizabeth's court included many whose names are still familiar to us today: the Earl of Southampton, that young and brilliant courtier with long red hair; the explorers Sir Francis Drake and Sir Walter Raleigh; and the stylish Edward de Vere, Earl of Oxford, wearing the latest Italian fashions and begging for court appointments in his thick rural accent, and when not in Greenwich practicing necromancy and pederasty. There were great ladies such as Philip Sidney's sister Mary, who had become Countess of Pembroke. She was known for her literary salon, her Christian piety, her affairs with men like Fulke Greville and Robert Cecil, and unspeakable sexual interest in her stallions. As John Aubrey puts it, 'She was very salacious, and she had a Contrivance that in the Spring of the yeare, when the Stallions were to leape the Mares, they were to be brought before such a part of the house, where she had a vidette (a hole to peep out at) to looke on them and please herselfe with their Sport.' Rather less salacious was Margaret, Countess of Cumberland, the richest woman in England, who spent much of her life settling her complex divorce from the earl, who was a well-known adventurer and explorer. There were secret service agents of various kinds, such as the queen's astrologer and magician Dr John Dee, the owner of the country's largest library, whose secret service number 007 would later be adopted by James Bond. Another one was Dr Lopez, a Marrano (or Converso) Jew, who was the royal physician and perhaps also a spy for his native Portugal. He would be executed on a trumped-up charge of attempting to poison the queen.

There were also less colourful characters who will be important to our story, such as Peregrine Bertie – the Lord Willoughby and England's most famous general. Lord Willoughby, a well-known amateur astronomer, had been an ambassador to Denmark and had later become Commander-in-Chief of the English forces in the Low Countries. When in London, he lived at his mansion Willoughby House, just outside the northern wall of the City, where the Barbican development is today. The name of the mansion is perpetuated on one of the tower blocks. As Thomas Pennant records in his *Some Account of London* of 1791, this mansion was 'of a great size' and had originally been a Roman watchtower. The site was later granted to the Earl of Suffolk and rebuilt under the name of the Base-Court.

This was also the London home of Lord Willoughby's sister Countess Susan Bertie after her husband the Earl of Kent died unexpectedly after only one year of marriage – until her remarriage a decade later, when she was in her late twenties. It was also the London home of their mother Catherine, Duchess of Suffolk, who was well known for her learning, her opposition to Catholicism and her interest in the Bible – she had even belonged to the Bible study group at court run by one of Henry's wives, and her library included several Bible translations.

Although the court was full of able men, the governing body – the Privy Council – was rather small. On taking the throne, Elizabeth had established her style of government and determined those upon whom she would rely. Elizabeth's first action had been to appoint her Secretary of State, William Cecil (later Lord Burghley), who would serve her for the next forty years. Together with Cecil, she determined that she would have a council of no more than twenty, and that they would be comprised of three groups with whom she needed to work closely. One group would be the ancient nobility, who naturally had a significant investment in maintaining the commonwealth. Another group would be the new blood, reflecting her personal loyalties and interests. The third group would be those with long experience of governance under her predecessors. Elizabeth appointed seven peers, most of whom had already held public offices. She added nine new men, including Cecil and Sir Nicholas Bacon, and four experienced commoners such as the diplomat Sir Thomas Wooton. To many of these men she give her own private nicknames, like 'Eyes' (Leicester), 'Lids' (Hatton), 'Sir Sprite' or 'Leviathan' (Burghley) or 'the Moor' (Walsingham). As her reign progressed, the queen concentrated all the serious titles and honours in a few hands instead of making them widely available to the whole nobility. Able men like Francis Bacon and even Robert Cecil went begging while Elizabeth piled honour upon honour in the hands of eight men – eight, out of a peerage of sixty-eight! And when she occasionally did give an especially able and handsome young courtier like the Earl of Essex an important government position, she would look over his shoulder for every decision, refuse to delegate, and generally make it impossible for him to exercise his authority.

These qualities and habits, in tandem with the queen's remarkable durability – her reign was more than twice as long as the average of her seven predecessors – generated a greater and greater degree of discontent in the court, but the queen was deaf to it. None of the nobles in their late twenties were being appointed to the Privy Council. Even lord lieutenants' positions went unfilled: over half the counties had no governor. Not only had her favouritism concentrated power in a few hands, the dissatisfactions and competition it engendered had also led to the development of two factions at court: on one side was a group of 'jumped-up book-men' led by Lord Burghley and his son Robert Cecil. On the other were men led by the Earl of Essex, who combined aristocratic values and tradition in domestic affairs with an aggressive approach to defence and foreign policy.

Now we come to a man who is in many ways the linchpin of our story. One of the lesser-known members of the Privy Council was Henry Carey, Lord Hunsdon – the queen's cousin, and rumoured to be the illegitimate son of Henry VIII and Mary, 'the other Boleyn girl', which Mary's biographer thinks is a 'high probability'.[3]

The queen was very close to his sister, Lady Catherine Carey Knollys, who was made a Lady of the Bedchamber. Her husband, Sir Francis Knollys, was made Vice Chamberlain of the Household and Captain of the Halberdiers, an infantry division of the English army. Their daughter, Lettice Knollys, would marry the queen's favourite, the Earl of Leicester. This small group of 'near and dear ladies' of the bedchamber were Her Majesty's friends and companions, and could exercise some patronage, although they 'never once durst meddle' in state affairs. Three other Boleyn relatives were also given appointments – Sir Richard Sackville as Under Treasurer of the Exchequer, John Fortesque as Master of the Wardrobe (who brought the queen's clothes to her ladies-in-waiting, who helped her dress), and John Ashley as Master of the Jewel House. Ashley's wife Catherine was appointed Mistress of the Robes and Chief Gentlewoman of the Chamber. Several of these offices concerned a central feature of the queen's performance – namely the costumes that she wore. As for Lord Hunsdon's daughter Katherine, the *Dictionary of National Biography* describes her as 'the Queen's most intimate female companion' and notes, very significantly, that the Careys in general were 'treated as members of the extended royal family'.

If Elizabeth was the charismatic leader of the court, and the leading actor in its theatrics, then it was Lord Hunsdon who, behind the scenes, was the chief dramaturg, responsible for all court performances and ceremonies both formal and informal – as well as for regulating the public playhouses.

Lord Hunsdon was therefore the senior member of the powerful and well-connected Boleyn faction. Although her Boleyn relatives were some of Elizabeth's closest kin, she decided to test out Henry Carey in other offices before inviting him to join the council, which did not happen until 1561. She did, however, make him a peer – Baron Hunsdon – in time for her coronation, and granted him £4,000 a year, as well as the Manor of Hunsdon. However, she would make him work hard for every penny – and on one occasion when he dared delay in reporting to her, she yelled and screamed abuse at him, as she would any other official who had displeased her.

There was, however, a disadvantage to his close Boleyn connection. The queen persisted in what one might call government by flirtation. To get anything done, a courtier had to go through a rigmarole of romantic love. It was absurd: the ability of a twenty-year-old courtier to flirt with the elderly queen should not, one assumes, determine government policy. Nevertheless, so it was. Lord Hunsdon therefore, was therefore at a disadvantage; he was precluded as her half-brother, as well as by his age, from participating in such romantic games.

Yet Elizabeth gave him a long succession of offices and responsibilities, including ambassadorial responsibilities in witnessing the signing of the Treaty of Troyes (1564), in dealing with Henry of Navarre, and especially in dealing with Scotland. She gave him several judgeships, several generalships, and the key position of being Lord Chamberlain – responsible for everything that took place 'upstairs' in the 'chamber' at court, most notably the court entertainment. The queen trusted him – just as long as he obeyed her – and after his victory over the rebel Leonard Dacre, she had expressed her pleasure that her half-brother had been appointed by God to be the instrument of her glory. Lord Hunsdon continued in his role as a prominent Tudor statesman, in which he played important military, legal and diplomatic roles almost without interruption, in a career at court which would span fifty-three years – longer even than that of Lord Burghley.

Hunsdon had no university education, nor formal legal training, but he had been well educated in a Cistercian monastery, and tutored by the French poet Nicholas Bourdon. Both Lord Hunsdon's mother Mary Boleyn, as well as his aunt Anne Boleyn (whose ward he had been from the age of two – presumably until he was ten years old, at the time of Anne's execution in 1536), had been educated at the French court, and knew the value of a French courtly education. Bourdon had been a serious tutor (he chose to have his portrait painted holding a pen). He was a friend of Erasmus, Rabelais and Clement Marot, one of the great French poets of the Renaissance, and he made sure that the young Henry Carey was educated in their works. Carey could hold his own with the men of both universities – and would prove it when he was made High Steward of Oxford and Recorder of Cambridge. Like many other noble lords, he was a member of Gray's Inn, which was both the professional and the training centre for the legal profession. Although he was first and foremost a general, a man of action, his cultural interests were wide, and he was a generous patron of the arts. Like Athena, he wore both the sword and the laurel crown.

He divided his time between Somerset House, and his official residence at the castle of Berwick-on-Tweed on the Scottish border, where he was Warden of the Marches, and to which he travelled up the coast in a royal navy vessel. But he was also constantly travelling through the Midlands after he became a judge of the forested Eyre south of the River Trent, the 'smug and silver Trent' (*Henry IV, Part 1*), sometimes visiting his country estates, including his land in Derbyshire, his stewardship in Middlesbrough, and the manor of Conisbrough Castle, near Doncaster in Yorkshire. Conisbrough had become a great castle in the twelfth century, although it had fallen into disrepair by 1540. It was, nevertheless, still liveable; it was a castle of many towers on a bed of stone. When he was in London, Lord Hunsdon lived in the great royal palace Old Somerset House on the Strand, the former residence of Elizabeth herself. He was married, but it was not an intimate relationship. Once he had become the Head Keeper of Hyde Park, and so entitled to its mansion, he gave this park mansion to Lady Anne as her separate residence, after which he might do as he wished.

This rather important man is important to us because, somewhere around 1582, he appears to have made what may seem to us today a rather unsavoury deal with the court recorder consort, the Bassanos, who as court musicians were under his control. He would extend them his protection at court and they would supply him with a mistress – a young Italian mistress. In Venice, after all, the intellectual courtesan, the *cortigiana onesta*, or 'honest courtesan', was a recognised profession. Such women were known for their knowledge of literature, their wit, and their skill at music as well as in the bedchamber. The role required knowledge of several languages, the classics, and fashion – as well as a sexual imagination strong enough for the engaged re-enactment of famous mythological rape scenes such as Leda and the Swan. The best practitioners could sleep with kings and make a fortune, while writing volumes of poetry in their spare time and effectively enjoying the single life.

Thus it was that around that time, at the age of fifty-six, Lord Hunsdon acquired a dark-skinned, thirteen-year-old mistress: Amelia Bassano. Brilliant, musical, multilingual and a highly ambitious poet, she would live with him for the next ten years, during which time he would love her and treat her well. Her fluent Italian made up for his lack of sparkling witty conversation, and since Her Majesty took to her and treated her kindly, having a young attractive woman on his arm strengthened Hunsdon's power at court, so long as he was not too blatant about it. There was of course no question of him marrying her: he had a wife already. But for as long as it lasted, it was an arrangement from which everyone benefited.

By the 1590s, Lord Hunsdon was one of the most influential men in the country. As can still be seen from various engravings, his palace, Old Somerset House, one of the royal palaces on the Strand, was in the most fashionable district, next to Lord Burghley's mansion and opposite that of Sir Water Raleigh. As was the case with many military and political leaders, he was 'very choleric' – one of the four sources of character recognised by Elizabethan medicine. It was this energy, the theory held, that gave him his ambition and passion. Despite his ambition, however, he was honest and not malicious; he was a down-to-earth, old-fashioned 'sword and buckler man'. He was known as a 'great swearer' for his bawdy talk. Perhaps, however, as Robert Nauton's *Fragmenta Regalia* suggests, 'his custom of swearing and obscenity in speaking made him seem a worse Christian than he was'. Certainly, his bawdy vocabulary would stand his mistress in good stead later on. A plain-spoken man, his letters show that he lacked the temperament to ignore the slights that were a perpetual feature of life at court. He was forever in danger of rebuking one of the queen's servants, whose report might do him real damage. He was not made for palace intrigue, and it appeared that practically nothing else went on in Whitehall. The whole palace was full of malice, envy and slander. As a break from the stresses of the court, one of Hunsdon's favourite occupations was his garden. Although the gardeners did most of the work, he most likely got his hands dirty as well, especially taking care of the more exotic species. He was well known as a collector of rare plants, and delighted in rare specimens brought to him from all over the globe. Together with Sir Walter Raleigh, Hunsdon even became the patron of John Gerard, England's leading botanist, when William Cecil (Lord Burghley) no longer wanted to support him.

Nevertheless, despite being known as a 'very passionate' man, Hunsdon must have had a steady hand on the tiller, otherwise he would hardly have survived the intrigues of Elizabeth's court as one of England's leading statesmen, soldiers and judges. In his capacities as the Governor of Berwick-upon-Tweed, Chief Justice in the forested Eyre, south of Trent (1589), Chief Justice Itinerant of the Royal Forces (1591), and of course Recorder of Cambridge (1590), there would have been a huge amount of administrative and legal work. This was not a job for any ordinary legal mind, but Hunsdon was intellectually capable of keeping up with his peers at Gray's Inn, and he knew how to delegate ruthlessly. As his Deputy Recorder Francis Brackyn would learn, it meant standing up for the causes of common law against the excessive claims being made by the Cambridge University lawyers, who were advocating civil law in their own favour, and slandering the Deputy Recorder as an unscholarly ignoramus. But fights were Lord Hunsdon's bread and butter. He would fight for the right cause, and he was not one to be awed by academic titles, language and regalia. Lord Hunsdon had a wide range of responsibilities, but he also had nine sons, along with other relations, and he believed in treating his family and household as part of his own miniature civil service, in order to support his various lucrative offices of state. In doing so, of course, he merely replicated, on a smaller scale, the system of nepotism that the queen herself used and on which his own power was based.

Hunsdon held other posts at the court of his cousin Elizabeth. Knighted in 1558 and created a baron in 1559, he was appointed Master of the Queen's Hawks in 1560, and made a Knight of the Garter the next year. He was responsible for court entertainment, for the operation of the chapel, and for the court musicians. Further honours followed, and his fortunes were established for good when he successfully put down the so-called Northern Rebellion in 1569–70, a Catholic conspiracy of several of the nobility.

Importantly for us, among his many posts, Hunsdon became Lord Chamberlain, taking on the responsibility of regulating – and censoring – all plays put on in England. In addition, he was responsible for an odd assortment of things: the royal doctors, the astronomers, the mole catcher and the rat-catcher, the serjeant painter and the court fools; he was the general in charge of London, and held three judgeships.

Such a list of responsibilities seems astonishing today, and yet Hunsdon's power, great though it was, was nevertheless circumscribed. None of his many offices addressed England's real problems. The country's foreign policy was in disorder; the economy was going to the dogs; inflation had gone through the roof, causing widespread hunger, profiteering and unrest. The court was widely regarded as corrupt, and the aging queen in her silk stockings and her famous wristwatch (the only one in England) was increasingly becoming irrelevant. Her slogan, *semper eadem* – 'always the same', only proved that she was incapable of responding to changing circumstances. She seemed to be living in the past, refusing to make difficult decisions. England needed a change. Rebellion was brewing, both at home and in Ireland. The old order was breaking down.

Over those last few years of Elizabeth's reign, Hunsdon had seen the idea of monarchy itself begin to be challenged, along with all the chivalry and codes of honour that went with it. In the future, instead of dealing with disputes by jousting in a tournament, or fighting a duel, men would resort to the law. A whole new group of lawyers were coming into existence. The New World was opening up the boundaries of the imagination. Perhaps the very model of the world that had been inherited from the ancients – a heavenly Christian order of the spheres, which was replicated and mirrored in the world below – was beginning to shatter at last. Copernicus had published his great heliocentric treatise, *On the Revolutions of the Celestial Spheres*, in 1543, and it would not be long before Galileo took up his cause.

Hunsdon himself was reported to be not a very good Christian, and like his son in law Lord Admiral Howard, was rumoured to be an atheist. We now know that Lord Hunsdon's private secretary, Henry Stanford, was writing blasphemous poems about the queen, while (the present book suggests) his mistress was writing covert anti-Christian dramas. So underneath Lord Hunsdon's surface compliance, which sustained him in his long career, like any good courtier, his true opinions were probably rather different. If Richard Cholmely was correct in his accusation of Lord Hunsdon in 1593 – that he showed 'profound witness' of being a 'sound atheist' – it is possible he may have even been willing to encourage provocative covert religious dramas.

It is in some ways surprising that these opinions did not impede his rise. For, more than most, Hunsdon prided himself on not entirely separating his private and his public self – he was, he said, not a 'flatterer' like those who surrounded the queen. Nevertheless, one took only gentle steps in this direction. One did not displease Her Majesty. Confronted with any opposition or disappointment, the queen would fly into a rage. She would not hesitate to insult her chief advisers such as Lord Essex, even boxing their ears, knowing that they could not hit back. As for her maids in waiting, she would hit them without qualm. She hit so hard that on occasion her blows would break their fingers, causing her maids to wail aloud. Her Majesty's flushed face made it quite clear that she was angry, and no-one wanted to be near the queen's anger; you would carry her words to your grave. You also had to be careful what you said, since Thomasina the dwarf had an eidetic memory and could recite your remarks to the queen even years afterwards.

If caution was required in the temporal sphere, absolute care was necessary in the spiritual one. In Her Majesty's opinion, the Plague of 1593 was not caused by rats carrying infected lice among the cramped muddy streets of crowded London. Plague, or Pestilence, the queen insisted, resulted from the lack of agreement between the parts of the body – in particular, between the temporal and spiritual parts. Every Christian who suspected himself of being diseased in this way needed first to cure the sickness of his soul, so that evil angels did not secretly glide into his body, creating their pestilential air. The queen read all the intelligence reports produced by England's very robust secret service. Some years before, she had instructed Lord Hunsdon to 'diligently intercept all letters of any seditious person that might stir up a mutiny'. She said, 'You shall do well by the speedy execution of two or three of them to make an example of terror to the others.' The queen insisted that government had to act swiftly to repress disorder, and to control the beggars and the masterless men, the separatists, and all those who erred in their religion. A new Royal Commission would be established to make sure that her new 'example of terror' was carried out properly.

When the Plague hit London that year, 800 people were dying a month throughout the city, but England could rest assured that Her Majesty was safe in Oxford busily attending debates on whether one man's soul was more excellent than another's, and 'whether the disagreements of citizens be useful to the State'.

Throughout 1593, Lord Hunsdon weathered the Plague in London and Oxford, and watched as it became a major problem. He saw the theatre companies of other nobles going out of business, because the public playhouses were closed as a safety measure. Lord Pembroke's Men attempted a tour of the country, but had been unable to mend their finances with travel and had been forced to pawn their clothes. Lord Strange's Men, under Edward Alleyn, had also gone on tour, but had broken up, some of the players joining The Lord Admiral's Men. Knowing that he could always come back to the Rose once the plague was over, Edward Alleyn himself stayed away from London, sending his wife little notes calling her his 'sweetheart' and 'little mouse', and advising her to clean the pavements, to hang rue in the windows as a defence against plague, and reminding her to take care of the parsley he had planted in the garden.

The plague was a problem for Hunsdon. He would be a Lord Chamberlain without any troupes of public entertainers left who could come to court to entertain Her Majesty. Players were the most cost-effective form of entertainment, roughly a quarter the cost of putting on a court masque, and the queen had long ago cut the entertainment budget, which made it necessary to provide her entertainments as cheaply as possible. He had been responsible for providing six plays a year to the court – a large number, as anyone who has run a theatre company will appreciate – and now, suddenly, his entire supply structure had vanished. In her royal boredom, the queen quickly made her displeasure known. Hunsdon even had his colleague Lord Burghley write to the chancellors of Oxford and Cambridge, asking if the student amateur players from the universities could entertain her 'by reason that Her Majesty's own servants in this time of infection may nor disport her Highness with their wonted and ordinary pastimes'. They couldn't.

Hunsdon knew that this was the time when his reputation for thinking and 'speaking big' would be tested to the full – as well as his management skills and his ability to deliver. The old industry model of the theatre simply no longer worked – it was impossible to leave it as vulnerable to any upset, and as dependent on touring, as it was. It needed to be re-established on a firmer footing. Permanent companies, with the stability offered by permanent theatres, were necessary. Moreover, it had to be done in such a way that the queen would get her entertainments, and that the popular opposition by the mayor and aldermen of London would be taken into account and neutralised. These people wanted to have plays banned from the city, and all playing in the pubs and inn courtyards closed down.

It was obvious to Lord Hunsdon that he would have to negotiate a political agreement with the mayor and his Puritan supporters. What needed to be done, despite the Mayor's opposition, was to establish two permanent companies, each of which would be a family-based business in which the major leading actor and the playhouse owner were close relatives. Each company should start off with a collection of plays, and then they could compete in a duopoly against each other. Their patronage should be kept close within his own family, because that would enable him to exercise greater control, and so be more assured of a stable and acceptable source of entertainment.

Hunsdon had several things on his side, however. First, the queen must be entertained. Second, the people needed their entertainment, too. It was one important way of suppressing dissent in Elizabeth's police state – dissent that seemed to be growing. Evidently the labouring classes of England did not all accept the official state ideology of Gloriana's majesty. 'Worse than Nero,' said one woman. 'A Turd for the Queen,' retorted another. Labourer Thomas Farryngton said that 'the Queen's Majesty was Anti-Christ' and she was bound for hell. Labourer John Feltwell said she was ruled by nobles and that 'we shall never have a merry world while the Queen liveth'. Labourer Jeremy Vanhill offered neither a theological nor a sociological interpretation and expressed himself more crudely: 'Shit upon your Queen. I would to god she were dead that I might shit upon her face.' He was quickly hanged, and the others imprisoned.[4]

The people had much to be upset about. The price of flour was rising rapidly. People were going hungry. In June 1595 alone, London would have twelve different uprisings; apprentices instigated riots against the Lord Mayor, against food prices, and against the imprisonment of their comrades. In the first riot, 300 apprentices rescued a silk weaver who had been sent to Bedlam – as insane – simply for protesting outside the Lord Mayor's house. In another riot, apprentices pulled down the pillories in Cheapside and at Leadenhall, and set up a threatening gallows outside the Lord Mayor's house: insanity indeed. Then a crowd of 1,000 apprentices marched on Tower Hill, looting shops along the way and threatening to kill the Lord Mayor himself. The Mayor instructed the householders to arm themselves: 'Every householder [was] to have a sufficient weapon at his core for preservation of her Maiesties peace.' He enforced a curfew:

That they keepe within their houses all their men servants and apprentices tomorrow from three of the clock in the morning untill eight at night, and the same householders be all that time ready at their door with a weapon in their hande.

The apprentices would receive 'open punishment for their lewd offence'. Five of the youths, who had been convicted of stealing stolen butter from the shops in Southwark, were taken to Tower Hill, hanged, and disembowelled.

Hunsdon kept working up to the last minute. Only a couple of weeks before he died he had been dealing with such trivia as the Bishop of Cork and Ross, who was vociferously complaining about the young vandals who had torn out the dedications to Her Majesty in a pile of Latin grammars in the local school. Then, in July 1596, he died, at the grand old age of seventy-two, at Somerset House, his palace in the Strand. Visiting her half-brother on his deathbed, the queen offered him the robes of the Earldom of Ormond. However, he graciously refused, saying,

'I will not take on my deathbed what Her Majesty had not seen fit for me in life.' A few days later, at the express orders of the queen, he was buried in Westminster Abbey with great and solemn splendour and much ceremonial procession along the route. She even found £600 for the monument – which was badly needed since the old man had left a 'broken and hard' estate. So she paid for him to have the tallest monument in Westminster Abbey. But once dead, soon forgotten. As soon as the burial was over, one of the first actions of his successor as Lord Chamberlain was to give in to pressure from the Mayor and completely ban all plays in the city – allowing only those in the suburbs in Shoreditch and Southwark.

Nevertheless, Hunsdon's vision had been achieved. He had established two theatre centres – the Rose Theatre on the South Bank for Marlowe's plays, and the Theatre/Curtain complex near Spitalfields in North London for Shakespeare's plays – and each had their own permanent theatre company. This decision would have vast, and unintended, consequences for the English theatre. Preventing any theatres from operating in the city simply generated a much greater demand for those theatres that remained, which translated into larger audiences, greater financial viability and much more attention for the plays that those theatres chose to promote.

Lord Hunsdon's achievement lived on, long after his death. He had created a stable infrastructure for England's new theatre industry, and that included music. The theatre did not merely require actors and staging, it also needed musicians to create the sound effects, to play the trumpets, drums, recorders and so on during the play, to provide music both before and after the show and during the interludes, and to be extras for walk-on parts when they were not doing anything else. As the court recorder consort, the Bassanos – who reported to Lord Hunsdon as the Lord Chamberlain – not only played music for the theatrical spectacles at court, but were also most qualified to supply musical services for the Theatre in Spitalfields. It was barely 200 yards away from their family home, which comprised three linked town houses in which they lived and made their musical instruments. The involvement of the Bassano family and their kin in music for stage plays is well established.

Baptista Bassano ran the family instrument business out of his home. It was located just north of Bishopsgate, in Spitalfields, in an area favoured by some of London's 100 or so Marrano Jews. ('Marrano' an insulting Spanish term, is used here rather than the more neutral 'Converso', because 'Marrano' was the contemporary Elizabethan term applied to them. Bishop Lancelot Andrewes, for instance, referred to someone as 'a very christened Jew. A Maran[o], the worst sort of Jew that is'.) Here, in Spitalfields, the Bassanos were right in the middle of the catchment area for six different theatres and inns that staged plays. The Theatre and the Curtain were 200 yards to the east. In Whitechapel to the south-west was the Red Lion Inn, where in 1567 Iacobo Burbage and John Brayne had built a stage scaffold to put on a performance of *The Story of Samson*. Immediately to the south along Bishops Gate, the main thoroughfare, were three of the other public houses that staged plays in the city.

Robert Johnson (who was most probably Amelia Bassano's maternal cousin) created half a dozen pieces of music or dances that appear in the late Shakespearean plays. For *The Tempest*, he wrote 'Full Fathom Five' and 'Where the Bee Sucks', for *Cymbeline* 'Hark hark the lark', and for *The Winter's Tale* the song 'Get you hence', and he composed the music for the anti-masque dances for several masques, which were then transferred into Shakespeare's plays. For instance, the satyrs dance from the Masque of Oberon was included as the dance of the leaping men of hair in *The Winter's Tale* (4.4.319–37). The witches' dance and Johnson's 'Come away Hecate' were taken from the Masque of Queens and included in *Macbeth* (5.3.34). Finally, the rural May dance, which was probably written by Johnson for the *Masque of the Inner Temple* (1613), was included in *Two Noble Kinsmen* (3.5.124–36). In each of these three cases the play incorporates a prior piece of music created by Robert Johnson. He also wrote music for other playwrights who worked with the Chamberlain's Men, or as it was later called, the King's Men – these playwrights included Middleton, Webster, Beaumont and Fletcher.

Another member of the family, Nicholas Lanier (who would become brother in law to Amelia Bassano) worked on at least seven masques involving actors from the King's Men, for which he sang the songs, designed the sets, or wrote the music. Alphonso Ferrabosco II (Amelia Bassano's sister-in-law's husband) also wrote music for seven of Jonson's masques. Ben Jonson praised him in the introduction to one of them, making a pledge to their friendship.

By the early 1600s members of the family had become established in senior positions in the provision of technical services – music composition, orchestral directing, performing and set design – for the King's Men. By 1633, as Michael Wilson has shown, at least half of the members of the King's Music were part of the extended Bassano family, being named Bassano, Lupo or Lanier. We know that the court musicians performed the incidental music for the masques staged at court, and presumably they also provided the same function for the performances given by the public acting companies there, and perhaps other plays as well. Susan E. James, for instance, believes it 'highly likely' that the music for *Roister Doister* (*c.* 1553) 'was originally played if not actually composed by the Bassanos'.[5]

Although court musicians at least had the social status of gentlemen, actors did not, being regarded as little better than vagabonds or vagrants. Similarly, playwriting itself was not a respectable occupation. Thomas Bodley, who was restoring the library at Oxford University, was always saying that play quartos were mere 'riff raff' and 'baggage books', which he refused to have on his shelves. Such was Elizabethan London, a glittering surface concealing deep social divisions, and held together by great spectacular processions and stage-managed events. It was in this context, over a period of about thirty years from 1576, that London would see the creation of a new theatre industry featuring the most complex and most brilliant stage plays that the world has ever seen, and in which the most brilliant plays of all were those credited to one William Shakespeare.

As the process of revisionist scholarship has begun to peer through the carefully constructed glamour of Queen Elizabeth and her court – what Julia Walker calls 'dissing Elizabeth' – so in parallel this enables us to see through the surface of the stage plays put on for popular entertainment, to understand better what they really were and why they were created. And it leads to the remarkable conclusion that for an entire decade the man who was most responsible for constructing that glamour, and the woman who was most responsible for deconstructing it, could be found at night sharing a bedroom in a palace on the Strand.

Finally, our sense of amazement at the extraordinary combination of different offices and functions that Lord Hunsdon united in his person may remind some of another sense of amazement (often remarked upon), at the many different kinds of knowledge displayed by the writer of the Shakespearean plays. Indeed, on detailed examination, the 'knowledge map' associated with Lord Hunsdon turns out to constitute a rather significant subset of the knowledge displayed by the great playwright. It is to that important and interesting fact that we now turn.

2

Shakespeare's Remarkable Mind:
A Shopping List

Most Shakespeare biographies elaborate on the relatively few facts we know about him to build up a semi-novelistic narrative that is filled out with information from the plays, parts of which are used to recreate his assumed life. In his recent book *The Truth about William Shakespeare: Fact, Fiction, and Modern Biographies*, David Ellis has shown that these 'biographies' are not biography at all. He rightly castigates a long list of academics who have produced such works – including Rene Weis, Peter Ackroyd, Jonathan Bate, Katherine Duncan-Jones, Stephen Greenblatt, and James Shapiro – for their 'general lowering of intellectual standards and the degradation of the art of biography'. The commercial success of these plays both in print and on the stage has distorted scholarly judgement to create an ideological apparatus; the assumed life of a financially astute playwright focused upon creating bestsellers at the box office. The distortion completely blots out entire areas of scholarship that have a different perspective on the plays, for example, the fact that they are exercises in religious criticism using Elizabethan literary technique. This alternative perspective is compatible with what is known both of the function of the theatre and also the patterns of symmetrical correspondences in Elizabethan thought, known as the Great Chain of Being.

Those so-called biographies reflect the same bias that is found in editions of the Collected Works, which often not only present the editor's preferred mash-up of the folio and quarto texts, with their own spellings, notes and extra stage directions, but give pride of place and primacy to those plays. Biographers and editors alike construct their versions of the 'Life' or the 'Works' of Shakespeare. However, they do so primarily for Shakespeare as Playwright and not Shakespeare as Poet, which is almost a banished topic in today's popular fabrication of Shakespeare as a comprehensible 'man of the theatre'. Like the handsome portraits that were later created by turning the First Folio cartoon into an imaginary portrait, this is an imaginary authorial persona founded largely upon the plays' financial successes – and entirely unrelated to their meaning. Yet, as Patrick Cheney has pointed out, the majority of contemporary references are to Shakespeare as a poet, and not as a playwright at all. Indeed, some of these testimonies, such as those by Barnfield and Edwards, 'place Shakespeare in the great tradition of the Elizabethan poets'.

In terms of what it reveals about the writer's interests and preoccupations, some of that poetry is even more revealing than the plays. The sixty-seven-line poem 'The Phoenix and the Turtle' most notably exposits what James Bednarz has called 'Shakespeare's poetic theology'. And while that theology uses components of Christian Trinitarian doctrine, it is very, very, far from a statement of adherence to the Christian faith. For example, even at the surface level of the text, one of the core elements, the co-mingling of the ashes of the turtle dove and the phoenix, is contrary to Christian practice. Although the poem uses Christian theology, it is very significantly *not* a devotional spiritual poem, but, as we shall see, something different – an allegorical religious satire. To be a religious satirist in Elizabethan London was very unusual – and risky. And a poetic requiem, a funeral mass, drawing both on classical and Christian elements, depicts the apparatus of death. If we follow the trail of breadcrumbs, this first lens on Shakespeare's skills, knowledge and interests will turn out to be of enormous help in filtering out not only who could have written this particular poem, but also the plays and sonnets that are universally agreed to be by the same writer.

The present chapter looks at the knowledge and skills that the playwright demonstrated in the works. Both the sociology of knowledge and the sociology of literature emphasise that knowledge is socially constructed through networks of relationships. Even the act of picking up a book and paying attention to it necessitates that one's social environment has given value or 'salience' to that particular subject rather than another.

Knowledge is gained in communities, so by understanding the kinds of knowledge that is demonstrated in the Shakespearean works, it is possible to work backwards to the communities of knowledge to which the primary author must have had access. Consider for a moment the very earliest plays, *Sir Thomas More* (designed for an unrealistically large cast) and *The Reign of Edward III* (designed for a cast of ten, probably for a private performance before Lord Hunsdon). In these examples we find a playwright in the early stages of his career, who was not yet writing for the public playhouses, but had special interests of two peculiar kinds – in the heraldry related to the Order of the Garter, and in the fate of foreigners or aliens in the Spitalfields area. Young playwrights write about what they know and experience in their communities: if we find the correct author of the plays they will probably have particular social ties to these two very differing communities of knowledge.

Furthermore, in a pre-industrial society the main means of social connection was through kinship networks, both real and what anthropologists call 'fictive' kinship. Early modern social networks are receiving some attention from scholars interested in the intellectual history of the Renaissance, who are even beginning to use sophisticated data visualisation techniques. A key question to ask is how the man from Stratford's kinship networks connected him to the various people the playwright knew, compared to the kinship networks of the other candidates.

In some instances, it is possible to quantify just how extremely unusual the playwright's knowledge is. For instance, a typical Shakespearean play makes fifteen times more references to falconry and three times more references to music than the average of other playwrights – both of which suggest that the playwright had an unusual association both with musicians and with falconers. Many have argued that the playwright's knowledge could have been derived from reading, but in many cases it is possible to prove that the knowledge must have been gained from personal experience. For instance, knowledge of practical musicianship demonstrated in the plays can only be learned by engaging with other musicians – and this is very distinct from the purely theoretical knowledge of music, demonstrated for instance by Sir Francis Bacon. Knowledge of seamanship could not have been gathered from books, since none were in existence on that subject at the time. The accurate accounts of Italy could not have been gathered from contemporary guidebooks on Italy, since these books were incorrect on some of the issues in question. As for the playwright's knowledge of falconry, at least some the details can be shown never to have appeared previously in print; indeed, a mention in a falconry handbook *subsequent* to the publication of the play in question shows that the playwright's usage was correct.

In these ways, by examining certain structural features of the plays and the specific knowledge that the playwright evidently possessed, it is possible to construct a map of the social communities and environment in which the playwright lived. This can be used to create a kind of 'shopping list', beginning with the rare knowledge and skills demonstrated in the plays, against which potential candidates can be evaluated. Whoever has a biography that fits can be a candidate for the authorship. This is a conventional methodology developed in the 1930s in the social sciences, where it is known as 'content analysis'. Ole Holsti, in his book *Content Analysis for the Social Sciences and Humanities*, defines it as 'any technique for making inferences by objectively and systematically identifying specified characteristics of messages'. Let us begin, then, with a look at the communities of knowledge Shakespeare clearly worked within.

The playwright had an extraordinary knowledge of the Bible, which was the source most frequently used in the plays. There are altogether around 3,000 religious and biblical references, using fourteen different translations of the Bible. These were large, heavy books, each weighing perhaps thirty pounds – they were not, that is, designed to be carried around. To use fourteen of them bespeaks access to a range of sources, and a level of sophistication in handling biblical texts that was utterly remarkable for the time. The playwright also extremely unusually used non-canonical biblical sources, such as the *Infancy Gospel of Thomas* used in *Romeo and Juliet* and the apocryphal *Gospel of Nicodemus* used in *Twelfth Night*. Finally, the playwright also used biblical literary and compositional techniques. For instance, as Jan Blits has beautifully shown, the structure of *Hamlet* resembles that of a book of the Hebrew Bible, written as it is as a series of linked rings, showing internal symmetry within each scene as well as overall symmetry between scenes. The playwright also appears to have read Church history; for instance,

Steve Sohmer argues that Sir Andrew's garbled phrase 'equinoctial of Queubus' (*Twelfth Night*, 2.3.23) refers to a judgement by Eusebius on the vernal equinox. The writings of the Church Father Tertullian are echoed both in the recorder reference in *Hamlet*, and the multiple references to Trinitarian theology in 'The Phoenix and the Turtle'. The playwright also had a deep and critical interest both in the Church and in theology; for example, the rites of exorcism. Mock exorcisms appear in both *Twelfth Night* and in *The Comedy of Errors*, while in *King Lear* there are about eighty different allusions to Harsnett's *A Declaration of Egregious Popish Impostures* (1603), which is an account of a fraudulent exorcism.

One distinctive characteristic of the plays is their very unusual attitude towards Judaism. The Jews had been expelled from the country 300 years earlier in 1290 by Edward I. Jews would appear in England only in sermons and literature – for example the blood libel in Chaucer's *Canterbury Tales* (1385); Croxton's *Play of the Sacrament* (1461); the play *The Jew* (1579), which attacked the greediness of usurers; and Christopher Marlowe's *The Jew of Malta,* in which the Jew Barabas talks about poisoning wells and is shown committing murders. All of these are within the medieval stereotype of presenting Jews on stage as devils, with hooked noses, red hair and beards.

Very oddly, the Shakespearean plays avoid such typical anti-Semitic stereotypes (see Appendix 7). They also make occasional use of Hebrew and even the Talmud. It is true that Shylock is presented using the stereotypes of the Jew as a miser and a moneylender. The action takes place realistically, in the ghetto. The playwright knows to distinguish Shylock's synagogue from others, that in Venice only military officers could bear swords, that a certain building has a 'penthouse' (which indeed still exists today), and that, contrary to what English audiences might suppose, Venice had horses – indeed, the stone tracks specifically designed for horse-drawn carts are still a feature of some of the streets today. Other Shakespearean Venetian references are to the characteristic gondolas and chopins – a kind of platform shoe – as well as to the Venetian calendar and judicial procedures. Regarding these stereotypes, however, in the autumn of 2010 a correspondence between Stephen Greenblatt and James Shapiro in the *New York Review of Books* discussed the New York Public Theatre's production of *The Merchant of Venice*. Each of these scholars made one very good point. Greenblatt pointed out how easily Shakespeare could have used the anti-Semitic language of the blood libel and the poisoning of wells – but chose not to do so. Shapiro noted that, whereas Marlowe's Jew was clearly an evil stereotype with a red wig, Shylock is not. The only representation of Shylock in a red wig is a nineteenth-century forgery by John Payne Collier. In fact, apart from his Jewish gabardine, a long garment still worn by the ultra-orthodox, 'there is nothing ... that visibly distinguishes Shylock from his Christian contemporaries'.[1]

This is very strange. For some reason, in *The Merchant of Venice*, Shakespeare completely breaks away from the two most widespread negative Renaissance stereotypes of the Jew common in anti-Semitic London. The marketing blurb on the cover of the Quarto describes the play as showing 'the extreme cruelty of Shylock the Jew towards the merchant in cutting a just pound of his flesh', but this would have been added by the printer and is no more accurate than the advertisements on the sides of modern buses. In any case taking the pound of flesh was not the playwright's invention, since it derived from the source text in *Il Pecorone*. The playwright presents a new, radical and positive image when the Jew makes his plea for equality ('When you prick us, do we not bleed?') which is unique to the English stage.

The playwright also demonstrates a familiarity with half a dozen languages, including Hebrew. In an article in *Shakespeare Survey*, Schelomo Jehuda Schöenfeld observed that, in *The Merchant of Venice*, Portia says 'I am lock'd' (3.2.40) and 'I am contain'd' (2.8.5) in one of the caskets. These are intriguing statements, because it is her portrait that is inside the casket and not Portia herself. One reading, of course, is that she is treating a representation of her as being she, herself. But a Hebrew speaker would know that Portia's name in Hebrew, a language typically written without vowels, is spelt PRT. They would see the lead casket, know that the word 'lead' in Hebrew is YPRT (*opheret* – the first letter is a soundless '*ayin*'), and realise that the Hebrew pun shows that Portia (PRT) is contained inside the lead (PRT). In addition, spoken Hebrew has been found hidden in the nonsense language used in *All's Well That Ends Well*. The interpreter says to Parolles, '*Boskos vauvado*. I understand thee, and can speak thy tongue. *Kerely-bonto*, sir, betake thee to thy faith' (4.1.75–7). In the allegory in the play Parolles is a Jew. Not surprisingly, then, the nonsense language the interpreter is speaking is actually Hebrew. If translated, the interpreter is saying something that makes sense in the context of the play. *B'oz K'oz* means 'in bravery like boldness', and *vah vado* means 'and in his surety' (*vah* means 'and'; *vado* = *vad*, meaning 'sure', plus an 'o' ending for 'his'). And so we get: '*In bravery like boldness, and in surety*, I understand thee, and can speak thy tongue. Similarly, *K'erli* is 'I am aware' (*ki* means 'since', *erli* = *er*, meaning 'aware', *li* is a grammatical suffix meaning 'to me') and *b'onto* is 'his deception' (*b'on(na)* means 'deception', with the grammatical ending 'o' meaning 'his'). Thus, '*I am aware of his deception* sir, betake thee to thy faith.' This use of Hebrew is supported by Parolles' allegorical Jewish identity, and his name, which amusingly echoes the French term for the scriptures. Another fascinating example is the allusions to the Talmud and the Tractate Nedarim in *A Midsummer Night's Dream*, which are discussed on page 44.

It has also been known for some time that Shakespeare used elements of Kabbalah. However it is not enough to point out, like Yona Dureau in her book *The Christian Cabbalah Movement in Renaissance England and its Influence on William Shakespeare* and Daniel Banes in his *Shakespeare, Shylock and Kabbalah*, that Shakespeare used sources found in Christian Kabbalah, such as Francesco Giorgi's *De Harmonia Mundi* of 1525. In addition, the playwright seems to have drawn upon the Lurianic Kabbalistic system which, at the time, was known only to a small number of Jews. It would not begin to become part of Christian Hermeticism for nearly another century. For example, in *The Merchant of Venice*, several characters in the play have names that suggest they represent the *sephirot*, but because they are sunk in the mud of decay they are rather degraded husks of what they should be. Thus the character Lorenzo, whose name means 'crowned with the laurel wreath of victory', is a combination which represents both the *sephir* KETER (crown) and the *sephir* NEZAH (victory). Yet instead of possessing deep mystical insight, as the crown energy implies, he is a 'dumb wise' man and says, 'I pray thee, understand a plain man in his plain meaning' (3.5.52), indicating he is only capable of understanding the plainest, *Peshat* kind of interpretation. This degradation of the *sephirot* is a teaching of Lurianic Kabbalah, not found in Christian Hermeticism.

Further, Shakespeare drew upon the Zohar, a key Kabbalistic text, and seems to have done so directly. Consider also how Jewish sources are used in *A Midsummer Night's Dream*. An important study by Alan Altimont published in *Notes and Queries* has identified the playwright's use of the Mishnah (the core of the Talmud). In *A Midsummer Night's Dream*, Helena questions her beauty, describing herself as being ugly as a bear, while Lysander calls Hermia 'tawny' – to which Helena replies that she herself is fair-skinned. The two women are then contrasted in terms of their height, one being dwarfish and the other a maypole. Thus the two women are successively contrasted in terms of their ugliness/beauty, their darkness/fairness and their shortness/tallness. In the Mishnah, in Tractate 'Nedarim', 9:10, there is a discussion about when marriage vows are made in error. The discussion concerns exactly these same pairs of qualities, and they appear in exactly the same order. Moreover, although Helena's absent father never comes on stage, he is twice referred to by name as 'Nedar'. *Nedar* is of course the Hebrew verb meaning 'was absent' – very appropriate for an absent father – but it is also a pun on the Hebrew word *nedarim*, meaning vows, which is precisely the name of the Tractate in the Mishnah that the playwright is using. Finally, *A Midsummer Night's Dream* culminates in an apocalyptic ending, an image alluding to the distribution of dew, which appears only in Jewish accounts of the apocalypse, such as the Zohar, when the Holy One revives the dead and will shower dew from his hair (Zohar, 1:131a).

The Zohar's teachings on the transmigration of souls include an extensive discussion of how male and female souls are sent into the world in pairs. In marriage, God joins two people together so they become one soul and one body, and a virtuous man may marry a man whose wife's soul emerged at the same time as his. Virtue is rewarded, since 'a man only obtains the wife he deserves' (Zohar, 91b–92d). In *The Merchant of Venice* there is also an odd discussion of souls being yoked together in like proportion of manners and spirit (3.4.10–15). Furthermore, one of the caskets used by the suitors for their wife selection is specifically inscribed 'Who chooseth me shall get as much as he deserves' (2.9.36). Other references in the plays to Hebrew mystical texts include a reference in *As You Like It* to Maimonides' 'seventh cause', concerning the ways in which writers can conceal their hidden meanings in texts.

By the end of their career the writer of Shakespeare's plays would be writing entire mystery plays of their own like *Julius Caesar*, *Pericles* and the other romances. At the start of their career, however, the playwright merely drew on the late medieval plays as a source, and presented their material as inset cameos. Out of the entire canon, about a fifth is represented by the eight history plays that make up the two tetralogies. Although the playwright's use of religious typology and allegory became much more sophisticated as time went by (see Appendix 9), its roots lie in these early history plays. Sherman Hawkins, in the article 'Structural Pattern in Shakespeare's Histories', argues that the two tetralogies (a classical term for a collection of four plays) are a secular version of the mystery cycles. As four-part series they are much more ambitious than the two-part plays like *Tamburlaine* that preceded them.

The way that Shakespeare parodies the mystery plays and their use of the New Testament is hard to see, even in the modern revivals that have performed the plays in a single program, as well as in the 'War of the Roses' condensations. In part, this is because the material is spread out episodically over multiple plays – comparable to the mystery cycle, where each New Testament event had its own play. Certainly both endeavours are of comparable scale and ambition. Whereas the York Corpus Christi play had 300 characters and 14,000 lines, the first tetralogy had 235 characters and 12,400 lines. This is comparable to the modern television series *Game of Thrones*, with its 257 characters. The unusual imagery of feet and walking, which John Rumrich has found across the second tetralogy, might even allude to the audience walking from one pageant wagon to another. But Shakespeare used this outdated medieval dramaturgy to create a parody.

Because of the climate of state censorship in Elizabethan England, writers often used what Annabel Patterson called 'strategies of indirection' to say one thing, but mean another. By using allusions, suggestions and 'hinting through trivial facts', a playwright might be able to communicate with the wiser sort in an audience and yet avoid imprisonment or death. This was in some ways akin to the 'thieves' cant' or 'beggars' cant' that beggars, criminals and those on the margins of society developed from at least the fifteenth century to communicate with each other by covert means. E. A. J. Honigmann has noted that coded meanings in the plays have been sought at least since the eighteenth century when Horace Walpole explained *The Winter's Tale* as an apology for Anne Boleyn. That claim, however, is a purely arbitrary explanation, of the kind that Richard Levin has rightly criticised.

But there was one kind of coding that was not arbitrary, and that was indeed almost standard in late medieval writing – allegorical biblical typology. Although the mystery plays primarily dramatise scenes from the Gospels, they also dramatise other Christian myths such as the rebellion of Lucifer, his seizure of the throne of God, and his fall from heaven, which opened all known examples of the mystery cycle. As John Cox observed in *Shakespeare and the Dramaturgy of Power*, this is a significant model for the history plays. In the start of the entire cycle *Richard II* opens with the king sitting in majesty on his throne, but he ends sitting on the ground. At the start of *Henry VI, Part 3*, the throne is occupied by the usurping York, accompanied by a debate that echoes the one between the good and evil angels about Lucifer's right to sit on God's throne. Indeed the act of the throne being occupied by someone other than the sovereign is constantly dwelt upon throughout the plays, for instance in Eleanor Cobham's (fictional) dream that she were 'sat in seat of majesty'.

In the first tetralogy the playwright was still developing a technique, and the allegories appear as discrete episodes – whereas in later plays they become deeply interwoven throughout the entire play text. The Greek model of the tetralogy comprised three plays about the gods and fate, and a fourth satyr play. So it is significant that the first tetralogy ends in what Theodore Weiss described in his book on the early histories and comedies as 'a kind of satyr play' in which Richard is the 'Dionysian satyr'.[2] Furthermore, this play also uses significant Pauline imagery and thus as an entirety follows the events in the New Testament accounts in chronological order. However, as David Frey notes in *The First Tetralogy: Shakespeare's Scrutiny of the Tudor Myth*, the playwright undermines any Christian concept of divine providence – such as the Tudor myth found in the chronicles – by showing events as the secular consequence of political expediency and opportunism. But there is more to it than that.

The start of the first tetralogy, *Henry VI, Part 1*, was heavily influenced by contemporary events in the French wars, and includes a short devil scene, probably by Marlowe. It mocks the Virgin Birth at the start of the New Testament sequence with Joan the Puzzle, Puzel or Pucelle (1.4), namely Joan of Arc, in what Albert Tricomi called an 'inverted saints play'.[3] Joan's unhistorical claim that she has been transfigured by a vision of the Virgin Mary establishes her association to the Virgin Mother, miraculously pregnant, and positions her heretically as her daughter (the child of the heavenly Virgin Astrey or Astrea), namely, a female saviour. If that were not blasphemous enough, she is even depicted as empowered not by God, but by devils, which we see her summoning onstage. This is the first of half a dozen parodies of the Virgin Mary throughout the canon.

The second play, *Henry VI, Part 2*, is both a miracle play and a rather odd saints play. The central character, the blessed King Henry, was the most popular late medieval 'saint' (he was nearly canonised during the reign of Henry VIII) and is shown visiting the shrine of England's first saint, St Alban. Henry was supposed to have performed 174 miracles, including several cures of blindness. However, the playwright introduces a parody of these miracles – the false miracle of Simon Simpcox of Berwick, the man who pretended he had been blind and was granted sight, and was then cured of his pretended lameness. The second half of the play depicts a parallel claimant for the throne, the rebel who was known by various names including John Mortimer, John Mendall and John Aylmere, but instead the playwright prefers 'Jack Cade', the nickname by which he is known in Stow. He appears in a country sequence that is at least a carnival, and almost a clownish play-within-the-play. His actual quasi-legalistic complaints were documented in writing in multiple sources, but the playwright does not reproduce these. Instead, in the play, Cade promises the common ownership of property, to reform the law, to multiply loaves of bread, to turn piss into claret, and he gets mocked for his pains. The significance of his initials 'J. C.' becomes obvious when he insists on being called 'Lord'. His surname not only refers to a container for fish, but specifically one that is also called a 'messe', suggesting that the playwright is parodying the life of Christ, whose title was identified in the early church with the Greek word for fish. There is even a comic crucifixion alluded to in Cade's proposal that the clerk 'Emmanuel' (a synonym for Christ meaning 'God is with us') should be hanged because he is literate and thus entitled to the 'benefit of clergy' of avoiding execution. Cade's own death in the garden of Iden (a proxy for Eden), conflates the coming of death to Adam, and to Cain, with the death of the Saviour. However, the entire operation is being masterminded by the Duke of York, father of Richard III (the vice or satyr in the tetralogy), who represents Lucifer, so the rebellion is that of the fallen angels. Earlier, York overthrew the Godlike Lord Protector, that 'noble shepherd', the Duke of Gloucester, but his victory would prove short-lived in the next part of the cycle.

Finally, a number of scholars have observed how the third part of the tetralogy offers a much more explicit parody of the Crucifixion. In writing *Henry VI, Part 3*, the playwright normally follows Hall's Chronicle, which, when it comes to the death of Richard, Duke of York, does not describe his dying, but notes that when men found his corpse they 'caused his head to be stricken off, and set on it a crown of paper, fixed it on a pole and presented it to the queen'. At this point, however, the playwright switches to the account in Holinshed's *Chronicles*, which describes York being caught alive and given a mock coronation while standing. It echoes another famous mock coronation:

> … and in derision made to stand upon a molehill; on whose head they put a garland in steed of a crown, which they had fashioned, and made of sedges and bulrushes; and having so crowned him with that garland, they kneeled down before him (as the Jews did to Christ) saying to him; 'Hail, king without rule; hail, king without heritage.'

In a 100-line passage Shakespeare conflates the accounts so York is given a powerful dramatic role. Echoing the hill of Golgotha, Margaret makes him 'stand upon this molehill here' wearing the paper crown from Hall's account. In

Shakespeare's additions, the molehill is compared to mountains, to which York had reached his 'outstretched arms'. His 'passions' move Northumberland, his face would not be eaten by cannibals (an allusion to the Last Supper), his blood is upon the heads of his killers (as in Matthew 27:25, the blood of Jesus was upon the heads of the Jews), and he is mocked.

As Emrys Jones notes in his book *The Origins of Shakespeare*, instead of saying 'Hail, king without rule' as in the chronicle, Margaret taunts York elaborately for imagining that he would be king (resembling the taunts by Caiphas in one of the Towneley Mystery plays), to which York, like Jesus, keeps a remarkable silence. York is thirsty, 'parched' like Jesus on the cross. Margaret mops his face with a napkin, impiously echoing the actions of Veronica in the *Acts of Pilate*, which was part of the apocryphal *Gospel of Nicodemus*, and is found in selected mystery plays. She asks him to 'make me sport' so that she may 'sing and dance', echoing the torturers of Jesus who dance around in the Wakefield plays. She even points out that the actors will receive a fee, referring perhaps to the actors who were specifically hired for their japes around the cross in the mystery plays. Then York is stabbed and he prays that his soul may enter the 'gate of mercy' (1.4.178), which might allude to a contemporary song, or to the gate of Jerusalem entered by Jesus before his death. We are also reminded, quite unnecessarily, that like Herod, his killer, Margaret, is the offspring of the King of Jerusalem since Rene of Anjou was the titular king of Naples and Jerusalem (1.4.123).

Thus the playwright has chosen a source that contains elements of the Crucifixion and has elaborated upon them in order to make the history play bear the weight of an allegorical typology. In this early example Shakespeare is *specifically rewriting the Crucifixion narrative* – a point which is of great importance to the argument in this book. It would be followed by other crucifixion adaptations, notably the comic death of Pyramus in *A Midsummer Night's Dream* (see page 182). Like Pyramus, the depiction is a mockery since although York ends *Henry VI, Part 3* by being crucified like Christ, he opens the play by sitting on the throne like Lucifer.

The religious dimensions in the second tetralogy (*Richard II, Henry IV* parts 1 and 2, and *Henry V*), have been discussed by several writers. These include Russell Astley in his thesis *The Structure of Shakespeare's Second Tetralogy with Special Emphasis on Christian Myth as a Model* (1982), George Morrison in his thesis *Shakespeare's Lancastrian Tetralogy* (1977) and Trudy Price Jones in her thesis *The Second Coming of the Second Tetralogy* (2006). All argue that *Richard II* shows Richard as a second Adam in a demi-Paradise, from which he falls, with the turn of fortune, like a bucket on a waterwheel. The following three plays show the redeemer coming to life, as Hal the prodigal son turns away from Satan and becomes Henry V, the mirror of a Christian prince. This is a typological equivalent to the biblical myth of the fall of Man, the wicked world, and the saving redemptive figure who is the apocalyptic hero.

Although this is generally correct, these broad strokes are far too simplistic. For one thing, the Vice figure of the satyr play is not located at the end in this tetralogy but in the middle, where a central focus is the *psychomachia*, or temptation, of Hal by the satyr Falstaff, with his witty parodies of Christian concepts such as his 'vocation'. In his article 'First catch your Satyrs', Anthony Stevens shows that Falstaff is modelled upon the satyr Silenos in Euripides' play *Cyclops*. In addition he is modelled on Bacchus in Nashe's pageant *Summer's Last Will*, the Glutton in *The Castle of Perseverance*, and the Vice in the morality play *Lusty Juvenatus*. Furthermore, these plays use the biblical imagery of Cain and Abel, the parable of Lazarus and Dives, and the parable of the Prodigal Son. This was a favourite subject for Renaissance tavern plays such as *Acolastus of Gnaphaeus*, and the *Comedy of the Prodigal Son* in which Satan/Despair and Hope contend for the prodigal's soul, complete with a pocket-picking scene.

The sequence starts with *Richard II*, which Robert M. Shuler has shown is a *reversal* of the events in the life of Jesus – which in the sixteenth century would have been regarded as an almost satanic mockery. The playwright takes an oddly selective approach which is focused on the downside of Richard's reign, since out of Holinshed's ninety-five pages the play uses only the last seventeen pages, beginning at page 493 – 'K. Richard his evil government' – plus the first nine pages of *Henry IV*. The playwright also replaces Holinshed's six biblical allusions with seventy-five new ones that are used to create a strange new set of imagery.

Overall, it is becoming increasingly clear that the religious allegories or typologies buried in the plays, and which have been studied since the 1930s, are actually anti-Christian in nature. These begin in the history plays, but become much developed in later plays, and will be examined in a separate book on the allegories. There are many examples buried in obscure scholarly literature. Steve Sohmer acclaimed *Julius Caesar* as Shakespeare's mystery play in his book of that title and Howard Felperin devoted an article to *Pericles* titled 'Shakespeare's miracle play'. *Othello* appears to parody a well-known early Jesuit after whom the play is named, and who is parodied as the Jealous Joseph figure from the mystery plays. *Macbeth* mocks a different Jesuit who was behind the Gunpowder Plot. As the work of Patricia Parker has shown, notably in her article 'Murals and Morals', far from being a play about sex as popularly imagined, *A Midsummer Night's Dream* is a religious satire (more on this later).

My favourite is a book by Linda Hoff, *Hamlet's Choice*, which essentially shows that the play is primarily an allegorical parody of the Book of Revelation, which I have staged under the title *Hamlet's Apocalypse*. A performance of the half-dozen heretical parodies of the Virgin Mary is described in my article 'A Meta-Theatrical Staging in New York City: Shakespeare's Virgin Mary Allegories'. Videos of *Shakespeare's Annunciation Parodies*, an extract from my staging of *Shakespeare's Gospel Parodies*, an extract from *Hamlet's Apocalypse* and other proofs of concept are available on the website of the Dark Lady Players. Most of these use a production aesthetic that deconstructs the surface of the play rather than burnishing it. The actor is treated as an 'uber-marionette', and the surface echoes the vital traditions of Kantor and Brecht as well as the nineteenth-century tradition of Shakespearean burlesque. The style appeals more to reason rather than to emotions, and actors make it clear that their characters are 'puppets' and not 'real people'. Some of these allegorical demonstrations are admittedly dark, such as the production of *Hamlet*, which demonstrated that Ophelia represents the Virgin Mary inseminated by the archangel Lucifer; the baby Christ was aborted off-stage, or the workshop production of *Othello*, which used research by Chris Hassel and Steve Sohmer to depict Desdemona as the Virgin Mary, thirty-three hours pregnant, being killed by her jealous consort on Easter Saturday. It makes one appreciate why Shakespeare has been regarded as a precursor of the Theatre of the Absurd.

Yet this absurd, macabre quality should not be surprising, since the heretical nature of the English stage was well known; in *The Anatomie of Abuses* (1583) Stubbes described it as 'Sathan's Synagogue'. Despite the playwright's intense use of the Bible and of Christian doctrine, there are no indications whatsoever that the writer actually believed or accepted Christian teachings. Helen Vendler notes that the sonnets scorn the 'consolations of Christianity'. Eric S. Mallin, in his book *Godless Shakespeare*, finds that Shakespeare's beliefs as demonstrated in the works 'show a mind and a spirit uncontained by (Christian) orthodoxy', which throughout the playwright's 'long godless career' undermined classic Christian notions such as God's omnipotence, the function of sacrifice, the meaning of conversion, the life everlasting, and mocked Christian ceremonies. So we need to seek for a playwright who possessed considerable theological and biblical knowledge, but who, far from applying it in a pro-Christian context, was doing completely the opposite.

Let me now take a detailed example – Shakespeare's peculiar idea of original sin as it is used across the works in the canon. The entire rationale for Christian doctrine lies in the idea of original sin, which supposedly came about in the Garden of Eden. This was a key element of the mystery plays, so by examining it we are addressing how the playwright treated the fundamental building block of Christian teaching. In his article 'Shakespeare in the Garden of Eden', Robert Law noted that 'the story of Eden and that of Cain held unusual interest for Shakespeare', since there are at least twenty-four references in the plays to the three initial chapters of Genesis. One of the most detailed of these is in *Richard II*. In the play there is a gardener, 'old Adam's likeness' (3.4.73), who compares the king to the gardener of England: 'This other Eden, demi-paradise' (2.1.42). He has not dressed and trimmed his land, so it has become filled with noxious weeds and caterpillars, and the queen complains at the implications, 'What Eve, what serpent hath suggested thee, / To make a second fall of cursed man?' (3.4.75–6). The implication is that Richard (as Adam) and the queen (as Eve) will both be expelled from their kingdom. However, what is noteworthy here is that there is no suggestion of Eve sinning. The fault is entirely Richard's, who, instead of taking an apple, takes Old John of Gaunt's lands. Eve is entirely sinless in this scenario; it is all Adam's (Richard's) fault and the punishment falls on him. This echoes *The Rape of Lucrece*:

> Let sin, alone committed, light alone
> Upon his head that hath transgressed so;
> Let guiltless souls be freed from guilty woe:
> For one's offence why should so many fall,
> To plague a private sin in general?

Similarly, in *As You Like It,* which begins in a version of Eden complete with an orchard and Adam, and in which rib-breaking is a sport for ladies, it is interesting that there is no Eve; she is deliberately avoided. Instead the location is imagined as the classical garden of the Hesperides, which was staffed by the daughters of Atlas. This is why, instead of one rib being broken to make Eve, nine ribs are broken (1.2.10–123) to create the nine daughters of Atlas. Yet only one, Hisperia, appears in the play and she is not expelled at all. This implies that the only apples that were picked were the golden ones of the Hesperides and they were picked not by Eve, but by a man, Hercules.

In *Henry V*, we find the possibility that only Adam might be expelled if the 'offending Adam' (1.1.28–31) could be whipped out of the king, leaving his body as Paradise, containing only celestial spirits, and presumably Eve. In *The Tempest* we find the 'Earth creature', Adam, in the character Caliban, who is called 'Earth' and is taught language and the names of the sun and moon; there is, however, no Eve on the island. Instead we get another classical equivalent, Plato's original androgynous human from *The Symposium*, with four arms and four hands, before it was separated into male and female, like an apple that is cut in half for pickling, as Plato puts it. So if Caliban is Adam, in the comic monster on the beach (2.1.20–34), Trinculo comically takes the place of Eve – and perhaps the apple as well!

Regarding Eve's sin, *Love's Labour's Lost* offers an unusual reading, since the 'child of our grandmother Eve' (1.1.255) is being pursued by the apple (Costard is a kind of apple) rather than the girl pursuing the apple as normally imagined, so the fault is the apple's! Alternatively, there is a suggestion that it was not Eve who tempted Adam, but the other way around:

> The gallant pins the wenches on the sleeve,
> Had he been Adam, he had tempted Eve

5.2.321–2

In *Two Gentlemen of Verona*, 'Eve's legacy' (3.1.341–3) is merely the original sin of pride rather than that of stealing an apple. In *Much Ado About Nothing* Benedick hides in the garden like Adam (5.1.181–2) and rejects Beatrice even if she were possessed with all that Adam had before the fall. For her part Beatrice (in the role of Eve) refuses to have anything to do with Benedick/Adam because she does not want to be 'overmastered with a piece of valiant dust ... a clod of wayward marl' (2.1.62–8).

In sum, the plays take a remarkably unorthodox view of the fall of man in Christian doctrine, and seem to be working towards a feminist and alternative reading. For a comparison to *Salve Deus* and to *Willobie His Avisa* see page 206–7. If these anti-Christian meanings of the plays had been discovered by the secret service in Elizabethan London, the author would have been imprisoned, tortured and executed – a very good reason to employ a play broker as an intermediary.

In some cases, the parodies of Christianity that appear in the plays have distinct resemblances to those in Marrano literature in Spain and Italy. Many Marrano dramatists, such as Juan del Encina and Nuñez de Reinoso, used pastoral and other idioms to conceal deeper religious meanings. So did the Marrano Fernando de Rojas in writing *La Celestina* (1499). One of the finest works of Spanish literature, it is a comic allegorical parody of Christianity. For instance, the old madam Celestina mediates between Calisto and his salvation – replacing the function of the Church with a bawd. The only defender of Christianity is the clown Sempronio, who turns it into a joke. The young man Calisto has abandoned the worship of Christ for the worship of Melibea, a young woman:

Sempronio   Are you not a Christian?
Calisto   Me? I am a Melibean. I worship Melibea.
              I believe in Melibea, I love Melibea.

This resembles some of the love dialogue in *As You Like It*. More clearly, however, the nurse (Angelica) in *Romeo and Juliet* is based on the bawd Celestina (meaning heavenly). The girl Melibea is a recognised allegory for the Virgin Mary – as is Juliet. Similarly, the passage where Juliet treats Romeo as if he were her straying falcon echoes a passage in *La Celestina* where the young man enters the girl's garden in search of his falcon.

There are also other Marrano influences on Shakespeare's work. 'The Phoenix and the Turtle' draws upon *Dialoghi d'Amore* (1535) by Leone Ebreo, also known as Leo Judaeus and Judah Abarbanel. Possibly the playwright's knowledge of the circulation of the blood ultimately derives from Servetus, the Marrano theologian and doctor Miquel Servet (1511–53). And *The Comedy of Errors* may owe something to the writings of yet another Marrano, Leone de' Sommi (Hebreo) who died in 1592. His most famous play for his community was an erudite comic Purimspiel, in Hebrew, the *Tsahoth B'dihutha D'Kiddushin*, meaning 'A Comedy of Betrothal', in 1550. Furthermore, in his book *The Development of the Theatre*, Allardyce Nicoll argues that some of the staging techniques in the Shakespearean plays show that the playwright knew de' Sommi's theatrical work, described in his book *Quattro Dialoghi in Materia do Rappresentazione Sceniche* (c. 1565), known as the *Four Dialogues*.

Another feature of the plays that is hard to explain is Shakespeare's knowledge of Italy and Italian. The playwright read the following sources in the original: Dante, Tasso's *Aminta* and *Jerusalem Liberated*, Bruno's *Il Candelaio and Lo Spaccio*, Bandello's *Novella*, Cinthio's *Epitia* and *Hecatommithi*, also *Il Pecorone*, *Il Filostrato*, Aretino's *Il Marescalo* and *Filosofo*, *Gl'Ingannati*, *Il Novellino*, *Il Cesare*, an Italian translation of Plautus' *Mostellaria* and possibly both de' Sommi's *Quattro Dialoghi* and the manuscript of Scala's *Flavio Tradito*. Orthodox critics assume that translations once existed of all these texts, but have subsequently vanished without trace, or else claim that Shakespeare's knowledge of Latin was sufficient to enable him to read Italian – most implausible granted the fluent knowledge of Italian that the plays demonstrate.

One example of the way in which these sources were used is *Julius Caesar*, which draws on Tasso's great epic about the siege of Jerusalem, *Gerusalemme Liberata* (1581). In 'Canto XI', the leader of the troops and his warriors are going up the Mount of Olives, and the caves create an echo: 'replicare s'udla / od di Christo gran nome' – 'one would hear the replication of the great name of Christ from the hills'. The playwright uses this phrase, which is the first use of the word 'replication' in English in this sense of reverberation, to describe the enemy Pompey's entry into Rome. In it, he describes how the curvature of the shore created an echo: 'To hear the replication of your sounds / made in her concave shores' (1.1.47–8). Two lines earlier in the play, the people of Rome are described as having greeted Pompey with a 'universal shout', which appears to echo a line in the same canto that refers to 'il grido universal' – the 'universal shout' of 100 soldiers. In *Measure for Measure* the image of hell as 'a thrilling region of thick-ribbed ice' comes directly from Dante. Another example is *Macbeth*. When the devil-porter at the hell gate says 'this place is too cold for hell', he is referring specifically to the frozen ninth circle of hell in Dante's *Inferno*, which was the fate awaiting those who – like Macbeth – killed their guests, their kinsmen or their lords. Even the order in which Macbeth names his victims is taken precisely from Dante's account. In *Coriolanus*, for example, the way that Hector uses the word 'whip' as a goad or incentive comes from a passage in the *Purgatorio* in which virtue is described as a whip, or *ferza*, that is wielded with love. In *King Lear*, the odd passage where Edgar meets his father (who is *sans* his eyes – precious gems – since they have been pulled out) also comes from a passage by Dante. He meets Forese who has also lost his eyes: 'parean l'occhiaie anella sanza gemme.' The playwright simply paraphrases this in describing Gloucester's eye sockets 'with his bleeding rings their precious stones now lost' (5.3.189–90), having earlier used 'sanza' in a French equivalent as 'sans'. In *Measure for Measure* the image of hell as 'a thrilling region of thick ribbed ice' comes directly from Dante.

Unusual Italian phrases also appear translated into English, such as the colloquialism 'by the ears' that appears in *All's Well That Ends Well* – the king says, 'The Florentines and the Senoys are by th'ears' (1.2.1). This is not an English expression, but seems to have been translated from the Italian '*si pigliano per gli orecchi*'. Similarly, the Italian expression '*sano come un pesce*' reappears as the rather odd 'whole as a fish' in *Two Gentlemen of Verona* (2.5.18). In *Twelfth Night*, the playwright gives yet another indication of thinking in Italian colloquialisms in the reference to the 'Lady of the Strachy'. The comic idea of a man being a 'Yeoman of the Wardrobe' (which was one of the offices at court) leads the playwright to jest that a man with such associations to hanging clothes might marry a lady of rags, namely the Italian expression 'la Signora delgi stracchi', referring to a poor but haughty woman.

In addition, the playwright read other Italian literature in translation (as well as possibly in the original). Take Boccaccio. *The Merchant of Venice*, the balcony scene of *Romeo and Juliet*, and of course *Two Gentlemen of Verona* were all adorned by his plots. Later on, *The Merry Wives of Windsor*, *All's Well That Ends Well* and *Cymbeline* would be as well. *Two Noble Kinsmen* would make use of his *Teseide*, while *Il Filostrato* would be used in *Troilus and Cressida*. Altogether, at least ten of the plots in the Shakespearean plays come directly from the *Decameron*. Although the playwright makes reference to John Florio's Italian–English Dictionary and his handbooks on learning Italian, these references come *after* the playwright had already demonstrated an excellent grasp of that language. Moreover, *Love's Labour's Lost* meanly parodies Florio as Holofernes, *Othello* parodies Florio's verse in his *Second Fruits,* and in the quarto version of *Hamlet*, Osric's mention of 'golden words' being spent parodies Florio's book titled *First Fruits … and Golden Sayings*. So the playwright felt confident criticising England's leading Italian tutor.

It is clear that the playwright had a detailed knowledge of Italy and Venice. We might begin a study of this by noting the playwright's unusual obsession with republicanism, catalogued in Andrew Hadfield's book *Shakespeare and Republicanism*, which is greater than in any other Renaissance dramatist. In Elizabethan England the most admired model of republican government was Venice, where the rule of the Doge offered an alternative both to that of Elizabeth and to the Pope. Hadfield finds a strong analogy between the classical and Venetian tales in the canon and the ideas associated with the revival of classical republicanism in Italian humanist thought.

In the case of *Anthony and Cleopatra*, the playwright depicts the Nile and Egypt in a way that reflects book learning and cultural stereotypes. In the case of the Italian plays, however, the level of detail is so specific as to suggest personal experience. Rather oddly, the playwright set nearly a third of the plays in Italy, and turned from the court history plays to writing Italian marriage comedies around 1593. Strangely, unlike other playwrights, Shakespeare does not depict Italy as a place of horrors, evils and wickedness. Also, unlike Webster or Jonson, who also set plays in Italy, the Shakespearean plays do not draw upon books to describe local geographical and architectural features. Indeed, no single example has been identified in which the details can be demonstrated as having come from a guidebook, thus, unlike other playwrights, the author chose not to use guidebooks. Indeed, as A. J. Hoenselaars notes in his essay 'Italy Staged in English Renaissance Drama', *The Merchant of Venice* and *Othello* are 'not representative of the Italian genre', which includes around eighty plays set in Venice, because, unlike those two plays, the others demonstrate 'outstanding geographical precision'. Yet, unlike Ben Jonson's Venetian play, that precision does not come from dropping names and architectural details taken from guidebooks every couple of paragraphs to create local colour.

Critics used to think that the Shakespearean references to a sailmaker in Bergamo and a waterway at Milan were errors because they did not match descriptions in English books. It was not until the early 1900s that Sir Edward Sullivan pointed out that they were not derived from the books, which were inaccurate, but actually matched the reality on the ground and the seventeenth-century Italian sources describing systems of inland waterways. Precisely accurate details of the topography of a canal system are so complex that they could hardly have been achieved simply through the imagination, or even through conversation with informants. Accurate geographical descriptions by other English authors, like Chaucer, do not reflect imagination but personal experience.

The playwright's very remarkable knowledge of Italy is covered in detail in Richard Roe's *The Shakespeare Guide to Italy*. After his lifelong and on-site investigation of the geography in the Italian plays, Roe finds dozens of instances in which the playwright has more detailed local geographical and historical knowledge than is contained in the books consulted by Shakespeare scholars, and indeed more accurate than the playwright's sources. Roe concluded – very remarkably – that the playwright *deliberately* went out of their way, 'pointedly naming or describing some obscure or unique place that might look like an invention or a mistake but which turns out to be actual'. Take, for instance, Act 1 of *Romeo and Juliet*. Benvolio says he had walked in 'the grove of sycamore / That westward rooteth from this city side' (1.1.119–20). Although the playwright used versions of the story by several other writers – Da Porto, Boaistuau, Paynter and Arthur Brooke – not one of them mentions this grove of sycamore trees. Today the grove of sycamores is subdivided by roads, but it still stands outside the Porta Palio. Somehow the playwright knew this tiny, dramatically unnecessary, detail.

Another example comes from *The Two Gentlemen of Verona*, where Valentine is setting off to sail from landlocked Verona to landlocked Milan in order to visit the court of the emperor. Despite their extensive book research, the very existence of this inland waterway system was not appreciated by Shakespeare scholars until the early 1900s. Some continued to ignore it, for instance the editors of the *Riverside Shakespeare* of 1974, who stated that 'Shakespeare seems to have supposed that Verona was a seaport'. Even Clifford Leech's Arden edition (1969) doesn't fully appreciate the playwright's knowledge. Initially, the play refers to Valentine being 'shipped' (1.1.54) and that he will 'embark for Milan' (1.1.71), and will meet his father at the 'road'. The Arden edition correctly recognises that 'road' is a term for roadstead where ships are anchored, and that the reference to a 'boat' and a dry 'river' (2.3.51–3) imply a river journey. However, the editor is mystified by the reference to a 'tide' and 'lose the flood', and suggests that the playwright is in error in believing that the river is tidal. Instead, as Roe points out, the playwright is referring to the canals and their locks. As anyone who has travelled on canals will know, the river is dry when the water is released from a lock, and it becomes a flood or tide when the lock is flooded to allow the boat to enter a higher stratum of the canal. From 1573 this canal system allowed a boat to sail from the Po up the Adda and then to use the Martesana canal and the Naviglio Interno canal to reach Milan. The author of the play was familiar with it, unlike Shakespeare critics until the early twenty-first century.

In addition, one part of Italy that is not covered in Roe's exhaustive analysis is the playwright's strange knowledge of the little town of Bassano. Roger Prior's article 'Shakespeare's Visit to Italy' demonstrates that the author must have visited Bassano and seen a fresco there. The detailed knowledge of this fresco found in *Othello* raises the further question of why the playwright would have had any reason to visit the small town of Bassano, which was completely off the normal tourist track. Furthermore this makes it likely that the Arden edition is probably right in suggesting Othello is named after – and a parody of – the headstrong Jesuit Girolamo Otello of Bassano (1519–81), whose family were pharmacists in the same town.

In sum, the playwright's knowledge of Italy was much more accurate than in the sources used to write the Italian plays. It was also more accurate than the information available in books – otherwise Shakespeare scholars would not have wrongly concluded from their exhaustive study of those same books that the playwright was in error. Since the playwright's obscure knowledge of Italy did not come from books, this leaves the alternative that it was derived from personal experience on the ground.

The primary author of the plays also had a deep knowledge of the Italian theatrical art form known as the comedy of the actors, or the *commedia dell'arte*. This was used not only in most of the comedies but also remarkably in *Othello*, which only appears to be a tragedy but underneath has a comic structure in which all the main characters match the stock types from the *commedia dell'arte*, according to Richard Whalen's article '*Commedia dell'arte* in *Othello*: A Satiric Comedy Ending in Tragedy', and Teresa Faherty's 'Othello dell'Arte: the Presence of "Commedia" in Shakespeare's Tragedy'. This is remarkable, since the only known *commedia* troupes in England were Drusiano's troupe in 1578 (when Mr Shakespeare was fourteen), and a court appearance in 1602, by which time many of the Shakespearean comedies had already been written. Not only were there no known books that could have explained in enough detail how the *commedia* operated, if such books had existed other playwrights would have used them also. It is, however, clear that Shakespeare had some very unusual knowledge and access, since the playwright used it so extensively for nearly half the plays in the canon.

Expert musicianship is another of the unusual features of the Shakespearean plays. As Tommy Ruth Waldo noted in *Musical Terms and Rhetoric: The Complexity of Shakespeare's Dramatic Style*, the 2,000-odd musical references in the plays makes them 300 per cent more 'music intensive' than those of any other contemporary playwright. There are, for instance, 110 musical mentions in *The Taming of the Shrew*, ninety-one in *Twelfth Night*, and eighty-one in *Much Ado About Nothing*. The plays are notable for their musical puns, such as Duke Senior's allusion to the song 'Rowland' and 'Welcome Home Lord Willoughby' in *As You Like It*, or Bottom's allusions to the song 'Monsieur' in *A Midsummer Night's Dream*. There are references to twenty-six different musical instruments and 100 songs in Shakespeare's plays,[4] the song most mentioned (four times) being 'King Cophetua and the Beggar Maid', in which the king meets and marries a poor black woman. It is equally remarkable that plays devoting so much attention to secular music pay no attention at all to Christian liturgical music of composers such as Tallis and Byrd.

A study of the dialects used in the plays – those passages, that is, when something other than what we might call 'standard' sixteenth-century court English, now termed Original Pronunciation, appears – shows that the Northern dialect, found towards the border with Scotland, is the dialect most commonly used in the plays. The Northern dialect in fact represents over 80 per cent of the dialect used in the plays. Under 7 per cent is in the dialect spoken in Warwickshire, where Stratford-upon-Avon was located, and at least half of that usage concerns terms used in print, which the author could have simply read. The only sustained passage of dialect in the plays is Edgar's speech in *King Lear* (4.6.231–42), which the Arden editor claims is standard stage West Country dialect, although both Gilbert Slater and Bradley claim it is Kentish. If the primary author of the plays was indeed a native Warwickshire dialect speaker then why is this not the dominant dialect in the plays? Out of a vocabulary of 25,000 words how is it that only *two* come from contact with a native Warwickshire speaker? (See Appendix 12).

In fact, Stratford-upon-Avon does not appear at all in the canonical plays. The lengths to which Stratfordians will go in attempting to create such a linkage can be illustrated by Caroline Spurgeon's attempt to link several lines describing the flow of water in the poem *The Rape of Lucrece* to the way that she observed water flowing under Stratford bridge in 1935. However, *Henry VI, Part 1* includes a mention – not in the immediate sources – of Sir William Lucy, which is assumed to be a reference to the Sheriff of Warwickshire at that period. Some have imagined that this implies the playwright's particular interest in Warwickshire, though it might also be an allusion to rumours that Mr Shakespeare had been a poacher of Lucy's game. Furthermore, there are references in *The Taming of the Shrew* (Induction 2, 18 and 21) to the locations Burton-heath and Wincot (Wilmcote), where Mr Shakespeare's aunt and mother lived. These have been used as supporting evidence for the Shakespeare-was-Shakespeare case. Anyone who would suggest otherwise ought, therefore, to be able to explain why these have been included, if the playwright did not come from round about. It is, therefore, worth looking at these references closely. First, *Shrew* links these towns associated with William Shakespeare with the character of Christopher Sly the drunken tinker who, at the beginning of the Induction, makes a comic allusion to his ancestor Richard the Conqueror (Induction 1.4). As far as the audience is immediately concerned, the point is that he is dull enough not to know that the leader of the Norman Conquest was William the Conqueror. There is a secondary meaning embedded here, for this 'mistake' actually refers to a compounding of names relating to an adulterous escapade of Shakespeare's, which was relatively well known since it was described in John Manningham's diary for 1602–3:

> Upon a time when Burbage played Richard the Third there was a citizen grew so far in liking with him, that before she went from the play she appointed him to come that night unto her by the name of Richard the Third. Shakespeare, overhearing their conclusion, went before, was entertained and at his game ere Burbage came. Then, message being brought that Richard the Third was at the door, Shakespeare caused return to be made that William the Conqueror was before Richard the Third.

The use of these Warwickshire towns would appear, then, to be made at William Shakespeare's expense.

Furthermore, Michael Egan speculates that Sly's series of occupations – working in the Bear Gardens, as a tinker, and as the maker of cards for wool carding – refer to Shakespeare's earlier occupations. Since the Bear Gardens amphitheatre was located in the manor of Paris Gardens, which was owned by Francis Langley (with whom Shakespeare would later be associated), this suggestion seems plausible – especially since Mr Shakespeare was actually living very near to the Bear Gardens until at least 1596, as we shall see (see Appendix 13). If there was enough interchange that Edward Alleyn could go from the Rose to being the Master of the Bear Gardens in 1604,[5] then presumably Mr Shakespeare could have moved in the opposite direction. The imagery of bear-baiting does actually appear in several plays, including *Macbeth* and *Julius Caesar*. It was, however, the subject of criticism by Puritans, who saw it as more of a foul den than a fair garden. In *Twelfth Night*, the play where it is dealt with most exhaustively, and in which Malvolio represents both a Puritan and one of the bears, this very common entertainment is depicted as rather problematic.[6]

Further, there is a much clearer piece of mockery aimed at 'William' in *As You Like It*. Superficially, the play seems to be set in France, in Arden (i.e. the Ardennes), which was where Lodge's story had taken place. Coincidentally, however, Arden was also an old name for a part of Warwickshire, where the Forest of Arden was located and Shakespeare's mother had once owned a house which she had then lost when the mortgage was foreclosed. The play presents a clown, William, who was born in the forest and who is associated with a saying about fools and wisdom that appears in Act 5, Scene 1. The same saying appears in Act 1, Scene 2, where it is oddly associated with a story about a knight and mustard. By association, the two identical sayings link William to the story of a knight and mustard. This is an allusion to Ben Jonson's play *Every Man out of His Humour* (1598), which parodies William Shakespeare in the form of a rural clownish character who gets a coat of arms with the motto 'not without mustard', parodying Shakespeare's coat of arms with the motto 'no, without right'.

We should also note in passing how odd it is that *Henry IV, Part 2* contains four characters called William, all of whom have non-speaking parts. One of them, an 'arrant knave' with the surname 'Visor' (a kind of mask) comes from Wilmcote, 3 miles from Stratford-upon-Avon – where another William character mentioned in *The Taming of the Shrew* had relatives, as the actor indeed did have. Finally, in *The Merry Wives of Windsor,* there is yet another William, a schoolboy who cannot comprehend page one of the Latin grammar book and has to be given lessons in basic Latin to make him into an educated 'page'.

In sum, then, the use of Warwickshire place names would appear to be part of a modest but systematic tendency on the part of the primary author of these plays to make fun of William from Warwickshire. Needless to say, this is not proof that Shakespeare did not write the plays; playwrights do occasionally put themselves in their own work in a self-mocking fashion. What is important, however, is that it is no proof at all that he *did* write the plays, or that the author came from Warwickshire.

Plays in Elizabethan and Jacobean London were generally written by playwrights who had no financial stability but were living hand to mouth, sometimes on a pay-by-the-page system. With the exception of Marlowe and perhaps a couple of others, plays were written rapidly and generally just consisted of the surface plot, without sub-plots or complex allegories. The very different composition of the Shakespearean plays suggests that their writer enjoyed much more economic security than other writers, since their plays reflect a long literary process of composition. As Lukas Erne has emphasised, these plays were written as literature, not by a working man of the theatre, but by a literary dramatist who frequently wrote many more lines than could be performed onstage. They could, however, be read in the study.[7] Then, as today, it would be up to the acting company to create a cut of the script that would work for them onstage – for instance, the surviving text of *Macbeth* may be missing a scene that was cut in production.

For a working actor to have been able to create these complex and often over-written plays seems unlikely, let alone being able to maintain such a pace for a period of twenty years – over which around forty plays were written. Only a handful of individuals of the period were both actors and playwrights – such as Kemp, Tarleton and Wilson – and none of them had the stamina to keep it up for more than a few years. The most successful of them, Ben Jonson, very soon abandoned working as an actor in order to concentrate upon his career as a playwright full-time.

It is clear however, that the primary author of these plays had considerable familiarity with the Lord Chamberlain's Men, and also with such technical issues as how many lines of dialogue to allow for the time when an actor goes offstage to change a costume. It is usually supposed that the playwright learnt these skills by watching and performing in the plays in the public playhouses. Yet, there are good reasons to doubt that the author's skills were gained primarily through participating in and watching plays performed onstage.

Firstly, out of all the plays that are used as sources, the majority had not appeared on the public stage within the previous five years, and a good number never could have done so since they weren't in English. Evidently, the playwright learnt most of their craft not by acting in plays, nor even by watching them, but by reading them (see Appendix 11).

Secondly, it is sometimes supposed that the playwright must have worked intimately with the Lord Chamberlain's Men because in some of our surviving texts the name of the actor was occasionally substituted for that of the character. For instance in the text of *Much Ado About Nothing* as we have it, instead of the character names Verges and Dogberry, the names of the actors Cowley and Kemp have been substituted. While these could possibly have been inserted by the playwright, they were much more probably put there by the theatre bookkeeper. As Andrew Gurr has shown, in all the play manuscripts of the period where such names of actors appear, a different hand has added them in, using different ink, strongly suggesting it was done by the bookkeeper or prompter responsible for the performing version of the script.[8]

Finally, while the plays have detailed stage directions explaining how actors should behave, these do not reflect the author's experience as an actor either. Many of them were created by the editors, including the scribe Ralph Crane, during the editing of the First Folio, and not by the playwright at all. For instance, the unusually specific stage directions in *The Tempest* are thought to reflect an observation of a past performance, rather than having been written to direct a performance that had not taken place.

Proto-Feminism

A remarkable feature of the plays is an unusually positive attitude towards women. On the one hand, women could possess economic power, worked as craftspeople and shopkeepers, made up nearly half the apprentices, and could freely appear in public, even in theatre audiences – where they might be specifically addressed by the actors, as in the Epilogue of *As You Like It*.[9] On the other hand, women were generally regarded as household possessions and as their husband's property; married women did not even own the clothes on their own backs, and very few women indeed were highly educated or highly literate.

So the playwright's treatment of women is distinctive. In 1664, Margaret, Duchess of Newcastle, who was herself a playwright, wrote a wondering letter which speculated about the true gender of the person who wrote the plays, and their remarkable ability to understand women's characters: 'One would think that he had been metamorphosed from a Man to a Woman for who could describe Cleopatra better than he hath done, and many other Females of his own creating?' Out of all of them, perhaps the best instance is the character of Emilia in *Othello*, which has been called the first feminist character in Western literature. Giorgio Melchiori in his article 'The Rhetoric of Character Construction: *Othello*' called Emilia's speech in *Othello* (4.3.83–102) 'the first feminist manifesto'.

The playwright was also oddly knowledgeable about girls' literature. For *The Taming of the Shrew* (and its predecessor), the playwright drew upon *The Knight of La Tour-Landry and His Book for His Four Daughters* (1484), which was available at court as a manual of etiquette for girls. The playwright also used *Penelope's Web* of 1587, which 'in a christal mirror of feminine perfection represents the virtues of women'. Parts of *Twelfth Night* drew upon Barnabe Rich's collection of stories for women, *Farewell to the Military Profession* (1581). This collection of stories began with a specific dedication on the title page – 'gathered together for the onely delight of the courteous gentlewomen both of England and Ireland' – and his first foreword is addressed 'to the Right Courteous Gentlewomen' for their 'honour, estimation, and all other their honest delights'. For *The Winter's Tale*, the author used *Mamillia: A Mirror or Looking-Glass for the Ladies of England* (1583). The primary author of the plays is also one of just a handful of writers to draw upon the *Heptameron* (1558) by Margaret of Navarre – the most popular book among the ladies at court – and Montemayor's *Diana* (1559), which was favourite reading among Elizabeth's ladies-in-waiting.

Not only are the plays pro-feminist, they also display a very unusual interest in menstruation. In *The Tempest,* the leaking ship is compared to a leaky 'unstanched wench' – that is, a woman having her period. In *Hamlet,* Ophelia's many herbs are mostly abortifacients, according to the medicinal handbooks of the time. As for *King Lear*, Colleen Kennedy, in a speculative article 'Deodorizing *King Lear*' claims it is 'a play with constant references to vaginal odors', and highlights the references in the play to menopause.

Even more interesting is how the women characters evolve over time. The first two major female characters can be found in *Henry VI*, written in 1589–90. These are Joan of Arc, an out-of-place, lower-class girl at the French court, and Queen Margaret, an out-of-place French queen at the English court. Both women are described as promiscuous, both have major English-speaking parts, both – very unusually – were generals, and each was described as a 'manly woman'. In Joan's case this was largely a reference to her actual male clothing, though Margaret was accused of having metaphorically 'stolen the breech(es)' (*Henry VI, Part 3* 5.5.24). As Howard and Rackin note in their book *Engendering a Nation*, Margaret upsets the normal order of things by taking her son away – despite him technically being his father's property, as she was herself.

While the role of Margaret in *Richard III* is not dramatically essential – some eighteenth-century stage productions and modern movie versions have dropped her entirely – her presence across the first tetralogy gives a role of 1,221 lines, comparable to Prince Hamlet. Although *Richard III* features three women alone on stage for an extended period (the only such example in Shakespeare and perhaps the only instance in Elizabethan theatre), the other women's roles in *Richard III* (written in 1591) are more domesticated, playing the roles of wife, of daughter, or of wife to be. By the time the playwright wrote the second tetralogy, women's roles had become even more domesticated, like Mistress Quickly or Queen Katherine in *Henry V*, who makes the same kinds of double entendres, except in French. By the time the comedies were written, we find intelligent, educated women, but they are not generals. Nonetheless, in a world where a talkative woman was regarded as a shrew, and horribly punished as such, the playwright was able to exploit the privileges of rank and fictive masculinity by presenting women characters as having royal blood, and by allowing them to speak in the guise of cross-dressed boys. These two strategies, which are prefigured in the roles of Joan of Arc and Queen Margaret in the first tetralogy, enable the women characters to speak more than audiences would normally expect. Indeed, the plays provide an unusual number of instances of women dressing up as men (or technically, boys playing women who dressed up as men as part of the plot, as women were not allowed on stage). This amounts to as many examples as had appeared in the whole of the English theatre up to this point.

Although the inferior social position of women in seventeenth-century England has often been exaggerated, the plays seem to go out of their way to provide representations of educated women who are literate and musical, who sing and play instruments, such as Katherina, Bianca, Viola, Beatrice and so on. Given that women were played on stage by boy actors, and there were only a fixed number of boys in the acting company, there were upper limits to the number of female roles that could be created. Furthermore, in many of the plays the playwright was following historical sources in which there were few women figures, and – history being what it is – was unable to invent new ones. However, still the playwright took steps (as indicated above) to give the women characters that did exist significant roles. Indeed, in at least three plays the woman lead speaks more than the male: Rosalind with 686 lines in *As You Like It*, Imogen with 580 lines in *Cymbeline*, and Helena with 451 lines in *All's Well That Ends Well*. And when the author was writing a play not based on historical sources, as in *A Midsummer Night's Dream*, *The Merry Wives of Windsor*, and *Love's Labour's Lost*, all of which were probably written initially for private performance not the public playhouses (and therefore were not constrained by the dedicated cast of the playing company), women have approaching a third of the roles – more than twice as many as in the rest of the canon. By contrast, in the pre-Shakespearean plays, the cross-dressing character of Neronis in the anonymous play *Sir Clyomon and Clamydes* (composed around 1580), who was used as a model for Rosalind, had only 267 lines.

We therefore have to explain two things, why the playwright gave such extensive roles to women at all, and secondly the process of evolution – in which the playwright began by showing powerful women at court like Joan and Margaret, but transitioned to writing domesticated roles like Bianca and even Katherine being tamed (perhaps) into the role of housewife.

Play Design: A Scholarly Process

Despite the eighteenth-century romantic notion of writers like Maurice Morgann that Shakespeare's plays were somehow written intuitively,[10] on the contrary, they were carefully constructed in a highly scholarly fashion. Less widely known, however, is how elaborately Shakespeare drew on a multiplicity of sources in writing the plays. For instance, Kenneth Muir has shown that, in *Midsummer Night's Dream*, the playwright drew on *eight* different treatments of the Pyramus and Thisbe story to create the brief version that appears in the play. We may conclude that the playwright's process was extremely scholarly, however powerful their intuition of human character. It is widely recognised that the plays draw from over 300 different books – a very large library in Elizabethan London – some of which the playwright appears to have read in several languages. The differences between the individual quartos, and between the quartos and the folio, also reveal that the playwright revised the plays constantly, adding in new material, altering other material, and in some cases making thousands of minor revisions.

This highly logical, scholarly, systematic approach to composition is also reflected in the way the plays were designed and structured. In his book *Shakespearean Design*, Mark Rose shows that *A Midsummer Night's Dream* is composed symmetrically, with a centre scene set in the wood, flanked by two scenes of the Mechanicals, which are flanked in turn by two scenes set at court in Athens (see Fig. 1).

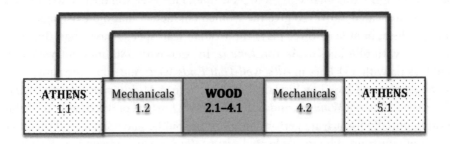

Fig 1: Internal Symmetrical Structure of *A Midsummer Night's Dream* (after Rose).[11]

The composition of *The Tempest* is even more sophisticated because, as Boika Sokolova's study, *Shakespeare's Romances as Interrogative Texts*, has shown, the play's symmetry is achieved not through the mirroring of scenes and acts, but by the grouping of the characters. At the centre is the pair of lovers, flanked by the grouping Caliban/Stephano/Trinculo, which in turn is flanked by Alonso/Sebastian/Antonio, the whole flanked by the outlying grouping of Prospero/Ferdinand/Miranda. The whole is bookended by the shipwreck. In an odd departure from this structure, a masque is inserted at 4.1, disturbing the overall pattern. It should not be surprising, therefore, that the masque is sometimes explained as a late addition (see Fig. 2).

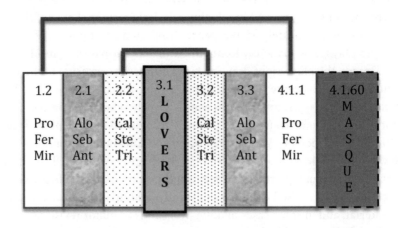

Fig. 2: Internal Symmetrical Structure of *The Tempest* (after Sokolova).[12]

We therefore have a very good way of assessing the work attributed to the various authorship candidates: it can be assessed by how far it resembles the very impressive symmetrical literary designs in the plays. This is a more reliable indicator than subjective comparisons such as verse style, and even more reliable than similarities of vocabulary, since literary design is so systematic.

Court Experience

Whereas most playwrights had at best a remote relationship with the patron of the playing companies for which they wrote, the writer of the Shakespearean plays appears to have had an unusually intimate relationship with Lord Hunsdon, one of the most powerful men at court, the man in charge of the English theatre and the patron of the Lord Chamberlain's Men. Take, for instance, *The Raigne of King Edward III*, which was printed anonymously but is now believed by scholars to be either in part or entirely by 'Shakespeare' and is now included in new editions of the collected works. In his article 'Was *The Raigne of King Edward III* a Compliment to Lord Hunsdon?', Roger Prior demonstrated that the writer not only compliments Lord Hunsdon, but used Hunsdon's own copy of Froissart's *Chronicles*, which was 'one of Hunsdon's most valued and consulted books'; he treated it like a family bible, recording the names and births of his many children on a blank leaf within it. The playwright gave particular emphasis to those passages which Lord Hunsdon found important. Indeed, Roger Prior plausibly argues that because the book was so prized by Lord Hunsdon it would not have left Old Somerset House, so 'quite possibly' the playwright actually composed this play in Hunsdon's library.[13] This, it seems, is the first time evidence has been put forward for the location in which any Shakespearean work was actually written. Furthermore, because the play reworks material from the Armada, in 'The Date of *Edward III*', Kurt Wentersdorf suggests it was written between 1589/90, while Eliot Slater dates it a year later to 1592, about the same time as *Henry VI, Part 1*. Amelia was living in Lord Hunsdon's residence at both these dates. Someone close to Lord Hunsdon wrote the play and she was in exactly the right place at the right time.

In general, of course, the playwright's accounts of courts are derived largely from the chronicles. Nonetheless, the way those sources are used, particularly in the history plays, suggests an intimate familiarity with politics, stagecraft (see page 25) and court power struggles. *Henry VI, Part 1*, for instance, is set entirely at courts and almost all the characters are courtiers. *Richard II* is preoccupied with court ceremonial rituals, which it inverts and parodies, most notably in the trial scene. Indeed the play seems to reveal an antiquarian knowledge of the actual pageantry employed in Richard's reign, including his apocalyptic entry into London, which was decorated as a heavenly city in which, as Steven Marx reminds us, Richard II played the anointed Christ. To take another example, *Antony and Cleopatra* shows knowledge of the ceremonial for welcoming a prince upon a ship of the Royal Navy, and so on. It is very clear when a character is just referring to something in a book – as in *Henry VI, Part 1*, when the child King Henry talks abstractly about civil dissension (3.1.71–3), referring to Cato's army in the deserts of Libya – since this contrasts with the harsh reality of everyday politics depicted in the rest of the action, even in the cases where the underlying source is Lucan or a chronicler.

The playwright also shows a remarkable knowledge of actual entertainments that had gone wrong on Her Majesty's visits to the court estates of the nobility. The plays tend to incorporate pageants and plays within the play modelled on the dramatic interludes that formed a key part of court life. For instance, the princess's hunting arrangements in *Love's Labour's Lost* allude to the queen's deer killing at a royal entertainment at Cowdray (1591). In a *tour de force* of a series of parodies of royal entertainments, the mechanicals in *A Midsummer Night's Dream* (1596) parody the disasters that occurred in the staging of historical court entertainments at Elvetham (1591), Kenilworth (1575), and Ditchley (1592). Other aspects of their play parody royal events at Whitehall (1581), Warwick (1574) and Stirling Castle in Scotland (1594).

Consider Kenilworth in 1575. In the entertainment put on for Elizabeth, an actor represented the mythical character Arion, who is thrown overboard by sailors on his voyage back from Corinth, and who saved himself by singing a song that attracted a friendly dolphin, which then carried him home. On this occasion, however, Harry, the actor who was supposed to play the role of Arion, stood stunned in an attack of stage fright. His voice had gone. When the time came for him to sing his lines and so summon the dolphin, it's not entirely clear whether he mounted the 24-foot-long mechanical dolphin (which was like a floating barge with wind musicians in its belly), or if he was able to begin his song. Either way, overcome, he quickly tore off his clothes and declared hoarsely to the whole assembly, 'I am not Arion, but only honest Harry Goldingham.' Fortunately for him, this pleased Her Majesty better than if he had gone through with the song in the normal way – so at least we know from informal accounts. Of course, the formal record, which was widely circulated, was a cover-up written by Robert Langham, the clerk of the council chamber door, who describes a 'delectable ditty' 'deliciously delivered', which was 'incomparably melodious'. In *A Midsummer Night's Dream* the playwright would allude to this event with the line 'I heard a mermaid upon a dolphin's back.'

The example from Warwick is similar and involves a pun on the recorder (the musical instrument) and the Recorder (a town official). Theseus, the duke, describes the event that echoes the Warwick entertainment. With a flourish of trumpets, the actor Quince then enters precisely to 'greet' the queen with a 'premeditated welcome' to the play within the play. His mis-punctuated prologue has periods in the middle of sentences and comes to an abrupt stop – precisely the problems that Theseus has just complained about. Also, the way the speech is delivered is oddly described as being 'like a child on a recorder' (5.1.122) – a pun clearly intended to link back to the event that took place in 1574, which involved a real Recorder in Warwick. He approached the Queen to give his speech, kissed her hand, but then got stage fright and forgot his lines. Fortunately for him, Her Majesty was in a playful mood, and was more forgiving than Theseus:

> Come hither little Recorder. It was told me that you would be afraid to look upon me or to speak boldly; but you were not as afraid of me as I was of you; and now I thank you for putting me in mind of my duty.

There are similar echoes of royal entertainments at Ditchley, Whitehall, and Stirling Castle. This raises the question of how the playwright gained access to this extremely unusual knowledge from diverse royal entertainments all over the country. As we have seen, the official records did not generally match actual events.

What is even more significant is the *timing* of this knowledge. This knowledge of the court, of statesmanship, and of national politics appears right in the earliest plays, in *Henry VI*, parts 1, 2 and 3, *Richard III*, and *Titus Andronicus*, all written before 1594. It is thereafter that the playwright began writing what one might call domestic 'bourgeois' plays, such as *The Taming of the Shrew*, *Twelfth Night*, *The Merchant of Venice* and *Romeo and Juliet*. Any authorship theory has to explain not only why the playwright began writing history plays, but why the writer then turned from statecraft to writing bourgeois comedies at this particular point in time.

Shakespeare's Many Types of Knowledge

Although some knowledge of the law was important for every educated person in Elizabethan England, the primary author has more than this. The canon provides descriptions of twenty-five different trials, along with references to issues like 'summer's lease' having 'too short a date', and querying why a short lease should be so expensive. At least 200 legal terms or concepts are mentioned 1,600 times in the plays, according to Sokol and Sokol's *Dictionary of Shakespeare's Legal Language*. It is the accuracy and nature of these Shakespearean usages, and the way in which the playwright appears to have actually thought in legal terms, that have led half a dozen experts to conclude that the writer had legal experience. One of the most significant views was expressed by Thomas Regnier, writing in *The University of Miami Law Review*, who pointed out that the use of inheritance law in *Hamlet* 'bespeaks a level of expertise that is not consonant with merely an

intelligent amateur', because it draws upon the manuscript notebooks of Sir John
Dyer – a judge – which were 'written in Law French, an archaic form of Norman-
English, and inscribed in law hand, a rare style of writing used by law clerks and
few others even back then'. Only someone who could read law hand could have
understood them.

Imagery referring to falcons appears again and again throughout the plays
– which contain *fifteen times* more falconry imagery than the plays of Ben Jonson,
Marlowe or Robert Greene. Unlike references to eagles or to pelicans, which
are derived from literary sources and cast in mythological terms, the falconry
references are always realistic. They cover not only wild falcons but also ones that
have been raised from the egg by a falconer. In *Othello*, Desdemona is a 'haggard'
or wild falcon, in *The Merchant of Venice*, Jessica is tethered to her family not
only with the 'jess', the silk or leather strap tied to a falcon's leg, but she even has
a turquoise ring, echoing the ring that attaches the jess to the falconer's leash.
In *Romeo and Juliet* on the other hand, there is a role reversal, and for once the
woman, Juliet, is the falconer and Romeo the bird. Romeo pleads that Juliet will
'cast off' her virginity like a falconer's lure to attract him, and like Katherina he
is to be given a new name. He flies on light wings and perches over walls, and
Juliet takes the bait of her virginity away from him in order to train him to her
liking.

Sonnet 78 refers to the process of adding extra feathers from a healthy bird into
a falcon's wing. It is a process known as 'imping', a technical term for repairing
a falcon's damaged wing feather. It appears again in the history plays where a
character wants to 'Imp out our drooping country's broken wing' (*Richard II*,
2.1.292). The plays also make numerous references to 'seeling', the process of
sewing a falcon's eyelids to accustom her to wearing a hood, which appears in
Othello, *Antony and Cleopatra* and *Henry IV*.

A more obscure example appears in *Hamlet*, where Gertrude is imagined
'stewed in corruption' and in 'the rank sweat of an enseamed bed' (3.4.90–91).
In the original source Polonius is cast from the queen's chamber into a toilet or
sewer to be eaten by pigs. In *Hamlet*, Polonius hides behind the arras (which is a
pun on *hara*, a pigsty). The word 'seam' means greasy, and 'enseamed' is a term in
falconry that refers to the process of giving a greasy laxative to a falcon so it will
release its bowels before it is ready to fly in order to reduce its weight. So, as Bill
Worthen observes, the playwright is referring to the queen's bedroom (alluding to
the original sewer) as if it were full of excrement from giving a colonic to a falcon.
Giving falcons colonics is a curiously specialist interest. This is something that
might concern a falconer, but hardly would be a common image in the mind of
someone who merely used falcons for hunting.

These examples show that the playwright not only had experience of participating
in hunts that used falcons, but – much more unusually – had extensive dealings
with people who were falconers, and probably with the birds themselves. Finally,

we should note that falconry was a sport that was traditionally stratified by social rank. At least in late medieval times there were strict rules about what rank one had to be in order to fly each particular kind of bird. Members of high ranks could fly birds associated with lower ranks, but not vice versa. The penalties for misappropriating a bird were extremely severe. So although the plays do refer to goshawks traditionally used by yeomen, they also refer appropriately to the flight of 'tercel gentles', also known as the 'tassel-gentles', or peregrines, which could only be flown by princes or barons. So the hawking references not only link the playwright to the activities of a falconer, but to the hawking techniques used by the very top layer of the English aristocracy.

Silk weaving is referred to in several of the Shakespearean plays, but was not formally introduced to England until the reign of James I, and mulberry trees, on which silkworms feed, were not generally grown in England until 1609. So until that date, the only source for the playwright's knowledge of sericulture, as it is known, would have been through someone involved in the silk-spinning industry, through those Italians involved in silk importing, or through a few specialists like Thomas Moffat, the author of *The Silkeworms and Their Flies* (1599).

It appears that Shakespeare drew on all these different sources of knowledge, especially in writing *A Midsummer Night's Dream*, which has extensive references to silk – but which was written several years before the appearance of Moffat's book. Moffat's book refers to the oval 'bottoms' of silk that the silkworms spin on the mulberry trees, and which the plays refer to as 'silken parcels'. In *Othello*, there is a reference to the 'worms ... that did breed this silk' (3.3.73). In *A Midsummer Night's Dream*, which makes an allusion to the 'weaving spiders' (2.2.20), the fates have cut Pyramus/Bottom's lifeline: 'shore / With shears his thread of silk' (4.1.334–5). The process of unwinding the thread is reflected in *The Two Gentlemen of Verona*, where it is used as a metaphor for love: 'unwind her love from him, / Lest it should ravel and be good for none, / You must provide to bottom it on me' (3.2.51–3). This unravelling is also mentioned in *Sir Thomas More*: 'When the thread of hazard is once spun / A bottom great wound up greatly undone.' A 'bottom of brown thread' appears in *The Taming of The Shrew* (4.3.137), together with a tailoring scene. As for Bottom himself, his occupation in *A Midsummer Night's Dream* is given as a weaver of homespuns. His name refers both specifically to the shapes made by the silkworm cocoons when they hang on the tree and also to the implement upon which their thread was wound. Images of silk cascade down the plays through the years in mentions of a 'silken thread' (*Much Ado*, 5.1.25), 'a twist of rotten silk' (*Coriolanus*, 5.6.95), and the 'idle immaterial skein of sleave silk' (*Troilus and Cressida*, 5.1.30). This very specialised and unusual knowledge in the plays implies that the playwright was associated with a distinctive network of individuals involved in the silk-weaving industry.

There are several hundred medical references in the Shakespearean works. To some extent the medical imagery in the plays – for instance the plague play *Romeo and Juliet* – is shaped by the playwright having lived through the plagues that closed the theatres in 1592–3 and killed nearly 20,000 Londoners. However studies by Robert Simpson and others on the medical references in the plays show that the early Italian plays, *Shrew*, *The Two Gentlemen of Verona*, and *The Merchant of Venice*, have on average an unremarkable five medical references per play. This is comparable to John Lyly's *Endymion* or Webster's *The Duchess of Malfi*, or similar plays of the early 1590s. However, this changed suddenly and dramatically in the group of plays of the later 1590s: *Romeo and Juliet*, *Henry IV, Part 2*, *Richard II*, and *King John*, which have on average twenty-two medical references per play. The extensive medical imagery in the plays continued from some years but slowly declined, until, by the final plays – *The Winter's Tale*, *Cymbeline* and *Henry VIII* – it had returned to the original conventional level of interest of about five mentions per play.

Several of the plays also refer to the circulation of the blood, such as *Coriolanus*, possibly written around 1605, and first published in the First Folio in 1623. This play specifically mentions the heart as the 'court' that distributes the blood to the brain and the other offices of the body:

> ... I am the store-house and the shop
> Of the whole body: but if you do remember,
> I send it through the rivers of your blood,
> Even to the court the heart – to th' seat o' th' braine;
> And, through the cranks and offices of man,
> The strongest nerves, and small inferior veines,
> From me receive that natural competencie
> Whereby they live ...
>
> *Coriolanus*, 1.1.32–3

This is problematic because the circulation of the blood was first announced in an obscure lecture in London by Harvey in April 1616, just a few days before the death of William Shakespeare in Stratford. Identifying how the playwright had medical knowledge of this kind is clearly, therefore, an important discriminator in demonstrating their authorship.

Whereas in Marlowe's plays there are just under three mentions of food per play, in the Shakespearean plays overall this doubles to six per play, or nearly nine per play if cooking and drinking are also included. Only Shakespeare's early court plays were comparable to Marlowe's, and the mentions of food suddenly increase around 1593/4. The most extensive discussion, which covers kneading, baking, boiling, stewing, frying, stuffing, larding, basting, and mincing, is in *Troilus and Cressida*. Other plays demonstrate knowledge of pastry-making: how to make a covered pie with a pastry cover (*Richard II*, 3.2.152), how to make a 'coffin pie' from pastry which would then be baked (*Titus Andronicus*, 5.2.185–8), how to pinch pastry (*All's Well*, 4.3.131), how to sugar a crust (*Hamlet*, 3.1.46) and even how to make a posset of hot wine and curdled milk (*Hamlet*, 1.5.68-9) to drink with it. The playwright was also oddly knowledgeable in baking and knew how to slow down the grinding of the wheat if you wanted to use the flour for making a cake (*Troilus and Cressida*, 1.1.14), and to sieve out the bran from the meal/flour before beginning (*Coriolanus*, 3.3.321).

Meat was the focus of the kitchen – geese, rabbit, hare, venison, mutton – with occasional fish. Whereas mutton appears in the plays twelve times, beef appears fourteen times, and venison (an aristocratic food) six times, there are only two references to pigs being roasted on a spit – even though this was the most commonly eaten kind of meat. Indeed, the word 'pork' appears only three times, in every case in *The Merchant of Venice* where it is used as an insult (pork being forbidden to Jews), similar to the insulting reference to 'bacon-fed knaves' in *Henry IV*. It seems reasonable to wonder why the playwright seemed to have an unusual aversion to England's most popular and tastiest meat.

The playwright also had some knowledge of generalship and soldiery: the plays use 400 words of special military vocabulary such as hoisting a petard, a technical term for positioning an explosive for demolishing a gate. One particular feature is that the earlier plays are those that demonstrate the knowledge of generalship, and the later plays those that demonstrate knowledge of the life of an ordinary soldier. There is a strange gap in the middle – the playwright does not refer much to the concerns of middle-ranking officers. *Henry V* uses a manuscript prepublication version of Sir Roger Williams' book *The Actions of the Low Countries* (not published until 1618). The playwright also demonstrates accurate knowledge of the preparations for war such as mustering, braying trumpets and loud churlish drums, but not of actual battles.

The playwright's knowledge of astronomical science and physics is very unusual. Moreover, an interest in science normally is established through exposure during the teenage years. As W. G. Guthrie has shown, over 100 astronomical mentions appear in the plays.[14] Take, for instance, geomagnetism, the magnetism of the Earth. This was announced, after nearly twenty years of work, in *De Magnete* by William Gilbert, who was president of the College of Physicians, and physician to the queen from 1601 to 1603. This discovery is referred to in *Troilus and Cressida* in two separate passages 'as iron to adamant (magnet), as earth to th' centre' (3.2.174) and 'the very centre of the earth, Drawing all things to it' (4.2.105). William Gilbert was also the only contemporary scientist who argued that tides were caused by the attraction of the moon. (Both Galileo and Sir Francis Bacon held different, incorrect, explanations of the tides.) However in *A Midsummer Night's Dream*, the playwright not only refers to magnetism, the 'hard hearted adamant' (2.1.196) but also refers to the moon as the 'governess of floods' (2.1.103) causing tides. Similarly, a discussion of the moon causing tides also appears in *Henry IV, Part 1*:

Falstaff   ... being governed, as the sea is, by our noble and chaste mistress the moon, under whose countenance we steal.

Henry	Thou sayest well, and it holds well too; for the fortune of us that are the moon's men doth ebb and flow like the sea, being governed, as the sea is, by the moon…

Henry IV, Part 1, 1.1.27–33

Since this understanding of the moon causing tides did not become an accepted scientific convention until after the publication of Newton's *Principia* in 1687, and William Gilbert's work on this was not published until 1651, the most likely explanation is that the playwright had some contact with Gilbert and learned about this research in 1596–7.

The playwright was also aware of a particular astronomical problem concerning the movement of the planet Mars. This is referred to in the early play *Henry VI, Part 1*, written in 1590, although in the section probably composed by Nashe and drawing on Cornelius Agrippa:

> Mars his true moving, even as in the heavens,
> So the earth, to this day is not known

Henry VI, Part 1, 1.2.1–2

Even if penned by Nashe, it was retained in the text that appears in the First Folio. It was, however, an extremely obscure astronomical problem that does not seem to have been under investigation by any English astronomers of the time. The astronomer who was heavily engaged in collecting data on the movements of Mars to solve this problem was Tycho Brahe in Denmark, who would give his observations to Kepler to analyse in February 1600. Kepler eventually published his laws of planetary motion in *De Motibus Stellae Martis* in 1609, showing that the orbit of Mars is an ellipse. So the most likely explanation of how the playwright became interested in this obscure astronomical issue was through having some early social familiarity with the astronomical work of Tycho Brahe, since this was too early to have been gained from Brahe's published letters *Epistolae Astronomicae*, of 1596, which some claim that the playwright had read.

Additional indications of the playwright's familiarity with Tycho Brahe include the appearance in *Hamlet* of his relatives Rosencrantz and Guildenstern. In *Troilus and Cressida* there is the figure of Troilus who may have a 'copper nose' (1.2.102). This extremely unusual feature has even led to the suggestion that Troilus is intended as a contemporary allusion to Brahe, who used a copper nose after having his real nose cut off in a duel. In the play, Ulysses advocates for the traditional cosmology in which 'the Heavens themselves, the Planets, and this centre (the Earth), observe degree, priority and place'. However the Troilus/Brahe character argues appropriately that this is all over and 'the bonds of heaven are slipped, dissolved and loosed.' That disruption was marked in 1572 by the supernova, a new star that shattered the idea of the Aristotelian fixed spheres, to which the stars were supposedly attached. This supernova, which Brahe observed and which led him to receive the funds to build his observatory, has been calculated by researchers at Texas State University to be the star that opens *Hamlet*.[15]

Further, as Peter Usher has indicated, *Hamlet* unfolds an astronomical allegory.[16] The Earth is represented by Claudius (Ptolemy), and initially surrounded by the Moon and 10,000 fixed stars. The 'moist star', the Moon, represented by Ophelia, will be taken away and together with Hamlet's father Jove/Jupiter, his eye of Mars, and the golden star Guildenstern, it will then become a satellite of the 'son of Hyperion', or Helios, the sun, namely Hamlet himself, who repeatedly puns on the words 'sun' and 'son'. This allegory would appear to be referencing how the geocentric Ptolemaic theory of the universe is being replaced by Tycho Brahe's distinctive model in which the sun is the centre of a mini solar system of planets, all of which then rotate around the Earth. The same model appears much more clearly in *Troilus and Cressida*:

> And therefore is the glorious planet Sol
> In noble eminence enthron'd and sphere'd
> Amidst the other.
>
> *Troilus and Cressida*, 1.3.92–4

As Hanno Wember observes in his paper 'Illuminating Eclipses', this passage both regards the sun as central, in that it is enthroned, but it is also attached to a celestial sphere so that it must be circling around something. This configuration precisely fits Brahe's model, where the sun, with its cluster of planets, circles around the Earth.

So in at least two instances the playwright used Tycho Brahe's rather unusual model of the universe as an alternative to the traditional Ptolemaic theory. Brahe published his geo-heliocentric model in *De Mundi Aetherei Recentioribus Phaenomenis* in 1588, and in 1590 sent two copies to the English astronomer Thomas Savile (who was travelling in Europe from June 1588 to 1591). However, Brahe's system remained largely unknown to the Copernican astronomers in England, including Dr Dee, William Gilbert, and Thomas Harriot. All the Gresham astronomy professors after 1597 were Copernicans. So there needs to be an explanation of how and why the playwright acquired this knowledge of Brahe's system.

There are other areas of knowledge in the plays as well, such as the familiarity that Shakespeare had with the potato, which at the time was grown only in a few rare-plant gardens and was a delicacy only eaten by courtiers. The playwright was familiar with explorers, navigation, map projections, rare plants, and Denmark, including the practical issues of Danish diplomacy and the administrative functioning of royal ambassadors. Several of the plays show some basic familiarity with accounting, which had been developed by the Venetian mathematician Luca Pacioli, whose book published in 1494 described the system of double entry bookkeeping used by Venetian merchants. In *Othello*, for instance, there is a reference to debtor, creditor and 'counter-caster', and in *Cymbeline* the neck of Posthumus is similarly identified with a ledger account awaiting 'aquittance'. The playwright also invented about 1,700 neologisms, many from Italian sources.

The playwright also had a distinctive interest in sex. As Andrew Hadfield observes in his book on Shakespeare's republicanism, both the long poems – the earliest works – depict a predatory sexual tyrant, a regal figure, who is described as a carnivore lustfully stalking their prey like a vulture or lion. Aside from this, the plays reflect a vast sexual vocabulary, documented in Partridge's *Shakespeare's Bawdy*, which lists over 1,000 entries. Frankie Rubinstein's *A Dictionary of Shakespeare's Sexual Puns and Their Significance* lists even more, including over 100 synonyms for vagina, quite apart from references like the one in *Love's Labour's Lost* to a woman having several 'lips'. (As Hugh Craig points out in his article 'Shakespeare's Vocabulary; Myth and Reality', the overall vocabulary used is so large – larger than Ben Jonson's – because the playwright wrote so many plays on such diverse subjects. When considered play by play, Shakespeare's plays use on average 1,664 different words, which is about average for Elizabethan playwrights: Webster used 1,827 and Jonson 1,727.)

Taken together, the various areas of skills and knowledge outlined in this chapter set out the criteria against which a candidate for the authorship must be evaluated. We will now turn to the leading and traditional candidate, 'William Shakespeare' of Stratford. It should be noted that the criteria I am using are entirely taken from the skills and knowledge demonstrated in the plays. This is the only reliable evidence, and this is based on a conventional social science approach, one that identifies the knowledge and skills possessed by the writer – knowledge and skills that must have been obtained through some kind of social and community existence.

Even the present book you are holding reveals something about the author: it reveals that it was written by someone who was academically trained in conventional Shakespeare scholarship, who has experience in directing a Shakespeare company, who has some knowledge of various languages, Roman history and Christian theology, who has worked in management in the area of strategy, who has been trained in social science, and so on. Each of these criteria acts as a kind of filter through which any candidate must pass. Only that candidate who can pass through all these filters can reasonably be put forward as the writer of these plays.

As the writer of *King Lear* put it, in a philosophical allusion to Lucretius and the process of creation, 'nothing can come from nothing' (1.1.92). For these last 400 years, the figure of Mr Shakespeare, as the man who presented the plays to the playing company and had his name on some of the printed copies, has been a sufficient explanation for the author. Whether or not he did anything more than that, the next chapter will show.

3

The Man from Stratford:
A Bad Buy

For the last 400 years, Mr William Shakespeare has been generally acclaimed as the author of the Shakespearean plays, even though, as a recent article in *The Times Higher Education* put it, 'we know virtually nothing about the man',[1] and what we do know, as Michael Posner observes in the Foreword, in no way resembles the material contained in the plays. This peculiar recognition rests, firstly, on the fact that his name began appearing on the printed play quartos (small paperback volumes) in 1598, and secondly because, when referring to the sonnets, the plays, or the long poems, various literary figures of the time, and the actors, assumed that they were Shakespeare's work.

The story begins when the Ovidian poem *Venus and Adonis* (1593) appeared with a dedication signed William Shakespeare, followed by a similar dedication in *The Rape of Lucrece* (1594). Both were printed by Richard Field, a former resident of Stratford-upon-Avon. Many kinds of fantasies – or 'biographical speculation' as Adam G. Hooks more kindly calls them in his paper 'Shakespeare at the White Greyhound' – have been built around this, including the proposition that William sought out his fellow Stratfordian as a publisher. This seems implausible since Field was a trade printer normally hired by other printers and booksellers, it assumes that William (and not the bookseller) arranged the printing, and Field had left Stratford-upon-Avon at least fourteen years before, when William was only fifteen years old. Furthermore, Field only printed *Venus and Adonis* for a year. For the next two decades it would be printed by Field's partner, John Harrison, at the sign of the White Greyhound.

As for the plays, Field was not involved in the printing of any of those at all. For an author seeking publication to first choose not a bookseller but a printer, and to do so because of the small home town that he came from actually seems a most unsound basis for judgement. For an author to select the bookseller and allow him to select a trade printer would have been a more sensible arrangement. If that happened, Harrison would then have chosen Field because of his reputation in printing a number of books with court connections, the anonymous *Art of English Poesie* (1589), which Field dedicated to Lord Burghley, Sir John Harrington's translation of *Orlando Furiosio* (1591), several issues of a pamphlet on the Armada for Lord Burghley, and an edition of Ovid's *Metamorphoses* (1589). Furthermore, although the early editions of *The Rape of Lucrece* were indeed printed by Field, Adam Hooks specifically concludes that this happened because Harrison hired him to do so. Later editions were printed by Harrison's successor William Leake, who went on to print *The Passionate Pilgrim*. Neither man had anything to do with Stratford-upon-Avon. Finally, as we will see below, if Richard Field were indeed familiar with William's family, which is quite possible, the name he would have known them under (previous to the granting of the coat of arms in 1596) was Shakspere, Shaksper, Shaxpere or Shagspere.

So much for the name 'Shakespeare' on the long narrative poems. It did not appear again for four years until the first quarto of *Love's Labour's Lost* (1598). It appeared in an odd form. Firstly, the spelling was not 'Shakespeare' as on both the long poems but rather dropped one letter and was 'Shakespere', which indeed resembles how the man from Stratford used it. Secondly, it did not claim that the play was actually *written* by him; it was merely 'newly corrected and augmented by W. Shakespere'. This strongly suggests that the play had existed earlier, and that the name 'Shakespere' was being applied in some supplementary capacity. However, as if to resolve this point, 'Shakespeare' subsequently appeared on reprints of the six earlier plays that had originally appeared anonymously, on almost all subsequent quartos, and on the First Folio (1623). In 1595, there appeared the first theatrical document that clearly mentioned Mr Shakespeare as a member of a theatrical company, namely a payment to him, William Kempe and Richard Burbage for performances at court the previous year.

One problem that is waved away by traditionalists is that the baptismal and marriage documents of the man from Stratford record him as Gulielmus Shakspere, Shaxpere or Shagspere (Gulielmus is the Latin for 'William'). Traditionalists argue that a name spelt many different ways could be spelt one specific way in the theatre. The documentary records show that his family name was actually spelled in about sixty different ways – which John Michell conveniently lists in his book *Who Wrote Shakespeare?* The spelling as 'Shakespeare' is rather rare in the family records, and indeed out of over 100 instances this minority usage appears only twice, in the October 1569 Harrison lawsuit, in which his father was accused of making a loan at an illegally high interest rate, and in the burial records of his brother Edmund in 1607. In none of these family records does William himself take the surname 'Shakespeare', and granted his Christian name, this is perhaps for very good reason.

In November 1596 it was under the name William Shakspere that he was accused – very notably *not* as a member of the Chamberlain's Men and their North London theatre in Spitalfields – but as an accomplice of Francis Langley, the gangster and owner of the Bankside Swan Theatre in South London, of threatening the life of William Wayte. It was under the same name that the following year he bought his mansion in New Place, Stratford.

On close examination, there also appear to be some problems with the theatrical record of 1595, which first mentioned, in a theatrical context, the name under which we know Shakespeare today:

To WILLIAM KEMPE, William Shakespeare and Richard Burbage, servaunts to the Lord Chamberleyne, upon the Councille's warrant dated at Whitehall XVth Marcij 1594, for two severall comedies or enterludes shewed by them before her majestie in Christmas tyme laste part viz St. Stephen's daye and Innocents daye xiijli vjss vijd (13 pounds six shillings and eight pence).

The most obvious oddity here is which Shakespearean plays these two 'comedies', suitable for a court performance, could actually have been. Discovered by Halliwell-Phillips, this document records a payment supposedly made to the Lord Chamberlain's Men for performing at court on 28 December 1594. On that date, however, the Lord Chamberlain's Men did *not* perform at court at Greenwich. They were the company of 'base fellows' that performed a site-specific *The Comedy of Errors* for an audience of drunken law students at Gray's Inn (where it was poorly received). Normally, entries in the Pipe Office Accounts, of which this is one, are backed by a parallel double-entry bookkeeping record. No such record exists. The record is not in the writing of the man who wrote the previous accounts, and the document passed through the hands of Collier, the notorious forger. While the document *may* be genuine, this is enough evidence to raise suspicions.

This evidence invites two opposing interpretations. In the first, the man from Stratford comes to London, and for some reason uses the name 'Shakespeare' to sign the two long poems, but continues to use his ordinary name Shakspere in his law suit and when buying his mansion, in legal dealings, and for baptism of his daughter and the burial of his son. Then, two years after its first usage, he uses 'Shakespeare' once again when he goes to collect money for the acting company – and then waits another four years, until 1598, to put that name on the plays.

In the second interpretation, the writer of *Venus and Adonis* and *The Rape of Lucrece* used 'William Shakespeare' as a pseudonym. At least two contemporaries thought that the name was a pseudonym, either for Marlowe or Bacon, as we shall see. *The Art of Poesie* is very explicit that because poetry and poets were despised, scorned, and not supported by Her Majesty's patronage, 'very many notable gentlemen of the Court' had their work published 'without their own names on it', lest the work be to their 'discredit'. Furthermore, Thomas Edwards perhaps implies that these particular poems were written by a poet at court who had 'golden words' and a 'bewitching pen' but was concealed by the purple robes that could be worn only by princes, the highest nobles, and Garter Knights.[2]

As Peter Dawkins notes, the surname might suggest Pallas Athena, the goddess of wisdom. She was also the goddess of poets, and Stephen Gosson, in his book *Plays Confuted in Five Actions* (*c.* 1582), quotes Tertullian to the effect that playwriting was dedicated to Athena. Her insignia was a spear, and among various other contemporary references, in *The Third Part of the Countesse of Pembroke's Yewchurch* (*c.* 1592) Abraham Fraunce wrote that 'Pallas was so called because she slew Pallas a Giant: or, of shaking her speare'. Similarly, Henri Estienne in his

Thesaurus Linguae Graecas (1572) says she is called a shaker of the spear 'hastae vibratix' because she is warlike. The name William comes from the roots 'wil' meaning 'desire', and 'helm' meaning a 'helmet' or protection, and could mean a desire for protection. For a poet seeking the protection of a pseudonym, Athena's helmet would have been very relevant, since it conferred invisibility. This is perhaps why Thomas Vicars, in the third edition of his manual on rhetoric, *Manuductio ad Artem Rhetoricam* (1628), refers to 'that famous poet who takes his name from "shaking" and a "spear"', indicating that the name was deliberately adopted.[3]

In this interpretation, after the man from Stratford arrived in London, he came to the notice of the author of the plays and was persuaded to use a specific variation of his name as 'William Shakespeare'. This is the name that the author first used on the long poems, at which point, though it might appear a common name, it was, in context, quite evidently a kind of pseudonym with classical associations to the goddess of poetry and playwriting. It also had another, less classical, association.

There is a huge difference between the name 'William Shakespeare' being used in print to sign off a pornographic poem like *Venus and Adonis*, and it being the name of an actual living person. The name did not only have abstruse mythological meanings: in its short form it actually had slang connotations that were entirely appropriate for a pornographic poem. In her book *Filthy Shakespeare: Shakespeare's Most Outrageous Sexual Puns*, Dr Pauline Kiernan notes that in Elizabethan slang the name 'Shakespeare' actually meant 'Wanker' or 'Masturbator', while the word 'Will' was slang for 'cunt', for 'prick' and for sexual desire in general. That might have been a good reason to use it as a pseudonym in dedicating a long pornographic poem, and it might explain why the dedication is so loving; it could even suggest that a sexual relationship existed between the poet and the Earl of Southampton. But to use that name in everyday life would have been a very different story. Not many people would want to be called 'Cunt Masturbator' or similar. Kiernan speculates that anyone who possessed such a name would have been 'mercilessly ribbed' for being 'a walking, talking, breathing, sexual pun'. This would have been a very good reason indeed for Gulielmus Shakspere to retain his perfectly serviceable original name. If he was going to change it at all, it would not have been to the ribald 'Will Shakespeare' unless he had some very powerful incentive.

In their private notes, booklists and inscriptions on title pages many contemporaries listed William Shakespeare as the author of one or more of the canonical works. These include title page inscriptions by Gabriel Harvey, George Buc (possibly a Collier forgery), Humphrey Dyson, William Burton, and private notes by Edward Alleyn and Gabriel Harvey. A list of contemporaries who made the same association in print includes the author of *Willobie His Avisa* (1594), William Covell's *Polimanteia* (1595), Francis Meres in *Palladis Tamia: Wits Treasury* (1598), John Weever in his *Epigrams* (*c.* 1599), and John Davies in *The Scourge of Folly* (1610). It has been claimed that Davies' epigram, which addressed Shakespeare as 'our English Terence', refers to the assertion by Roger Ascham in his book *The Schoolmaster* (1570) that two of Terence's comedies were actually the work of other writers. This, however, seems implausible. The epigram most likely simply invokes Terence's skills in writing comedy – and perhaps some element that Shakespeare borrowed from his literary style. It is unclear, however, that any of these attributions were made based on detailed personal knowledge of Shakespeare and his writing. They are more likely to have been repeating a generally accepted assumption – and one which was not necessarily correct.

The people who were closest to William Shakespeare and his writing processes, and on whose testimony we must therefore place most weight, were the other actors in the Lord Chamberlain's Men. The acting company that received the plays from Mr Shakespeare's hand evidently thought he was the author, because they admired the fact that the copies he gave them were almost without a blot. In other words, Mr Shakespeare handed them plays that looked like fair copies, but must have claimed that these were his original working papers ('foul copies'), which normally would have been full of crossings out ('blots'). Otherwise the praise he received in the epistle to the First Folio (credited to the actors Heming and Condell), that his 'hand and mind went together, and what he thought, he uttered with that easiness that we have scarce received from him a blot in his papers', would have made no sense.

It is surprising that this extremely famous observation about Shakespeare's work has not received more careful attention. At a time when people wrote with feather quills and ink, having almost no crossings out would be quite remarkable for *any* document – let alone over thirty different 100-page play manuscripts drawing from so many sources. For instance, Mr Shakespeare's will, an important legal document that would have commanded special attention, and which is only three sides in length, has a good number of blots and crossings out on every page. Blots also appear on the collaborative manuscript of *Sir Thomas More*, suggesting that Shakespeare's 'foul copies' were indeed foul. The inescapable conclusion is that Mr Shakespeare was falsely claiming that the unblotted documents he handed the playing company were his original 'foul papers'.

This is confirmed by Ben Jonson's famous diary entry, published posthumously:

> I remember, the Players have often mentioned it as an honour to Shakespeare, that in his writing, (whatsoever he penn'd) he never blotted out line. My answer hath been, would he had blotted a thousand. Which they thought a malevolent speech. I had not told posterity this, but for their ignorance, who choose that circumstance to commend their friend by, wherein he most faulted.

Ben Jonson was evidently aware of the concealed religious allegories in the Shakespearean plays concerning the Emperors Titus and Vespasian (see Appendix 8) because his *Epistle Dedicatory*, with its peculiar references to country hands, leavened cakes, and dedications to temples, is recognised by several scholars as a rewriting of Pliny's dedication of his *Natural History* to Titus Caesar. Jonson's satires of the man from Stratford, for instance in *Every Man out of His Humour* (1598), make it quite clear that he did not think that Mr Shakespeare was the true author. Yet his eulogy makes it very clear that he admired the writings as those that 'neither Man, nor Muse, can praise too much'. So although the ignorant actors interpreted Jonson's reference to blots as a malevolent speech – indicating that he thought the verse was poor and should have been corrected and rewritten – what Jonson was really saying to 'posterity', as he put it, was quite different. Jonson was saying, in his typical cryptic fashion, that the players praised Mr Shakespeare for giving them clean *unblotted* manuscripts, but this is something for which Shakespeare is to be faulted; Jonson wishes that Shakespeare had *blotted* (written original verse with crossings out and revisions) a thousand. In other words Jonson is saying that he wished Shakespeare had actually written the original verse for which he is receiving praise simply for handing over fair copies.

So much for the documentary evidence. Like it or not, it does not stand up to scrutiny. Ghostwriting is a well-established practice today, and it was well established in the sixteenth and seventeenth centuries. In their book *Shakespeare Bites Back*, Edmondson and Wells refer to the 'novels of Mark Twain' as literature that was based on biographical life experience. The problem is that Mark Twain was a pseudonym concealing the author's true name, which was Samuel Clemens. So the appearance on the cover of the name that the man from Stratford later used in London does not demonstrate in any way that he wrote the Shakespearean works.

Over 17,000 literary works have been published under pseudonyms or similar devices, and in the sixteenth and seventeenth centuries, as Archer Taylor and Frederick Mosher point out in their book *The Bibliographical History of Anonyma and Pseudonyma*, albeit with some exaggeration, 'almost every writer used a pseudonym at some time during his career'.

Very many of those pseudonyms had classical associations of some kind. One of the most humorous examples is the way in which Sir John Harington, in his book in which he invented the flush toilet, *A New Discourse upon a Stale Subject; The Metamorphoses of Ajax* (1596), concealed himself behind a Greek-style pseudonym *Misacmos*, or 'Hater of Filth'. Physician Robert Burton published *The Anatomy of Melancholy* (1621) under the name Democritus Junior. Joseph Hall wrote his Menippean satire *The Discovery of a New World* (published in Latin in 1605–7) under the name Mercurius Britannicus. Robert Fludd wrote his *Summum Bonorum* (1629) under the name Joachim Frizius. Poet Richard Braithwaite published *A New Spring Shadowed* (1619) under the name Musophilus, and published *The Smoking Age* (1617) under a different pseudonym, Eucapanus Nepenthiacus. John Barclay published *Virtus Vindicata* (1617) under the name Polienus Rhodiensis; the satirist and co-author of *The Isle of Dogs* Thomas Nashe published under the humorous pseudonyms Cuthbert Curryknave and Pierce Penniless; and actor Robert Armin published his joke books *Foole upon a Fool* (1600) and *Quips upon Questions* (1609) under the transparent pseudonym Clonnico de Curtain, meaning the clown of the Curtain Theatre.

However, these are pseudonyms that generally announce themselves by their oddity. Under the heading of 'straight' pseudonyms, we may include satirist Gabriel Harvey, who published *The Trimming of Thomas Nashe* (1597) under the name Richard Lichfield, and antiquarian Elias Ashmole, who edited *Fasiculus Chimicus* (1650) under the almost anagrammatic pseudonym James Hasolle. Those of unorthodox religious views especially turned to pseudonyms: John Frith published *A Pistle to the Christian Reader* (1529) as Richard Brightwell, Jesuit Thomas Everard's translation *The Sum of Christian Doctrine* (1623) appeared under the name John Heigham, Catholic Roger Anderson published *The Converted Jew* (1631) under the name John Clare, Jesuit Joseph Cresswell published *A Proclamation Published under the Name of James King of Great Brittany* (1611) under the pseudonym B. D. De Clerimond, and dramatist John Marsden wrote two poems under the pseudonym W. Kinsayder.

A smaller number of texts, it is true, were published under allonyms, that is, the name of another living person. For example, the writer Sir Thomas More used the allonym of William Ross to write his controversial *Responsio ad Convitia Martin Luther* (1523). In the *True Report of the Late Discoveries* (1583), parts of the text and the nine testimonial poems supposedly written by Sir Francis Drake, Martin Frobisher and others, were actually written by George Peele, Matthew Roydon and their friends as ghostwriters. The writer of *Willobie His Avisa* pretended to be the living Henry Willobie as well as two fictional preface writers. In the theatre world, the poet John Taylor mentioned a 'learned brain' who passed his plays off under the allonym William Fennor, and recruited Fennor to distribute his manuscripts to interested knights. But it is worth noting in this regard that 'Shakespeare' is not a true allonym: it was rather, at least initially, an alias.

So we may reasonably conclude that then, as now, the name on the cover is not a reliable indication of who wrote a work, but that it may take decades for an identification to be established, even today. For instance, the 1967 bestseller *Coffee, Tea or Me?*, which was supposedly written by the two air hostesses Trudy Baker and Rachel Jones, was exposed by the *New York Times* in 2003 as the work of popular novelist and ghostwriter Donald Bain. In the case of the Shakespearean plays it has taken very much longer – hundreds of years – because of the complexity of the situation.

In the theatre, the situation was especially complicated. As Knapp and others have shown, plays were very often created by multiple people. For instance, teams of writers created the plays at the Rose Theatre, each specialising in certain kinds of roles, rather like screenwriting today. Because there was no system of unionisation, of accreditation, or residual rights, and because many plays were published anonymously, sometimes only one of those writers would have his name on the cover, and often none at all. Ben Jonson, in his play *Volpone*, describes an entire apparatus of collaborators. He distinguishes a coadjutor (an equal collaborator), a novice, a journeyman or a hack, and a tutor (possibly meaning a superintendent of a team of writers). Jonson, however, regarded himself as the primary writer, did not mention the names of his co-authors, and rewrote their contributions when the plays appeared in print. At the Rose Theatre, a study of Henslowe's diary shows that on average about 60 per cent of the plays produced were actually written by multiple authors, although only 2 per cent of all plays acknowledged their co-authors on publication. In other words, only 40 percent of plays printed were by a single author, but almost all plays appeared under a single name – while the names of the other author(s) were suppressed.

This complexity is reflected in some of the Shakespearean plays. For instance, Shakespeare's *Henry VIII* was written in part by John Fletcher, yet it appears in the First Folio in the section of the histories entirely as the work of Shakespeare. *Pericles* does not appear in the First Folio at all, but did appear in quarto form under the name of Shakespeare alone in 1609, though it appears to have been written between 1607 and 1608 with some contributions by George Wilkins. Similarly, *Timon of Athens* appeared in the folio as the sole work of Shakespeare, but was probably a collaboration with Middleton. Only *The Two Noble Kinsmen* (which also did not appear in the First Folio, but was published in quarto form in 1634) appeared under both its authors, 'The memorable Worthies of their time Mr John Fletcher and Mr William Shakespeare.' So, as Jeffrey Knapp notes in his article 'Shakespeare as Coauthor', 'even though multiple authors often collaborated on writing plays in the commercial Renaissance theatre, contemporaries typically assumed that the plays were written by single authors', because the names of the other writers were almost always left off. In the case of *Titus Andronicus*, Ravenscroft recorded theatrical gossip that Shakespeare merely gave the play some 'master touches'. So, having his name on the cover is far from being a reliable indicator of Mr Shakespeare's sole authorship, and may not indicate any kind of authorship at all.

The only literary figure who seems to have actually known Shakespeare personally was Ben Jonson, the editor of the First Folio. The actor Shakespeare is listed as having acted in his play *Every Man out of His Humour*. Significantly, Jonson parodies Shakespeare in this very play as the rural, clownish character Sogliardo (whose name in Italian means 'filth'). He has just got a coat of arms (as Shakespeare had in 1597), the motto of which is 'not without mustard' – an allusion to Mr Shakespeare's motto, 'not without right'. This depiction is linked to the clownish character William from Arden appearing in *As You Like It*, who lives in the Forest of Arden and is associated with a saying about wise men and fools that in turn links to Jonson's mustard joke. Jonson's depiction is not of a genius, but rather of a rural, comic figure. It is telling that a character in the play suggests that a hobby horse should be placed over Sogliardo's tomb, saying it is 'an excellent trophy to hang over your tomb'. Hobby horses did various tricks and antics and concealed a real person inside.

It is possible that Ben Jonson may have also written an earlier play also parodying William. The play's author is given only as the innocuous initials B. J., but is not included in Jonson's collected works. On the other hand, he would only have been in his late teens when he wrote it and might have rejected it as juvenilia. In any case, the play is *Guy, Earl of Warwick* and is dated to the early 1590s. The plot comes from a fourteenth-century medieval romance and concerns a major Christian hero, Guy from Warwickshire, one of the Nine Worthies. The playwright has given him a comic and cowardly servant called Sparrow (pronounced Spear-o) who comes from Stratford-upon-Avon, but abandons his pregnant wife to travel the road to be a 'high minded sparrow' and chase pretty wenches.[4] A couple of lines refer to the dog Crab in *The Two Gentlemen of Verona*, and several lines parody the play *Mucedorus*, which was later published as a work by Shakespeare. So as Alfred Harbage first suggested in 1941, this may very well be an early parody of Mr Shakespeare (see Appendix 13).

Something of the same irreverent conception of Mr Shakespeare is shown in the Cambridge University play *The Return from Parnassus* (1601), which wonders that 'mimick apes' should be lifted up by the world to 'high degree' by 'mouthing words that better wits have framed' (see Appendix 14). Other well-known poets would also join in this chorus of criticism. In his book *Satires Virgidemarum* (1597), Joseph Hall, who criticised the author of *The Rape of Lucrece* for beginning too many lines with the words 'Oh' and 'But', also accused the author of being someone who could not be complained against because he wrote under 'another's name'. So the contemporary evidence shows that there were literary figures who regarded Mr Shakespeare either as a comic rural clown, or as the frontman for plays that had been created by someone else.

This becomes clear in the next example, a collection of satirical poems titled *Skialethia: Or, a Shadow of Truth* (1598) by Everard Guilpin. This was two years before William Shakespeare had acquired his coat of arms, and one of the epigrams relates to a certain 'Titus', who 'vaunts his gentry everywhere' and makes references to cooling the volcano Etna, which had appeared in *Titus Andronicus*. In his first satire, Guilpin also alludes to the poet's statement in Latin on the title page of *Venus and Adonis*, that they would drink from Apollo's 'Castalian Spring', the fountain of poetic inspiration, rather than please the vulgar. Clearly this poem is referring to William Shakespeare, yet Guilpin describes a poet whose very brain is composed of Castalian dew, but whose 'outward show' is very different, since he appears to have been born in a year when there was a dearth of wit.

Finally, as Feldman notes in her book on the apocryphal plays,[5] the anonymous author of yet another play, *Arden of Faversham* (1592), chose to repurpose two characters who appeared in Holinshed's *Chronicles*, one called Black Will and another called Shakebag. The playwright – who Vickers argues was Thomas Kyd – took both of these characters and presented them in a central role as incompetent hit men. Arden was the name of Mr Shakespeare's mother (and is echoed in *As You Like It*). Since 'bag' in Latin is 'pera', the names Black Will Shake(pera) taken in combination would appear to be referring to the actor, especially since the playwright invents him dying in Southwark. This theatrical record is notably *not* obviously parodying William as an actor, nor as a frontman for the plays. On the contrary, it seems to be an early allusion to Shakespeare working as a hit man in Southwark for Francis Langley – a fact that would otherwise only appear in the legal records four years later. Since London was full of minor criminals, to satirise one in a play implies that he also had some, unspecified, theatrical association.

Turning now to our shopping list, one important requirement for a candidate is to have had a relationship with and knowledge of the Lord Chamberlain's Men. On this point, William Shakespeare is in the strongest possible position. He was listed as a member of the company on an official document in 1595, was mentioned by Jonson as an actor, and is listed later on various documents relating to the sharers in the Globe Theatre and the Blackfriars Theatre. He was unquestionably an actor, and may still have been acting in the plays in 1601, at which time he may have played the minor part of Adam in *As You Like It*, according to a tradition deriving from one of Mr Shakespeare's 'weak-minded' elderly relatives in Stratford. So for at least some of the period in which he was associated with the Chamberlain's Men he worked as an actor. Of course he could have had other additional functions, and was described by the Stratford Parish Clerk a century later as having started in the theatre as a 'servitor'. He also left gifts of gold rings to his 'fellows', other actors in the company, by an insertion in his will in 1616. While he does not appear in the records of any theatre company previous to the Lord Chamberlain's Men, if he is the W. S. mentioned in *Willobie His Avisa* in 1594 as already being an 'old player', then he would have had some previous theatrical experience, possibly through Francis Langley at the Bear Gardens amphitheatre (see Appendix 13).

Although this association with the Lord Chamberlain's Men is a very positive factor in support of his authorship, it also has some negative implications. How could a working actor have found the leisure time to research and write these extremely complex plays and consult the large number of bulky books required? Moreover, if the plays were written by a working actor, one would expect that the plays used as main source material would be those that were acted in the public play houses. That however, is not true: many of the plays that were used as Shakespearean sources were ones that could *not* have been publically acted, because they were not written in English (see Appendix 11). Furthermore, although he had an association with the playing company, there is no evidence that he enjoyed a close relationship with Lord Hunsdon, which Roger Prior has pointed out as being something that the writer of *The Raigne of King Edward III* must not only have had, but must have had at a very early date – namely five years before the formation of the Chamberlain's Men.

Professor Bart van Es has recently argued that the developing interpersonal nuances in the playwright's writings after 1594 were due to being a shareholder in the Lord Chamberlain's Men and the financial stability that this brought. Certainly the playwright had a detailed knowledge of the Lord Chamberlain's Men, as it seems that certain parts were written for specific individual actors, and remarkably Shakespeare's casts seem to age as the actual Chamberlain's Men themselves grew older.

However, the more sophisticated interpersonal dynamics in the plays after 1594 might simply reflect the playwright's exposure to the *commedia* in Italy, or the benefits of writing for a consistent cast of actors who were a known quantity. Dekker's plays, for instance, drew upon an intimate knowledge not simply of the Admiral's Men, but also of the items in their prop wardrobe – which he could do simply by knowing the company well. Financial security as a sharer in the Chamberlain's Men can be dismissed as a factor that facilitated writing more complex plays, since the most complex plays of all were the two tetralogies – eight plays, in two series, not written for any stable group of players nor for any single commissioning producer. This was an extraordinary risky and ambitious thing for an early career playwright to do unless they were well off and not relying on selling their play scripts. Yet when the tetralogies were written, Mr Shakespeare was not in such a financial position. In other words, the financial stability of the playwright that enabled them to write complex literary plays was not something that appeared suddenly in 1594, but was there from the start.

There is good evidence that Mr Shakespeare was literate. A letter exists addressed to him (about money lending) from Richard Quiney. Furthermore, as an actor – even if he only took minor roles – he had to read his part. Yet we know from modern studies that children brought up by illiterate parents do not do as well scholastically as those whose parents are able to read to them. Cognitive development in later life is critically dependent on having an experience of a linguistically rich environment in early childhood. Since Stratford-upon-Avon was an out-of-the-way town and Mr Shakespeare's parents were both illiterate – since they signed with marks – one would not expect such a household to produce a highly literate child.

In their desperation to claim that Shakespeare possessed books, Stratfordians unfortunately even resort to complete invention and fantasy. Josina Reaves reports that in a debate at the New Yorker Festival in October 2011, Professor James Shapiro claimed not only that he possessed books but that 'Shakespeare had indeed left books and manuscripts to his son-in-law … on the second page of his will'. This statement may have allowed Shapiro to win the debate; but it is an utter and complete fabrication, as anyone can check by consulting one of the copies of the will that are conveniently available online.

It is highly significant that no books appear in Mr Shakespeare's will. With a few exceptions, the majority of educated individuals disposed of books in their wills. For instance, Sir Thomas Smith, a man from a poor background who became Vice Chancellor of Cambridge, specified that the University of Cambridge were to send carts within twelve days of his death to collect his books, and even specified how they needed to be packed for the journey. We know that books were very important to the playwright because, as Patrick Cheney has noted, they are mentioned 130 times in the canon, roughly three times in each play, together with fifteen mentions of 'volume', thirteen mentions of 'text', three mentions of 'library' and words like folio, edition, print, publish, and press. Yet, separate from the works in the canon, there is no evidence of Mr Shakespeare reading any books at all. None of the 100 or so pieces of paper that have survived refer to him buying or owning any books. His will signed in 1616 makes no mention of any manuscripts, nor blank paper (then very valuable), nor any books, nor any bookcases or book trunks in which they might have been stored. It is sometimes suggested that the books might have appeared in a separate appendix, but as Bonner Miller Cutting points out in her article 'Shakespeare's Will ... Considered Too Curiously', that would not be normal legal practice. Although not everyone who possessed books mentioned them in their wills, books were valuable, and were usually listed in the body of a will. A number of actors left books in their wills, such as those contained in E. A. J. Honigmann and Susan Brock's book *Playhouse Wills 1558–1642*, even though these actors had read far fewer books than the author of the plays.

Moreover, other writers took great care to dispose of their manuscripts, especially unpublished works. The scientist Thomas Harriot, for instance, gave specific orders to his executor that his 7,000 pages of manuscript should be placed in the Earl of Northumberland's library. Sir Francis Bacon instructed that his own papers be bound and placed in half a dozen specified libraries. But Shakespeare's will makes no mention of manuscripts or unpublished works at all. Indeed, as Diana Price has shown in her book *Shakespeare's Unorthodox Biography*, none of Shakespeare's many surviving personal papers have anything to do with literary matters or literary friendships at all – which is very unusual among Elizabethan writers.

It is sometimes suggested that Shakespeare derived his knowledge of books by browsing bookstalls, and memorising the books he wanted, which is why he possessed no actual books. However, it is hard to imagine that one could make 3,000 references to fourteen different, very heavy, translations of the Bible by perusing the contents of bookstalls, even if his memory was such that he did not need to buy any books. Elizabethans did have remarkable skills in memory and developed particular techniques for the 'art of memory'. But to remember 300 books, plus play translations, plus fourteen translations of the Bible for twenty years would stretch the memory even of a genius – one would have expected occasional inaccuracies. Of course, this wouldn't have been the case if the actual books were used, and indeed, there are no such inaccuracies. Moreover, the way that multiple sources are used together to construct sentences drawing on multiple materials suggests that the playwright was sitting with them open at a table going from one to another. In any case, there is no evidence that Mr Shakespeare had an exceptional memory, for instance, when he was making his will several months before his death he was unable to remember the name of his own nephew. Or any books.

Besides the heavy Bibles, many of the other books used in the plays were extremely large items, such as Holinshed's *Chronicles*, or the various herbals, such as Batman's *Herbal*, John Gerard's *Herbal* or Dioscorides' *Herbal*. They could not easily have been carried on tour or backwards and forwards between Stratford-upon-Avon and London.

Furthermore, both of Shakespeare's daughters were illiterate (one could not read her husband's handwriting and the other signed with a mark). Their illiteracy would suggest that they grew up in a house without books – this is normal for illiterates. Children who grow up in a house with books are likely to learn to read, so his children's illiteracy suggests that Shakespeare's house in Stratford-upon-Avon lacked books. As for the possibility that he kept books in London, when his possessions were evaluated for taxes in 1596 they were valued at only five pounds in total, which after allowing for clothes and furniture, would have covered at most one or two books.

It is true that Mr Shakespeare's heir, the doctor John Hall, who married his daughter Susanna and who lived in the same house, mentioned having a 'study' of books in his will in the 1630s. However, as a doctor he would naturally have had some medical books, and would have inherited additional ones from his own father, also a doctor. There is no reason to suppose that *any* of those books had belonged previously to William Shakespeare. Very occasionally, a book does appear at auction which is put forward as having the supposed signature of Shakespeare on it, and which might appear to have come from his book collection. Unfortunately, all half dozen or so of these have proved to be nineteenth-century forgeries from the likes of Collier and Ireland.

Then there is another problem with Mr Shakespeare's verbal fluency. There is no explanation for how and why Mr Shakespeare developed the skill of inventing 1,700 new words, many from Italian roots. Inventing neologisms was an essential part of the skill of a courtier. But Mr Shakespeare's biography shows he was never a courtier. The record for creating new words was set by Chaucer, a fourteenth-century civil servant and courtier to Richard II, who invented 2,004 words, such as 'bed-head'. But many of these were probably not new – they just had never before appeared in print.

Different Types of Knowledge

It is sometimes proposed that the source of Shakespeare's medical knowledge
– indicated by 712 medical references – was John Hall, who was a doctor and also
a herbalist, and that Shakespeare was 'assisted in his researches' by Hall. There
are two problems with this: the dates, and the actual nature of Hall's medical
knowledge.

Hall graduated from university in 1597 and then went to France until 1600, after
which he settled in Stratford-upon-Avon, becoming a member of Shakespeare's
family in 1607. The early Shakespeare plays – those written about 1590 – have
an average number of medical references for plays of the time. But this number
expands significantly about 1595, and lasts for several years. By 1607 the medical
references return to a level comparable to those of other playwrights. The dates
suggest that Hall was not a medical source for Shakespeare.

Secondly, as R. R. Simpson notes in his book *Shakespeare and Medicine*, 'there
is no evidence that Hall influenced the medical references to be found in the plays
of Shakespeare'. For instance, Hall's writings demonstrate no knowledge of the
circulation of the blood, nor of the *pia mater*, a membrane in the brain mentioned
several times by Shakespeare. Once again, Hall does not appear to have been a
source of medical knowledge for Shakespeare. More telling for our purposes is the
fact that the world-class medical knowledge the man from Stratford supposedly
possessed did not influence his son-in-law, even though the two of them were for a
while living in the same house.

There is no evidence to suggest that Mr Shakespeare had any special interest
in music. He left behind no musical instruments in his will – and people of
Shakespeare's socioeconomic bracket tended to bequeath such instruments
individually. We know of no close friends who were professional musicians
(although one London acquaintance played the trumpet). In fact, we know
that Stratford-upon-Avon, a town of about 1,500 inhabitants, appears to have
numbered only two people who possessed any musical instruments. So there is no
evidence that he grew up learning music or being exposed to sophisticated music
before he arrived in London at the age of twenty-five or so around 1590.

By 1593, however, he would have had to learn enough to make knowledgeable
musical references. For *The Rape of Lucrece* he would not only have had to be
familiar with common terms such as 'discord' and 'descant', but be aware of
technical terms in Pythagorean music theory such as 'diapason', which was used as
a term for the range or compass of the voice, and in the poem is related to the term
'burthen' which was the technical name for the under-song or dirge that existed
below the melody. Similarly, for *Titus Andronicus*, the playwright demonstrates
significant musicianship in punning on the name Philomena, which means 'music
lover', making puns on Lavinia's lack of a cord to hang herself and the term
'chord', and composing the entire Lavinia episode as a rewriting of a fragment

of a Greek comedy about the rape of Music, which is preserved in Plutarch's *Moralia*. So, if he did begin learning music on arrival in London, he must have done so amazingly quickly to develop greater musical expertise than any other dramatist of the period. It is also impossible to show that he knew or was in any way connected to Robert Johnson, one of the major composers of the music for the plays. It is also odd that his favourite song, 'King Cophetua', should be about a young black girl who has the King of Africa fall in love with her.

There is no evidence that Mr Shakespeare knew any Italian. Italian was not taught at Stratford Grammar School (if indeed he even attended it, which is not documented). It is of course possible that he learnt Italian on coming to London, but he is not known to have been a pupil of London's leading tutor John Florio, who taught the Earl of Southampton. Indeed, the plays show that the playwright had good Italian *before* mentions of Florio's books on learning Italian begin to appear in the plays. It is of course conceivable he could have studied with another tutor. What is not conceivable is Schoenbaum's suggestion that that the Italian in the plays is no more than could be picked up at a local Italian restaurant, run by Paolo Marco Lucchese in Hart Street – nor Shapiro's suggestion that a few conversations with Italian visitors would have been sufficient. Further, Shakespeare seems to come to his Italian full-blown: that is, the plays do not show the trajectory one would expect of a playwright starting with poor Italian and improving gradually. Given this fact, it is particularly important that it is quite clear when Mr Shakespeare could have gone to Italy for an extended period, who he would have gone with, why he apparently studied a painting by Bassano in the little town of Bassano, and thought it so significant that he devoted an important speech of Iago's to it in *Othello* (more on this later).

Similarly, there is no evidence that Mr Shakespeare knew Hebrew, which was taught at just a few public schools and to some students at Oxford and Cambridge. It was not taught at any grammar school, including Stratford Grammar School. The one Hebrew-speaking community in London was the Marrano (Converso) community – but there is no evidence that he had associations with it whatsoever.

Such an observation might seem even to Stratfordians, let alone the lay reader, to be entirely irrelevant: who, exactly, has maintained that Shakespeare knew Hebrew? In fact, scholars have noted Hebrew puns in *The Merchant of Venice*, and of course there are references to the Talmud in *A Midsummer Night's Dream*, which were described in the previous chapter; these findings have both published in leading scholarly journals.

There is also no evidence to suggest that Mr Shakespeare was in any way interested in what we would today call feminism. We can judge, certainly, from how he treated the women in his immediate family. Firstly, in his will he does not refer to his wife Anne by her personal name – as is usual practice – but only in terms of her social and legal role as his wife. Secondly, he kept all the female members of his family illiterate. This is hard to reconcile with the depictions of literate, educated and musical women in the plays – but easy to substantiate, since in witnessing a deed in 1611 Judith signed, with her mark, a doodle which resembles a pair of spectacles, after which the scribe wrote the name 'Shakespeare'. Equally, Susanna was unable to recognise her husband's handwriting. This would be understandable if they both grew up in a household without any books. Thirdly, Mr Shakespeare also treated his daughters unequally, favouring the married daughter, as was traditional in the patriarchal society of the time (glorious virgin queen or no). Nor can it be maintained that Shakespeare was a literary genius who paid no attention at all to his daughters, for he took the trouble to specify the interest rate that one daughter would pay another if money transfers were delayed in the settling of his estate. Clearly, his concern here was the money, not the women's independence – something matched in the man from Stratford's deep interest in pecuniary matters.

The matter of Shakespeare's court knowledge should be prefaced by observing that the case for Oxford – indeed, for all aristocratic candidates – appears to rest to some extent on a rather snobbish conviction that a commoner could not render court life as accurately as Shakespeare. The present author harbours no such snobbery, but wishes only to observe that it is extremely hard to understand how a commoner could have gained the knowledge about the court that would have been necessary to the playwright – since access to the 'upstairs' world at court was restricted to about 500 to 600 nobles and top officials. Shakespeare is imagined arriving in London perhaps in 1589–90 as a twenty-five-year-old actor. In that very same year, he would have had to have been writing the history plays, all of which concern courtiers, and the first of which, *Henry VI, Part 1*, has a cast almost entirely of nobles and is set partly at the court of France. The same is true of *Love's Labour's Lost*, written not long after. How could he possibly have become familiar practically immediately with a setting largely closed to commoners and the thousands seeking admission? And how would he have got detailed inside information about contemporary French courtiers?

Faced with the obvious difficulty, orthodox Shakespeareans have suggested that Shakespeare obtained his knowledge of court from performing there as an actor. James Shapiro stated in the *Wall Street Journal* (9 April 2010) that 'Shakespeare performed at court over 100 times probably in the course of his career … he's in a better position than many, as a court observer, than those who were at court themselves.' What Shakespeare did 'in the course of his career' is entirely irrelevant. *Henry VI* parts 1, 2 and 3, along with *Richard III*, all of which extensively incorporated knowledge of the court, were written in the period from 1589 to 1593. The first of these plays is set entirely at court. According to the documentary evidence, Mr Shakespeare does not appear in the records of *any* company that performed at court at that time. As for the period 1594 to 1596, when *Richard II* and *Henry IV, Part 1* were written, John H. Astington lists in his helpful book *English Court Theatre 1558–1642* the number of times the Lord Chamberlain's

Men played at court. That number is six – not much for the level of knowledge Shakespeare demonstrates. It is an additional oddity that, at the very point when the Chamberlain's Men were established and beginning to perform at court, Mr Shakespeare should begin writing Italian marriage comedies, a new genre.

The plays appear to have been written by someone who mocked and parodied the Gospels, the Church, and Church ritual. This is hard to reconcile with what is known of Mr Shakespeare. He trusted the church sufficiently to invest several hundred pounds in buying an annuity from parish tithes. He was, as he needed to be, a member of Holy Trinity, his local parish church. Neither of these is remotely definitive, of course. What is striking is that, as a 'lay rector', he was buried in a private plot beside his nearby monument. In addition, the introduction to his will reflects Orthodox Church of England wording without any special qualifications, reservations, theological caveats or special use of any particular Bible translation (which would have indicated non-traditional beliefs). It is believed that his father, John Shakespeare, was a recusant (secret) Catholic, and there was a remote family connection to Jesuit Robert Southwell. The most powerful evidence is that in 1757 a 'spiritual testament' titled 'The Contract and Testament of the Soul' which follows the formula of St Charles Borromeo's *Last Will of the Soul*, was supposedly found in the attic of Shakespeare's birthplace. In it his father makes a formal profession of his Catholic faith. Although this document (which is now missing) may have been a forgery created by John Jordan to deceive Edmond Malone, in the seventeenth century Richard Davies wrote that Shakespeare had 'died a Papist'. This suggests that Shakespeare was perhaps from a family of a recusant Catholics – something advocated by a number of scholars in the late twentieth century, though the evidence is rather thin.

On the other hand, some of those who have recognised the Jewish content of the canon have attempted to argue that Shakespeare himself must therefore have been a Jew. Neil Hirschorn, in an article in *Midstream*, concluded that the playwright was 'descended of forcibly converted Jews … and resented that condition'. David Basch, in *Shakespeare's Judaica* and other books, reaches a similar conclusion. More recently, Ghislain Muller's book *Was Shakespeare a Jew?: Uncovering the Marrano Influences in His Life and Writing* has focused on the Langrake lawsuit of 1569, in which Shakespeare's father made illegal loans. He is named as 'John Shappere alias Shakespere from Stratford Upon Haven', which Muller considers to be a version of the Jewish name Shapiro. The problem is that there are around sixty different versions of Shakespeare's family name. Indeed, the same informant brought another law case in 1572 against John 'Shaxspere' of 'Stretford super Haven'. The word 'shappere' appears in the poem 'Piers Plowman' meaning a 'shaper': there is no reason to suppose it is Jewish. Furthermore, there is no evidence of a Marrano (or Converso) community of any kind in Stratford-upon-Avon, so it would have been impossible to have a *minyon* for prayer. We can dismiss the speculations about the man from Stratford being Jewish, which are based on the physical characteristics of the non-contemporary Chandos portrait, or which assume that Shylock was a self-portrait. The fact that Shakespeare's father was a moneylender does not make him Jewish (many moneylenders were not). None of this counters Richard Wilson's arguments in his book *Secret Shakespeare: Studies in Theatre, Religion and Resistance* that the family were recusant Catholics, which would be completely incompatible with him knowing Hebrew, creating anti-Christian parodies, studying passages from the Talmud or reading the *Zohar*.

In order to hunt legally, one had to have a certain rental income from land. Mr Shakespeare met those criteria for at most one year of his life: in 1602, he bought some land that might have met the rental requirement for that year. It would have fallen short the next year, when the legal minimum was raised to ten pounds under the game laws. Shakespeare, then, was not a hunter. The plays make many references to hunting, yet, as Berry's book *Shakespeare and the Hunt* observes, the playwright appears opposed to hunting, seeing it – in *As You Like It*, for instance – through the lens of Cornelius Agrippa as a cruel art.

The falconry references in the plays are oddly specific; they are always realistic and cover not only wild falcons but also ones that have been raised from eggs by a falconer. In *Othello* Desdemona is a 'haggard' or wild falcon, in *The Merchant of Venice* Jessica is tethered to her family not only with the 'jess', the silk or leather strap that is tied to a falcon's leg, but she even has a turquoise ring echoing the ring that attaches the jess to the falconer's leash. In *Romeo and Juliet* on the other hand, for once the woman, Juliet, is the falconer and the Romeo is the bird. Romeo pleads that Juliet will 'cast off' her virginity like a falconer's lure to attract him, and like Katherine he is to be given a new name. He flies on light wings and perches over walls, and Juliet takes the bait of her virginity away from him in order to train him to her liking. This suggests that the playwright's experience was not necessarily that of someone who hunted with falcons, but someone who was very familiar with falconers and the way that they cared for the birds.

Nor is there any evidence to link Mr Shakespeare to the army. There is certainly nothing to suggest – as the order of the plays does – that his early experience with military men was with generals and that he only subsequently became acquainted with common soldiers. More importantly, there is nothing in his biography to suggest any specific knowledge of the military at all.

The plays make over 100 astronomical references, including a number to Tycho Brahe's astronomy. An interest in science is normally acquired during the teenage years, but the new astronomy would not have been taught at Stratford Grammar School (even the syllabus at Cambridge University taught only Ptolemaic astronomy as a branch of mathematics). The best explanation that Stratfordians have been able to offer for the knowledge of astronomy and navigation in the plays is that one of those who contributed a poem to the First Folio was the poet Leonard Digges. His grandfather and father had been astronomers, and his mother subsequently married Thomas Russell whom Shakespeare appointed in

1616 as an overseer of his will. There are two separate arguments here, each with substantial problems.

In terms of Mrs Digges as an indirect channel, we don't know what, if any, relationship existed between Russell and Shakespeare previous to 1616. Secondly, to imagine a chain of transmission of astronomical knowledge via the deceased astronomer, through his wife, to Russell, and thence to Shakespeare seems convoluted. Thirdly, the astronomical knowledge in the plays appears *before* the mother's remarriage in 1603, and is not therefore dependent on any knowledge Russell gained from Mrs Digges.

In terms of the poet Leonard Digges being a direct channel of information, his only known association with Shakespeare is the publication of the posthumous poem in the First Folio. There is no evidence that he actually had an interest in astronomy nor that he even knew Shakespeare at all, let alone that he passed his father's astronomical knowledge on to him. In any case his father, Thomas Digges, became a Copernican early on, praising that system in his books *Alae seu Scalae Mathematicae* (1573) and *A Perfect Description* (1576), and he is not recorded as supporting the astronomy of Tycho Brahe, whose system was published in 1588.

As for the knowledge of the law in the plays, it has been held to be superficial; it has been suggested that all of it derives from Shakespeare's early days attending a local Stratford court over which his father presided, and that he used legal language casually. In fact, as Sokol and Sokol show in their book, *Shakespeare's Legal Language: A Dictionary*, the plays demonstrate 'a quite precise and mainly serious interest in the capacity of legal language to convey matters of social, moral and intellectual substance'. Simply watching the operation of a local court in Stratford-upon-Avon is not likely to have supplied this background. Further, the scope of the legal issues in the plays is much greater than anything that would have appeared in cases at the local Stratford county court. Perhaps the definitive proof of this is an article by J. Anthony Burton 'An Unrecognized Theme in *Hamlet*' published in *The Shakespeare Newsletter*. Discussing the gravedigger's scene in *Hamlet,* Burton observes it is a 'parody of legal reasoning in a forty-year old decision written in the corrupted version of Norman-English known as Law French'. This was expanded upon by Thomas Regnier's remarkable article in *The University of Miami Law Review,* which makes a cogent argument that the knowledge of inheritance law crucial to the plot of *Hamlet* 'bespeaks a level of expertise that is not consonant with merely an intelligent amateur', not least because it appears quite clearly to draw upon the manuscript notebooks of Sir John Dyer, a noted jurist of the time. These notebooks were 'written in Law French, an archaic form of Norman-English, and inscribed in law hand, a rare style of writing used by law clerks and few others even back then'. It is quite incorrect to claim, as Stratfordians do, following Dr Johnson's preface to the *Complete Works,* that 'the legal knowledge which he displays might easily have been caught up in conversation'.

Many Elizabethans had some legal knowledge – and consequently made their own wills. Despite Shakespeare's interest in money saving, he evidently did *not* feel he had sufficient legal knowledge to make his own will, since he hired a lawyer. Nor would his personal legal experiences – seeking the repayment of a seven-pound loan from John Clayton in 1600, suing the local apothecary for one pound nineteen shillings in 1604, recovering a debt of six pounds from John Addenbroke in 1608, and acting as a witness in a marital case Belott *versus* Mountjoy (1612) – have provided him with the legal expertise demonstrated in the plays.

Mr Shakespeare's primary connection to the silk weaving industry is that, in 1609, like thousands of other people throughout the country, he planted a mulberry tree. This followed a proclamation by King James that all loyal landholders should plant mulberry trees to promote the cultivation of silk worms. The tree was finally cut down in the mid-eighteenth century. Furthermore, Stratfordians argue that in 1602 Mr Shakespeare lodged with the Mountjoys in London and may have observed them turning raw silk into coloured silk yarn for their hat-decoration business. This hypothesis does little to explain the many earlier silk-weaving references in, for instance, *A Midsummer Night's Dream* written in 1596.

Stratford Links and Style Matching

There is also the issue of how the plays compare to a small example of Mr Shakespeare's poetry outside the canon. There might be just one instance of verse that was clearly composed by the man from Stratford. To understand it requires a little background.

The main legal moneylender in Stratford, John Combe, was lending at the 10 per cent legal rate, and owned the largest house in town (Shakespeare owned the second largest). It was his family who sold 127 acres of land to Mr Shakespeare in 1602. John Combe wanted to ensure that he had a good tomb, and, when he died in 1613, left the large sum of sixty pounds in his will for the Southwark stone carver Gheerart Janssen to create a suitable tomb in Stratford parish church. It seems reasonable to assume that there was a good relation between John Combe and Mr Shakespeare, since there is no evidence to the contrary, Shakespeare was also a practicing moneylender, and there is no evidence of any complication of the 1602 sale of land. When he died, John Combe left Mr Shakespeare five pounds in his will, which was organised by Collins the lawyer and signed on every page.

Janssen appears to have built Combe's monument, a recumbent effigy, over the period 1614 to 1615. Evidently, Mr Shakespeare was taken with having Janssen create his own monument – the one that still survives in Holy Trinity Church – and commissioned him to do so. Shakespeare also emulated his friend Combe in using Collins to create his own will on 25 March 1615. Again copying Combe, he signed his will on every page, leaving his sword to Combe's brother when he died one year later in 1616. When a Lieutenant Hammond visited the church in 1634, he noted that 'some witty and facetious verses' were written on Combe's monument, claiming that they had been composed by Shakespeare himself. The verses no longer survive on the monument, but they are well documented since in 1673 Robert Dobyns recorded them as follows:

> Ten in the hundred here lieth ingraved
> A hundred to ten his soul is ne'er saved
> If anyone ask who lieth in this tomb
> 'Oh ho' quoth the devil, 'tis my John-a-Combe.'

These lines are of course a joke, since Combe charged the conventional interest rate of 'ten in a hundred', which then reappears reversed as the 'hundred to ten' odds of his going to heaven. There is also an inscription on Shakespeare's tomb, which was first seen by Dowdall in 1693, who wrote in a letter that it had been made 'a little before his death' by Shakespeare himself:

> Good friend for Jesus sake forbear
> To dig the dust enclosed here!
> Blest be the man that spares these stones,
> And curst be he that moves my bones.

Two bad, and somewhat stylistically similar, verses appear on two tombs. Two visitors, sixty years apart, are told the verses are by Shakespeare. It was unlikely to have been known that Combe and Shakespeare were friends, or had parallel wills, or that both their monuments had been created by the same stonemason, and that there were indeed reasons to link these two tombs. Just possibly, popular tradition could be right. These two inscriptions might be the only known instances of poetry composed by the man from Stratford. It is, needless to say, unlike any of the poetry normally credited to the playwright. But it is a fair stab at gravestone verse from an actor and moneylender with a local grammar-school education. It also suggests, as Sabrina Feldman has recently claimed, that he might have written some of the apocryphal plays that were credited to him, which is discussed in the appendices (see Appendix 13).

Stratfordians have claimed that the plays refer to Shakespeare's father, an alderman, wool dealer and a glover in Stratford-upon-Avon. Yet A. J. Pointon, in his book *The Man Who Was Never Shakespeare*, has pointed out that these references are in fact faulty and prove the playwright's *lack* of accurate knowledge on the matter. As for the references to weighing wool in *The Winter's Tale*, these concern matters that would interest a shepherd rather than a wool broker. A reference in *Romeo and Juliet* to an alderman wearing his ring of office on his forefinger is not correct since it is worn on the thumb. As for the glove references

in the plays, it is sometimes argued, for instance by Ron Rosenbaum in his article
'Glove Me Tender: Shakespeare in the Skin Trade', that the plays make fifty or
so references to gloves because Shakespeare's father was a glove maker. That is
to ignore the fact that gloves were a common element of Elizabethan clothing,
and were referred to about as often as the plays refer to 'dress', so they have no
special significance. Barely a couple of these mentions refer to the process of
leather-working and for instance, the mention in *Twelfth Night* of the stretching
properties of chervil, a kind of leather made from kids' skin, is hyperbolic and
technically incorrect. Moreover Feste's reference to a glove in that play is used
as a metaphor for sexual ambiguity, and for the turning of a woman into a man
through wit, by alluding to Elizabethan sexual theories of how male and female
sexual organs were formed in the womb. This is hardly something that can be
traced to John Shakespeare's Stratford workshop.

It has also been argued that the reason the plays contain so many examples
of twins is because Mr Shakespeare was himself the father of twins. In his RSC
edition of *Twelfth Night* (2010), Professor Jonathan Bate argues that the court
performance of this play on the festival of Candlemas, 2 February 1602, was on
the seventeenth anniversary of the baptism of Mr Shakespeare's twins Hamnet
and Judith. By incorporating a pair of twins in the play, and by showing the male
twin (Sebastian) returning from a watery grave to be united with the female twin
(Viola), Bate argues that 'Shakespeare allowed himself the consoling fantasy of
a seventeenth birthday reunion'. Such a superficial reading is implausible for
several reasons. Firstly, why should the playwright chose to commemorate the
anniversary of the twins' baptism rather than their birth? Secondly, the play does
not incorporate the imagery of Candlemas and was not written for that occasion.
On the contrary, as the name indicates, it was primarily written to be performed
on the festival of Twelfth Night, which concludes the twelve days of Christmas,
namely 5 January. This is why, for instance, one of the songs is a parody of 'the
Twelfth Day of Christmas' (2.3.85). From other references to the liturgical
calendar, Steve Sohmer has argued it was originally written to be performed on
two different dates, 5 January and 3 February 1600: neither is the baptismal
anniversary of Mr Shakespeare's twins.

Although the above discussion shows that there is very little fit between Mr
Shakespeare's biography and the knowledge demonstrated in the plays, there is
one large blank area in the biography, the so called 'lost years' or 'missing years'.
This assumes he did not spend the decade from 1582 to 1592 at Stratford in his
father's business, but used this period to somehow acquire the skills demonstrated
in the plays and became equipped with them for his arrival in London around
1592. There have been various efforts to discover Mr Shakespeare in a situation
during this period that could have provided him with the knowledge in the plays.
Let me take three instances: one in which Mr Shakespeare is imagined as a soldier
in the Low Countries; one as a young tutor/actor in Lancashire; and one connected

with Italy. As the reader will see, the creators of these scenarios recognised some of the problems with the knowledge in the plays.

Alfred Duff Cooper in his book *Sergeant Shakespeare* recognises the large amount of military knowledge, including generalship, in the plays, and the familiarity with campaigns in the Low Countries. He therefore concludes that Shakespeare served as a soldier under Lord Leicester in the Low Countries between 1585 and 1592. As evidence he provides a letter from Philip Sidney referring to 'Will, my Lord of Leicester's jesting player', which Cooper supposes, without any supporting evidence, to be the young William Shakespeare. Another soldier theory was antiquarian W. J. Thoms's discovery in 1859 that a different 'William Shakespeare' was listed among those serving as conscripts in the Low Countries in 1605 and identified him as the playwright – ignoring the difficulty that Shakespeare was at the time in London for the operations of the Globe Theatre and the playing company, and that the references to generalship are in the early plays, written well before this time.

As well as a soldier, he has been identified as a schoolmaster. Aubrey, in his *Brief Lives*, states that the playwright 'had been in his younger years a Schoolmaster in the Country.' Accordingly, E. A. J. Honigmann, in *Shakespeare: The Lost Years*, argued that Shakespeare travelled to Lancashire, where he served as a tutor in the household of the Houghton and Hesketh families under the name William Shakeshaft. In 1581, after he had been employed a few months, Hesketh died, leaving young Shakespeare/Shakeshaft a large sum, and commending him as worth employing. In the preceding sentence of his will, Hesketh mentioned both musical instruments and 'play-clothes' or costumes. From this juxtaposition, Honigmann infers that, in addition to being a tutor, Shakeshaft was a musician and an actor, and that at some point he met a company of players associated with Lord Derby, and moved to London. However, Shakeshaft was a common name in Lancashire. There is no reason to suppose that Hesketh's mention of music and costumes had any relationship to Shakeshaft, nor that, even if it did, it implied he was an actor. There is also no evidence to suggest that this Shakeshaft moved to London and became an actor, let alone that he took the name William Shakespeare. Nor is there any evidence that this experience of working as a tutor gave Shakespeare (Shakeshaft) the knowledge of the various skills demonstrated in the plays.

Yet another suggestion is that during these missing years Shakespeare went to Italy. Gaenor Cimio suggested Shakespeare must have attended the University of Padua,[6] Lewis Einstein in *The Italian Renaissance in England* suggested Shakespeare was a sailor on an English merchant ship that stopped at Venice, and Aelwyn Edwards suggested Shakespeare worked in Italy as an agent for the merchant adventurer William Harrison.[7] The subject 'Did Shakespeare Visit Italy?' takes up a chapter in Georg Brandes' book *William Shakespeare: A Critical Study*. He also endorses work by Karl Elze that suggested that Shakespeare visited Italy in 1593. Quite a few English people did visit Italy, including the actors Antony

Munday and Will Kempe. When might Shakespeare have visited Italy? In his article 'Shakespeare's Visit to Italy', Roger Prior suggests that Mr Shakespeare joined the Bassano brothers on their three-month visit to Italy in 1593, and suggests that he went there to investigate business opportunities in the leatherworking industry. On such a visit he could have learned both Italian and Hebrew, and much about Italy. There is, however, no evidence of Mr Shakespeare knowing the Bassano brothers, let alone any plausible explanation of why this close-knit Jewish family would have invited Mr Shakespeare – newly arrived in London from Warwickshire, and speaking the dialect to prove it – to accompany them on such a trip. Not to mention the implausibility of learning two different languages on a three-month visit.

Another alternative source for Shakespeare's knowledge of Italian is put forward in the *Encyclopaedia Britannica* of 1902 in an article entitled 'Shakespeare Continues His Education', by Thomas S. Baynes. It argues that, on arriving in London, Shakespeare became a friend of Florio, the teacher of Italian and member of Southampton's household. Baynes bases this claim on the supposition by W. Minto in 1895 that one of the sonnets contributed by an unnamed friend to the preface of Florio's *Second Fruits* (1591) was by Shakespeare. In his book *William Shakespeare*, however, E. K. Chambers rejected the claim that this sonnet is by Shakespeare, which compromises Baynes' argument. In addition, many of Florio's pupils are documented: William Shakespeare is not among them.

Perhaps the most fantastic explanation for the 'missing years' is put forward by Sicilian literature professor Martino Iuvara in his book *Shakespeare Era Italiano*. As summarised by Karolina Rakoczy in the *Times of Sicily*, he argues that William Shakespeare of Stratford died an early death and never went to London at all, and that the person who turned up as an actor in the early 1590s was actually an Italian called Michelangelo Florio Crollalanza, who had been educated in Latin and Greek in a monastery, and who changed his surname on his arrival in London to its English equivalent, 'Shakespeare'. Although this would explain the playwright's knowledge of Italy and Italian, among the very many problems with this 'explanation' are how Crollalanza suddenly learned perfect court English, and why he would have bought a mansion in Stratford-upon-Avon, and become part of the family of John Shakespeare.

All of these accounts of Shakespeare's 'lost years' attempt to find a way to explain how he acquired one or more of the areas of knowledge demonstrated in the plays, for which no alternative explanation exists. All these explanations are easily shown to be unsound. There is one, much more interesting, possible explanation for the 'lost years', put forward by Sabrina Feldman, although because it does not deal with how he could have gained the sophisticated skills, I consider it in an appendix (see Appendix 13).

One imaginative argument, put forward by Tina Packer of Shakespeare & Co., admits that Mr Shakespeare did not possess any of these areas of knowledge listed, but argues that he had Amelia Bassano as his mistress and that she supplied him with all these kinds of material as 'pillow talk'. To this I object that he would have had to be running to her every few minutes for a musical or classical reference or Italian pun. He would also have had to do it continuously over twenty years, first while she was living with Lord Hunsdon, and then when she was living with her husband. Anyway, if the material was all hers then the fact that he transcribed it does not make him the creator of these plays. The underlying flaw in this explanation is emphasised by the problem of timing.

In addition to the substantial areas of mismatch between Mr Shakespeare's biography and the content of the plays, there is a problem of timing. It is generally understood that Shakespeare died on 23 April 1616 in Stratford-upon-Avon, several days' journey from London. If it could be shown that the plays were still being rewritten after that date *in the authorial hand,* this would rule him out as the author. Now, there were thousands of purely editorial changes, widely understood to have been made by Ben Jonson, Ralph Crane, the printer and the compositors during the publishing of the First Folio. It has also been suggested that some changes were made to the text of the folio by John Florio, who could possibly have been involved in an editorial capacity,[8] such as editing out an unflattering parody of himself that had appeared in the quartos of *Hamlet.*

There are also, however, several examples of substantive, non-editorial changes in content that have now been identified, and identified as having been made after April 1616. These are the references in the plays to the circulation of the blood; the writing of part of *The Taming of the Shrew* in 1621; changes made onto the actual 1622 quarto of *Richard III*; and the 163 lines added to the text of the 1622 quarto of *Othello* when it appeared a year later in the First Folio. Stratfordian writers usually ignore this problem, and it is left to writers like Archie Webster, who pointed out in his article in *The National Review* (1923) that 'such plays as *Othello* (1622); *King John* (1591–1622); *Richard III* (1597–1622) and others seem to have been substantially altered and revised within the year preceding the folio of 1623'.

Taken together, these examples suggest very strongly either that Mr Shakespeare did not write the plays, and that the true author survived him and made these changes, or that Shakespeare had an associate – someone not yet identified – who co-wrote the plays, and who went on making changes after his death. The excuse sometimes offered that these changes were simply non-authorial minor changes is not sound.

Let us take these issues one by one. First, while William Shakespeare was lying on his deathbed in Stratford-upon-Avon in April 1616, Dr William Harvey, who discovered the circulation of the blood, was on the 16th to the 18th of that month giving the Lumleian lectures on anatomy in London. Tempting though it might be to imagine a scenario in which the knowledge came to Shakespeare's attention, causing him to make some last-minute changes to his work, the original notes of

Harvey's lecture, analysed in Witteridge's *British Medical Journal* article, 'Growth of Harvey's Ideas on the Circulation of the Blood', show that Harvey did not refer to the circulation of the blood, although he would discuss the subject in various later anatomical lectures (on which occasions it would be regarded as a dubious theory). Harvey would not publish this discovery until his book *On the Motion of the Heart and Blood in Animals* appeared in German in 1628; the book was not available in English until 1653.

Yet, at least half a dozen of Shakespeare's plays – all having to be written by 1616 if written by Shakespeare – refer to the circulation of the blood. The clearest example is the passage in *Coriolanus*, not published until the First Folio in 1623, which specifically mentions the heart as the 'court' which distributes the blood to the brain and the other offices of the body:

> ... I am the store-house and the shop
> Of the whole body: but if you do remember,
> I send it through the rivers of your blood,
> Even to the court the heart – to th' seat o' th' braine;
> And, through the cranks and offices of man,
> The strongest nerves, and small inferior veines,
> From me receive that natural competencie
> Whereby they live ...
>
> > *Coriolanus*, 1.1.138–44

There is also a clear reference to the heart pumping blood around the body in a passage added between 1594 and 1623 to *Henry VI, Part 2*:

> See how the blood is settled in his face.
> Oft have I seene a timely-parted ghost
> Of ashy semblance, meagre, pale, and bloodless
> Being all descended to the labouring heart
> Who in the conflict that it holds with death
> Attracts the same for aydance 'gainst the enemy
> Which with the heart there cools and ne're returneth
> To blush and beautifie the cheek againe.
> But see his face is blacke and full of blood.
>
> > *Henry VI, Part 2*, 3.2.160–8

There are several possible explanations of this problem advanced by Stratfordians. That this and the other passages do not refer to the circulation of the blood. Or that Harvey *did* refer to it in his lecture, and Shakespeare used that information to rapidly revise the plays just days before he died. Or that Harvey discussed the matter in an earlier talk, date unknown. Or that others (possibly the scientist

Walter Warner, a retainer of the Earl of Northumberland) knew about the circulation of the blood before Harvey, and Shakespeare learnt of it from them. Or that Shakespeare had access to the sources that Harvey himself used – lectures given at Padua Medical School, which Harvey had attended.

Obviously, these are not compelling suggestions.

A similar problem appears in *The Taming of the Shrew*. In his article 'The Anachronistic Shrews', James J. Marino suggested that at least a major section of *The Taming of the Shrew* was composed around 1619–20, several years after Shakespeare's death. One supporting example is the reference to Soto (Induction, line 86), which appears to refer to a character in Fletcher's *Women Pleased*, not published until 1620.

Finally, the changes to *Richard III* and *Othello* are generally accepted as being in the authorial hand. The idea that the playwright left these changes behind on a separate piece of paper, or on an alternative version of the play (claims that have been made), are not credible in the absence of accompanying evidence that can explain all the other difficulties.

Of course, many of the quartos were corrected after they were published, and several of them were significantly expanded. For instance, nearly 1,000 extra lines were added in aggregate to *The Merry Wives of Windsor*; *Henry V*; *Henry VI, Part 2*; *Henry VI, Part 3* and *King John*. However, in none of these cases is there evidence of the date at which the additions were made. By contrast, in *Richard III* and *Othello*, there is compelling evidence that the changes were made between 1622 and 1623, which raises grave doubts about Shakespeare's authorship, given that he had been dead some six or seven years.

The sixth quarto of *Richard III* was printed by Thomas Purfoot in 1622. By the time the play was reprinted in the First Folio the next year, it had had 193 new lines added, along with 2,000 minor changes. The most significant addition was the fifty-four-line passage in which Richard promises that his wife will be 'Caesar's Caesar' (4.4.288–342), emphasising the otherwise understated Caesar allegory in the play. We know that the changes were made directly onto a copy of the 1622 quarto, because twelve of Purfoot's printer's errors were carried along with these changes into the First Folio. This proves that the changes were made between 1622 and 1623. This was the subject of a number of studies in the 1950s and there is no question that the 193 new lines are authorial, because of the style in which they were written. The timing is confirmed by their not having appeared in any of the previous quartos. Mr Shakespeare had plenty of opportunity while he was still alive to add these extra lines in to the quartos published in 1598, 1602, 1605, or 1612, but he did not do so. So either the publisher of the folio possessed another, longer, manuscript by Mr Shakespeare with 193 extra lines in it that nobody had known about for twenty years or so, but chose *not* to use that manuscript as the copy for the printer, preferring Purfoot's error-ridden quarto, or these were 193 new lines added by the true author directly on to the 1622 quarto, together with the other changes.

Finally, *Othello*. This is a more complicated affair.[9]

First, the additions. An extra 163 lines were added to the 1622 quarto of *Othello* and carried into the First Folio in 1622/23. The major additions are shown in any good modern edition, and especially affect Act 4, where they double the number of lines in the quarto: in Act 1, three passages, especially (1.1.119–35; 1.2.72–7); Act 2, two passages, especially (2.3.275–7); Act 3, three passages, especially (3.3.386–93); Act 4, eight passages, seventy-six lines, especially (4.1.38–43 and 172–4, 4.2.74–7 and 153–66, 4.3.29–52, 54–6, 59–62, and 85–102); and Act 5, five passages, twenty-seven lines (5.2.147–50, 181–90, and 244–6). Among these additions several things are of note. They strengthen the character Emilia: the lines in 4.3.85–102 – that if wives fall it is the husband's fault – are rather feminist in tone. More importantly, however, in the quarto there is a passage that mentions the willow song but does not provide an opportunity to sing it:

> My mother had a maid call'd Barbary,
> She was in love, and he she loved proved mad
> And did forsake her: she had a song of 'willow;'
> An old thing 'twas, but it express'd her fortune,
> And she died singing it: that song to-night
> Will not go from my mind
> Harke who's that knocks?
>
> *Othello*, 4.3.24–31

In the First Folio, thirty-two new lines are inserted after line 29. In these lines Desdemona sings that a poor soul sat sighing by a 'sycamore tree' (an obvious pun on 'sick a moor', since the Moor Othello, whom Desdemona loved, was indeed proving mad) and was singing 'willow willow willow'. In the same way that her mother's maidservant 'called Barbary' (the home of the Moors) died singing this 'old' song, so Emilia says in another addition that she will do likewise: 'I will play the swan / And die in music. (Sings) Willow, willow, willow' (5.2.245–6). The word is spelt 'willough' in the folio, an oddity we will return to, as well as to the fact that this is clearly a depiction of a swansong – a term that has come down to us today with a general meaning of 'final performance,' but which at the time meant the final work of a great poet or musician. English literary references to this effect go back to Chaucer, and were used in a madrigal by Orlando Gibbons in 1612.

For some reason, then, a swansong about 'willough', which refers to a woman whose love proved mad, was deliberately added into the First Folio text of *Othello* in 1622. It has been suggested that there were two versions of *Othello*, but the only possible justification for such a claim is to avoid the obvious interpretation of the handwritten changes on the 1622 quarto: that the changes were made after Mr Shakespeare had died. If the only 'proof' that the changes were made before

1616 is that Shakespeare died in 1616, then they cannot prove that Shakespeare made the changes: the argument is entirely circular. It would also be extremely odd for two versions that differed in this slight way to exist in parallel.

The only explanation that makes any sense is that these lines were added in 1623 – and since they were not added by the ghost of Mr Shakespeare, they were put there by someone else, someone who had a very good reason for making these very particular changes, whose meaning is discussed in a later chapter that will suggest the character Emilia is a contemporary allegory for the presumed playwright Amelia Bassano. It is supported firstly because of the importance of the character as a feminist, but secondly because she has variously been identified as having an almost authorial role in the play as a director or puppet-master pulling the strings of the characters.[10]

This review clearly suggests that Mr Shakespeare did not have the access to many of the key areas of knowledge used in the plays. The proposition that he got these areas of knowledge from books falls down firstly because he did not demonstrably own any books, and secondly because you cannot learn fluent Italian, or gain the knowledge of musicianship evident from the plays, simply from books. It has to be learnt in a social context. Even where books were involved, such as in the playwright's knowledge of feminism, there has to be a social context that would have made the playwright read a manual of court etiquette for girls, and search out the obscure works of Christine de Pizan or various works written to be read by girls. Since Mr Shakespeare kept his own daughters illiterate, he clearly has no match for that social context.

As an actor and theatre businessman, as well as the son of a prominent Stratford-upon-Avon businessman and politician, Mr Shakespeare certainly had friends and acquaintances who were moderately well educated. His daughter married Richard Quinney, who had financial dealings with him and who read Erasmus, Terence and Cicero. Lodging in his house was for a while, his 'cousin' Thomas Greene was a member of the Middle Temple and friend of the playwright John Marston and the poet Michel Drayton. The overseer of his will, Thomas Russell, was born into a family with personal ties to the courtier Sir John Harrington. However none of these associations would have brought the very specific kinds of knowledge that can be demonstrated from the plays.

Now it is perfectly reasonable to argue that after 400 years there are gaps in the records, and that most playwrights of the period have lives that are significantly undocumented. However in the case of Shakespeare that is not an argument I would make. His life is actually very well documented, with about 100 documents – they just do not record anything about him writing or researching the plays. In other words, for some reason, unlike the documentation on other writers, there is a systematic bias in the existing documentary record that fails to substantiate his career as a writer. It is only these particular documents and any references to them that seem not to exist.

The Shakespeare myth is invested in the romantic myth that a poor boy from a small rural town could have a 'rags to riches' story, and through writing plays transform himself into a very rich man, and his home town into a kind of 'Shakespeare Shrine', as it has been called. The problem with this myth is that John Shakespeare was not poor; he owned at least three houses in Stratford, additional houses and estates at Snittersfield and Asbies, and he was routinely making illegal loans for large sums of money at illegally high interest rates. For instance, in 1568 and 1569 he was lending the equivalent of £75,000 in a single loan, and in 1572 was also making illegal wool purchases in similar amounts. So as well as being a glover and mayor of his home town, John Shakespeare was a crook, an illegal wool and money dealer. It is therefore not surprising to find that on arriving in London his son also became a moneylender, and an associate of Francis Langley's crime syndicate on the South Bank.

He did very well, became the second-richest actor in the country, and returned to Stratford-upon-Avon to buy the second-largest house in town. That, however, has no correspondence at all to the biographical information contained in the sonnets – that the writer feels like a woman who has been branded and banished for harlotry, that the writer's name is stigmatised, that they are despised and rejected. While being sensitive to rejection is common in the theatre, this does not fit at all with the fact that at the time those sonnets were being written the Shakespearean plays were actually receiving their greatest exposure ever at the court of King James.

Granted this lack of fit between the man and the knowledge demonstrated in the plays, and in the biographical information in the sonnets, it is surprising that so many scholars have created biographies of Shakespeare, when what we really know of him could be summarised in under a dozen pages. Early historians had an opportunity around the 1660s to gather information from those who had known him, including his daughter. However the only one who seems to have any success at all was Ravenscroft, who gathered only from those 'anciently conversant with the stage' that *Titus Andronicus* was a play which had not been written by Mr Shakespeare, but had been brought to him by a 'private author' to be acted.[11] But this has not stopped modern writers who have determined to create a biography of Shakespeare as a playwright. As James Shapiro has pointed out in a lecture, in 1796 Goethe published an influential novel, or *Bildungsroman*, titled *Wilhelm Meister*, in which a sensitive young man learns acting and begins to model his life on Prince Hamlet. This has been followed by an avalanche of biographies, all of which have created their own fictional accounts of what the man Shakespeare must have been like, and how that life must have mirrored the canonical plays. They are all, however, essentially romantic fictions, but academics are attached to them, as Shapiro observes, *not because they are historically true* – but because they are good stories, and are easy to use in the classroom to inspire students.

None of them, however, explains the fact that in addition to writing plays and private sonnets Shakespeare remained a public poet, writing 'The Phoenix and the Turtle' around 1600, a highly sensitive, mystical, theological, allegorical and apocalyptic poem that parodies Catholic liturgy. It is a commentary on scholastic philosophy that borrows ideas from the *Dialoghi d'Amore* (1535) by Leone Ebreo, also known as Leo Judaeus and Judah Abarbanel. An Italian Marrano Jew, he had written his own poem about a female phoenix and a male turtle and neo-Platonic theories of love roughly a century earlier. So Shakespeare's poem, rather in the manner of one of the French authorities on the same subject *Le Phoenix de Jean Edward du Monin* (1585), fuses those neo-Platonic ideas with Christian theology and doctrine – and does so in order to provide a brilliant comic parody. Yet if biographers abandoned their romantic plots and gave proper weight to this evidence, it would lead them to the similar controversial religious material in the plays, which is invariably overlooked, and hence to an entirely new line of inquiry, such as the one that has been pursued here.

4

Some Rotten Alternatives

James Joyce comically merged the different authorship candidates together as a single individual called Rutlandbaconsouthamptonshakespeare. However, as the case for Mr Shakespeare fails, we must carefully distinguish between them to seek a candidate who actually meets all the criteria explicitly and implicitly set out by the evidence both outside and inside the plays. We will look at some of what have been called the 'Top Possible Authors for the Works of Shakespeare'.[1]

As we investigate the major alternative candidates we will need to avoid the distractions of interesting anecdotes that do not amount to evidence. We must consider each candidate against the key criteria that scholars have identified in the plays and which were listed in an earlier chapter. The weaknesses in the case for Mr Shakespeare as the author of the plays that bear his name have led to the development of almost an entire industry, which has put forward around eighty different candidates. Each of them involves some kind of conspiracy theory and the case for each of them is, if anything, even weaker than the case for Mr Shakespeare. Here I deal at length with the three most popular cases, and more briefly with some of the others.

The Earl of Oxford

In their lengthy statistical article 'Oxford by the Numbers' in the *Tennessee Law Review*, Ward Elliott and Robert Valenza concluded that none of the individuals they tested could have written the Shakespearean plays, either as individuals or as a group. They concluded that apart from the sections which were written with known collaborators, the plays were written by *another* single author who had a 'consistent, countable profile-fitting pattern'. It was, however, not the Earl of Oxford, despite being the leading authorship contender. They regard his poetry as being 'light years apart' from that of the Shakespearean works, and conclude that the likelihood of being struck by lightning is greater than the likelihood that Oxford wrote the plays.

Yet it is easy to see why the leading candidate, Edward de Vere, 17th Earl of Oxford, has attracted attention, because he is in some ways the antithesis of the man from Stratford and his perplexing black-and-white First Folio engraving.

Combine a flashy, dangerous, sexy and exciting life with the colourful portrait of a dashing and elegant young man, in a fashionable yellow doublet, and he may seem the very model of how we might imagine an Elizabethan playwright. This has certainly helped gather interest in Oxford as a candidate, and there is even a Shakespeare Oxford Society with their own annual conference and journals devoted to him. One Oxfordian, Percy Allen, was so interested in this possibility that in 1942 he hired a medium, Mrs Hester Dowden, to channel both Oxford and Shakespeare to explain how they had collaborated on the plays.

Nonetheless, the objective evidence for Oxford is at first glance rather promising. As an earl, he was familiar with the court. He had MA degrees from Oxford and from Cambridge. He was a literary patron. He had his own company of musicians in his house, Fishers' Folly, and there is a record that suggests his own musical accomplishments were of a professional standard. As a member of Gray's Inn he might have been expected to have some legal training. Sobran has claimed that a quarter of the legal terms mentioned in the plays reappear in Oxford's surviving letters – although according to Alan Nelson the earl merely 'parroted' terms he had heard, and did not use them correctly. Oxford also is known to have possessed books, including three or four that corresponded to those used by the author of the Shakespearean plays, namely a Geneva Bible and copies of Chaucer, Plutarch, Plato, Cicero, as well as a number of books in Italian. Until he was forced to sell it in 1589, the earl ran his estate, Fisher's Folly, a massive affair with pleasure gardens and bowling alleys, as a sort of literary salon where there were 'more rare qualified men and selected good Scholars than in any Nobleman's house that I know in England'.[2]

He also knew Italian, and had travelled in Italy for ten months between May 1575 and March 1576. The standard biography, Alan Nelson's *Monstrous Adversary*, shows that he lived in Venice, visited Padua, Sienna, Genoa and Milan. There, he devoted much of his time to sexual liaisons with the prostitute Virginia Padoana and a sixteen-year-old choirboy Orazio Cogno, whom he brought back to London and lived with for a year. Doubtless these experiences improved his Italian and also broadened his sexual vocabulary.

Finally, it appears that Oxford was very far from a believing Christian. Nelson's biography assembles comments from two witnesses: Lord Henry Howard said that Oxford thought 'the Trinity a fable ... Scripture [is] for policy', and Charles Arundel condemned Oxford's 'most horrible and detestable blasphemy in denial of the divinity of Christ our saviour'. In addition, Howard reports that Oxford practiced necromancy, attempting to raise the spirits of the dead, and claimed 'that he hath oft times copulation with a female spirit.' That certainly suggests that Oxford would have had no qualms about creating the kinds of anti-Christian satires that are found across the Shakespearean plays.

Oxford was also connected to the theatre. He employed the playwright of allegories John Lyly as his secretary, and was publicly known to have written comedies. Yet those to whom he gave patronage, like John Lyly, Thomas Greene and Antony Munday, praised him in their book dedications for his birth and generosity – but not as a writer. Gabriel Harvey in an epigram in 1578 told him to put away his 'feeble pen' and become a soldier instead. Most lists of contemporary Elizabethan poets exclude Oxford – such as those by Richard Carew (around 1595), Richard Barnfield (1598) and Thomas Cutwode (1599). There are, however, two exceptions. In 1589, George Puttenham's *The Arte of English Poesie* listed him as one of a number of nobles who wrote 'excellently well'. This was followed in 1598 by Francis Meres who listed the best playwrights of the time: 'The best for Comedy amongst us be, Edward Earle of Oxforde, Doctor Gager of Oxforde … eloquent and witty Iohn Lilly, Lodge, Gascoyne, Greene, Shakespeare, Thomas Nash, Thomas Heywood, Anthony Mundye … and Henry Chettle.' That Meres, at least, considered that the comedies that the earl wrote were distinct from those written by Shakespeare does not indicate anything either way – for if there is anything to the notion that Shakespeare was a frontman, universally understood to be the author of the plays, there is no reason Meres should think of Oxford and Shakespeare as the same man. However, the Oxfordian argument that Edward de Vere had to conceal his authorship of the Shakespearean plays behind a pseudonym because writing plays was somehow not permitted for an aristocrat is demonstrably a false argument. Francis Meres explicitly acknowledges Oxford as a writer of comedies, for which he required no pseudonym, and indeed places him very visibly at the head of his list of playwrights precisely because of his social rank and status.

The evidence that Oxford did *not* write the Shakespearean plays, on the other hand, is much more substantial. It begins with his lack of ties to the Chamberlain's Men, the differences between the nature of his interest in the Bible and that shown in the plays, the substantial differences between his poetry and that of the Shakespearean canon, and, most significantly of all, the lack of chronological fit between his career and the dates on which the plays were written.

The first major problem is that Oxford had his own playing companies, Oxford's Men and Oxford's Boys. One of them even performed an apocryphal Shakespearean play, *The Weakest Goeth to the Wall*. At first blush, this would seem to make part of the case for Oxford: he was intimately associated with the theatre. In fact, it suggests the opposite. Oxford was always hard up for money because he was extravagant, so it is difficult to imagine why he would have written very popular plays and then passed them on to another theatre company to be performed instead of giving them to his own and making money from the productions – even if he did so under someone else's name.

Oxford's poetry and use of English are another problem. His verse, of which around twenty short poems survive, is all very personal – none of it has religious, historical or philosophical implications. One of the best known is 'In Praise of a Contented Mind', of which we may consider an extract:

Were I a king, I could command content
Were I obscure, unknown should be my cares
And were I dead no thought should me torment
Nor words, nor wrongs, nor loves, nor hopes, nor fears.

The problem with Oxford's poetry is that it is not radical or experimental, but rather conservative. For instance, several of the poems use the outdated structure of fourteeners, fourteen-syllable lines that had been popular in the 1540s but that had given way to iambic pentameter as the universal language of Elizabethan theatre.

Further problems appear when his seventy-four surviving letters are examined. Nelson notes that Oxford wrote, and therefore spoke, a dialectical form of English, not the standard English used by Shakespeare. His biographer therefore concludes that Oxford was 'not a fully competent practitioner of his native English'. Clearly, therefore, this excludes him from having written the Shakespearean canon.

Oxford's Bible has survived, and is currently in the Folger library. It is a copy of the Geneva Bible, the Old Testament dated 1570, the New Testament dated 1568, and the Psalter dated 1569. It is bound in red velvet and decorated with metal plates, and an oval section on the cover reproduces Oxford's coat of arms. That Bible is marked with underlinings which were first studied by Roger Stritmatter, who had suggested that these corresponded to the Shakespearean plays. A further analysis by David Kathman, however, shows that only 8 per cent of the verses in Oxford's Bible overlap with verses used in the Shakespearean plays. For instance the underliner, presumably the earl himself, focused on 1 Kings, 1 Samuel, 2 Samuel, 2 Macabees, and 2 Esdras, all of which are barely used in the Shakespearean plays, but marked only one line in each of Genesis, Acts and Proverbs, which the plays draw upon heavily. Because this Bible marks only 1,000 lines, and the Shakespearean plays make at least 2,000 biblical references (ignoring those to the Church and Christianity), out of all the biblical verses used by Shakespeare only 4 per cent are marked in Oxford's Bible. That is less than the overlap between the verses in Oxford's Bible and the biblical allusions in Spenser's *Fairie Queene*, and so not enough to demonstrate anything at all. The markings in Oxford's Bible actually show that his biblical interests corresponded very little at all to those of the author of Shakespeare's plays.

As for his education, Alan Nelson has noted in his biography *Monstrous Adversary* that the Earl of Oxford did not have a BA, although he spent five months at Queens' College, Cambridge, at the tender age of eight. He obtained his MA from Cambridge at the age of fourteen and his MA from Oxford at the age of sixteen, in both cases because he was part of the queen's entourage that visited the university. The degrees were a kind of souvenir, and not given for academic achievement. Furthermore, although the earl was indeed a member of Gray's Inn, he seems never to have been in residence there. The errors in his use of legal Latin terminology do not suggest great familiarity with the law.

Finally, there is the issue of chronology. It is documented that the Earl of Oxford died in 1604. For the plays that were written collaboratively, and which appeared after his death, such as *Henry VIII*, *Two Noble Kinsmen* and *Pericles*, Oxford would have had to be the author whose work was taken over after his death by the collaborator. For *Pericles* at least, this does not seem to be what happened, since it appears Shakespeare took over material from Wilkins rather than the other way around. Sir Henry Wooton and Henry Bluett, who saw *Henry VIII* performed in 1613, describe it as a 'new play', rather than Fletcher's updating of a manuscript that, if written by Oxford, would by then have been at least nine years old and somewhat out of date – and would presumably have appeared so to the viewer.

As for the plays written by one hand, as most were, they would all have to have been completed before 1604. Those who support the Earl of Oxford have offered their own re-datings of the plays: none of these address the evidence that changes were actually being made up to 1623. Moreover, there is evidence to tie some of the plays very specifically to a date after 1608. In that year the King's Men (formerly the Lord Chamberlain's Men), the group that performed the Shakespearean plays, moved into a new indoor playhouse, the Blackfriars. Shakespeare's plays of this time had technical features that exploited the particular technical capacities of this theatre, for instance the descent from the roof of Jupiter in *Cymbeline*, and the disappearance of the feast in *The Tempest*, accompanied by the noise of the stage machinery. There is no reason why these features should appear in the scripts if they were created before 1604, when the King's Men only had access to the outdoor Globe Theatre, since those features could not have been performed onstage until the Blackfriars was built.

Even more convincingly, several of the plays are referred to by scholars as the 'British' plays, including *Macbeth*, *Lear* and *Cymbeline*, all of which touch on the issue of the unification of Britain as a single kingdom. This, however, was not a concern of Elizabethan state policy, instead being a concern of the government of King James, and largely after 1604, the date of Oxford's death.

There is yet more detailed evidence. Of all of the plays, the one that can be dated most clearly is *Macbeth*, which was written after the Gunpowder Plot of 1605 – and could not, therefore, have been written by someone who died in 1604. The evidence is quite clear. Today, we associate the Gunpowder Plot with Guy Fawkes, but in 1605 to 1606 Londoners saw it rather differently, as a plot masterminded by the Jesuits, Fawkes being merely the man who procured the explosives. The Jesuit rationale for equivocation was spelled out in the manuscript *Treatise of Equivocation*, written by a Jesuit named Henry Garnet. Garnet was the confessor for two of the Gunpowder plotters. His manuscript was also found in their possession, which led to Garnet being tried for treason and hanged, drawn and quartered. In the early 1600s, it wasn't Guy Fawkes but Garnet who attracted literary attention in connection with the Gunpowder Plot. This invites a particular focus when we look at *Macbeth*. Why? Because the idea of 'double meaning', or equivocation, is central to 'The Scottish Play'. The standard definition of 'Equivocale' in Florio's dictionary is 'of diverse significance, of double meaning'. In Cotgrave's dictionary, 'Equivoque' is defined as 'a double or divers sense of one word'.

This word 'double' is of course famous in *Macbeth* from the chant of the witches, 'Double, double, toil and trouble'. Shakespearean plays are usually symmetrical. Structurally, in *Macbeth*'s witches' scenes, it is clear that the knocking and the references to 'double double' are symmetrically matched later on by the knocking and references to equivocation during the Porter's scene. Thus, the witches' repetitious chant 'Double, double, toil and trouble' (4.1.9) is paralleled by the Porter's repetitious line 'Here's an equivocator ... come in equivocator' (2.3.9–11). In the Porter's scene, the footnotes in the standard Arden edition explain that the characters whom the Porter admits to hellmouth are the equivocator (Garnet himself), his alias (Mr Farmer), and the Tailor – who was associated with the image of Garnet's face that supposedly appeared miraculously on a bundle of straw following his execution. Furthermore, the three apparitions in the witches' scene – namely the head, the bloody child and the child holding a tree – appear to be derived from the imagery of Garnet's portrait on that miraculous straw. In other words, the apparitions summoned by the witches are a clear reference to Garnet's seventeenth-century Jesuits – something that could not have been written about before 1605, and so not until after Oxford's death.

The standard Oxfordian response to this is offered by Mark Anderson in his book *'Shakespeare' by Another Name*. He claims that '*Macbeth* makes no allusions to equivocation that can be tied to the Gunpowder Plot specifically', an observation that is clearly not correct, as I have demonstrated above. In support of his argument, he is obliged to maintain that, in 1606, 'equivocation was hardly a novel concept', i.e., that the word could have come from some source other than the Gunpowder Plot. Fortunately it is possible to settle the matter by running a statistical analysis of the appearance of the term in the literature of the period. My analysis shows that the term 'equivocation' was used only twenty-seven times in the decade 1594–1604, namely two or three times a year. It then rose by 100 per cent to fifteen uses in 1,157 printed records from 1605–6. The six uses in *Macbeth* would have amounted to 40 per cent of all uses in the previous decade, and would have been the only example that – for some reason – made so many uses of the term in a single document. So the term 'equivocation' was still extremely rare in 1605–6, but spiked in the wake of the Gunpowder Plot. This suggests that Father Garnet's trial indeed influenced Shakespeare, whose use of the term was part of this small explosion that took place over a two-year period.

Oxfordians also try to deny that the plays make reference to anything else datable after 1604. For instance, in his article 'The Case for Oxford Revisited', Ramon Jimenez claims that 'the discovery of Jupiter's moons [by Galileo in 1610] ... go unmentioned in the plays'. However, Scott Maisano in 'Shakespeare's

Last Act: The Starry Messenger and the Galilean Book in Cymbeline' presents astronomer Peter Usher's finding that the descent of Jove in that play, surrounded by four spirits, is indeed an allusion to Galileo's 1610 discovery. As the editor of the Penguin edition of *Cymbeline* remarks, this was 'no accident'.[3] This is yet another piece of evidence that Oxford could not have written these plays. So is the fact that *The Winter's Tale* appears to incorporate elements from the staging of *Mucedorus* in 1610, not to mention the references to circulation of the blood or the authorial changes made to certain plays in 1622.

And so we come to Oxfordian attempts to re-date the plays in order to make them all significantly earlier. What is supposedly a 'major statement' for the Oxfordian case, as the *Shakespeare Oxford Newsletter* (Winter 2012) described it, is found in Katherine Chiljan's book *Shakespeare Suppressed*. The newsletter claims that Chiljan provides 'devastating' evidence that the plays date from a time in the 1570s when the man from Stratford was an infant. The reviewer concludes that the book presents a 'challenge which demands a major answer'. So to address one of Chiljan's examples, material in *The Two Gentlemen of Verona* matches three plays which were performed at court during the 1570s. The likely reason is that *The Two Gentlemen of Verona* used those texts as sources. Similarly, phrases from Thomas Nashe's *Strange News* (1593) reappear in *Much Ado*, *The Comedy of Errors*, *As You Like It* and *Hamlet*, which used it as a source. The likelihood that Nashe combed four *unprinted and unperformed* plays as sources to select just these phrasings is infinitesimal, especially since all of them can be dated later than 1593.

There is also the Marlowe problem. Nearly a dozen of the Shakespearean plays show very close relationship to Marlovian plays written in the early 1590s. The proposed Oxfordian re-dating would require that Marlowe was somehow influenced by a dozen Shakespearean plays *that had not been performed and had not been printed*. For instance in Shakespeare's *Romeo and Juliet* the 'gallop apace' speech parallels the speech, 'Gallop apace bright Phoebus through the sky', which comes from Marlowe's *Edward II* of 1592. There is therefore no way it could have been written in the 1560s. The Marlovian correspondences are perhaps the strongest nail in the Oxfordian coffin, stronger even than the fact that Oxford died in 1604 before half the plays were written.

Finally, yet another eccentric Oxfordian proposition about the dating of the plays surfaces in Roland Emmerich's movie *Anonymous*, that Edward de Vere wrote *A Midsummer Night's Dream* in 1560 at the age of ten. Firstly, the idea that a child could have written such a profound philosophical work on the nature of poetry, and a complex allegorical anti-Christian satire, is totally ridiculous. It would be implausible for an English earl at such a tender age to have learned Hebrew and to have made frequent visits to Westminster Abbey to study England's only copy of the Talmud – a source for the play – all while being kept under house arrest by his teachers as a ward of Lord Burghley. Furthermore, as Professor

Stephen Marche remarked in his review 'Wouldn't It Be Cool if Shakespeare Wasn't Shakespeare' in the *New York Times* on 21 October 2011, the suggestion is completely impossible since this would require *A Midsummer Night's Dream* to have been written before the very genre of English secular comedy – of which it is part – had even been invented.

In addition to the inherent implausibility of *Midsummer* being written in 1560 when its author was ten, or *Romeo and Juliet* being written in 1561 when he was eleven, there is another problem concerning craftsmanship. Both of these plays are mature works. At what age are we to suppose that Oxford began playwriting and learning his craft? Furthermore, if he could write amazing work like *Midsummer* or *Romeo and Juliet* at the age of eleven, why did his verse then degenerate when he got older and started writing under his own name? In any case, why would Oxford have created these plays twenty years before his own theatre company, the Oxford's Men, was active? Why he did not then give his plays to them, waiting instead thirty-six years for *Midsummer* to be performed in 1596? Furthermore, some of the plays actually have the real names of the Chamberlain's Men actors written into the script – for instance John Sincklo is mentioned as acting in *The Taming of the Shrew* and *Henry VI*, parts 2 and 3. Most probably the names were inserted by the playhouse bookkeeper, but if not, then how could Oxford know thirty years beforehand which actors would be performing the plays?

Of course Paul Streitz has claimed that Oxford did not die in 1604 at all but was banished to the island of Mersea in the English Channel, off the coast of Essex, where he continued to write both the plays and also the King James Bible – for this fantasy, needless to say, there is no evidence at all. Though he left no will, in June 1604 Oxford began settling his affairs, granting the custody of the Forest of Essex to a relative, and on 24 June he died. Three days later his name was deleted from the list of peers in the House of Lords. On 6 July he was buried, and the burial was recorded in two different burial registers. On 18 July the dowager countess distributed a few shillings to two local parishioners, his son Henry became the 18th Earl, and no friend, no tradesman, no family member records that they ever heard from him again.

In this sad morass of material on the Earl of Oxford, there is, however, at least one oddity that is helpful in identifying the true author. Craig Huston, in *The Shakespeare Authorship Question*, examined similarities of language between Oxford's writing and the Shakespearean works. Most such similarities were very common: the word 'deluded', for instance. However, there were a small number of expressions that were rather rare. For instance, Oxford's phrase 'gentle hearts', which is paralleled in Sonnet 20 as 'gentle heart', appears in only twelve records out of the 4,500 printed between 1600 and 1610. Oxford's phrase 'gaze on beauty', which is paralleled exactly in *The Rape of Lucrece*, is even rarer, appearing in only five records out of 8,500 published over the period from 1590 to 1610. This does not show that the Earl of Oxford wrote the plays. What it does suggest, however, is that the Earl of Oxford and the author of the plays belonged to the same small social network of people who used these unusual expressions.

Since the Earl of Oxford is the leading candidate for the authorship, apart from Shakespeare, I have felt obliged to discuss the evidence at length. He was first put forward as a candidate in 1920 by J. T. Looney, in *Shakespeare Identified*, but he was certainly not a genius, nor a feminist, and his letters show none of the intellectual and theological concerns that underlie the Shakespearean plays. Most to the point, he could have written neither the tragedies nor the romances that were created from 1605 onwards because he was lying dead in his private tomb.

Christopher Marlowe

Being dead should be an insuperable problem for a claimant to the Shakespearean authorship. Yet it has not stopped backers of Christopher Marlowe. Marlowe died, as far as the records show, in a brawl in a Deptford pub at the age of twenty-nine – a brawl probably started as the cover-up to a government-sponsored murder. This violates one of the most basic requirements for the authorship, that to have written the plays the candidate needed to be alive for the whole period from 1589 to 1623 (in order to make the changes to *Othello* between 1622 and 1623). There is a large financial prize, the Calvin Hoffman prize, offered each year for anyone who can prove that Marlowe wrote the Shakespearean plays, but despite the financial incentive it has not been awarded. Marlowe's backers claim, however, that Marlowe faked his death in order to avoid the accusations of the Atheism Commission, and went abroad under a false identity, from whence he wrote the Shakespearean plays.

Marlowe is certainly a credible figure. He knew Italian and the classics, and he was a great playwright – second, in fact, only to Shakespeare. He was an atheist, and claimed that the figure of Jesus was a 'deceiver' in 'vain and idle' tales, and that the Holy Scriptures were 'all of one man's making' and had been created as a matter of 'policy' (see Appendix 8). Marlowe would have had no problem in writing the religious allegories in the Shakespearean plays – indeed, in many ways they continue the allegories and religious views in his own works.

There is also a piece of evidence which suggests that at least one contemporary thought Marlowe had indeed written some of the Shakespearean works. Ros Barber observes that William Covell's *Polimanteia* (1595) praises the author of *Venus and Adonis*, *Lucrecia*, and eloquent Gaveston, the latter being presumably the character in Marlowe's *Edward II*.[4] There are very close resemblances between Marlowe's plays and the early Shakespearean works, and it is likely that he collaborated on several of them. However, as a series of excellent pieces of research by Thomas Merriam on the verbal similarities have demonstrated, those resemblances disappear after the early years.

It is not inconceivable that Marlowe could have faked his death and that as a spy he might have had the skills to do so. There are dozens of examples, both ancient and modern, all over the word of those who fake their deaths. These days, it tends to be to get out of credit card debts or other financial problems. Then, Marlowe's likely trial for heresy would have been a much more pressing reason. However, the circumstances of his death, in which the two witnesses were informers and members of the secret service, and which are examined in Charles Nicholl's book *The Reckoning*, are not in dispute. The only question that they suggest is whether his death was a deliberate murder by the secret service, or was, as the inquest found, accidental. The idea of a corpse being substituted for his body so he could escape to Europe to live under a false identity has no factual foundation.

Nonetheless, different proponents of the idea that Marlowe had a posthumous existence have fantasised him living under at least three different identities in Italy, Spain and France. Robert Ayres would have it that Marlowe did not die but went to live in Venice under the name Gregorio de'Monti, a secretary to the English Ambassador. Unfortunately, de'Monti did not speak English, and was described by the Venetians as a Venetian. The fact that he ran off with the Spanish actress Micaela de Lujan and wrote a dedication to one of Guarini's comedies does not qualify as sufficient theatrical experience to be the secret author of the Shakespearean plays. Another supporter, John Baker, finds Marlowe living under the name John Matthew at the English Catholic Seminary at Valladolid, Spain, with the support of Sir Robert Cecil, but returning to England and being pardoned in 1604 and discharged from prison under the name of Marley. Marley is a common name, as well as being a variety of Marlowe.[5] But this is very thin stuff on which to hang a theory of Marlovian authorship of the plays.

Nor is it likely that Marlowe was masquerading as a French spy, as argued by A. D. Wraight in her book *Shakespeare: New Evidence*. That a spy called Monsieur Le Doux was found with a crate of books, some of which were identical to those used to write the Shakespearean plays, could have many explanations less outrageous than that Le Doux was Kit Marlowe in disguise carrying away the raw materials with which to write the Shakespearean canon. Because the number of books in common use in Elizabethan London was only a couple of thousand, and Shakespeare used such a high proportion of them, it is practically inevitable that some books that Shakespeare used would appear in any reasonably sized trunkful. Le Doux was an established spy in the employ of the King of France and had an entire documented career as a secret agent: writing plays to be performed in English theatres does not feature in his career trajectory. Nor is there any explanation why Marlowe (as Le Doux) should have written the early histories at court and then switched to writing Italian marriage comedies around the year 1593, nor why he would make references to his own death in *As You Like It*. Nor is it clear how to reconcile the conflicting claims that Marlowe became Le Doux who became John Matthew who became Gregorio de'Monti – or the other way around.

Even if Marlowe had another afterlife as a French spy, or a French monk, this would not explain him developing the musical knowledge necessary to write the plays. It also does not explain, for instance, why the stereotyped perspective of the Jew as a red-wigged devil found in *The Jew of Malta* is suddenly rejected and replaced by the plea for equality found in *The Merchant of Venice*.

The Marlowe theory is not based on factual relationships between the kinds of skills and knowledge shown in the plays and a living playwright. As far as we can tell, there was no living playwright after 1593. Nonetheless, Marlowe and his religious beliefs, or lack of them, are unquestionably a part of resolving the mystery of Shakespearean Authorship, as we shall see. For there are other possible explanations of why Marlowe's influence is so prevalent in the plays, why it declines, why his religious ideas and uses of religious allegories are developed, and why *As You Like It* goes out of its way to comment on his death. Marlowe died in 1593. But his influence did indeed live on. As we shall see, the person who wrote the Shakespearean plays, and so continued Marlowe's work, was not Marlowe himself – but someone very close to him: his pupil, protégé, and, it appears, probably his lover.

Sir Francis Bacon

A recent history of the Authorship Controversy, James Shapiro's book *Contested Will*, goes into some of the details of how in the nineteenth century people first began to suspect Bacon as a possible author of the Shakespearean plays, and the extraordinary efforts that they went to in their search for evidence. His account covers the cipher machines built by those who were convinced that secret codes had been embedded into the plays by Bacon. There were other supporters of Bacon who dredged the River Wye, convinced by the ciphers that hidden manuscripts sat in lead boxes at the bottom of the river, and that finding them would reveal the truth about Bacon's authorship of the plays. Supporters of Bacon seem to favour ciphers: others conducted an analysis of the cryptograms buried in the sixpence admission tickets to Shakespeare's burial site in Holy Trinity Church and deciphered the secret location at which Bacon is said to be buried together with the original manuscripts of the plays in his handwriting. And so it goes on.

It is a pity that the case for Bacon has been marked by such eccentricities, because he compares very positively on many of the different areas of skills and knowledge identified in the plays. Bacon was undoubtedly brilliant: He meets the intellectual requirement. He also was alive in 1623, unlike Oxford or Marlowe or William Shakespeare. He owned books and in his will he made a bequest of his 'books of orizons or psalms' to his friend the Marquis Fiatt. Further, the second paragraph of Bacon's will goes into great detail about how his own manuscripts must be preserved. He calls them 'the durable part of my memory which consisteth in my works and writings' and instructs how they shall be bound into books and placed in half a dozen libraries of record. He also left money to establish university lectureships and specified the required qualifications of the lecturers. Unlike the will of the man from Stratford, Bacon's will is that of an intellectual concerned about his intellectual legacy. It is also possible that John Marston may have referred to him, in 1598, as the unseen lawyer 'Labeo', who Marston may have suspected to exist behind the Shakespearean works – though this does not mean Marston was right, any more than William Covell in 1595 was right in suspecting that Marlowe had written *Venus and Adonis* and *The Rape of Lucrece*.

Bacon read many languages and his commonplace book contains quotations in English, French, Italian, Spanish, Latin, and Greek. He also possessed two Hebrew grammars interleaved with pages of his handwriting. He seems to have visited Italy (according to Pierre Amboise, his first biographer, in 1631). As England's leading lawyer, he would have all the necessary legal skills to write the plays. He had apparently made some study of medicine. He also appears to have owned a collection of about twenty play quartos, including eight Shakespearean quartos of *Titus Andronicus, Richard the Third, Richard the Second, King Lear, King John, Romeo and Juliet, Hamlet* and *Henry IV.* A courtier, philosopher and writer, he produced a number of works on science and philosophy. His book *Tracts of Law* covers some of the areas that appear in Shakespeare's plays. He wrote an essay on gardens naming some of the same flowers that appear in the plays. Bacon was also a friend of many of the leading thinkers and intellectuals of the time, including William Herbert, Earl of Pembroke, Ben Jonson, Beaumont and Fletcher, Sir John Davis, Fulke Greville, the Earls of Surrey and Essex, and at one point the Earl of Southampton.

However, Bacon did not have any particular skills in or practical knowledge of music, nor did he live as a member of an intensely musical social network. Certainly, he wrote about music. In *New Atlantis* he predicted the recording studio: 'We have sound-houses, where we practice and generate all sounds, and their generation. We have harmonies which you have not, of quarter sounds and lesser slides of sound. Divers of instruments of music likewise to you unknown ... We represent small sounds as great and deep; likewise great sounds extenuate and sharp.'

However none of this, nor his comments on the design of choirs or how music and medicine could work jointly in healing, would have enabled him to write the Shakespearean plays. Andrea Luppi, in an article 'The Role of Music in Francis Bacon's Thought', emphasises that his was a theoretical interest in composition, linked to mathematics, acoustics, astronomy and engineering. Bacon saw music as operating upon the laws of science. As he stated, 'Music in the practice, hath been well pursued, and in good variety; but in the theory ... very weakly.'

Likewise, Bacon would not have created the anti-Christian allegories in the Shakespearean plays. He adhered to Christian belief, believing that it was necessary to ensure the safety and stability of the kingdom. Marlowe or Oxford would have been willing to create the anti-Christian allegories, knowing that their effect would be to destabilise Christian belief. This is not something that Bacon would not have done. His essay on the unity of the Church reflects his orthodox Christian conservatism.

Timothy H. Patterson, in his article 'On the Role of Christianity in the Political Philosophy of Francis Bacon', emphasises that Bacon did look for the human mastery of nature, and explores the possibility of Bacon as 'an anti-Christian writer' with 'antireligious intentions', which had previously been explored by Howard White in his book on Bacon's political philosophy. However, to the extent that this is sound, it relates to Bacon's long-term intentions in establishing a world that was ruled by rational, scientific methodologies. This philosophical focus is very different from the Shakespearean plays, which, as we shall see, were concerned with deconstructing Christian beliefs. If Bacon took any action it was by writing his legalistic and reformist tract for King James, titled *Certaine Considerations Touching the Better Pacification and Edification of the Church of* England, in 1603. This deals with issues such as confirmation, music in church, use of the ring in marriage, thefts of church funds, the use of the word 'priest', and whether clergy should wear caps and surplices. It is light years away from the kind of concerns that the playwright had, in undoing fundamental assumptions of New Testament criticism.

Unlike the Earl of Oxford, Francis Bacon wrote in standard English. But his poetry and attempts at drama were stilted. His poetry is modest, and shows no resemblances in wording, composition or style to Shakespeare. Unlike Mr Shakespeare, Bacon had no connection to the Lord Chamberlain's Men or any of the other acting companies. He had no known experience with writing plays, although he did create several masques and allegorical 'devices'. His device for Lord Essex, *The Conference of Pleasure* (1595), included a hermit, a Secretary of State, a soldier and an esquire. In 1595 Bacon produced another masque for Lord Essex, *The Masque of the Indian Prince, or the Darling Piece of Love and Self-Love*. It featured a praise of the Virgin Queen that included the following verse:

> Seated between the old world and the new,
> A land there is no other land may touch
> Where reigns a Queen in peace and honour true;
> Stories of fables do describe no such
> Never did Atlas such a burden bear
> As she in holding up the world oppress't
> Supplying with her virtue everywhere
> Weakness of friend, errors of servants best.

If this were not enough, we might usefully turn to two manuscript documents and consider what they imply for how Bacon worked, and whether they hold any relevance to the plays. The first is Bacon's private diary or commonplace book, *The Promus of Forumularies and Elegancies*, which has 2,000 entries in several languages. It nowhere suggests that he was working on writing any of the Shakespearean plays, nor that he was working on their publication in the First Folio. The most it suggests is that Bacon collected words and expressions such as 'good morrow' and common sayings such as 'a fool's bolt is soon shot' or 'to drive out a nail with a nail', some of which appeared in the Shakespearean plays.

Secondly, the so-called Northumberland Manuscript, found in 1867 and now at Alnwick Castle in Northumberland, must also be mentioned since it is traditionally used to support Bacon's authorship. It is a twenty-two-page manuscript that includes speeches and essays by Bacon, and a letter by Philip Sidney. The cover page is full of scribbles, many in Latin, as well as the name William Shakespeare, a list of several Shakespearean plays, together with the name of Henry Neville at the top, and his family motto and a poem about it. This document suggests that the owner had literary and historical interests. In any case, in the centre of the folder, writings by Francis Bacon are listed to the left, while writings by William Shakespeare, namely *Richard II* and *Richard III*, are to the right, followed by *Asmund and Cornelia*, and Nashe's *Isle of Dogs*. *Asmund and Cornelia* is a non-existent play, but is referred to by Bacon in his *Conference of Pleasure* – apparently a misremembrance of *Gismund and Cornelia*. This mistake makes it likely that the person who wrote on the folder was indeed Bacon, but possession of this folder does not mean that he wrote the plays.

Finally, let me return to the predilection for codes, which led one of Bacon's early supporters to camp out at Shakespeare's grave hoping to get it opened to search for manuscripts that would confirm the Baconian case. One simple example of this obsession with codes is the Latin word *honorificabilitudinitatibus*, meaning the condition of being able to achieve honours. It is spoken by Costard in *Love's Labour's Lost,* and it has been argued that it conceals an anagram which reads (in bad Latin) '*Hi ludi, F. Baconis nati, tuiti orbi*', meaning 'These plays, the offspring of F. Bacon, are preserved for the world.' Or else perhaps '*Pro bono orbis F. Bacon e nemo*', meaning 'For the good of the world F. Bacon is nameless.' Unfortunately for the anagram makers, this word, despite looking as if it were made to the purpose, was not invented by Bacon. The *Oxford English Dictionary* records the first usage around 1300. It was used by Dante in *De Vulgari Eloquentia* around 1302. It appears in *Love's Labour's Lost* because it was an existing word undergoing something of a revival: it was used by Nashe at the same time. There is no justification for supposing it was being used in order to encode bad Latin anagrams.

In summary, Bacon possessed a number of the skills and areas of knowledge demonstrated in the plays. Most importantly he was a genius, but not a literary genius. Several things precluded him from writing the Shakespearean plays. Bacon's religious values were different, he lacked the poetical skill to write

Shakespearean verse or prose and he lacked any serious practical knowledge of music. Nor, ultimately, did he have the time. He was a busy statesman holding a succession of high legal offices (even, in 1617, ruling England as the Lord Keeper of the Great Seal, while King James was in Scotland for six months). He was also writing major works of scientific philosophy and the law that demanded all his attention: there are fifteen volumes in the standard edition of Bacon's works. These objections effectively rule out Bacon as a candidate for the authorship of the Shakespearean works.

Some Other Authorship Candidates

If one were writing a history of the authorship controversy, one could go down many other fascinating avenues, such as an inventive book on Ann Whateley, who is chiefly fascinating because she did not actually exist, but is the product of a spelling mistake on Mr Shakespeare's marriage documentation. I will not go through all the remaining seventy plus candidates for the authorship because their cases are even weaker than those that have been reviewed so far in this chapter. However, some of them can be touched on briefly.

Queen Elizabeth was first put forward as an authorship candidate in 1857 and was subsequently the subject of tongue-in-cheek article by Gulick 'Was "Shakespeare" a Woman?', and also a book by George E. Sweet, *Shake-speare the Mystery*. His argument amounts to little more than that the queen was very smart and had a large vocabulary. He might have added that she was a poet, though not a very good one, spoke Italian, knew Greek, translated part of at least one classical play, and had a good knowledge of theology as head of the Church of England. Unfortunately for this theory, unlike, say, Queen Margaret of Navarre who did indeed write plays, Elizabeth was busily engaged in governing the country, and had her own theatre company, The Queen's Men, who she would have written for if she wrote for any. All her spare time is accounted for, she never travelled to Scotland, had no opportunity to acquire a knowledge of the Northern dialect, and as a pious Christian would have had no motivation for writing anti-Christian religious allegories into the plays. She died in 1603, so she could not have written either *Macbeth* or *Cymbeline* which are clearly dateable to after her death. Nor is it clear why she would have begun by writing court plays and then suddenly changed to writing Italian marriage comedies. And as the richest and most honoured woman in the country she hardly can be made to fit the playwright's self-description in the sonnets of being poor and despised, lacking honours and proud titles.

The case for **William Stanley, 6th Earl of Derby,** was put forward in 1891. His initials conveniently parallel those of William Shakespeare. A Jesuit spy had reported in 1599 that the earl was 'busied only in penning comedies for the common players'. He also had first-hand knowledge of the court of Henry of Navarre – which appears allegorically in *Love's Labour's Lost*. He studied law and may have known Italian. Unfortunately no literary works authored by the earl survive, so it is impossible to know anything about his literary capacity. Further, if the Earl of Derby wrote plays at all they would most likely have been for his brother the 5th Earl's playing company, Lord Strange's Men, which in 1593 was renamed Lord Derby's Men. Needless to say there is no reason why he would have incorporated Jewish religious allegories into the plays, or how he learned Hebrew, or why he made so many musical references or referred to falconry from the perspective of a falconer. Nor, as an earl, does he fit the playwright's self-description in the sonnets of being poor and despised, lacking honours and proud titles. Nor is it clear why he would have begun by writing court plays and then suddenly changed, and begun writing Italian marriage comedies.

The case for the **Earl of Rutland** was put forward in 1912. He is known to have visited Denmark in 1603, and visited Italy in 1596. He was classically educated, had a library in his family castle, and was familiar with Italian and the law. Correggio's painting of *Jupiter and Io* was on display in Milan only between 1585 and 1600, and is referred to in *The Taming of the Shrew* – although a copy existed in Rutland's castle, suggesting he had a special familiarity with the painting. Like Derby he left behind no writings, so it is not possible to know if he wrote poetry or plays, nor is it possible to make any assessments about his style. As with Oxford, there is no evidence that he was a child prodigy, which he would have had to have been since he was only sixteen when *Venus and Adonis* was published. His visit to Denmark in 1603 was too late to write the first quarto of *Hamlet* since that was the year the play appeared in print. His visit to Italy in 1596 was too late to give him the local knowledge to write *Romeo and Juliet* or *The Two Gentlemen of Verona* in 1594–5. There is no reason to suppose he knew Hebrew, or had any reason for writing anti-Christian religious allegories. Nor as an earl does he fit the playwright's self-description in the sonnets of being poor and despised, lacking honours and proud titles.

The case for **Mary Sidney, the Countess of Pembroke** was put forward by Gilbert Slater in *The Seven Shakespeares* (1931) as one of the seven individuals he thought wrote the plays as a sort of aristocratic playwriting collective. His argument was mainly based on the feminine influence he detected in the plays, especially their female characters. Subsequently, Robin Williams in *Sweet Swan of Avon* argued that Sidney was the sole author. She was a poet, and did translate one play from the French. She also spoke Italian, played several musical instruments, and had her own theatre company, Pembroke's Men, which did indeed perform a couple of the earliest Shakespearean plays. However there is no evidence of how Sidney could have acquired the detailed legal and military knowledge, the knowledge of Denmark, or the knowledge of Judaism shown in the plays. She did indeed visit Italy, but only in 1606, after which many of the Shakespearean plays set in Italy had already been written. Nor is the fact that Sidney played the violin and maintained a set of virginals evidence that she had the very high degree of musical knowledge, especially of the recorder, found in the plays. Sidney's poetry shows no similarities in linguistic content or structure, to either the sonnets or the plays. She was only a minor poet in any case, writing three original poems totalling around 250 lines in all. It is impossible to imagine that the Marrano satires were created by Mary Sidney, since apart from her unorthodox sexual practices, she was a pious Christian full of 'faith and pietie', as Amelia Lanier noted, who studied divinity and made Wilton House a place 'where first, God daily served, religion truly preached', as noted by Nicholas Breton in *Wits Trenchmour* (1597). Nor as a countess does she fit the playwright's self-description in the sonnets of being poor and despised, lacking honours and proud titles.

Some other candidates have also been put forward recently. Partly on the basis that his name appears on the Northumberland folder, there has been an attempt to suggest **Henry Neville** as the author of the plays[6] but since there is no evidence of him being a playwright or poet this is implausible. He also did not read or speak Hebrew, nor did he have any connections to the theatre in general, nor to the Lord Chamberlain's Men. The case for **Thomas Sackville**, put forward by Sabrina Feldman in her article 'The Swallow and the Crow', is interesting since he was a poet, a lawyer, and was publicly known for writing the play *Gorboduc* (1561), a major source for the Shakespearean plays. He also had travelled in Italy. However, he died in 1608 and could therefore not have written *Cymbeline*, which refers to Galileo's discovery of the moons of Jupiter in 1610, nor other plays that were written to be performed in the Blackfriars Theatre, built in 1608. As Baron Buckhurst and Lord Treasurer he also is no match for the self-description in the sonnets, and had no connection to the Lord Chamberlain's Men. The case for **John Florio**, put forward by Lamberto Tassinari, is interesting because Florio not only knew Italian, but was also of Jewish origin. But he falls short on the other key criteria. For instance, the fact that upon one occasion he was asked to recommend a musician does not demonstrate he had any more musical knowledge than any educated Elizabethan.

In conclusion, all the leading authorship cases fall down and the evidence for the others is even weaker. Of the leading candidates, only in one of the cases was the candidate a major poet – and he was dead. None of the leading candidates had exceptional exposure to musicianship. None of them had any unusual associations with falconry. Two of them were atheists and might have created anti-Christian allegories – if they had not been dead. All knew Italian. None of them knew anything about silk weaving, or generalship. Or rare plants. Or girls' literature. Or feminism. Or Judaism. Only one knew Hebrew. Two had knowledge of the theatre and one had an involvement in staging masques – but none of them had any association with the Lord Chamberlain's Men.

We therefore need to look for a new candidate – and there is one on the TopTenz list – who does meet all these biographical criteria and who was also a major experimental poet.

5

Amelia's Early Life: 1569–1582

In London, in the late sixteenth century, it was an established fact of life that women could not write plays. The best that England could offer was occasional women's improvisations such as that of Alice Mustian in Salisbury, who in 1614 gave a one-woman show featuring the irregular sex lives of her neighbours. She set up her stage on boards across two barrels and charged admission of 'pins and points' for her performance, which attracted a large crowd – and complaints from those she insulted.[1]

Europe was more sophisticated. Moderata Fonte's musical and allegorical play *La Feste* had been performed in Venice before the Doge on St Stephen's Day in 1581, and Isabella Andreini performed her partly improvised comedy, *Isabella's Madness*, for the Florentine court in 1589. But London was not as socially liberated as Venice. Even to think of translating a play one would have to be a countess, like Mary Sidney, Countess of Pembroke, who translated Robert Garnier's tragedy *Marc Antoine* (1592) from the French. No woman would publish an original play until Elizabeth Cary, Countess of Falkland, who wrote *The Tragedy of Miriam* (1613), which was never performed on stage and was published only under her initials. It was not until the 1650s that Margaret Cavendish, Duchess of Newcastle, actually wrote plays to be performed commercially. But even at this date the idea of a woman being involved in this male occupation was so extraordinary that Samuel Pepys called Cavendish 'mad' and 'ridiculous'. Other people, to her annoyance, criticised her spelling. So was it that, in late sixteenth-century London, to have any involvement in playwriting one would have had to be a countess or a duchess. A small, dark-skinned Jewish girl from a family of Italian court musicians would have seemed to have no chance at all in this venture, let alone the chance of becoming the greatest playwright of the age. This chapter begins to tell that unlikely and amazing story.

The story begins in Italy in the early 1500s in a small town called Bassano del Grappa, about 40 miles north of Venice. In some ways Bassano was a small medieval town like many in the region. It was the home of a famous dynasty of painters that included Jacopo de Ponte, better known as Jacopo Bassano. It was also the home town of a remarkable dynasty of Jewish musicians, who were then known as the Pivas, and who specialised in making and playing musical instruments. Their name, as the Bassanos' biographer Roger Prior has shown in his article 'Shakespeare's Visit to Italy', means both 'bagpipes', 'big-nose' and 'penis'. Jokes to the effect appear in *The Merchant of Venice,* in which all three concepts of nose, bagpipe and penis are associated in the lines: 'And others when the bagpipe sings i' th' nose / Cannot contain their urine' (4.1.48–9). The same jokes also appear in *Othello*, where the musicians are told to put their pipes in a 'bag' (3.1.19), and asked whether they speak in the 'nose' because their 'tail' has been in Naples and caught a venereal disease there (3.1.3–9).

As a town, Bassano had many attractions. In the main square, there was an apothecary's shop known as 'The Moor' after the large sign of a Moor's head that hung outside. There was also another apothecary's shop in the square, which until 1591 was run by Giovanni Otello. Several other members of the Otello family lived in the town and two of them, both notaries, ordered pictures from Jacopo Bassano, the town's most famous artist. Another smaller square in the town was known as the Piazza of Salt. Prominent in this square was a building with many windows, covering the front of which was a remarkable fresco. As Roger Prior shows, it has a fascinating relevance to *Othello*.

The fresco could only be properly seen in the early morning, when there was good light, and all the window shutters were closed. When opened, these shutters, known as *gelosie* (literally 'jealousies'), would have blocked out much of the artwork. The fresco was painted in 1539 by Jacopo Bassano. Until 1583 the house was owned by the philosopher Zuanne Corno, an ambassador to the Venetian Senate, whose title was the Count Palatine and who was known for writing a sonnet about weeping. His name, Corno, meant 'Mr Horns', the Elizabethan image of cuckoldry. His son-in-law Zanetto, a salt merchant, operated his shop out of one of the ground-floor storefronts.

The details of this unique and remarkable fresco on the building, which still survives today, are recorded in Iago's speech in *Othello*, as he goads him with an image of Desdemona and Cassio engaged in sexual intercourse, offered under the guise of something he could not successfully arrange for Othello, however far gone the two lovers were:

> What shall I say? Where's satisfaction?
> It is impossible you should see this,
> Were they as prime as **goats**, as hot as **monkeys**,
> As **salt** as wolves in pride, and fools as gross
> As **ignorance made drunk**. But yet, I say,
> If imputation and strong circumstances,
> Which lead directly to the **door of Truth**,
> Will give you satisfaction, you may have't.

> 3.3.404–11

Now consider the fresco in the piazza. As Roger Prior explains, it is divided into several bands. At the top is a series of animals, with a prominent sheep, and next to it a large *goat* underneath which there is seated a *monkey*. (The theme reflects the New Testament warning that people will be divided into the sheep and the goats, but there is no equivalent significance to the monkey). Roughly beneath the monkey there is a large painting of a naked woman, *Truth*, who stands in between two of the arched windows. She can of course only be seen when the shutters are closed: at other times, the shutters form a *door* and cover her over. To the left of Truth is another large allegorical figure, with two faces and a snake around her arm, signifying Prudence. Finally beneath Truth is a painting of the drunkenness of Noah, and to the left the daughters of Lot after their escape from Sodom.

Not only does the figure of Otello the apothecary in the main square match the unusually frequent references to drugs and medicine in *Othello*, but this fresco about sexual desire, with its implications about cuckoldry, clearly informs Iago's speech. Further, the house was owned by the Dal Corno family, the term 'corno' meaning 'horn', which was the standard symbol of cuckoldry in Elizabethan England. Proceeding from the goat to the monkey, the speech moves on to the door of Truth. 'Salt' (the phrase 'as salt as wolves' appears nowhere else in English literature) would appear to refer to the salt shop on the ground floor, and 'ignorance made drunk' is a very clear biblical reference to Lot's intercourse with his daughters when he was drunk and naked after leaving the Ark. The fresco was painted in 1539, and is today on display in the local civic museum.

Unfortunately, as was indicated by their anti-Semitic nickname 'Pivas,' or penis, Jews were not very welcome in Bassano. The town voted in 1510 to expel its Jewish residents and by 1524 they had succeeded in doing so. Sometime in this period, therefore, the Pivas packed up their musical-instrument-making business and moved to Venice – although they would keep a house on the Borgo di Lion in their hometown until the 1570s. Because the curfew in the ghetto would have precluded them from playing at concerts, playing on the Sabbath, or taking part in the active musical life of the city from which they derived their income, they did not move into the ghetto as practicing Jews. Instead, they settled just east of the Ponte Vecchio outside the ghetto. This meant that they could not practice their Judaism openly. They became Marranos or Conversos, hidden Jews (see Appendix 5).

Obviously, the Pivas dropped their anti-Semitic name as soon as they could, renaming themselves after the town they came from as Bassanios, or Bassani, which later became simply Bassanos.

Bassano was one of the centres of the silk-farming and silk-weaving industry. Bassano silk was even finer than Chinese silk, and the women reelers of Bassano were thought to be more excellent than any others in the world in reeling silk. Their silk was exported all over Europe, including to London, where Henry VIII's wives demanded elegant silk dresses. Because of its quality, the demand for Bassano silks was very high and they were more expensive than other kinds. We can judge their popularity in London because the purchases that London 'silkwomen' made from the Venetian silk merchants are still recorded in the account rolls in the Public

Record Office. The silkwomen would buy 'fardels' (bundles) of raw silk and thread, and take it back to their homes, where they and their apprentices would convert it into made up goods, such as dresses. According to David Lasocki and Roger Prior, who wrote the definitive biography *The Bassanos*, the family may have had some involvement in the silk industry, a common Jewish occupation. The coat of arms that they eventually would take, and which is mentioned between 1588 and 1597, featured what were described in contemporary heraldry as butterflies above a laurel tree. If this is really a mulberry tree with silk-worm moths on it, this could allude to the town of Bassano's importance as a centre of the silk trade.

By 1515, some if not all of the Bassanos had moved from Bassano, and were involved in concerts and processions in Venice and with music groups like Il Concerto Palatino. As the Bassanos were developing a reputation for becoming 'all excellent and esteemed above all others in this city' as musicians, in England, Henry VIII was seeking to strengthen the musicianship at his court so that it would be comparable with that of any other prince. He made his first attempt in 1525 when he acquired five new sackbut players, some from Venice. Then, in 1531, 'four new minstrels' appeared, some of them members of the Bassano family, but they then returned to Venice for reasons unknown. Finally, in 1539, when the king was very despondent about his marital situation, his agent Edmund Harvel recruited the entire family of five Bassano brothers, the youngest of whom was Baptista, as Henry's court recorder troupe, inviting them to move with their entire families to London. Harvel's plan worked, and the king began celebrating with his musicians each evening – and planning his next divorce.

Under both Henry and Elizabeth the recorder troupe flourished, as did their businesses in making musical instruments and in composing music. At the time of his death in 1547, King Henry had a collection of at least seventy recorders, and of the music that the second generation of Bassanos composed – much of it was for different kinds of woodwind instruments. About twenty different pieces survive, providing a good indication of the music played at court. These would have included music for the queen's dances in the morning, music to accompany the midday meal, and the evening music to accompany court entertainments such as pageants or the occasional stage play. There is a woodcut of recorder players in Venice which forms the frontispiece of Silvestro Ganassi's *Opera Intitulata Fontegara* (1535), which has been variously identified as members of the Ganassi family or conceivably the Bassano brothers before they left Venice.

There is one instance in a Shakespeare play in which an attempt is made to teach a musical instrument at some length. In *Hamlet* (1600), the prince attempts to instruct Guildenstern in the recorder. The players enter 'with recorders' and Hamlet demonstrates expertise in the art of playing the recorder: 'Govern these ventages with your fingers and thumb, give it breath with your mouth, and it will discourse the most eloquent music. Look you, these are the stops' (3.2.348–51). Not only does Hamlet demonstrate knowledge of the backstop on the recorder, but he seems to be paraphrasing an obscure Latin poem on how to play a 'flatu' (the Latin term for a kind of flute) by the fifth-century bishop St Paulinus of Nola. Just as Hamlet instructs his listener to 'govern those ventages with your fingers and thumb', St Paulinus's poem applies the term '*regit*' (govern) to the fingers: '*mobilisque regis digitis*'. Hamlet then says 'give it breath with your mouth', using language reminiscent of the way in which God blew breath into Adam – a rather odd resonance, but one echoed in Paulinus. Only a wind instrument player interested in the history of music would have such detailed knowledge.

Finally, the First Folio version of *Hamlet* claims that the recorder music will not be eloquent but will be 'excellent' and repeats that in a man/recorder there is 'excellent voice' (3.2.350, 359). Not only does this reflect Tertullian's obscure second-century theological conceit that a pipe or 'tibia' in Latin can be imagined as a human being, the very word 'excellent' is a pun on 'exilent', the name of the smallest kind of recorder. Further details are provided in Christopher Welch's *Six Lectures on the Recorder* from which I have drawn these examples.

During the mid-1500s, the Bassanos married into both the Nasi family, who were probably the prominent Jewish banking family headed by Donna Gracia Nasi, and the Lupo family of Iberian Jews led by Ambrose Lupo. As Roger Prior showed in his article 'Jewish Musicians at the Tudor Court', some of the Lupos were arrested as Marranos under the reign of Henry VIII. We know that some of the Portuguese Marranos in London observed Passover and Yom Kippur rituals, and there is a documented instance of one of these families holding a *bris*, or circumcision. We also have a report that, in the 1530s, another of the Portuguese Marranos, Alves Lopes, was holding 'a synagogue in his house and lives in the Hebrew manner, though in secret'.

We can, therefore, suppose that experience of the Bassano family, and their community, was the source of the strange fact that *The Merchant of Venice* does not use the two standard anti-Semitic stereotypes – that of the blood libel or the Jew on stage as a red-headed devil, but instead creates a new, radical and positive image of the Jew when Shylock makes his plea for equality for Jews as human beings.

I am a Jew. Hath not a Jew eyes? Hath not a Jew hands, organs, dimensions, senses, affections, passions? Fed with the same food, hurt with the same weapons, subject to the same diseases, healed by the same means, warmed and cooled by the same winter and summer, as a Christian is? If you prick us, do we not bleed? If you tickle us, do we not laugh? If you poison us, do we not die? And if you wrong us, shall we not revenge? If we are like you in the rest, we will resemble you in that.

The Merchant of Venice, 3.1.52–61

As hidden Jews, we know almost nothing of the extent to which the Bassanos practised Judaism – beyond a reference in the records of the Inquisition that the second generation, Anthony's sons, were distributing heretical books. We have documentation of them writing letters to the queen in Italian and of some of them cursing soldiers in that language on the street. However Belkin, in *Leone de' Sommi and the Performing Arts*, has found that Italian Jews spoke Hebrew as their first language, so it is conceivable that the Bassanos both read and spoke some Hebrew. If so, this may be the source of the scattered uses of Hebrew in the plays. One instance, identified by Florence Amit, is the first soldier's speech found in *All's Well That Ends Well*:

> *Boskos v'vado* [In bravery, like boldness], I understand thee, and can speak thy tongue. *Kerely-bonto* [I am aware of his deception], sir, betake thee to thy Faith or seventeen poniards are at thy bosom ...
>
> *All's Well That Ends Well*, 4.1.60–3

Would knowledge of Hebrew have been limited to the male members of the family? It is impossible to know. There certainly is evidence from Jewish communities in Europe of girls knowing and writing Hebrew. The records of the Inquisition describe imprisoning women who helped to set the lettering of Hebrew books both in 1485 and the middle of the sixteenth century. Donna Reyna established her own Hebrew printing press in Constantinople in the late 1500s, which produced a prayer book, a tractate of the Talmud and thirteen other works. And in the early 1700s, in Amsterdam, Berlin and other cities, the daughters of Moses of Holland helped set his Hebrew typeface when they were eleven and nine years old. So for the female members of the Bassano family to have known some Hebrew is not out of the question, and if they did they would have studied the Torah. Of course, there is no documentary evidence of any of the Bassanos studying the Torah, but there is one intriguing suggestion.

The play *The Merchant of Venice* features a suitor of Portia named Bassanio. One of Bassanio's tasks is to choose the casket in which Portia is concealed – whatever exactly that means, for Portia is of course standing beside the caskets setting Bassanio the riddle. That this episode (and indeed the larger play) is an allegory about religious choices is emphasised by there being three caskets, an idea taken from the *Gesta Romanorum*, a well-known and popular thirteenth-century book of stories for preachers. There, a maiden (an allegory for the soul) has to make her choice from three caskets in order to wed the emperor's son (an allegory for Christ). The soul's choice is between life and death, something echoed in *The Merchant of Venice* when Portia urges, 'Confess and live'. Bassanio meditates successively on the caskets of gold, silver and lead:

> ... in a word
> The seeming truth which cunning times put on
> To entrap the wisest. Therefore, thou gaudy gold,

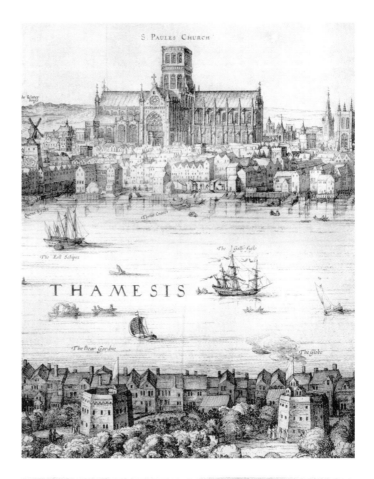

Top: 1 Claes Visscher's Panorama of London.

Bottom: 2 The church of St Mary Overy, Southwark, London Bridge.

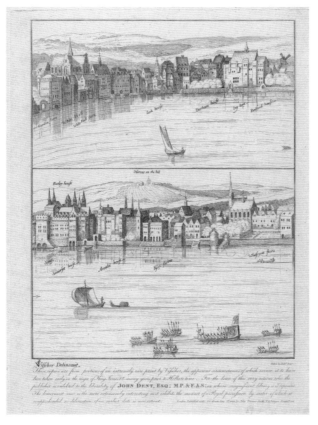

3 Prospect of London by Richard Sawyer after Claes Visscher.

4 Whitehall Palace by Thomas Sandby (*c*. 1760).

5 *An Allegory of the Tudor Succession.* Unknown artist (*c.* 1590).

6 *Procession of Queen Elizabeth*, George Vertue (1742).

C.B.I.

RAY FOY ACQUERANT.

BERGEN OP Z

LORD WILLOUGHB
BORN OC 12 1

Opposite: 7 Portrait of Peregrine Bertie, 11th Baron Willoughby de Eresby (1555–1601).

Right: 8 Susan Bertie (1567).

Below: 9 *Old Somerset House,* Thomas Theodosius Forrest

Above: 10 *View of the Savoy, Somerset House and the Water Entrance to Cuper's Garden*, after Samuel Scott.

Below: 11 *Somerset House* by Leonard Knyff.

12 Old Somerset House, drawing by Samuel Wale.

13 *Henry Carey, Lord Hunsdon* (1592).

Above: 14 Possible portrait of Amelia on a locket (*c.* 1591).

Opposite: 16 Amelia's lover, the Earl of Southampton (1594).

15 Berwick Castle (Lord Hunsdon's northern residence).

1585

VOD ME NVTRIT.
E DESTRVIT

17 Amelia's lover, Christopher Marlowe.

18 Venetian recorder players (1535).

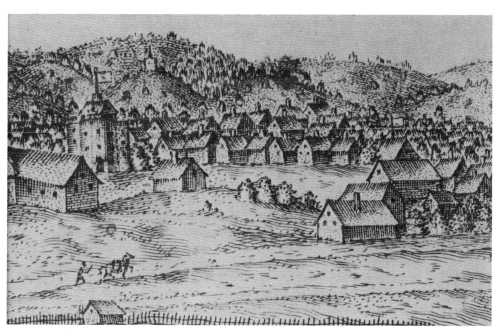

19 The Shoreditch theatres (pre-1599).

20 The Globe Theatre and the Bear Garden, Bankside.

Below left: 21 Theatre interior, Bankside (*c.* 1595).

Below right: 22 Shakespeare satirical cartoon in the First Folio (1623).

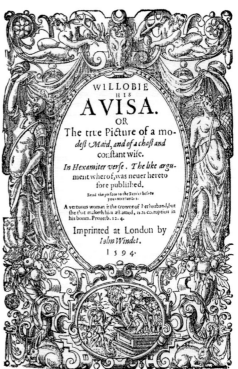

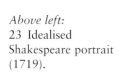

Above left:
23 Idealised
Shakespeare portrait
(1719).

Above right:
24 *Willobie His
Avisa*, frontispiece
(1594).

25 Amelia's
successful brother-in-
law, Nicholas Lanier
(1620s).

26 Household of the Countess of Cumberland by Jan van Belcamp.

Next page: 27 Amelia remains buried in the parish church of St James, Clerkenwell, where she has lain since 1645.

Hard food for Midas, I will none of thee;
Nor none of thee, thou pale and common drudge
'Tween man and man: but thou, thou meagre lead,
Which rather threaten'st than dost promise aught,
Thy plainness moves me more than eloquence,
And here choose I: joy be the consequence!

The Merchant of Venice, 3.2.99–107

One oddity is that Portia herself is supposedly 'inside' the lead casket (in reality only her portrait is). Her name would be expressed in Hebrew as the consonants PRT. The initial letter 'peh' can be pronounced F with a prefix. Now to understand that Portia is 'inside' the lead casket, we simply have translate 'lead' into Hebrew – namely, the word oFeReT – which repeats the letters of her name and sounds like 'ferret', a technical term for reading Torah. So this Hebrew pun, one of many that are identified in Schelomo Schoenfeld's article 'A Hebrew Source for the *The Merchant of Venice*', suggests that the author is taking the traditional story of the caskets as an allegory for choosing Christ, and turning it into something rather different by creating a set of references to Hebrew and to the interpretation of the Torah. And the successful interpreter is called Bassanio: can this really be a coincidence?

Once he was settled in London, Baptista began living with his common-law wife Margaret Johnson, an English woman, and apparently the daughter of a well-known lutenist. Her brother's son, Robert Johnson, trained in the household of Lord Hunsdon's son Sir George Carey, and remains well known as a lutenist today, largely on the strength of a series of well-known musical compositions that are still frequently recorded. Perhaps most famous is Ariel's song from *The Tempest*:

Full fathom five thy Father lies,
Of his bones are Corrall made.

Robert Johnson wrote songs for other Shakespearean plays as well – for *Cymbeline* ('Hark hark the lark'), and for *The Winter's Tale* ('Get you hence'). In addition, when masques became fashionable in the reign of King James, Johnson composed music for several masques – music that was then used for the masque sequences in other plays. For instance, the satyrs dance from the *Masque of Oberon* was included as the dance of the leaping men of hair in *The Winter's Tale* (4.4.319–37). The witches' dance and Johnson's 'Come away Hecate' were taken from the *Masque of Queens* and included in *Macbeth* (5.3.34). Finally, the rural May dance, which was probably written by Johnson for the *Masque of the Inner Temple* (1613), was included in *Two Noble Kinsmen* (3.5.124–36). Of course Johnson also composed music for a range of playwrights including Middleton, Webster, Beaumont and Fletcher.

For us, the point is that the Bassanos would come to have a strong connection to the major composer for Shakespeare's plays. Of course, that lay some years in the future. But it meant that when Baptista had a child, it would be born into one of the important musical families in England. This is significant, because various studies have begun to show that early musical experience can very positively impact both brain size and cognitive functioning.

So we must imagine a highly musical extended family of Marranos or Conversos, still associated with people involved in silk manufacturing, speaking Italian and Hebrew, and returning every few years to visit Italy, where they maintained a house in their home town of Bassano. To this family, Baptista Bassano and his common-law wife added a baby girl in 1569. They called her Amelia, meaning 'industrious one'. It was a name that would prove predictive.

Life must have been exciting growing up in Spitalfields, which was right in the middle of the theatre district. The Bassanos were within the catchment area for six different theatres and inns that staged plays. Apart from the purpose-built theatres, a few hundred yards to the south-west was the Red Lion, where in 1567 Jacob Burbage and John Brayne had built a stage scaffold to put on a performance of *The Story of Samson*. Immediately to the south along Bishops Gate, the main thoroughfare, were three of the other public houses in the city that staged plays. So even as a girl of five she would have seen her family intimately involved in theatrical music.

Then in 1576, after two purpose-built theatres were erected to supplement the informal theatres in neighbouring pubic houses, the area became even more of a theatrical centre. It had elements of a red-light district, and the family home (today buried under a major London station) was only 200 yards or so east of London's first two purpose-built theatres. The Curtain certainly, and possibly the Theatre also, can be seen in a peculiar engraving known as *View of the City of London from the North Towards the South*, which is in the University of Utrecht Library (illustration 19). Comprising three horizontal sheets of paper, this is a panoramic map viewed from a point in North London looking southwards. There is no river Thames. At the extreme east is Westminster Abbey, and at the extreme west is the Shoreditch area, which when seen in detail shows at least the Curtain Theatre, surrounded by small houses. Whether the other building is the Theatre – later known as the Globe – or a pageant house, depends on whether the print is to be dated before or after 1599, and is discussed by Herbert Berry in 'The View of London from the North and the Playhouses in Holywell'. The Spital, after which Spitalfields was named and at which the Spital Sermons were given, as mentioned twice in the early Shakespearean play *Sir Thomas More*, was literally outside the Bassanos' house.

The little area would be flooded each afternoon with 4,000 playgoers, along with all the ancillary businesses, such as crime, prostitution, costume hire and food sellers, that attended the theatre. While the Bassanos would have seen this as an expansion of their business opportunities for performing music in the theatres, it also had become a less conducive environment in which to bring up a young girl.

About Amelia Bassano's early life we know very little, other than that she mentioned to her physician Dr Simon Forman (fortunately an early keeper of case notes) that her father's business had begun to decline by the time she was born, and that, by the time he died in 1576 when she was seven, 'he began to be poor and miserable in his estate'. We do, however, know that her family possessed books – heretical books – because a contemporary record from the Inquisition states they were known for sharing these books with others. Dr Nicholas Patricca, Professor Emeritus of Theatre at the University of Loyola, has even claimed that the Bassanos' library also included the specific copies of the Italian novellas by Bandello and Da Porto that were used to write *Romeo and Juliet*!

Initially on arriving in London, the Bassanos were housed in temporary accommodations in Charterhouse. Shortly afterwards, however, they found their own lodgings. Two of the brothers went to live in Mark Lane, which was where the Portuguese Jewish community lived under their leader Hector Nuñes.

However, Baptista Bassano moved to Spitalfields, London's silk-making district, where he bought three connected houses in a row very near to the Spital, a former monastery and now a hospital. Because silk making was part of the Bassanos' own history, it is probably not a coincidence that Baptista Bassano bought a house which, as a contemporary map indicates, was close to the silk workshop owned by the Vaughans. This was where Mrs Margery Vaughan made the dresses for Henry VIII's wives, who conveniently forgot to pay the bills. Relations between the families were close: one of the Vaughans would act as the overseer on Margaret Bassano's will. Spitalfields would later become something of a production centre for the whole craft of silk making, where lived exotic characters with names like Job the Venerable, the silk weaver, or Jehu the Throwster, who twisted the silk thread. This meant that the Bassanos were part of one of the very few communities in London, perhaps the only one, in which there was any knowledge of silk weaving. This was one of the key areas of knowledge found in the plays, but the industry was not formally introduced to England until 1607. There are at least thirteen references to silk in the plays, including 'silken thread' (*Much Ado*, 5.1.25), 'a twist of rotten silk' (*Coriolanus*, 5.6.95), and the 'idle immaterial skein of sleave silk' (*Troilus and Cressida*, 5.1.30). *A Midsummer Night's Dream* makes an allusion to the 'weaving spiders' (2.2.20), and the Fates have cut Pyramus/Bottom's lifeline, 'shore / With shears his thread of silk' (4.1.334–5). As for Bottom himself, his occupation is given as a weaver of homespuns and his name refers both to the shapes made by the silkworm cocoons when they hang on the tree and to the implement upon which their thread was wound.

Margery Vaughan's husband Stephen was a Tudor diplomat who was an agent of King Henry during the 1530s, and held the Office of the King's Books, procuring new items for the libraries and transcribing a manuscript copy of Tyndale's *Answer to More* for His Majesty. Although some suspected him of heretical Puritan leanings, Vaughan affirmed his loyalty to Henry's Church. He ended his days as Crown Agent in Antwerp – where he raised money from bankers, including the Fuggers. He also probably assisted with Henry VIII's loans from the Nasi family, Marranos who managed the Mendes Bank and were prominent among the 100 or so local Jewish families in Antwerp. This may be the same Nasi family into which two of the Bassano brothers were married.

One would not normally imagine that a decision about the education of a seven-year-old child would be critical to the future of Western literature, but in this case that is exactly what it was. If the Bassanos' business had been doing a little better or if Amelia had been practically inclined to woodwork or silk weaving, she might have remained in the Bassano home in Spitalfields. If that had happened, literary history would have been rather different. As it was, his business was failing, and she was not so inclined. It was now that the Vaughan family, next-door neighbours to the Bassanos, had a decisive influence over her future.

After Margery and Stephen Vaughan had died, their son, Stephen Vaughan the younger, had taken over the great house and its silk business. Amelia's mother, Margaret Johnson, trusted him enough to make him the overseer of her will, in which she left his wife a ring worth twenty shillings; the bulk of the estate went to Amelia. Baptista Bassano had also done a land deal with his next-door neighbour 'to the use of Margaret Bassany alias Johnson for her life', which would revert to Stephen Vaughan upon her death in the summer in 1587. Both Stephen and his sister Anne had been well educated in the great house in Spitalfields during the 1540s by a Dutchman, Stephen Cob, who knew Latin, Greek and French, but had been brought up before the Privy Council for translating a commentary on the Gospels that was considered to contain heretical opinions. He had run a little private school in Spitalfields in the Vaughan's house, and in addition to the three Vaughan children, students included a son of George Brooke, Lord Cobham and possibly another girl boarder.

Educated by a heretic, and having a father accused of heresy, it was Anne who was the clever one in the family, and the one most skilled at theological thinking. James Sanford, writing in *The Garden of Pleasure* (1576), called her one of England's top four 'noble Gentlewomen famous for their learning'. After her marriage she had left England and lived in Geneva for some years, where she knew Knox and Calvin, and translated some of Calvin's sermons, to which some of her sonnets would be appended. They are some of the finest religious sonnets produced during the Renaissance. They show that Ann Vaughan Locke was the creator of the sonnet sequence that others would later make so famous. Titled *Sermons of John Calvin, upon the Song That Ezechias Made* (1560), Locke's translation and the attached sonnets were dedicated to 'the Right Honourable, and Christian Princesse' Katherine Willoughby, Duchess of Suffolk, the mother of Susan and Peregrine Bertie. Both had been tutored by Calvin's friend from

Geneva, the Bible translator Miles Coverdale, unlike their older stepbrothers, who had been tutored by John Wilson, author of *The Art of Rhetoric* (1553), whose work would be parodied in *A Midsummer Night's Dream*.

Ultimately, however, the credit for Amelia's education probably goes to Anne's brother, Stephen Vaughan. When faced with the plight of the brilliant but fatherless seven-year-old, he may have been the person who had the idea that would change Amelia's life. She should be 'adopted' and educated by a countess. It may seem strange to us today but the age of seven was exactly when promising children in the upper echelons of Elizabethan society were sent away to live in noble families, and that is what happened to Amelia.

Education by a Countess: 1576–82

Susan Bertie, the Dowager Countess of Kent, had married her husband the earl at the age of sixteen, and was widowed just a year later. She lived part of the time in her country house in Greenwich, and the other part at Willoughby House, the vast mansion owned by her brother Lord Willoughby on the site of the modern Barbican. There she stayed with her mother, the radical feminist and Protestant thinker Catherine, Duchess of Suffolk. It was the duchess who had befriended both John Foxe and the playwright John Bale in the 1540s when she had been a young woman. The work of both of these radical reformers would influence the early plays, where it would be used to construct the comic allegorical parody of Christ as Oldcastle/Falstaff based on Bale's account of his death, and the parody of King John based on Bale's allegorical play *King Johan*.

Married so briefly, Susan Bertie had not had children. She was now still single at twenty-two, with no obvious prospect of marriage, and she wanted a child. It was a straightforward match between a lonely feminist countess and a small, brilliant seven-year-old girl. And it would have the most profound consequences. For roughly the next six years Amelia would live 'with the Countess of Kent', as she put it, receiving the sort of education normally given only to the uppermost echelons of English society.

Willoughby House was located right next to two of the city gates, Cripple Gate and Alders Gate, a large Italianate street of handsome houses. Next to Alders Gate was St Botolph's church, and next to that, the local bedlam, which afforded many hours of fascinating character study. The poor, mad inhabitants, 'distraught in their wits', who were maintained by their friends at the 'hospital for distracted people', were a common subject for Elizabethan writers. Some of them would end up as cameo portraits in characters like Tom O'Bedlam, the Jailer's Daughter, Malvolio and Ophelia.

Since Willoughby House was only a mile away from the instrument workshop and family home at Spitalfields, Amelia presumably saw her relatives there from time to time, in addition to seeing them at court. She describes the countess as 'the Mistris of my youth, / The noble guide of my ungovern'd dayes'. But most of the time it is safe to assume she was being put through the rigours of an Elizabethan upper-class education in history, logic, rhetoric, Greek, Latin, literature, the classics and so on. It is hardly a commonplace experience to have a young girl, the daughter of a deceased professional father, raised by a countess; there were, after all, only a handful of English earls, hence only a few countesses. Yet, oddly enough, this extraordinary situation is replicated in *All's Well That Ends Well*, where a young girl is living in a household with a general of the horse, Bertram (equivalent to the general Peregrine Bertie), and a dowager countess (equivalent to Susan Bertie). In the play the countess describes how a professional father left her 'his sole child, my lord, and bequeathed to my overlooking. I have those hopes of her good that her education promises' (*All's Well That Ends Well*, 1.1.29–30.)

The play describes something of what it would have been like to be reared as an orphaned girl, like a 'foreign seed' (1.3.142), by a dowager countess. It describes a skilled professional father whose young girl is 'bequeathed' to the 'overlooking' of a dowager countess upon his death. The countess has hopes of her education, and her 'fair gifts' since the girl is a 'pretty lady' 'whose words all ears took captive' (5.3.17). The countess indeed regards her as a daughter, since 'her father bequeathed her to me' (1.3.98), and loves her entirely.

Furthermore, in the discussion of the Earl of Oxford we identified that Oxford shared some unusual vocabulary with the author of the Shakespearean works, and therefore had to belong to the same sociolinguistic community or social network. As indicated above, Amelia Bassano lived from the age of seven with Countess Susan Bertie in her country house, and at Lord Willoughby's London mansion, Willoughby House. Lord Willoughby, the head of the household, was married to Oxford's bad-tempered sister, Mary de Vere. So there was probably a close relationship with the Earl of Oxford's extravagant household at Fisher's Folly, in Bishopsgate about a mile away, which might explain the similarity of vocabularies.

Feminist readings: Christine de Pizan

As a young girl Amelia who would have occasionally gone to court with Susan Bertie, so she would have had to study *The Knight of La Tour – Landry's Book for His Four Daughters*, which was the guide for young girls at court, and which would be an important source for *The Taming of the Shrew*. Since she was living with two proto-feminists, the Duchess of Suffolk and the Countess of Kent, they would probably have supported her in reading girl's literature, and would have acted as highly intelligent, literate and musical female role models, of the kind that are found in many of the Shakespearean plays. Since Amelia Bassano was the first English feminist poet, it is easy to understand how she might have created the figure of Emilia in *Othello*, which has been called the first depiction of a feminist in English literature.

One book that she probably found in Susan Bertie's country house at Greenwich was Christine de Pizan's *The Book of the City of Ladies*. Reginald Grey, the 5th Earl Grey and deceased husband to Countess Susan, had inherited his title and estate from his uncle Richard Grey (the 3rd Earl), who had been had been the book's patron and is mentioned in the introduction. In addition, the son of the translator, also called Brian Aynsley, lived in the parish of Lee in Lewisham, near Countess Susan's country home in Greenwich. His senile attempts to give the whole of his estate to his daughter Cordelia were contested by his other daughters, and became part of the inspiration for *King Lear*.

The concept of a community of women was something that Amelia would eventually use in the poetry she published under her own name. *The City of Ladies* was written as an answer to a man who argued that women could not become lawyers, and it also refutes the idea that women should be condemned for the sin of Eve, a point which Amelia would later echo in her poetry. However Pizan's books were also used by only one other writer in contemporary English literature, Shakespeare. Pizan's poem on Joan of Arc was used in *Henry VI, Part 1* (1.2.83–4), and her version of the Pyramus and Thisbe story was used in *A Midsummer Night's Dream*. A passage from her *Epistle of Othea*, in a translation made around 1450, which claims 'the sinne of ingratitude is like the wind' was turned into the song in *As You Like It* about the wind not being as unkind as man's ingratitude (2.7.175–9). So living with Susan Bertie was almost certainly how Amelia gained access to knowledge of this little-known feminist writer, whose works were used in the Shakespearean plays. Quite possibly she kept the copy of *The City of Ladies*, since she would be using it so many years later.

Peregrine Bertie, the owner of Willoughby House and the Lord Willoughby, on the other hand, was a different story. He was one of England's most famous generals and his victory in the Low Countries was celebrated in the tune 'Rowland' for the song 'Welcome Home Lord Willoughby', which is alluded to in *As You Like It*. There is a famous portrait of him on horseback, followed by an African servant holding a skull, which gives a nuance to Amelia growing up in the household.

Lord Willoughby (Peregrine Bertie) is indeed probably caricatured in the play *Love's Labour's Lost* as the famous soldier Armado. A pun in the play calls him 'too peregrinate' (5.1.114), a pun the queen often made herself. At the time the first draft of the play was being written around 1591, he had finally come home after fighting for Henry of Navarre and capturing three fortresses. However, he was not in a good state, owing to his expenses not being reimbursed by the treasury, and with his troops half dead from hunger and cold. The problems in his campaign in France are echoed in *Henry VI, Part 1*, written about the same time.

The Taming of the Shrew goes into some detail about the 'course of learning and ingenious studies' (1.1.9) that a student could find in Padua to quench an intellectual thirst. Tranio advocates a certain eclecticism, including the use of enlivening poetry, and he is perhaps referring to the first two years of Padua's medical syllabus in which students covered logic and natural philosophy, mainly using the texts of Aristotle, since he warns his master not to be 'so devote to Aristotle's *Ethics* / As Ovid be an outcast quite abjur'd (*Taming of the Shrew*, 1.1.31–3). Susan Bertie's father, Richard Bertie, had visited Padua in 1554 as well as visiting Venice to inspect the treasury of St Marks. Evidently he had passed on his love of Italy to his family (his grandson Robert Bertie would head the English contingent as *Consulianus* at the university in 1603). A close relative, Richard (Riccardo) Willoughby, although a Catholic, was even a leader of the English contingent at the university. Indeed, he headed it as *Consulianus* for seven different years from 1584 to 1595, and was a friend of several of the leading thinkers in the city, notably Galileo and Paulo Gualdo, the Dean of the Jesuit University, with whom Galileo corresponded on sun spots. Richard Bertie's son, General Peregrine Bertie, the Lord Willoughby (and brother of Susan Bertie) would visit Venice in 1594.

This was the university where the circulation of the blood – so important to the Shakespearean plays – was being discovered. Fabricus was a fantastic teacher who attracted everyone's admiration. That was how he would manage to hold his academic position at Padua for fifty years. He would lecture on the anatomical method, and do dissections not just of humans but of animals as well. His work on the circulation of the blood and the valves in the veins that control the flow of blood would be published in *De Venarum Ostiolis* in Padua in 1603. It was not, however, a new discovery, having been experimentally demonstrated by Realdus Columbus (1516–59), his predecessor at Padua, in his book about anatomical things, *De Re Anatomica*, published in Venice in 1559. Indeed, it had been discovered even earlier by Servetus, the Marrano theologian and doctor Miquel Servet (1511–53), who had worked in Paris with Vesalius immediately before the latter took up his appointment at Padua Medical School in 1537. Overall, it seems most likely that Padua was the source of Harvey's knowledge, although it has been claimed that the English mathematician Walter Warner (who worked for Henry Percy, Earl of Northumberland) was the origin of Harvey's knowledge, and conceivably could have been the playwright's source well before Harvey's announcement in 1616.

So the Willoughby household was part of a network of English noble families that sent on average four or five people a year to study in Padua. This was a fashionable and luxurious university of the rich young nobility, many of upper Italy and southern Austria, some of whom lived a wild and extravagant lifestyle. The University of Padua was the world's leading centre for studies in medicine (especially anatomy), and astronomy, and had strengths in law and in botany. Lord Willoughby would himself matriculate from Padua University at the age of forty-one in 1596, and quite possibly this connection was the source of the unusual knowledge of the circulation of the blood that appears in the Shakespearean plays.

Journey to Denmark: 1582

And so we come to another critical year in Amelia's life when she reached the age of thirteen, the Elizabethan age of consent.

Quite suddenly Susan Bertie had fallen in love and was going off to the Low Countries to get married. What was to happen to Amelia? Perhaps Lord Willoughby had the answer. In addition to being a famous general, and interested in the University of Padua, Lord Willoughby had one other important job. He was Ambassador to Denmark and needed to go to there very soon for a visit. It was a large delegation that went, including his friend Dr Thomas Moffet, the silkworm expert (and the author of the book on silkworms that so influenced Shakespeare); Robert Glover, the Somerset Herald; Mr William Waad; Sir Gilbert Detick, the Garter King of Arms; plus fifty other gentlemen and 'his whole traine' as Holinshed described it, which presumably included servants and women. Since the only business to be conducted was to visit Elsinore Castle in Copenhagen and install King Frederick II with the Order of the Garter, it was expected to be a celebratory, festive occasion, something of a vacation and sight-seeing tour in fact.

So what was to be done with Amelia? She was an adult and could do with a trip overseas to broaden her mind. Why, Lord Willoughby must have wondered, should he not take her to Denmark in 'his traine' as part of his retinue? They would not be away long. In reality, after a massive storm or 'tempest', and problems with pirates that forced them to return to Hull on 12 July, they finally left on 22 July and were away for two months, returning to Norfolk on 27 September 1582. So it is possible that Amelia accompanied him when she was thirteen years old. It was a terrible voyage, as Peregrine Bertie reported in a letter to Sir Francis Walsingham:

> Iff misfortune of tempest had not spoyled my second shippe wherein my stuff and necessaries was, breaking har topmast and driving her to sutche a leake as she and har company was in danger, besides contynuall winds against us ... we have no occurrences of importance save only of pirates mutche daily complained on.

It was this personal experience of living through a 'tempest' and observing how the boatswain and seamen dealt with it that Amelia perhaps recalled many years later. She would so vividly reflect it in her play that some would think the author had to have been a professional seaman. It resembles the description in *The Weakest Goeth to the Wall*, in which the devil bursts the bawling chaps: 'Come dog, come devil! He that scapes best let him take all, and split, and roar.' This would later be echoed in *The Tempest* in the extended passage: 'incharitable dogs ... hang cur ... what care these roarers ... we split, we split' (1.1.43–63). In the storm the boatswain says 'take in the topsail' and 'down with the topmast' (1.1.6 and 34) because they fear sinking in a (feminine) ship that, to use a most unusual and personal comparison, is 'leaky as an unstanched wench' (line 48) at the time of her menstruation – a very unusual metaphor, but one that a thirteen-year-old girl might be very concerned with.

Although it was still being built, the castle at Elsinore was very fine. Apart from the problems in persuading the king that it did not compromise his dignity or his sovereignty to put on the regalia of another monarch's honours, the trip to Elsinore went well. The Order of the Garter, which would reappear in the early play *Reign of Edward III* in an allusion to Lord Hunsdon's own role as a Garter Knight, was duly administered. As Lord Willoughby put it:

> the King, very royally prepared, received the robes with his own hands, and with great contentment accepted and wore the Garter, the Collar, and the George ... This being done we royally feasted, and the King all the ordnance of the Castle given us.

That is, there was a salute of cannon after every toast, and being Denmark, there was a lot of drinking. Willoughby and his friends enjoyed the hospitality but found the drinking customs problematic, since it was Danish custom to hold one's water and not leave the table to urinate, since, as he put it, to 'relieve oneself during the evening was a terrible violation of etiquette'. However, the two state dinners were an opportunity to meet the local nobility, including Petrius Guildenstern and Georgius Rosenkrantz. Petrius Guildenstern was evidently a relative of the Swedish Ambassador to England in 1559–62. By 1588 there were nine members of the Guildenstern family and three members of the Rosenkrantz family at court. Both families were quite ancient, and were also related to the famous Danish astronomer Tycho Brahe. It would have been easy to arrange a visit.

Evidently Lord Willoughby's conversations with the Danish nobles went well, since the visits to Brahe would be one of the highlights of the trip. Indeed, after his visits to Uraniborg, Brahe's grand country house built on a private island 9 miles south of Elsinore, Lord Willoughby would make the astronomer one of his closest friends and correspondents. Willoughby would describe how Brahe's laboratory was admirably furnished with 'rare huge and admirable instruments' which do 'nightly watch the stars', and in which he himself participated, in studying the new comet that appeared on 18 October and lasted to the 15 November 1585.

Brahe had no telescopes, but he did have certain very large brass devices, known as mural quadrants, which allowed him to measure and note the positions of 777 fixed stars. As the leading observational astronomer of the sixteenth century, he had also created at least four types of observing machinery, known as armillary spheres, described in his *Astronomiae Instauratae Mechanica* (1598). Brahe had persuaded the king to have the house built because of a remarkable astronomical occurrence – the appearance of a supernova in Cassiopeia in 1572. Brahe had proved that this had taken place beyond the Moon, in the crystalline sphere of the fixed stars of the Primum Mobile, which was, according to Christian theology, supposed to be unchanging. Naturally, this was deeply worrying to governments all over Europe. It implied that Christian theology and the traditional Ptolemaic view of an Earth-centred universe was wrong. In the future, Lord Willoughby would keep closely informed on affairs in Denmark, and would spend a total of five months there, including his second trip in 1585 to negotiate military support for Henry of Navarre.

The aspects of *Hamlet* that are perhaps directly traceable to the thirteen-year-old Amelia's visit to Elsinore in 1582 most likely include the layout of the castle, the platforms where the guns were located (1.2.213), the arrangement of the rooms, including the 'Queen's Closet', the 'lobby' (2.2.161), which is reached by going upstairs (4.3.36–7), the floral garlands or 'crants' worn at Ophelia's funeral, and the depictions of the 111 dead kings of Denmark that were on the tapestries hanging on the wall of the banqueting hall. Some of her other recollections included the way that dawn comes so early over the flat and dreary Danish landscape, the closeness of the castle to the sea, as well as the Danish drinking customs punctuated by cannon fire, and the rowdy drunkenness. As the 1603 quarto puts it, 'And there's no health the king shall drink today / But the great cannon to the clouds shall tell.' And most of all, of course, the star that opens the very first scene of *Hamlet* has been identified by scholars as that very same supernova identified by Tycho Brahe. The deep astronomical allegory in the play precisely concerns the subject of the work of the Danish astronomer: the move from a geocentric to a heliocentric universe. Only a close relationship with a well-informed astronomer could have given the playwright a knowledge of astronomy that included familiarity with the theories of Tycho Brahe, knowledge of the precession of the equinoxes, the heliocentricity of the solar system and Galileo's discovery of the moons of Jupiter, which is referred to in *Cymbeline*. While most of the several hundred astronomical references that W. G. Guthrie found in the plays are not technically specific, these ones are.

It is even conceivable that this background would have given Amelia an initial interest in astronomy. She could have continued in this interest after 1582, since the royal astronomers reported to Lord Hunsdon, and also because London's leading astronomer, the mathematician Thomas Harriot, a rival of Galileo and the first man to observe the moon through a telescope, held his classes on astronomy and navigation in a house on the Strand that was a few doors down from where she was living.

The visit to Denmark would have put off the problem of Amelia's future for a few months, but there was no question of her continuing to live at Willoughby

House on her own. Educated and brilliant, at the age of thirteen she had reached the age of consent and sexual maturity in Elizabethan London. To whom could she be married? No noble would want to marry a commoner without a dowry, and being so highly educated she could hardly be married off to any ordinary man. What was to be done with Amelia? So now we come to the second major event in Amelia's life and the one which gave her a passionate interest in the theatre. Lord Willoughby knew that Lord Hunsdon was lonely. As the queen's half-brother and the Lord Chamberlain responsible for the 'Chamber' (essentially the court), he had split from his wife, who was living in her own separate mansion, so he could not take another wife. But there was nothing stopping him from taking a mistress – a brilliant, educated, musical young Italian mistress, who would help reinvigorate his life – an 'honest courtesan' as the role was referred to in Italy. The Bassano family would only have welcomed such a relationship because of the additional protection it gave then at court.

And so it was that while Susan Bertie headed off to live in Europe with her new husband, Amelia moved once again. Around the age of thirteen she left Willoughby House and moved to the Strand into the princely palace Old Somerset House as the mistress of one of the most powerful men in England: Lord Henry Hunsdon, the Lord Chamberlain and the man in charge of the English theatre.

6

Amelia at Court: 1582–1593

Unlike the case for Mr Shakespeare, the case for Amelia Bassano Lanier can be substantiated both by her life circumstances and by the fit with her own poetry. This led Dr William Green – an expert on theatre research as a former Professor of English at Queen's College, CUNY, the past President of the International Federation for Theatre Research, and former Secretary of the American Society for Theatre Research – to describe the present findings as 'absolutely fascinating and supported by a huge amount of documentary evidence'.

Amelia's upbringing up to the age of thirteen gave her the core foundation that would enable her to become a great playwright. Her family background provided her with the role model of Italian woman playwrights. It gave her knowledge of Italian, Hebrew and of Judaism, and a positive image of what it meant to be a Jew. It gave her the knowledge of silk weaving found in the plays. It connected her to the person who invented the sonnet sequence. It connected her to the town of Bassano in Italy. The man who wrote most of the known music for the Shakespearean plays was her close relative. Her musical background not only gave her the knowledge shown in the plays but, because of the impact of music on the brain functioning of children, may have contributed to the development of her genius. Spitalfields gave her the experience of the 'low life' found in some of the plays. Her education from the age of seven in a noble, proto-feminist household connected to the great Bible translator Miles Coverdale gave her an education befitting a countess, as well as familiarity with the nobility, and encouraged her interest in the Bible and Bible translations, as well as the study of girls' literature and early feminist ideas including the writing of Christine de Pizan. Life in the Willoughby family also introduced her to astronomy, and to Denmark, provided a connection to the University of Padua, gave her the experience of living through a tempest, and a little knowledge of the strategic military issues that concern generals to be found in the early plays, and perhaps also knowledge of Henry of Navarre.

This was an extraordinary background, an existence on the boundaries of many different social worlds from the red-light district to the highest echelons of the court. For the next decade, living between the ages of thirteen and twenty-three as mistress to Lord Hunsdon, Amelia would build even more sophisticated skills: knowledge of gardening and rare plants, of the Northern dialects, of the law, of generalship, and of falconry. In addition to the experience of court diplomacy gained through living in the household of Lord Willoughby, Ambassador to Denmark, she would now live for a decade with a man who was an informal Ambassador to Scotland, and whose son-in-law the Lord Admiral was a former Ambassador to France. In addition to diplomacy, this decade would be the source of a vast knowledge of court ceremonial and ritual (such as that found in *Richard II*), court theatre, plays, and the show business of theatrical staging, which was such a prominent part of court life and for which Lord Hunsdon was directly responsible. It was also a foundational experience, which she idealised in the reflection on the memory of Queen Elizabeth I that makes up over half the dedication. Stefani Brusberg-Kiermeier, in her paper '"Never shall my sad eies againe behold those pleasures": Aemelia Lanyer and Her Idealization of Tudor Court Life', compares her to two other commoners – Mary and Anne Boleyn – who tried to make a life for themselves at court, and she argues that 'the courtesan should be regarded as a form of the female courtier'.

It is worth noting that the orthodox Shakespearean James Shapiro, shaking off observations that Shakespeare as we know him had no chance to learn all these things, makes an appeal to the power of imagination. However knowledge is knowledge, and no amount of imagination can substitute for it.

As the movie *Dangerous Beauty* (1998) noted about Veronica Franco, a famous sixteenth-century Venetian courtesan, 'courtesans are the most educated women in the world'. As Lord Hunsdon's mistress, Amelia would have the strange position of being an observer at court who was not really part of that world. One the one hand, she would have behaved as a courtier. She would have been familiar with court theatrical interludes, and with games such as French tennis, chess and lawn bowls. She would, for instance, have engaged in the practice of making up new words, which, however odd it may seem to us today, was a requirement for the excellent courtier, as Castiglione noted in *The Book of the Courtier*. The Shakespearean plays contain nearly 2,000 neologisms according to some reckonings, many of them created by making an English version of an Italian term. On the other hand she was also, from the colour of her skin alone, an outsider. Similarly, she had no title; her family were, after all, mere gentlemen. In the English system of social stratification, that came very far down. Yet she had lived for five years with the wife of an earl, and a duchess who was addressed as 'princess', and now this dark-skinned woman was living with a man who was a kind of prince in his princely palace, half-brother to the queen. It might explain very well why she liked the song 'King Cophetua and the Beggar Maid' – the most popular song in the Shakespearean plays – about a young black beggar maid who had been plucked out of the gutter to marry a king. She would have lived in Lord Hunsdon's palace almost as part of his collection of curiosities from around the world. In the cultural context of Elizabethan London, her dark skin – if we may risk a biographical reading, Sonnet 130 describes her breasts as 'dun' meaning of a dark colour, black or brown – would have made her stand out at court, where women normally treated their faces, necks and breasts with Venetian ceruse, or Spirits of Saturn, a thick, white face powder made from vinegar and white lead. This would have contrasted with their stuck-on black eyebrows made from mouse skin.

Amelia occupied, then, an ambiguous position. On the one hand, her being Hunsdon's mistress put the Bassanos in the strong position of feeling they had a friend at court who would offer them protection against the discrimination that they would otherwise have faced as Jews and as 'blackamoors'. Yet both these kinds of discrimination were extremely powerful. Indeed, within a few years, black 'Moors' were being deported in order to keep England white. Two stories are illustrative. In 1596 the queen issued a proclamation to the Lord Mayor noting that 'there are of late divers blackamoores brought into this realm, of which kind of people there are already here too many'. Five years later in 'her princely wisdom' she issued yet another instruction:

> Whereas the Queen's Majesty is discontented at the great numbers of Negars and Blackamoores which are crept into the realm since the troubles between her Highness and the King of Spain, and are fostered here to the annoyance of her own people ... In order to discharge them out of the country, her Majesty hath appointed Caspar Van Zeuden, merchant of Lubeck, for their transportation ... This is to require you to assist him to collect such negroes and blackamoors for this purpose.
>
> *Orders to Expel Blackamoors & Negroes* (1601)

Shortly after Amelia became Lord Hunsdon's mistress, in 1584, Arthur Bassano and others were disrespectful to officers of the former Sheriff of London: 'one of them – a little black man who was booted – answered in a very despiteful manner, together with another of them, being a tall black man', who said: 'We have as good friends in the court as thou hast and better too ... Send us to ward? Thou wert as good kiss our arse.' Later Arthur Bassano confidently informed the Recorder of London, 'You were as good eat the sole of my boot as send us to Newgate.' Their confidence was misplaced however; they were arrested and sent to prison for contempt. But they were not deported. Similarly, the following year, another member of the family, Mark Anthony Bassano, spoke in Italian in the street and cursed the four or five soldiers who pursued him with drawn swords.

Clearly the Bassanos were perceived as 'black', most likely because of their Moorish ancestry, and the relative darkness of their skin. If they had been suspected of being Jews this would, of course, have only accentuated the perception that they were dark. As Tudor Parfaitt has shown in his recent book *Black Jews in Africa and the Americas*, Renaissance Christians viewed Jews as dark, and akin to Moors. Further, some Jews themselves adopted the same viewpoint; Isaac ben Judah Abranel even explained their swarthiness as part of a divine punishment, while others claimed the lack of ruddiness in their faces was the result, due to Jewish law, of a lack of red menstrual blood at the moment of conception.

While Amelia was clearly a Bassano, a foreigner, the Willoughbys were the cadet branch of the Tudors, and Lord Hunsdon was the (albeit illegitimate) son of Henry VIII, one of the most powerful members of the Tudor dynasty. So in one sense the Tudors were her family. When conversations at court turned to historical precedent, they would turn to events in Tudor history. It is often said that young playwrights begin by writing about things that they know best. In the case of Amelia she would begin to write about the Tudors in *Henry IV*, *Henry V* and *Henry VI*, the so-called 'history plays'. To Amelia, the events she wrote of from the fourteenth and fifteenth centuries were not ancient history: this was her family, and by the time the first history play was being written she had spent nearly a decade learning about it.

Built in 1549, Old Somerset House, Lord Hunsdon's royal palace on the Strand, was one of the earliest examples of Renaissance architecture in the country. Years before, when she was still a princess, Queen Elizabeth had lived there herself. The two-storey building, which was still being completed in the late 1590s, was built round a quadrangle, in part from stone taken from the demolition of the old St Paul's Cathedral. The palace was known for its great gardens stretching down to the river, and it was at least partly open to the public. Every day the gentlemen of London came to visit the long gallery of royal sculptures. Contemporary accounts describe how they would admire the statues, commenting learnedly on their meanings, comparing them to woodcuts of famous sculptures elsewhere or even conversing with them as if with ancient heroes. However, it was the gardens that were a special treat and they are shown in several illustrations, most notably the engraving by Leonard Knyff. Lord Hunsdon was quite well known as a collector of rare plants, and delighted in rare specimens brought to him from all over the globe. He even became the patron of botanist John Gerard when William Cecil (Lord Burghley) was no longer able to support him.

Gerard would often say how pleased he was to have a patron like Lord Hunsdon, who took such a deep interest in botany. Gerard was known for having his own garden of 'all the rare samples' and 'all manners of strange trees, herbs, roots, plants, flowers and other rare things'. This was a passion he shared with Lord Hunsdon, who was known for his 'curious keeping of rare and strange things from the farthest parts of the world', including, of course, Amelia herself. He generously gave Gerard samples and seeds of such rare specimens as the Peruvian balsam tree – though the tropical plants were often not able to survive the first approach of the English winter. Gerard profited from Hunsdon's patronage. Although much of the really important work on botany was going on among a small group of scholars in Lime Street, to which he did not belong, it was Gerard's botany, not theirs, that would be reflected in the Shakespearean plays. In one case, the plays would even refer to a wholly imaginary plant that Gerard had described in his *Herbal*.

These plays would also feature the rare American potato. This was first grown in Italy by C. Clusius in 1585, but was introduced to London by Sir Walter Raleigh from America in the same year, and grown in Raleigh's own mansion on the other side of the Strand opposite Old Somerset House. It was, apparently, only by accident that his gardeners realised it was the tuber, not the leaves, that were edible. Altogether, the plays would also set thirty scenes in gardens and refer to over 200 different kinds of plants as well. Spurgeon argues that Shakespeare was the only English playwright preoccupied with practical gardening issues, for example, the way in which frosts and sharp winds can nip new buds (*Henry IV, Part 2*, 1.3.37), or how gardeners should manure the roots that are most delicate (*Henry V*, 2.4.37),or to complain about cankers that destroy the bloom of roses. (Although *The True Chronicle History of King Leir* does refer to blossoms 'nipped with winter's frosts'.)

One of Lord Hunsdon's many honours was that in 1561 the queen made him a Knight of the Garter, the chivalric order founded by Kind Edward III in 1348, which includes the monarch, the Prince of Wales and twenty-two other worthies. A Garter ceremony was held every few years, whenever one of the members died and had to be replaced. Hunsdon would have worn the dark cloak with the insignia on the shoulder, the heavy gold chain, a black Tudor bonnet with ostrich feathers, and the garter itself strapped around his left calf. He was entitled to wear purple robes not only in his own right because of his own royal blood, but also as a Garter Knight.

As an honour involving only twenty-four men from the highest ranks of European society, the Order of the Garter was a highly specialised matter. One would imagine it would not normally enter into a playwright's consciousness. Strangely, however, the Shakespearean plays demonstrate a special interest in this remote chivalric honour. In *Richard III*, King Richard swears 'by my Garter' and is told that he has dishonoured it. *Henry V* makes allusions to the battle of Crecy, where many of the first knights of the Garter fought. In *Henry VI, Part 1* people wish to tear the garter off Falstaff's craven leg, and in *The Merry Wives of Windsor* there are numerous references to the Garter Inn and villagers who dress up as fairies to clean Windsor Castle for the ceremony, while quoting the motto of the Order of the Garter, and flowers whose colours even match the Garter insignia (*The Merry Wives of Windsor*, 5.5.64–72).

However the Garter theme begins, as Melchiori has observed, right in one of the earliest plays, the *Reign of Edward III*, written about the year 1590. It is hard to explain the playwright's interest if they had never seen a Garter ceremony and did not have personal links to a member of the Order. There are also some very peculiar features of the account in that it notably ignores the traditional dramatic story of the Countess of Salisbury and her rape by the founder of the Order of the Garter, King Edward himself.

We have considered earlier the possible motivations for writing *The Rape of Lucrece*. In *Venus and Adonis*, the boy is raped, and there is the horrific rape of

Lavinia in *Titus Andronicus* – these plays were all written in the period from 1592 to 1594. As a mature woman Amelia would write her Crucifixion poem, which has been described as a rape of Jesus and a rewriting of *The Rape of Lucrece*. The sonnets describe the poet's 'maiden virtue rudely strumpeted' (Sonnet 66). Did Amelia see the experience of being pandered to Lord Hunsdon at the age of thirteen as a rape, and could this have influenced the writing of *Reign of Edward III*?

In Jean Le Bel's book *Vrayes Chronicles* or the true chronicles, we are told how King Edward fell in love with the Countess of Salisbury, and when her husband was away he 'raped her so savagely that never was a woman so badly treated'. Melchiori argues that the full, brutal, account 'sounds like a crude anticipation of the narrative of the rape in Shakespeare's *Lucrece*'. The historical account also describes the countess losing her garter at a dance, and the king picking it up and making it the centre of his new chivalric order, but most oddly these events are nowhere to be found in *The Reign of Edward III*. If, as Roger Prior has argued, this play was written for a private performance before Lord Hunsdon, himself a Garter Knight, then the two notable historic omissions are explicable. By ignoring these events and replacing them with unhistorical depictions of the Black Prince being ceremonially armed and created a knight, the playwright is ironically contrasting the heraldic, theatrical, imagery of honour with the actuality of the behaviour of those men who wield power.

Lord Hunsdon did not live only in London. He was also Warden of the Scottish Marches and governor of a castle in the fortress town of Berwick on the border with Scotland. The castle itself was beautiful, although it had a sombre history. In the eleventh century it was where Duncan had stayed before setting out with his navy to be killed by Macbeth. In 1296 King Edward I, 'the Hammer of the Scots', besieged the castle and the town, killing almost all the inhabitants, and only stopping after watching his men hack a pregnant woman to death. The castle had a whole staff, including a marshal, treasurer, a mayor and officers, eighty horsemen, 500 soldiers, eighty gunners, grooms, a preacher, and forty-two footmen. The food, unfortunately, was not so good, since Robert Vernon, Surveyor of the Victuals, had problems in getting top-quality supplies. But Berwick had regular postal services to London and acted as the centre for secret service operations in Scotland. Every so often, mysterious spies and informers would appear, together with large sums of money being sent by couriers for some special diplomatic purposes. Although it was far away, and the queen herself would never visit Scotland, control of the border was critical – which was why the government was willing to spend almost 10 per cent of their budget, around £14,860 a year, supporting Berwick and its operations.

When at Berwick, Lord Hunsdon and his son Sir George Carey were frequent visitors to the Scottish court, and got to know King James well, which is perhaps how he came to be burlesqued as Bottom in *A Midsummer Night's Dream*. As

Marion A. Taylor observed in her book on contemporary allegory in the play, *Bottom Thou Art Translated: Political Allegory in* A Midsummer Night's Dream *and Related Literature*, there are a number of parallels to King James. Bottom is a 'mechanical', a sort of tradesman, which echoes the way James described himself as an apprentice in *The Essays of a Prentice in the Divine Art of Poesie* (1584). Bottom sends a fairy to get honey from a thistle, because he thinks it a fair flower – as it was to a Scot, whose national flower it became in 1540. He eats oats, because everyone knows how much Scotsmen love their porridge oats. He mispronounces 'Thisbe' as 'thisne', because James had a thick voice and an over-large tongue and would mispronounce his words. He itches and scratches, because James had a very thin skin which continually itched – not helped by his lack of washing. Even Bottom's rude manners match those of James, who was known to be 'countrified and extremely rude both in his eating, dress and interests.' Bottom is a weaver because this was Scotland's national occupation. Because James liked them, the play even uses exaggerated alliteration and repetition, 'alack, alack, alack' and 'Now die, die, die, die, die' (*Midsummer Night's Dream*, 5.1.295 and 170). James is on record as saying that 'when it comes to purpose it will be comely to repeat such a word eight or nine times'.

Having become Lord Hunsdon's mistress sometime in 1582, Amelia would have joined him on his six-month-long visit to Berwick from August 1584 to February 1585. However, Scotland was an ignorant backwater, a long way from London and civilisation. With nothing social to do, there was lots of time to be spent listening to the Northern dialect and to read Lord Hunsdon's unpublished state papers on Scottish affairs dating back to the 1560s. These papers covered the murder of Lord Darnley, King James's father, which would reappear decades later in *Macbeth*.[1] The state papers and other testimonies note that the murder was committed in the silence of the night and that the murderer went back to bed and pretended to be asleep – as occurs in *Macbeth*. Lord Hunsdon returned to London for 1586, but would be back again in February 1587. Indeed, until spring 1588 he was generally active in the north of England, as the general responsible for the Middle and the Eastern Marches, and for putting down unrest at home and readying a Northern army in anticipation of any Spanish invasion.

Scotland aside, it was necessary that the whole realm be well guarded, and put in a state of readiness. An army had to be assembled. For that reason the Privy Council had charged Hunsdon and the other lord lieutenants to rally the forces under their charge, to muster and put in readiness a force of soldiers together with their arms and armour. The first priority was to take an audit of the forces and what was to be furnished, and to send to London a certification of the men and the weapons that would be ready. In the evenings, there would doubtless be many discussions of military strategy among men, both those who thought that learning could come from books and who were 'knowledged and literatured in the wars', and those who only valued practical experience.

Initially, Lord Hunsdon was given the responsibility of mustering the army in Wales, so for Amelia, the next year or so would have been an experience not of battle, but of preparations and rehearsals for it. In *Henry IV, Part II* she would describe how musters were gamed by the locals, full as they were of fake names: 'a number of shadows to fill up the muster bank' (*Henry IV, Part 2*, 3.2.45–6), or a 'muster-file, rotten and sound upon my life, amounts not to fifteen thousand poll' (*All's Well*, 4.3.188). She would watch Lord Hunsdon deal with captains leading their 'rag-o-muffins', and 'there's not three of my hundred and fifty left alive' because the others were fake characters put down to enhance the muster roll. Typically the local parish sent in five men, only two of whom would be able-bodied. But the two who were able-bodied would bribe the corporal and be dismissed. Then, in order to meet his target, the recruiting officer would take the three others, claiming, with all manner of rationalisations, that the one with very thin legs would be excellent at reloading pistols, that the other is so thin that when he stands to the side no bullet can hit him, and as for the third who is brave as a mouse, he will prove most excellent in retreat, as the play comically puts it. 'Just give me the spare men,' says Shakespeare's corporal, 'and spare me the great ones' (*Henry IV, Part 2*, 3.2.288). These 'fiery voluntaries' who bore their birthrights on their backs were out 'to make a hazard of new fortunes' (*King John*, 2.1.66–7) but would give any general nightmares.

Recruiting officers, like the individual she would depict as Falstaff, ended up with a 'charge consist[ing] of ancients, corporals, lieutenants, gentlemen of companies ... and such as indeed were never soldiers, but discarded unjust serving-men, younger sons to younger brothers, revolted tapsters and ostlers trade-fallen' (*Henry IV, Part 1*). Moreover, many of them were half naked and had just been let out of jail. When they reached the meeting place, the mustering involved much parading around and inspection, with soldiers and officers decked out in ribbons. Barrels of ale were usually supplied, and the event would culminate in a mock battle or two. There would be gunfire and drums, but the only injuries were usually accidental.

It is this experience, of mustering an army in Wales and of the Welsh people, that is reflected in *Henry IV, Part 1*. In that play, the character of Lady Mortimer sings in Welsh, and there is Welsh conversation between her and the famous Welsh leader, Owen Glendower. The latter is the 'irregular and wild' Welsh leader, and a 'great magician'. A talkative, quick-tempered man, Glendower of the play is passionate about poetry and history and cannot bear 'crossings'. The English Hotspur refuses to understand him: 'Let me not understand you then; speak it in Welsh' (*Henry IV, Part 1*, 3.1.117). Here, Wales and Welsh appear noble and mystical. Of course, Amelia may also have developed some of this knowledge through a kinsman of the Willoughby family, Sir Robert Salisburie, a Member of Parliament and 'one of the Esquires of the bodie to the Queen'. He was the largest landowner in North Wales, with extensive landholdings in

Lleweni, Denbighshire, and was a well-known sponsor of Welsh poetry. It was to him that Robert Chester dedicated a volume of poetry, *Loves Martyr*. Over 100 pages long, it included contributions from various poets on the theme of the phoenix and its mythical flirtation with the turtle dove – one of which would be Shakespeare's 'The Phoenix and the Turtle'.

By March 1588 however, it was clear the Spanish attack was soon to come. Preparations had not gone well. There were still twenty-five counties, of which Wales was one, that had not sent in their certificates describing their preparations. Of those that had been sent in, another fourteen were deficient, lacking details of horse, or ammunition, or the numbers of untrained men. The next month Her Majesty appointed Lord Hunsdon to come down to London to be the General in Command of the army responsible for her personal protection, and to supervise the mustering for Norfolk and for Suffolk. Over the next three months he had to work extremely quickly. By July, he had assembled an army of 28,900 men divided into fourteen regiments, headed by men such as Sir William Knowles and Sir Thomas Cecil. But then, Lord Hunsdon was good at things military. For the most part, his army was of good quality, with men of valour eager for battle. Excitement had reached such a pitch that in London even lads as young as eight or nine years of age would form themselves into bands, choose their own officers, and march around with flags flying, banging on drums and practicing with miniature weapons.

On 28 July 1588, in order to be better protected, the queen moved from Richmond Palace to London. The army of 34,000 men under Lord Hunsdon's command surrounded her palace, camping out in St James's Park. London was now an armed encampment. Streets were barred with chains, and crossroads guarded. The Thames was prepared against invasion from sea, and coastal places fortified. England was almost ready to repel the Spanish invasion. Awaiting the expected battle, and awaiting an invasion from Dunkirk, on 19 August 1588 Her Majesty was encamped at Tilbury, where a second army of 22,000 foot and 1,000 horse guarded the coastline. The queen rallied her hungry troops (she had not paid the merchants' bills), by giving them a feast of words instead. She gave it dressed like an Amazon queen, buskined and plumed, with a golden truncheon and gauntlet. Her speech was doubtless a piece of theatrics that helped make her men forget their hunger. Of course, the version that was later put into circulation, with its famous lines, 'I know I have the body of a weak, feeble woman; but I have the heart and stomach of a king', was simply a brilliantly written piece of propaganda.

Fortunately, the invasion never came: the Spanish Armada was routed at sea by storms. Yet for Amelia, this experience of preparations for war would leave another indelible impression. Her vocabulary would have absorbed another 400 words of military jargon. She would have learnt all about the preparations for war (when she had actually to describe a battle, for instance in *Henry V*, she would look elsewhere). As for sixty-four-year-old Lord Hunsdon, the end of the war meant a certain disappointment, in that he had not seen action. For all his effort, the queen gave him the right to export 20,000 woollen cloths – not much, but nearly three times more than she gave Sir Walter Raleigh for his work on the fleet. She also awarded him the great jewel that would become known as the Hunsdon Onyx, an Italian carving showing Perseus descending from the sky with the head of the Gorgon on his shield, in order to rescue Andromeda.

Next, Lord Hunsdon would be given a series of legal appointments, and these would also leave their mark on Amelia's plays. In 1589, Hunsdon became Chief Justice in the forest of Eyre, South of Trent, just below Manchester. Amelia got to know the Midlands area, admiring the 'smug and silver Trent' in *Henry IV, Part 1*. She had probably also accompanied Hunsdon not just to Berwick, but on some of the visits to his country estates, including his land in Derbyshire, his Stewardship in Middlesbrough, and his manor of Conisbrough Castle near Doncaster in Yorkshire. From these visits would come Amelia's exposure to the Northern dialects (see Appendix 12), which are prevalent in the Shakespearean plays, and possibly also her exposure to some of the mystery plays, which were still being occasionally performed in the north of England.

A considerable part of the country still was governed by forest law and forest courts, instituted for the government of the forest and for the punishment of all injuries done to the sovereign's deer or venison, to the 'vert' or 'greenswerd', and to the cover in which such deer are lodged. As Chief Justice of the forest of Eyre Lord Hunsdon had to hear and determine, as the law codes stated, 'all trespasses within the forest, and all claims of franchises, liberties, and privileges, and all pleas and causes whatsoever therein arising', and to try presentments in the inferior courts of the forests. Of these, there were several kinds, including the court of attachments, wood-mote, or forty-days' court. The latter, for example, has to be held before the verderers of the forest once in every forty days and was 'instituted to inquire into all offenders against vert and venison.' Amelia's early interest in legal issues and disputes concerning the treatment of deer forests would appear both in *The Merry Wives of Windsor* and in the forest in *As You Like It*, in which Time appears as an Old Justice (4.1) rather like Lord Hunsdon himself, and which uses legal words like 'purlieu' to refer to the outskirts of a forest (4.3.84).

In addition, Lord Hunsdon had his other legal roles as Recorder of Cambridge, as well as Chief Justice Itinerant of the Royal Forces, and like many others he was a member of Gray's Inn. After Hunsdon's death, clearly taking advantage of his land deals, leasings of manors and all the other legal cases and trials that had passed through his office over the years, the plays would provide descriptions of twenty-five different trials, and refer to issues like summer's leases having too short a date, querying why a lease so short should have so large a cost. The author would even refer to the struggle that was going in her own soul in legal language that was borrowed from the allocation of freehold land, as if her eyes and ears were tenants of her heart, and 'impannelled a quest' (engaged in an inquest) for the rights to the proper 'title' (Sonnet 46). She would write enough on the law that an account of the over 200 legal terms she uses in 1,600 different places would be sufficient to be gathered up into a dictionary.

All Lord Hunsdon's legal work was done by the law clerks working for him in his household, in Somerset House. Christine de Pizan, a significant contemporary source, had argued that women should be free to become lawyers. So if Amelia gained her legal experience by working on some of his legal cases, Lord Hunsdon was simply doing what that literary prince, Lord Clotten in *Cymbeline*, would do: 'I will make one of her women lawyer for me, for I yet not understand the case myself' (2.3.71–3). It was an experience that later in life would lead her to choose an untranslated Italian source – recognised by all Shakespeare scholars as Giovanni Fiorentino's *Il Pecorone* – for one of her plays, in which there is a lady who arrives in Venice 'dressed like a lawyer'. She would turn the plot into *The Merchant of Venice*, featuring the lawyerly disguises of Portia and Nerissa. It was a legal training that later in life she would put to good use in major lawsuits of her own, including one against a prominent attorney, and another decade-long lawsuit against her husband's relatives, in which she would twice petition the Privy Council.

Although the early years in which Amelia was mistress to Lord Hunsdon would be occupied by military preparations and the legal work from his three judgeships, there was also time for recreation, such as hunting. In part, this is reflected in the plays, in which falcon imagery would appear again and again; the plays contain fifteen times more falconry imagery than the plays of Ben Jonson, Marlowe or Robert Greene. When he was in London, Lord Hunsdon often went for exercise to Hyde Park, London's most favoured hunting ground, which was specially stocked with deer. Keeping the park operational was one of his many responsibilities as Keeper of Hyde Park. He was first appointed Assistant Keeper by the queen in 1574, for which he was to receive the sum of four pence a day, plus the food for the deer – a miserly allowance (less than an actor's day rate!), though he subsequently became Head Keeper at eight pence a day and of course had many other sources of income.

A more important fact, however, was that Lord Hunsdon was also England's leading expert on falconry, having been made Master of the Royal Falcons in 1560. This was just a few years before Turberville wrote his *Booke of Faulconrie or Hawking* (1567), and the two men were probably acquainted: the book was dedicated to Lord Hunsdon's son-in-law. Turberville was also an innovative poet and translator, both of Boccaccio and of Ovid's *Heroides (The Heroines)*, which appeared as *The Heroycall Epistles of the Learned Poet Publius Ovidus Naso* (1567), a collection of imaginary letters by neglected or abandoned women advocating a woman's point of view, which Amelia was presumably happy to read. They were, moreover, letters that appeared to have been written by women, but which had actually been written by a man, a device that undermines the characteristic male heroes of conventional epic and foregrounds women's concerns. This comic gender inversion would be alluded to in the *Shrew* play when, for instance, Lucentio (a man) imagines himself in the role of Dido of Carthage (a woman), in love with Bianca (a woman) in the improbable role of an old man, Aeneas (1.1.445), right before he begins to explicitly use the *Heroides* in his courting. All of this suggests to the alert reader that *Shrew* is a rewriting of the *Heroides*, in that it is a depiction of a neglected or abandoned heroine. No surprise, then, that it should have been written by a person of one gender pretending to be another. Furthermore, there was a tradition of rewriting the *Heroides*, and the person who most recently attempted it was the leading Venetian courtesan Veronica Franco, whose conquests included Henry III of France, and whose volume of poetry *Terze Rima* had been published in 1575. It appears that the playwright was following in her footsteps.

Amelia would also make extensive use of Turberville's translation of the *Heroides* in writing the women's parts in *A Midsummer Night's Dream*. However in writing *The Taming of the Shrew*, Amelia was obviously also thinking also of Turberville's work on hawking, and in particular of his introduction. He presents the texts of his translation as if they were dishes at a banquet: 'Bid thee [I say] to a base banquet to sharpen thy stomach.' He hopes that the reader will not 'scorne or loth any dish' although he acknowledges that they are a curious kind of 'cates' (delicacy): 'For doubtlesse the cates of themselves in their kind are passing curious.' The reference would reappear in the jokes on 'kate' and 'cate' that concern another falcon or 'haggard' in *The Taming of the Shrew*.

Evidently, Hunsdon's activities as the royal falconer were so substantial that it led Amelia to make *fifteen* times more falconry references than any other playwright – including unique references made from the viewpoint of a falconer such as a reference to imping, the process by which a falconer repairs a bird's wing feather. Finally, it appears that while living at Old Somerset House Amelia would have had a perfect opportunity to learn about the practicalities of looking after the birds. Not only was Lord Hunsdon the royal falconer, but the actual falconries remained at the Charing Cross Mews (the current location of the National Gallery), where the royal stables had also been located, at most, two minutes' walk from the house.

Four years younger than Amelia, the Earl of Southampton, Henry Wriothesley, had for many years been a ward of Lord Burghley, and had lived next door to her in Cecil House. She would probably have visited there regularly to use Burghley's outstanding library of about 1,700 volumes, which was then three times the size of the library at the University of Cambridge. The only direct evidence that the earl cared to help support Amelia's family dates from his writing a letter of support for her husband in 1607. However, the two long poems, *Venus and Adonis* and *The Rape of Lucrece*, were both dedicated, lovingly, to the Earl of Southampton in 1593 and 1594. Both are signed William Shakespeare. Since that name was not being used at this time by the man from Stratford, we need to look elsewhere to find the poet who was Southampton's friend.

We can find a clue, perhaps, in the earliest layer of *Love's Labour's Lost*, a play about noblewomen's unwillingness to marry that can be dated to perhaps 1591. It was possibly written as an interlude to help persuade the queen not to force Southampton to marry Lord Burghley's granddaughter Elizabeth against his will, and it was inspired by Sir Philip Sidney's *The Four Foster Children of Desire* (1581), which had been successful in communicating to the French that the queen was not yet ready to marry. Because both the Earl of Essex and Earl of Southampton were themselves foster children or 'wards' of Lord Burghley, the analogy was perfect. Amelia would set her French lords at the court of Navarre, which is where Essex already was and where Southampton wanted to be. As a clue that the French lords were English nobles, allegorically speaking, she would call their king Ferdinand, which would call to mind Ferdinando Stanley, the name of Baron Strange, 'Prince Ferdinando, Earl of Derby and King of the Isle of Man' (although in the later printed versions this name survives only in one stage direction to the 1598 quarto and in one heading). She also caricatured her step uncle Peregrine Bertie, Lord Willoughby (brother of Susan Bertie), as the famous soldier Armado. Like Armado, Bertie was a famous solider – in fact, England's most famous soldier. He had also been fighting for Henry of Navarre. She would emphasise the point with a pun calling him 'too peregrinate' (*Love's Labour's Lost* 5.1.114), a pun the queen often made herself in reference to Lord Willoughby.

As for the precise workings of the allegory, in the play, the character 'Berowne' (an allegory for Biron) cannot marry 'Rosaline' until such time as the princess/queen marries the king. Biron is the historical Duc of Biron, but is also Southampton refusing to marry. Yet beneath that, as should now appear to the alert reader, appears to be a further allegory as to the identity of Lord 'Berowne' (a pun on the colour brown as well as on Biron), and the lady 'Rosaline' he cannot marry. In a play in which so many things are turned preposterously back to front, it is possible to change the names around to get identities as Lord Rosaline (or Rosely, as Wriothesley was pronounced) and the Brown Lady (Bassano means base or black, from the root *basso*). That is why she is 'black like ebony' and dark as the ink in the full-bodied letter 'B' in a manuscript in the play (5.2.41–2). It hardly seems an accident that the reference is made to the letter B, her initial. All of a sudden, it becomes extremely clear why the Earl of Southampton is unable to marry the 'Brown Lady', since at the time she was mistress to Lord Hunsdon, and in any case as a commoner could never have married an earl. This is despite the fact that a proxy for Henry Wriothesley (H. W.) describes their affair, claiming that his tongue and hand and hart, his love, her limbs, have all done what they ought (*Willobie His Avisa*, canto LXXIII).

Many different aspects of Lord Hunsdon's household would influence Amelia, (not least his large vocabulary of sexual obscenities). It is significant that Lord

Hunsdon's many diverse responsibilities, including even his minor ones such as his responsibility for the court musicians, the court doctors and apothecaries, astronomers, gardeners, mole catchers and fools, map so neatly on to the knowledge areas in the Shakespearean plays. This influence included not just contemporary knowledge, but also oral history about the past, about Henry of Navarre, about the mistakes that had been made in court entertainments of the past, and about Lord Hunsdon's quelling of the Northern Rebellion in 1569, which would affect many of the plays, but none more than *Henry IV, Part 1*, which begins, curiously for the plays, with the allegorical figure of Rumour, who represents the seditious tale-bearers whose whisperings had stimulated the rebellion. It also included the presence of fools, including stories about the fool Monarcho, the queen's favourite fool for six years from 1569 to 1575.

The Shakespearean plays are notable for transforming the figure of Vice from the mystery plays into the figure of the fool. A number of fools, including Touchstone and Feste, have prominent roles. One who is mentioned only in passing is Monarcho. Intriguingly, he came from the Italian town of Bergamo, about 100 miles from Bassano, but within the same region of the Veneto. Bergamo was known for the slowness of its porters, the stupidity of its peasants, and for its amusing rustic dances, hence the 'bergomask' that Bottom offers to dance in *A Midsummer Night's Dream*. It was an appropriate town for a fool to come from. The queen, in her characteristic ironic fashion, gave him the nickname 'Monarcho', or 'little monarch'. He is commemorated by name as a 'phantasime', or fantastical person, in *Love's Labour's Lost* and Amelia puns on his name in *Twelfth Night*. There was a common Elizabethan saying 'hoods make not monks', which is quoted in English in *Henry VIII* (3.1). It is also quoted in Latin by Feste in *Twelfth Night*: 'Lady, *cucullus non facit monachum.*' Although he had died when she was only eleven years old, Amelia is remembering the motley fool 'Monarcho' as a pun on *monachum*. Why would she otherwise have Feste mistranslate the Latin as 'I wear not motley in my brain' (1.5.58)?

Last, but not least. The single factor that would influence her most was that, as Lord Chamberlain, Hunsdon was responsible both for court entertainment and for regulating the English theatre (see Appendix 6). From 1594 he would become patron of the Lord Chamberlain's Men – the company that was given the rights to perform the Shakespearean plays. Lord Hunsdon's own company of players, Hunsdon's Men, had originally been formed in 1567, although it was closed down in 1583 when some of its members moved to the Queen's Men. Hunsdon nevertheless had experience managing theatrical entertainments. Choosing the court entertainment and overseeing its production was a hard task, made harder by his frequent travel on military and legal involvements. Hunsdon could not afford to make a mistake while Her Majesty was peering down, eagle-eyed, from under her canopy of state.

Few understood how hard a job theatre was: getting groups of actors to work together so that the illusion of the performance would capture the audience's attention almost as if by magic. Even walking across a stage or standing or sitting still required great skill. The art of the office subsisted in managing productions and supervising their staging. This would have required managing people who understood the skill of devising, and being a good judge of various genres, including histories, comedies, tragedies and other kinds of shows, all combined with a sense of space and architecture and, of course, knowing what material would please Her Majesty. Then you had to choose a company of players who would also please Her Royal Highness, which meant knowing her taste very well. Lord Hunsdon also had the complicated job of ensuring that the plays being put on in the public playhouses were not breaking the law, and he had to deal constantly with the objections of the Puritans and from the City of London who wanted to close the theatres down. The Office of the Revels and its censors reported to him, and he would have taken a personal interest not only in the quality of the plays, but in how they were staged and whether they were communicating using secret allegories, or bug-words, as they were called.

Amelia's relationship with Lord Hunsdon would have given her access to the Office of the Revels, which was the only place in England where plays were taken seriously, and where reading plays took place as a real discipline. Readers constantly had to be aware whether a play was heretical or insulting to any of the great nobles, which made for a kind of literary criticism. However, reading plays, as it is reasonable to assume Amelia did, would not have been enough. To become a great playwright she would have needed a mentor. For that, there was really only one man in England equal to the task.

Christopher Marlowe: Collaborator and Lover (1589–1592)

The early Shakespearean plays are remarkable for having been very substantially influenced by Marlowe; indeed, Marlowe may even have collaborated on some of them. Like Shakespeare, it is highly significant that Marlowe, too, embedded in his plays a system of allegories, albeit fairly crude ones. These allegories reflect, as do those in the Shakespearean plays, the knowledge that Christ was not a historical figure but merely, as Harold Bloom would later put it, the world's best-known literary character.[2] The Gospels were works of literature, not of history, and Christianity itself was therefore was a false religion (see Appendix 8). This was why Marlowe described the literary character Jesus as a 'deceiver' in 'vain and idle' tales – literary fictions, not true histories – which, as he told Simon Aldrich, were 'all one man's making'. That is, they were devised by the Emperor Vespasian as a matter of 'policy' after the Roman–Jewish war, as the character of Barabas indicates in *The Jew of Malta* (2.3.9–10). Barabas's remark alludes to what is today known as the 'Flavian hypothesis', as expressed by the historian Tacitus: 'It was only after the rise of the Flavians that we Romans believed in such stories'.[3] That the author of the Shakespearean works followed Marlowe in creating dangerous allegorical heresies alluding to the Roman–Jewish war is confirmed most notably in *Titus Andronicus*, where the parallels identified by J. J. M. Tobin and others form the underlying system of meaning in this remarkable play. So there was a very close intellectual affinity, bespeaking a very close meeting of minds, between Marlowe and the author of Shakespeare. Was there anything more?

As to whether Amelia and Marlowe became lovers, Amelia had lived for many years with Lord Hunsdon. We also know that Lord Hunsdon was notable for his 'obscenity in speaking', corresponding perhaps with the diverse and extensive sexual vocabulary shown in the Shakespearean works, which is the subject of several dictionaries. She would have become accomplished in the theatrical sex games that went with the job of being an upmarket 'honest courtesan', according to the Venetian model. (Out of nearly 12,000 prostitutes in Venice perhaps 200 deserved this title.) According to Christina Valhouli, the Venetian favourite was enacting the bestial rape scene of Leda and the Swan, in which Zeus takes the form of a swan to rape the girl.[4] In both of these facts may lie the answer to the odd reality that the first works to be accredited by name to Shakespeare were the two long pornographic mythological poems, one about a man (Tarquin) raping a woman (Lucrece), and the other about a goddess (Venus) trying to rape a man (Adonis). One provenance for enacting such fantastic material may have been Lord Hunsdon's bedroom at Old Somerset House, and it speaks of Amelia having a vivid sexual imagination.

While we know nothing directly about relationship between Amelia and Marlowe, both were well aware of the classical works on sexual instruction. Marlowe was the translator of the first three books of Ovid's *Amores*, in which the poet asks help from the muse in writing his amorous verse, and which presents the poet as a lover. Later books even give useful advice to the poet's mistress on how to deal with her husband and avoid his attentions. Marlowe's translation was banned as pornographic and burnt by the public hangman in 1599. However, the Shakespearean plays show familiarity with Ovid's much more explicit *Ars Amatoria*, 'the art of love'. This work not only treats men and women as sexual equals, but gives specific instructions on simultaneous orgasm and techniques for men to have multiple orgasms. Lucentio offers to use it to instruct Bianca in *The Taming of the Shrew* (4.2.8) and Juliet paraphrases it when she says 'At lovers' perjuries, / They say, Jove laughs.' This 'precious book of love' may be alluded to early on in *Romeo and Juliet*, a play notable for its sexuality.

It is conceivable that Amelia and Marlowe also left references to each other in their works. In *Dr Faustus*, Marlowe unnecessarily describes a 'beauteous paramour' as having one particular odd physical characteristic, she 'had a wart or mole in her neck' (*Dr Faustus* A, 4.1.62–3). According to her surviving medical records from Dr Simon Forman, Amelia also had a wart or mole at the pit of her throat, which would normally be covered up with a piece of jewellery. Conceivably, then, Marlowe wrote her description into his play.

Maureen Duff, however, goes further than this. It has long been known that Robert Greene's final satire accused Marlowe of atheism, as the 'famous gracer of the tragedians'. In addition, Duff argues that Marlowe, who had recently translated the works of Lucan, is also the figure of Lucianio in Robert Greene's satire *A Groats-Worth of Wit Bought with a Millionth of Repentance* (1592). This tells how a 'poor penniless poet' 'Lucianio' meets a beauteous courtesan called L'Amilia (similar to Simon Forman's spelling of her name). She is living in the suburbs, 'pleasantly seated' in a house with a pleasant garden and a drawing room decorated with goodly portraits. She first appears like a 'second Helen' sitting at her window singing a sonnet with a delicious voice. The refrain to the song is:

> Fie fie then on fancie,
> It hinders youthes joy,
> Faire virgins learne by me,
> To count love a toy.

After eating and dancing, and being given a diamond, L'Amilia then tells a fable of the fox and the badger. Duff concludes that 'Greene is saying that Marlowe embarked on an affair with Emilia Bassano prior to September 1592', when she got pregnant and was thrown out of court.

A more reliable indication, however, can be found in the Shakespearean canon. If we read the poem *A Lover's Complaint* autobiographically, it would appear to be a poem about a girl betrayed by a man rather like Marlowe. Borrowing its literary style from Samuel Daniel's 137-verse poem, *The Complaint of Rosamund* (1592), about a fair young woman who comes to court and gets exploited, Amelia describes her unnamed lover as one who, like Marlowe, had taken 'holy vows' to be a priest, and was therefore at university doing a degree in theology. The lover was a poet whose lips issued silken parcels, a reference perhaps to Marlowe's verse. Yet he was irreligious and broke his holy vows. The poem suggests that her affair with Marlowe – shown in his portrait as a fair-skinned, beardless man with long brown hair, as described in the poem – left Amelia sad, angry and wistful:

> His browny locks did hang in crooked curls;
> And every light occasion of the wind
> Upon his lips their silken parcels hurls
> [...]
> Small show of man was yet upon his chin;
> His phoenix down began but to appear,
> Like unshorn velvet, on that termless skin
> [...]

His qualities were beauteous as his form,
For maiden-tongued he was, and thereof free
[...]
What with his art in youth, and youth in art,
Threw my affections in his charmed power,
Reserved the stalk, and gave him all my flower.
[...]
This false jewel, and his amorous spoil.
                    A Lover's Complaint, 85–8, 92–5, 99–100, 145-47, 154

One other, more substantial piece of evidence is found in *As You Like It* in the character of Touchstone. Like Amelia, he is a former courtier, who is very smart, something indicated in Elizabethan psychology by his having a 'very dry brain' (2.7.39–40), yet he is a 'motley', as the playwright described herself in Sonnet 110. Touchstone is also a poet who discusses the nature of poetry (3.3.14–17) while standing among Audrey's goats. He compares himself to that most 'capricious' (from the Latin *caper*, a goat) poet Ovid, among the uncomprehending Goths (3.3.7–9), and complains that his verses are not understood. The word 'Touchstone' in Greek is '*basanos*'. As if to push the point home, Touchstone refers to being put on trial: 'put me to my purgation' (5.4.49), which was a special sort of trial by torture, for example by water, fire or combat, which in Greek was also *basanos*. It seems that Amelia wrote herself into the play through a double pun as the *basanos*, or Touchstone, who would be married of a vicar Martext (Marlowe the theology student) who then goes away suddenly – a passage that always looks very strange when it is acted on stage, and which should therefore indicate something particular being signified.

There are a number of elements in the play that support the association between *As You Like It* and Marlowe, in that Marlowe is clearly associated both with the unhappy fate of literary lovers and with the Martext figure. Touchstone, as the girl, is left singing the song *Sweet Oliver* about a man who leaves behind the girl who wants to marry him – which is why the character is given the name Oliver Martext. This is precisely what happened when Marlowe was killed, leaving Amelia behind. The literary structure of surrounding allusions to Marlowe set up the association, specifically to his poem about the untimely death of the young lover Leander, and place at the centre the desire by Touchstone/Basanos/Amelia to have married him. The structure is demonstrated by several allusions:

- The reference to ladies being young and fair and having the gift to know it echoes a passage in Marlowe's *Hero and Leander* in which Hero is glad she has such loveliness and beauty to provoke his liking (2.7.37–9).

- A man being struck dead and the great reckoning in a little room, which allude to Marlowe's murder, supposedly over the 'reckoning' or bill (3.3.12–13).

- **'I were better to be married of him than another'** (3.3.82–2, emphasis my own).

- A quote from *Hero and Leander*, 'who ever loved that loved not at first sight' combined with a reference to him as a dead shepherd, since Marlowe was the author of *The Passionate Shepherd to His Love* (3.5.81–2).

- A comic inaccurate summary of *Hero and Leander* and their deaths (4.1.90–5).

Of these allusions to Marlowe, the references to his poem about the untimely death of the young lover Leander and to his murder are particularly clear. We can then infer not only that Marlowe was the person who helped to teach Amelia the craft of playwriting, but that he was also probably her lover, and that she wanted to marry him – an ambition necessarily curtailed when he was abruptly killed to stop him testifying to the Atheism Commission. We might also note that in the folio version of *The Merry Wives of Windsor* the theme of exile – in a reference to Psalm 137 'By the rivers of Babylon' describing the Jews after the destruction of the first Temple – is also associated with Marlowe and love, by referring to his song 'Come Live with Me and by my Love'. This also has watery connotations since it derives from the wooing song of the Cyclops to the water nymph Galatea in the *Metamorphoses* of the exiled poet Ovid, and involves a pun on the shallowness of justice.

It would appear, then, that in her early twenties, somewhere in the period from 1589 to 1592, Amelia was having an affair with Christopher Marlowe, right under the nose of Lord Hunsdon, now in his mid-sixties. This is significant because in June 1592 came the next major event in her life. She became pregnant. She had previously had several abortions, or 'false conceptions' but her physical condition now required that she have this baby. And one thing that was very clear at court was that if Queen Elizabeth couldn't have a baby, she didn't want to be reminded blatantly that other women could. Lord Hunsdon could not keep his pregnant mistress. It would be a public scandal. She would be sent to prison or hauled through the streets for flagrant immorality. So, as Lord Hunsdon put it, Amelia would have to be married off 'for colour' – that is, to keep up appearances. That way everyone could pretend that the child had been conceived in matrimony. It was the way it had always been done: Usually, the maids of court would go scarce twenty weeks with child after they were married. It was of course enormously hypocritical and unfair, as would be noted in *Two Noble Kinsmen*:

Lords and courtiers that have got maids with child ... They shall stand in fire up
to the navel and in ice up to the heart and there th'offending part burns and the
deceiving part freezes. In troth, a very grievous punishment.

                                                           Two Noble Kinsmen, 4.3.40–5

On 18 October 1592, Amelia entered the sacrament of holy matrimony at St
Boltoph's, Bishopsgate, with Alphonso Lanier, her cousin and a court musician.
Alphonso was the son of Amelia's aunt Lucretia, who had married Nicholas Lanier
twenty years earlier at All Hallows Church, Barking. Nicholas was a modestly
successful lute player, and they had several children. Alphonso, aged twenty at
the time of his marriage, and so three years younger than Amelia, was one of the
eldest. She was marrying a cousin and a Christian. With the money she had been
given by Lord Hunsdon as a payoff, they were able to take a house in a fashionable
part of Westminster. In that house, she would go into labour a few months later, in
January or February 1593.

Amelia claimed that her estate at the time she married Lanier was £4,000, or
about £4 million in today's money, which was about Lord Hunsdon's annual
income. Amelia probably exaggerated, but the amount must have been substantial.
Since she had inherited only £100 from her father, and her cash allowance from
Lord Hunsdon had been £40 a year, which would have represented only £400 in
total, most of this sum would have come in jewels, gifts, and the dowry Hunsdon
provided. As Lord Hunsdon put it, he would give her enough to make her 'seem
well off' to the man who married her, if not quite as well off as she implied. She
was, however, clearly well off enough, from the late 1580s to around 1608, to
have the leisure to write complex plays without the pressures of trying to sell play
manuscripts!

It would not be a happy or a well-managed marriage. Over the period of a
decade, Alphonso Lanier would waste and squander her wealth – in bad land deals,
to finance his participation in overseas expeditions in search of treasure, and in a
number of other ways – until there was almost nothing left. He illustrates well the
profligacy and waste that are satirised in the plays. Around 1594, he tried to buy
up the rights to the property of fugitives who had fled the country – but ended
up spending over £100 trying in vain to claim their properties. By 1602 he was
involved in a lease with Sir Robert Wroth, a wealthy landowner with whom he
struck his biggest and most unsuccessful deal, using £300 from Amelia's estate to
buy land from Sir Thomas Knollys that was subsequently valued at only £50 a
year. He tried for the next several years to sell it on for £500, but was unable to find
a buyer. So Amelia was right in her claim that he squandered her estate and drove
them into poverty. By 1602, she would need to take up work as a tutor in a noble
household, and would later turn her hand to teaching at school (see Appendix 10).

It has often been observed that many of the plays are obsessed with marriage,
but that the resulting marriages are problematic – Desdemona's marriage, for

instance, is unconsummated, while the marriages at the end of *As You Like It* or *Twelfth Night* do not even happen.[5] Is it possible that some of the unhappy marriages shown in the Shakespearean plays are autobiographical? Amelia, or Emelia (the Elizabethans did not have standardised spelling), is not a common name. Yet it appears an unusual number of times in Shakespeare's plays. In her paper 'Shakespeare's Emilias and the Politics of Celibacy', Dorothea Kehler noted the 'special associations' of this name in the Shakespearean plays, where it 'recurs for women whose legal or emotional status as wives is ambiguous or who are involved with another's failing marital relationship, or who foresee their own unhappiness as wives'. The name appears eight times in nearly a quarter of the plays, including *Othello*, *The Comedy of Errors*, *The Winter's Tale*, *Two Noble Kinsmen* and in a male form in *Titus Andronicus*. That rate of appearance is fifty times more than would be expected if the name reflected a random distribution. From the sheer number of appearances, it looks as if Amelia was indeed writing herself into the plays, and depicting an unhappy marriage. We do know that in 1595 she was investigating the Talmud for regulations on how to dissolve marriage vows in a Jewish marriage, because the section would be used in the composition of *A Midsummer Night's Dream*.

One obvious example is the character of Emilia in *Othello*, which as we will see was substantially strengthened by the 163 extra lines that were added to the 1622 quarto of the play. Her unhappy marriage to the deceitful Iago forms one of the subplots of the play. On the other hand, she is not defined by that marriage, and Richard B. Zacha, in his article 'Iago and the Commedia dell'Arte', suggests that her position of watching the play, and her apparent foreknowledge of what is to happen, implies that she almost seems to be the author of what transpires. Furthermore, her dropping of the handkerchief at almost the centre point of the play means she functions almost as a designer of its architecture. A similar point is made by Solomon Iyasere, in his article 'The Liberation of Emilia', who sees Emilia as an unusual heroic figure, speaking up for what she really believes and (like Amelia Lanier) espousing feminist values against male opposition.

Another example is *Shrew*, where the central dynamic is again that of a wife wanting to speak freely against male opposition, which defines her as a shrew. Amelia had begun a 1,500-line earlier version, *A Pleasant Conceited History Called The Taming of a Shrew* (published in 1594), before she evidently visited Italy in late 1593. It was a major innovation, as Eric Sams observes: 'The first modern comedy in English.' It involves the comic device of masters and servants changing roles found in the contemporaneous *The Comedy of Errors* and *The Two Gentlemen of Verona*. It possibly incorporates input from Greene and Marlowe – or is written to give that impression of collaboration – for it reworks elements of Greene's *Menaphon* and *Orlando Furioso*, Marlowe's *Tamburlaine*, and the unpublished *Dr Faustus*. It is set in Athens, and in it Christopher Sly calls the Lord Simon 'Sim', which indicates that the playwright is drawing upon the 1530 Italian translation of Plautus's play *Mostellaria*, which is also set in Athens and includes an old man referred to as Sim. An intermediate version, which included some elements of *The Taming of the Shrew*, was in existence in 1593 (because it is quoted then by Anthony Chute and in *A Knack to Know a Knave*). This intermediate version seems to have been a step towards evolving the text of *Shrew* in the First Folio, which was printed using the old licence for the earlier version, indicating that they were considered to be different versions of the same play. At the end, Kate gives a long monologue about the creation of the world, derived from Guillaume de Salluste's *La Création du Monde ou Première Semaine* (1578), which includes a reflection on Adam and Eve, in which Adam's authority is satirised.

This early version is seemingly autobiographical; it is about a man who woos a wife because she is well off, and a rapid marriage occurs. It is an account of an old man Alphonso and his daughters Kate, fair Emilia, and Philema. Writing about it in 1596 in his book *The Metamorphosis of Ajax*, theatre-lover Sir John Harrington refers to the way in which the play has 'made a number of us so perfect' in taming their shrewish wives. It was while revising this play, setting it in Italy and renaming it *The Taming of the Shrew,* that Amelia would add in aspects of the *commedia* and would change the names of the characters. Emilia, daughter of Alphonso (her husband's name), disappears and is subsumed by Kate, now daughter of Baptista (her father's name). Kate's sister is no longer Philema but Bianca, a literal blank (Bianca comes from the Latin *blancus*, meaning blank or white). Excluding the blank, the names give us her true identity as Emilia daughter of Baptista (Bassano), the name under which she had been baptised. Beginning in the earliest, 1,500-line, version, Kate most oddly becomes treated as if she were a falcon being tamed. 'Kate' was the name of a famous falcon of the period and was owned by Henry, Lord Berkeley, whose son married Lord Hunsdon's granddaughter. On marriage Amelia took on her husband Alphonso's surname Lanier – a French word meaning 'falcon', or more precisely, according to the *Oxford English Dictionary*, a French word meaning a species of falcon in countries bordering the Mediterranean, a word that is also found in Middle English with the spellings lanier, lanner, laner, etc. She literally became Mrs Falcon. So the *Shrew* plays tell the story of Amelia, daughter of Baptista, who gets unwillingly connected to A. Lanier (Falcon); it is a kind of literary signature, of which we shall see more later.

So we can look at *The Taming of the Shrew* in some ways as autobiographical. It is the story of a strong, independent woman married against her will to a rather crude man determined to control her and make her obedient, against whom she uses her gifts of wit, language and intelligence, in the end becoming an actor, pretending to be tamed for a man who does not know the difference. In the early play, however, the Christopher character is not parodied as Mr Shakespeare, since this is before the formation of the Chamberlain's Men.

In 1593 we now come to one of the most critical junctures in the life of the author of the Shakespearean plays. Quite a number of those plays, for example

The Comedy of Errors (1594), no longer exist in their original form because they only appeared in the First Folio, by which time they had probably undergone extensive revision. We can only definitely assess the skills of the young playwright through the evidence of the two long poems, and of three plays for which we have a datable early text – one history play, one tragedy and one comedy. *The First Part of the Contention* (widely recognised as an early version of *Henry VI, Part 2*), *Titus Andronicus*, and *The Taming of a Shrew* all appeared anonymously in print in 1594.

The *Shrew* play is described as having been performed by Pembroke's Men, and *Titus* by a combination of Derby's, Pembroke's and Sussex's Men. No performance information is provided for *Contention*. None of these plays shows any significant in-depth knowledge of Italy, where the Bassano family evidently visited in September 1593 (a few months after Marlowe's death in May 1593). The names that appear in the *Shrew* play (and its later rewriting as *The Taming of the Shrew*) show Amelia's hand, and mean that it must have been composed after her marriage in October 1592 but before she left for Italy in September 1593: the entry on the Stationer's Register was made on 6 May 1594. Amelia's hand in *Titus Andronicus* is also clear, because of the characters Emillius and Bassianus, and it must have been largely complete by the time it was entered on the Stationer's Register on 2 May 1594. Both plays were presumably registered because they would form part of the repertoire of the newly formed Lord Chamberlain's Men.

In his essay 'The Influence of Marlowe on Shakespeare', Eric Sams describes this entire period as one in which the Shakespearean author experimented with the parody, imitation and quotation of Marlowe in developing the emerging Shakespearean style. The collaboration between Amelia and Marlowe may have begun in 1592 when, perhaps, a 341-word passage describing Joan's invocation of spirits was added by Marlowe to *Henry VI, Part 1*. Allison Gaw, in *The Origin and Development of Henry VI, Part 1*, suggests that Marlowe's contribution was even more extensive. All of the *Henry VI* plays employ Marlowe's dramatic depictions of victory and success, capturing the heights of heaven or dramatic failure.

In *Titus Andronicus*, although Marlowe possibly designed the extensive Marlovian allegorical subplot concerning the Roman–Jewish war, his influence upon the verse is limited. As Robert Logan notes in his book *Shakespeare's Marlowe*, the character of Aaron in *Titus* is derived in part from the figure of Barabas in *The Jew of Malta*, while Aaron's first major speech ('Now climbeth Tamora Olympus' top') echoes *Dr Faustus*, who 'Did mount him up to scale Olympus top'. The short 1,500-line play *The Taming of a Shrew*, on the other hand, was written while Amelia was still deeply under Marlowe's influence, but before she had learnt to incorporate his style, and simply borrowed forty-eight lines from Marlowe in sixteen places, especially from *Tamburlaine* and *Dr Faustus*. For instance, 'the centre of my soule whose sacred beauty hath enchanted me' (*The Taming of a Shrew*, 4, 52–6) was adapted directly from 'no Centre of my soule, Her sacred beauty hath enchanted heaven' (*Tamburlaine, Part 2*, 3051–7). Not enough research has been done to know if the echoes of Marlowe and Greene reflect their collaboration or the playwright's imitation of their style.

We must therefore see Amelia in the seven-month period from October 1592 to May 1593 as going through a series of major life transitions: the end of her relationship with Lord Hunsdon, her expulsion from court, her unhappy marriage, the birth of her baby boy, and the murder of her lover and mentor. Despite having worked with Marlowe for over a year, her plays were still not very good – only in a few places does the quality of *The Taming of a Shrew* match those of the scenes it would eventually be turned into. It would have been Amelia's travel in Italy and her experience of the *commedia* that enabled her to take the next step in her development as a playwright.

A good writer can write a tempest without ever going to sea, and there have been many attempts to identify purely literary sources of the storm described in *The Tempest*. But it certainly does no harm to note an occasion when the author may have experienced one. More importantly, as we have noted before, when the question at hand is a matter of *knowledge* rather than *imagination*, then experience, either first-hand or through reading or conversation, is an absolute requirement. The likely visit to Denmark would have provided the experience of living through a tempest. Amelia could well have accompanied Lord Willoughby on his voyage to Denmark in July 1582, when she was thirteen years old. It had been a terrible voyage, as Peregrine Bertie reported in a letter to Sir Francis Walsingham (now available in the Report of the Historical Manuscripts Commission in the British Library, where I was amazed to find it):

> Iff misfortune of tempest had not spoyled my second shippe wherein my stuff and necessaries was, breaking har topmast and driving her to sutche a leake as she and har company was in danger, besides contynuall winds against us ... we have no occurrences of importance save only of pirates mutche daily complained on.

It could well have been this personal experience of living through a tempest and observing how the boatswain and seamen dealt with it that Amelia vividly recalled many years later, and which she would so vividly reflect in her play that some would think the author had to have been a professional seaman.

Furthermore, accompanying Lord Hunsdon as he sailed up the coast to Berwick Castle would have given her the unusual knowledge of how princes are welcomed on board ships of the royal navy, knowledge she demonstrates in *Antony and Cleopatra*. Finally, her passage to Italy would have given her experience of merchant shipping. Alexander Falconer, in his book *Shakespeare and the Sea*, has shown that familiarity with both kinds of shipping is demonstrated in the plays, together with knowledge of seamarks and sea buoys. Amelia stayed for a while in the household of the Countess of Cumberland, who was very interested in navigation, and Lord Hunsdon's daughter Katherine was married to Charles Howard, the Lord Admiral.

Travel to Italy: 1593

Amelia's baby boy, Henry, was born in January 1593. As soon as she had recovered from the pregnancy, she would have left the baby with his nurse, as was the Elizabethan custom. Because her marriage was intolerable and because London was in the middle of a plague outbreak – 10,675 people, or about 5 per cent of the population, would die between December 1592 and December 1593 – she seems to have left for Italy as soon as she could.

For pleasure-seeking tourists, Venice was the capital of Europe, known for the delicacy of its entertainments, the beauty and pomp of the city and a superfluity of delights. Nashe described it in his *Unfortunate Traveller* (1594) as 'the Paradise of Earth and the Epicure's heaven' from which one may bring various arts, including 'the art of atheism … the art of epicuring, the art of whoring'. Visitors found that the pleasures and diversions of the city were a sure way to empty their pockets. Apart from minor drawbacks like stinking canals and vicious ferrymen at the Rialto Bridge, it was a city of art and architecture at the peak of its glory. Religious ceremonies were celebrated with great pomp and magnificence, as were the feast days that glorified the myth of the city. At carnival, everyone enjoyed three days of masked dancing and festivity. The loveliest masquerades were held, in which people were able to assume any sort of disguise and enjoyed a very great liberty. Women were even free to dress in men's clothes if they chose. In his book *The City and Republic of Venice* (1699), de Saint-Didier would later write that

> the liberty of Venice makes everything authentic, for whatsoever the life is, or religion one professes, provided you do not talk, or attempt anything against the State or the nobility, one may be sure to live unmolested.

Now 600 years old, Venice was a city of small squares full of entertainments. The streets were largely safe and the congested canals, packed with passing ships and 5,000 gondolas, each with their little shelter in the middle, offered a form of constant public theatre. In the Palazzo Ducale acrobats would practice their human pyramids, and in front of St Mark's a floating circular 'theatre of the world' (*teatro del mondo*) had been moored. It would be towed up and down the Grand Canal, and could host performances at different places in the city.

Amelia's stay in Italy would influence the whole of her writing. On the one hand it contributed pieces of background information, like the Venetian shoe styles or *chopins* that she mentions in *Hamlet*, the gondola in *As You Like It*, the correct language to describe Venetian officials, and obscure knowledge that provided local colour, such as the length of the 'Lombardy mile' and her understanding of the unique Venetian calendar, the *More Veneto*. But of greater importance is that it enabled her to go to the theatre and gain first-hand experience of the *commedia dell'arte*. On leaving court she would write no more court history plays for several years. Instead, she turned her attention to something much nearer home: domestic life reflected in Italian marriage comedies and a servant comedy, *The Two Gentlemen of Verona*.

The records show that three of the Bassanos, Arthur, Edward and Andrea, took a leave of absence from court in September 1593. Since this was a plague year, it is most likely that they travelled to Venice – which the Bassanos frequently visited and where for a long time they owned a house – and stayed in Italy for the next three months or so. Although no travel authorisations have been found, Amelia most likely went with them. If so, it would have been on this trip that she visited the little town of Bassano and saw there the fresco that she used in *Othello*, and experienced all the things that would be reflected in the quarter of the plays that are oddly set in Italy, and which, even more oddly, unlike the average English drama set in Italy, show remarkable geographical accuracy.

7

Amelia, a Poet in Exile: 1594–1610

The co-author of the definitive biography of the Bassano family, Dr David Lasocki, has concluded that 'the circumstances of Amelia's life, the knowledge she could have picked up from them, and aspects of her own writings all fit numerous features of the plays well'. That extraordinary fit begins in the history of the Bassano family and Amelia's life at court, and then continues with the evidence of her own writings. Similarly, Dr Andrew B. Harris, an award-winning theatre historian who formerly chaired the Theatre department at Columbia and two other universities, concludes that the present research provides 'fascinating evidence that the poet Amelia Bassano Lanier had a hand in crafting what we know as Shakespeare's plays'.

Exile from court must have been one of the most traumatic experiences of Amelia's life, as her status changed in a few weeks from a kind of princess to a very ordinary housewife. It was a decline and fall the she would reflect on for the rest of her life. It is perhaps no coincidence that the work of another poet in exile, Ovid's *Metamorphoses*, was used as a model to create *Venus and Adonis*, published in 1593. It is an exile that would specifically be alluded to in *As You Like It*, where Amelia's lookalike Touchstone the *basanos* (Greek), is exiled from court to live among the goats in the way that 'the most capricious poet, honest Ovid was among the Goths'. There is perhaps an allusion here to Amelia's challenge to the hypocrisy that a nobleman's mistress is chaste. Beneath the pastoral surface there is much more than meets the eye, and as Charles Nicholl notes there is at least a triple pun: Ovid's name means 'sheep' in Latin, his chastity or 'honesty' was unlikely, since he was exiled for writing a sex manual, and he is capricious or lascivious, from a Latin term meaning goat.

This transitional period of her life with Lord Hunsdon, her affairs, and even her work as a playwright may be hinted at in another poem, published anonymously in 1594. It requires a little background, however.

If we were to flash forward fifteen years in the future, in 1610–11 Amelia Lanier would publish her book of poetry, *Salve Deus,* under her own married name. There her cast of characters includes Juno, Pallas, Venus, Lucrece, Susan(na), Rosamund, Cleopatra, Cresed, a phoenix and King Solomon. Her main poem, also titled 'Salve Deus', is in some ways a rewriting of Shakespeare's *The Rape of Lucrece*, which it even quotes. It is a long satirical parody of the Crucifixion, explicable because she came from a family of Marrano Jews, who had migrated from Venice sixty years before. To recapitulate, their family symbol was apparently a rabbit's foot, and their family home was in Spitalfields, just opposite the theatre district. In her youth, as we have seen, she had been a member of the Willoughby family, having been brought up by Susan Bertie, Countess of Kent and sister to the Lord Willoughby. Thereafter she had become mistress to the queen's illegitimate half-brother, the Royal Falconer and Lord Chamberlain, Lord Hunsdon, and lived with him in his palace, Old Somerset House. There she enjoyed an allowance of forty pounds a year until in 1592 she became pregnant. She was thrown out of court, and was married off to a man named Lanier, a French word meaning 'falcon' (as noted before, according to the *Oxford English Dictionary*). Her book of poetry shows the ability to handle multiple poetic styles, and is dedicated to the noble ladies of England and to her former patron the Countess of Cumberland, whom she describes as 'the Articke Starre that guides my hand'.

However, fifteen years before, in 1594, another, more mysterious, book of poetry was published, under an allonym, by an unknown author.[1] The cast of characters also includes Juno, Pallas, Venus, Lucrece, Susan(na), Rosamund, Cleopatra, Cresed, a phoenix and King Solomon. Titled *Willobie His Avisa*, it was also a rewriting or parody of *The Rape of Lucrece,* and is the first work to refer to it. It appears to be largely an account of the sexual adventures of a married woman, 'Avisa', but also contains a peculiar theological satire in which Avisa, together with two other birds, ascends into the 'christal' skies like a new Trinity. It makes several Hebrew puns, and quotes Italian proverbs. It also has the most complex frontispiece of any book published that year, which is partly based on an Italian engraving and incorporates two large rabbits. Avisa is described as living near or in the theatre district. She is also, through a pun, an 'a-visa', an unseen bird, associated with a member of the Willoughby family. One of her lovers is an elderly prince, who in canto ten refers to her as a 'haggard hawk', and offers her forty angels 'to begin' if she will live in his palace. The book employs multiple poetical styles, is dedicated to a community of women and concludes with a poem that mentions 'the Articke pole that never moves', like the 'ever-fixed pole' and its guardians in Ursa Minor in *Othello* (2.1.15).

These points of resemblance between the two books suggest that 'Avisa' was really Amelia, and that she actually wrote the earlier volume as a kind of sexual comedy, or perhaps a comic sex diary. This is confirmed in several ways. Firstly the poem hints that the true name of the lady rhymes with Avisa, as Amelia does to some extent. Secondly, the poem implies a relationship to Diana, noting that 'we to Diana gave the maid' and referring to her as 'Dian's nymph'. Diana is shown nude, bathing with her ladies, on the frontispiece. The name of Diana's priestess was Emilia according to Richard Edwards's play *Palamon and Arcite* (1566), and Abbess Emilia served a religious institution at Ephesus, the site of Diana's famous temple in *The Comedy of Errors*. When we are told that Avisa has a sire who is the 'mayor' of the town, the term 'sire' can refer to a nobleman, and 'mayor' can simply refer to a high official. We are told that on the house where she lives hangs the badge of England's saint, namely the flag of the cross of St George, which hung on every royal palace, presumably including Old Somerset House.

The significance of Amelia Bassano Lanier being the author of *Avisa* as well as the title character lies in what else we know about her. Avisa was acquainted with an 'old player', W. S., who appears in the poem as a rather unpleasant character that expresses interest in her sexually, and is conceivably William Shakespeare, then aged thirty, who would just have joined the Chamberlain's Men. The three-way dialogue is modelled on the contest for the soul by a good and evil angel from the mystery plays. It also contains echoes of the conversation between Olivia and Malvolio, and between Margaret and the Earl of Suffolk in *Henry VI, Part 1*.

The poem also could imply, right from the outset, that she was writing for the North London theatres. Canto one states that Avisa's tongue 'should allure' and 'draw great numbers to the field', meaning the 'playing places in the field' as the two theatres in Finsbury Fields in Shoreditch were known. This is also the theatre complex that is indicated when the poem mentions the two brothers renting part of a former castle (monastery) near a holy well. This suggests Avisa's activity not only as a poet but as an 'invisible' (a-visa) playwright drawing crowds at the playhouses.

That those plays were early Shakespearean works is consistent with other evidence. We have no record of where *The First Part of the Contention* (an early acting version of *Henry VI, Part 2*) was performed, but its companion piece, *The True Tragedie of Richard Duke of Yorke* (*Henry VI, Part 3*), was performed by the Pembroke's Men, who did work at the Shoreditch Theatre in 1591–2. The close association between the parts implies that the earlier play was performed there, and it is known that this is where they performed *The Taming of a Shrew*, an early version of *The Taming of the Shrew*. So I agree with Andrew Gurr's suggestion that Pembroke's Men were active at the Theatre and the Curtain in 1591 under Richard Burbage. Evidently it was these early versions of *Henry VI* which attracted unusually 'great numbers': Nashe would later estimate that *Henry VI, Part 1* performed at the Rose was seen by over 10,000 people.

The link between Amelia's poem and the Shakespearean plays is suggested by several other clues. Firstly, *Avisa* was published in 1594, at the same time as the *Shrew* play was, which also centres upon a woman who can be identified as Amelia Bassano; she is also referred to in falconry language as a 'haggard', she is remarkably strong willed, and she consistently rejects a suitor for her hand. We may also see *Willobie His Avisa* as a remarkably theatrical poem – it was indeed the model for William Haughton's play, *Englishmen for My Money*, which was the first city comedy.

Specific words in *Willobie His Avisa* anticipate Shakespeare. For example, the three references in *Willobie* to 'labours lost' are among the earliest usage in print of this expression, other usages appearing only in five sources, and it would appear four years later in the title of a Shakespearean play. *Willobie*'s term 'nature's frame' had only been used before in print by four writers, but appears six years later as 'frugal nature's frame' in *Much Ado About Nothing* (1.5.51) and 'Nature hath fram'd' (*The Merchant of Venice*, 1.1.51). Next, *Willobie* refers to 'Lavine land' and declares in canto 47 that Avisa

> ... is no saint, she is no nonne
> I think in time she may be wonne.

Henry VI, Part 1 has 'She's beautiful, and therefore to be wooed; She is woman, and therefore to be won.' *Titus Andronicus* describes the character Lavinia in similar language, concluding that she is 'loude' or lewd:

> Shee is a woman, therefore may be woode,
> Shee is a woman, therefore may be woonne
> Shee is *Lauinia* therefore must be loude
>
> Quarto, 2.1

Willobie also makes a reference to Josephus's book on the Jewish–Roman War – so important for all the plays – with the uprooting of the mandrake, or 'Baras root', which parallels the uprooting of the mandrake in *Romeo and Juliet*, which was written in 1595.

Furthermore, in *The Merchant of Venice*, written in 1596, the order of Portia's suitors is identical to those in *Willobie His Avisa*. The play takes Avisa's five different suitors and simply expands or 'bombasts' the list to turn it into Portia's nine suitors.

Near the top of Avisa's list of suitors was the Italian *cavaliere* or cavalry officer, called Cavaliero. Toward the top of the list in *The Merchant of Venice* he reappears split into two separate characters, a horsey Italian prince from Naples and a horse-loving Frenchman, Monsieur le Bon (*The Merchant of Venice*, 1.2.38–52). At the very bottom of Avisa's list was the *Italo-Hispalensis* man, whose name indicates he has affiliations with Italy and Spain (specifically Seville). He also would be split into two characters at the bottom of Portia's list, namely the Italian Lord Bassanio (*The Merchant of Venice*, 1.2.110), and the Spaniard, Prince Arragon. Immediately above the last character on Avisa's list of suitors was DH *Anglo-Germanus*, whose place on Portia's list would be taken by the German nephew of the Duke of Saxony (*The Merchant of Venice*, 1.2.80). He would be preceded on Portia's list by the only two Anglos, namely a Scottish lord and the English Baron Falconbridge (*The Merchant of Venice*, 1.2.63), who is a proper picture of a man but no conversationalist. These two men had been expanded out of the single Anglo on Avisa's list, namely the 'olde' 'Courtier', an English nobleman of 'riper years', who had a princely palace and offered her forty pounds a year to win her before her marriage.

That this elderly nobleman is a reference to Lord Hunsdon is confirmed in two ways in *The Merchant of Venice*. Firstly, his name is Falconbridge. Similar to its use in *King John*, this puns on Lord Hunsdon being Keeper of the Royal Falcons. Secondly, he was also indeed a kind of Scottish Lord, since he was warden of the Scottish Marches and Governor of Berwick Castle. Since *The Merchant of Venice* confirms that Lord Hunsdon is this elderly courtier, this means Avisa was definitely Amelia. She did indeed live with him (for around a decade), on an allowance of forty pounds a year, and was evidently writing plays for the public playhouses in the field.

From Princess to Housewife

We come now to a series of snapshots of Amelia's life from the age of twenty-four, in the working-day world. She was living outside the court, in an unhappy marriage, responsible for managing a household, and, when she did not have to work in tutoring and teaching in order to make some money, she devoted her lonely spare time 'in sorrow's cell', as she put it, to writing. We will touch on the dynamics of her relationship with Mr Shakespeare, the likelihood that Lord Hunsdon probably did not understand the deeper allegories, and begin to explore the relationship between the poetry published under her own name and the Shakespearean works.

Since the age of seven, Amelia had lived in a branch of the Tudor aristocracy where conversations were about politics and government, about statesmanship, war and alliances, and grand ideas. This experience gave her the raw material for the early plays. The personality of Lord Hunsdon, the Royal Falconer and bastard son of Henry VIII, who had been involved in the Dissolution of the Monasteries, coloured that other bastard that was likewise shown as sacking the monasteries in *King John*. Lord Hunsdon's accounts of his battles against the Percys in the Northern Rebellion of 1569 similarly coloured the descriptions of battles against the Percys 200 years earlier that appeared in *Henry IV, Part 1*. Young playwrights write about the subjects and issues that are important in their environment, about which they have knowledge and expert informants, which explains why Amelia's early plays were about court intrigue and the origins of the Tudor dynasty. Living in the households of two different generals – one the Ambassador to Denmark and a general of the troops fighting for Henry of Navarre (Lord Willoughby), and the other Lord Hunsdon, she had acquired the specific insight into generalship and international relations that appears in *Hamlet*, *Macbeth* and *Love's Labour's Lost*. Hunsdon was not only the general in charge of London and informal Ambassador to Scotland, he was also an occasional diplomatic emissary to King

Charles IX of France and later to the Duc d'Alençon and d'Anjou, brother of Marguerite, Queen of Navarre. In 1591, with Lord Howard of Effingham and Lord Buckhurst, he negotiated a peace treaty with France, precisely the time when details of the conflict in France were being used to write *Henry VI, Part 1*.

Amelia had also lived for a decade as one of the small number of women at court, which was an erotically charged environment of constant flirtation, innuendo, and illicit sex. Together with Lord Hunsdon's broad vocabulary of sexual obscenities, this had equipped her with an extensive sexual vocabulary, including, for instance, over 100 synonyms for vagina. But now in a flash that was all over. It was a major life transition.

In 1592, instead of the carefree life of luxury she had enjoyed at court, Amelia became a housewife. She bitterly resented this change in her fortunes. The sexual freedoms and independence that were possible for women at the licentious Elizabethan court (and that are supported in the feminism of the *Salve Deus* collection) would not have sat well within any traditional Elizabethan marriage. As Judith Cook observed of the women in the plays, 'one of the most striking qualities is their independence'. Women are especially unruly, and have a greater presence, in the plays where the author was not confined to historic sources, such as *Love's Labour's Lost* and *The Merry Wives of Windsor*. It is also notable that two of the early plays, namely *Romeo and Juliet* and *The Taming of a Shrew*, both deal with the problematic consequences of an arranged marriage. Both were written within a year or two of Amelia's arranged marriage, 'for colour', to Alfonso. Further, in her book *Broken Nuptials in Shakespeare's Plays*, Carol T. Neely emphasises how many of the plays are characterised by what she calls 'broken nuptials'. These include parodies of weddings, irregular weddings, premature or postponed consummations, mock deaths and other forms of disruption. In addition the women use trickery, escapes, bed-tricks, wit and disguises in order to escape male commands and control.

Not only do the plays after 1593 turn to Italian marriage comedies, the amount of cooking imagery in the plays increases. This is the time when Amelia would have had to manage her own household of servants. Because of the coincidence of names in the 1,500-line *The Taming of a Shrew* and the 3,000-line *The Taming of the Shrew*, there is reason to suppose that some aspects of the households depicted is autobiographical. Furthermore, as Caroline Spurgeon has observed, the plays demonstrate an 'extraordinarily close' knowledge of 'different kinds of cooking – the kneading, baking, boiling, mincing, stewing, frying, stuffing, larding, basting and distilling ...' *Troilus and Cressida* alone refers to twelve different kinds of cooking processes. Furthermore, the plays show what would for a male playwright be a most unusual interest in sewing and mending, in babies and children, and in everyday household tasks, all of which the mistress of the household had to supervise. Overall, as Spurgeon notices, the plays contain an unusually large number of images of housework ranging from washing glass to tidying up cracked china, preparing food, seeping, sewing, scouring, turning and remaking clothes and so on.

We may see in these references something of Amelia's concerns in managing a household, quite possibly of unruly servants who would have been rather different from the elite royal servants she had commanded in Old Somerset House.

The plays are remarkable for their interest in medicine, but as recent work in the social history of medicine has shown, in Elizabethan London medical care was mostly done in the household and it was the responsibility of the mistress of the house. Recent studies of medicine books show that elite women in particular frequently developed medical expertise and were often involved in neighbourhood and charity-based medicine. A recent essay by Seth Stein LeJacq, 'The Bounds of Domestic Healing; Medical Recipes, Storytelling and Surgery in Early Modern England', notes that women owned manuscript books of traditional remedies, which were the first place that members of the household would turn. Domestic medicine even included minor surgery, involving everything from a cure for severe burns to the head, to one for being run through with a sword, or healing a thumb almost severed at the joint. Mostly ingredients were available in gardens or apothecary shops, and were expected to cure everything from plague to smallpox. The mistress of a house would be expected to have skills in distillation and the preparation of these medicines. So the medical knowledge in the plays might be expected, on the face of things, to reflect a woman's technical knowledge of housekeeping.

Mr Shakespeare, Play Broker (1594)

If Amelia returned from Italy with the other Bassanos, the musicians Andrea, Edward and Arthur Bassano (who took a leave of absence from court from September 1593 to March 1594), she would have returned to London at about the time Lord Hunsdon was making his decision to set up the duopoly of two permanent theatre companies: one at the Rose to perform mainly Marlowe's plays, which were immensely popular, and one, The Lord Chamberlain's Men, at The Theatre, who would be given rights to perform the Shakespearean plays. A year later, Mr William Shakespeare is first recorded as appearing on the scene in person, in an official document issued on 15 March 1595, referring to performances at Christmas time in 1594. This is the first and only reference to Mr Shakespeare in connection with the Chamberlain's Men that exists in Elizabethan court records and in modernised spelling. It reads as follows:

> To WILLIAM KEMPE, William Shakespeare and Richard Burbage, servants to the Lord Chamberlain, upon the (Privy) Council's warrant dated at Whitehall 15th March 1594, for two several Comedies or Interludes showed by them before

Her Majesty in Christmas time last part viz St. Stephen's Day and Innocents Day, 13 pounds, 6 shillings and 8 pence.

Public Record Office, Pipe Office, Declared Accounts No. 542, Folio 207b

The document is a warrant for payment for two performances at court on St Stephen's Day (26 December 1594) and Innocents Day (28 December) by the Chamberlain's Men, following their establishment in March 1594. Problematically, however, this document is not supported as it normally would be by a duplicate entry in the double-entry bookkeeping system. The entry is not in the treasurer's handwriting. The dates are also problematic, because on 28 December the company performing at court was the Admiral's Men, and that same day the Chamberlain's Men were performing *The Comedy of Errors* at Gray's Inn. This document is also known to have passed through the hands of the forger Collier, who put a great deal of energy into forging Shakespeareana when he couldn't find anything original.

If it is genuine, this is the first document to associate Mr Shakespeare with an acting company of any kind and also the first to call him 'Shakespeare' (the name that had previously appeared on the long poems). This is a rather sudden high-level appearance on the theatrical scene, since his name does not appear as an actor – in any spelling whatsoever – on the internal records of any of the previous playing companies that had trained the other actors for the Lord Chamberlain's Men. On the other hand, he may have been the writer/actor/manager of a small company, as recent research has suggested (see Appendix 13).

It is unlikely that Robert Greene's *Groats-Worth of Wit* obliquely alluded to him in 1592 as the 'upstart crow', and one of London's leading actors. It is much more likely Greene was again criticising Edward Alleyn, as shown by A. D. Wraight in her book *Christopher Marlowe and Edward Alleyn*, and in Daryl Pinksen's follow-on article 'Was Robert Greene's "upstart crowe" the actor Edward Alleyn?'. The references to the player thundering his verse and having acted in the role of Hercules make the identification with Alleyn very specific. Dying in poverty, Greene is protesting against a system in which playwrights get no residual royalties, and in which actors can become rich by repeating their words in a successful production.

Even if Greene's target had been William Shakespeare, hitherto unknown either as playwright or actor, he is not being conceived as a dangerous rival playwright who deserves Greene's deathbed invective. Rather he is being disparaged as an actor, who were known as crows, encompassing Aesop's crow who is a mimic, an actor dressed up in other birds' feathers; and Horace's crow, whose words are the words of others. Since this was a period when most plays were collaborative products, and were published anonymously if at all, and when their authorship was rarely of concern, Greene's point is not that the 'crow' was reciting plays that had been 'plagiarised', since *Henry VI, Part 1*, for instance, was not published. The main point is that the 'crow' was reciting the words of others, not his own – as Alleyn clearly was when he performed the speech from *Henry VI, Part 3*, to which Greene alludes, and which he had not written.

By 1594 Shakespeare was now thirty years old, and this warrant records his appearance to collect money with two well-known and established actors, each with between five and ten years of documented acting experience. All appear as members of The Chamberlain's Men. Collecting money, at least, is something we know Mr Shakespeare was good at. It is compatible with the many other existing documents detailing his obsession with money. However, he probably would not have appeared in the capacity of a playwright since he had no such public reputation at the time; none of the plays had appeared with the name 'Shakespeare' on them, and no literary commentators had suggested that he was the author of any of the plays that had so far either been performed or appeared in print.

Indeed, even during the years 1594 to 1597, while Mr Shakespeare was, by inference, a member of the newly-founded Lord Chamberlain's Men, not once did any commentator of any kind suggest that he wrote any of the canonical plays. If it were not for the 1595 warrant, then the first unquestionable legal document to place Mr Shakespeare in theatrical circles would be one from 1596. It is a writ of attachment dated 29 November for a court case against William Shakspere – but oddly not as an associate of the Lord Chamberlain's Men at all. Remember, Lord Hunsdon had established a duopoly so that the Chamberlain's Men had Burbage's theatre in North London, and the Admiral's Men had the Rose Theatre on Bankside in South London. During the year 1596 the playwright was occupied with several plays – *A Midsummer Night's Dream*, *The Merchant of Venice*, *Richard II* and *King John* – which were being finalised and/or performed by the Chamberlain's Men. The acting company was also fully occupied in giving several court performances, in getting used to a new patron after the death of Lord Hunsdon, and in public performances of their repertoire at the North London theatres.

Yet most curiously in this 1596 legal case, William Shakespeare appears as an associate of Francis Langley, the goldsmith and gangster who was building the Swan Theatre. This was a different, rival, theatre on the South Bank, which would seat 3,000 people. It was described (and sketched) by a Dutch visitor Johannes de Witt in his *Observations on London* as the 'finest and biggest of the London amphitheatres'. On the other hand, the Lord Mayor described it as a hangout for 'thieves, horse-stealers, whoremongers, cozeners (confidence men), connycatching persons (swindlers), practisers of treason, and such other like'. We know a great deal about Langley, thanks to William Ingram's fine biography *A London Life in the Brazen Age; Francis Langley 1548–1602*. Like William Shakespeare, he was an active moneylender, and both he and his associates engaged in extortion. He used his government position as a clothing inspector to waylay those in the cloth business, to extort money and even to break into their houses. The 1596 law case

accuses 'Shakspere' and Langley of having threatened to murder the stepson of
William Gardiner, the Justice of the Peace who was supposedly responsible for the
law and order of Bankside, a dubious responsibility since it was largely composed
of brothels, taverns, theatres and bear-baiting parlours. In reality, Langley and
Gardiner were rivals, each seeking to get their share of the profits from the
various illegal activities of the theatre district. This law case does not suggest
that Shakespeare was an actor but rather, like Langley, a businessman, perhaps
involved in some of the side businesses associated with the Bankside theatres.

Supporting this association with Langley and the Swan Theatre is a document
now lost, but consulted by Edmond Malone, which shows that as of July 1596 Mr
'Shaksper' was actually living in the Bear Gardens area on the South Bank, quite
near to the new Swan Theatre. This in itself is strange, since it was so far from the
established North London theatre district where the Lord Chamberlain's Men were
based. In the first two years of building the company there, 1594–6, there would
have been substantial work for many hours each day. Yet to commute to where
The Chamberlain's Men were performing would have required crossing the river
in a water taxi and then a walk of several miles. It is true that by October 1596
he lived slightly closer, as a 'householder' in the parish of St Helen's Bishopsgate,
but this was still some distance from the theatres. Many of the other actors in
The Chamberlain's Men, like Burbage and Tarlton, are documented as living
actually in Shoreditch so as to be close to each other and their theatre workplace.
But there is no evidence that Mr Shakespeare did so – only an unsubstantiated
rumour gathered later by John Aubrey about what might have taken place nearly
a century previously. Moreover, after the building of the Globe, when residence
on the South Bank might have made sense, Mr Shakespeare was instead staying
with Christopher Mountjoy – well known for his side businesses in the sex trade.
In sum, if Shakespeare was fully committed as an actor and playwright in the Lord
Chamberlain's Men between 1594 and 1596, there would have been little reason
either for him to be living on the South Bank, or for his curious relationship with
the owner of the Swan Theatre – near where the Tate Modern is nowadays – since
this was a location in which the Chamberlain's Men were legally precluded from
performing.

The identification of Mr Shakespeare as a playwright would not occur until
1598, when the name 'Shakspere' would first appear on the cover of *Love's
Labour's Lost*, after which time literary commentators would quickly associate
his name with the other plays. However, in that same year, Mr Shakespeare
would evidently act in Ben Jonson's play *Every Man out of His Humour* (1598),
because when Jonson's collected works were published, Shakespeare is listed
as having done so. Yet significantly, this is a play that parodies Mr Shakespeare
as the country bumpkin Sogliardo, with the comic coat of arms and motto 'not
without mustard', and also as being a 'hobby horse', a kind of exterior trapping
presented to do tricks for the public, concealing the true creator underneath. This

is one of a handful of occasions in which Ben Jonson signalled his knowledge that Shakespeare had not written the plays credited to him. Our earlier review of Mr Shakespeare's access – or rather lack of access – to social networks and critical areas of knowledge suggests that Ben Jonson is exactly correct.

Conceivably, over this period from 1594 to 1598, Mr Shakespeare would have given the play scripts to members of the acting company. If he was Amelia's 'play broker', functioning as an intermediary to anonymously convey the plays to the playing company and ensure their production, it makes sense that he would have been so from the beginning of the company. The two long poems, *The Rape of Lucrece* and *Venus and Adonis*, had appeared a couple of years before under the name Shakespeare, which can be inferred to be Amelia's *nom de plume*, since, as discussed earlier, contemporary documents mentioned spear shaking as having connotations of Pallas Athena, the goddess of poetry and playwriting. Given the evidence presented that Shakespeare really cannot have written the canonical works attributed to him, and the evidence, some yet to be presented, that Amelia Lanier wrote them, it is likely that she found a theatre businessman who was baptised as Gulielmus (the Church Latin for William) Shakspere, and, out of over fifty known alternative spellings of his surname, persuaded him to henceforth employ the one that matched the long poems. Those poems would establish him as a credible poet who could take the risk of fronting these heretical plays – either because he did not know what they contained, or because he did know but was being paid so well that he was prepared to take the risk of being discovered. If he did knowingly take that risk then he showed himself to be very astute, as he was in many other financial matters, since he was of course never discovered and retired happily to enjoy his mansion. It is also possible that he was an existing actor/manager/playwright, either at the Bear Gardens or at a patron's private theatre company, and that he might have been looking for new plays to expand his repertoire (see Appendix 13).

One clue as to what Amelia may have been feeling about Mr Shakespeare at this time may be found in the account of Touchstone and William in *As You Like It* (*c.* 1600). The character Touchstone – a kind of stone for assessing gold – is *basanos* in Greek, and he is put through his purgation, which in Greek is also *basanos*. He has also been exiled from court and abandoned among the goats in the countryside. He is compared to Ovid among the Goths (3.3.7–9), who complained there was nobody to understand his poetry. Most important of all, he is very brilliant because he has a dry brain, he discusses the nature of poetry (3.3.14–17), and he is equated to a great poet whose work is not understood. In all these respects it is suggested that here we have a portrait of Amelia Bassano, writing as a poet in disguise, from exile, and whose work is not understood, because its allegories are not solved.

Most conclusively of all, Touchstone hates and mocks the rural clown character William, who through the references to fools and wise men, as well as to Arden, is identifiable as a contemporary parody of William Shakespeare. Indeed,

Touchstone/Basanos fills up William's empty 'cup' with rhetorical figures, and wants to kill him in 150 different ways. The allegory is really quite simple. We may conclude from this something of Amelia's barely hidden feelings towards the man who was brokering her plays to the world.

Many articles, such as the one by Eric Sams, 'Hamnet or Hamlet, That Is the Question', or Stephen Greenblatt's 'The Death of Hamnet and the Making of *Hamlet*', have reminded us that the play *Hamlet* is actually based on the Scandinavian character Amleth. They also point out that William Shakespeare had a son, who died aged eleven in 1596, and who had been named after a local tradesman in Stratford-upon-Avon, variously called Hamlet or Hamnet. From this it is assumed that the play was named after the boy, and this has frequently been seen as evidence that the play was necessarily written by the man we call William Shakespeare. However, the fact that the play happens to have the same name as Mr Shakespeare's son is not proof of anything. The fact is, 'Hamlet' is simply an anglicised version of Amleth, and the playwright generally kept the names of the main characters in the stories or plays from which the plays were constructed. However, if one were to make the argument that the name 'Hamlet' carries a biographical implication for whoever wrote the play, as many Stratfordian scholars do, then it suggests that Mr Shakespeare probably wasn't the author.

Granted, a serious artist follows the artistic logic of his or her work, wherever it should take him or her. And so whatever happens to Prince Hamlet will be whatever Shakespeare thinks *should*, or better *would*, happen to him, taking into account the sources. But let us pursue the argument that the author consciously named his hero after his deceased son, for whom he did not care enough to erect a tombstone on his grave. Is it plausible that the author, three years after the death of his son, would want to memorialise him on stage as an adult contemplating suicide, jumping in and out of the grave, and then being slaughtered? Similarly, although other plays do parody William as a clown and a fool, this play portrays Old Hamlet – who would therefore represent William himself – as deceased, a devil and in hell. Furthermore, the play depicts him as damned (1.5.76–7) because he is 'unhouseled' (he did not receive Last Communion) and he is 'unaneled' (he died without receiving the oil of the Last Rites). It seems extraordinarily unlikely that a presumed Catholic like William Shakespeare would want to depict himself on stage, in a play that his own theatre company would be performing, in a situation which, in the words of the play, really is 'horrible, most horrible'. On the other hand, the person who might be tempted to depict him and his son in this frankly cruel fashion, as a contemporary allegory, might well be the person whose plays he was fronting, and who wanted to kill him in 150 ways. It might very well reflect her resentment, and she appears to have left her signature on the play in another contemporary allegory, as we will now demonstrate.

Prince Hamlet mysteriously lies about the origin of the play within the play, *The Mousetrap*. He says an Italian woman set the events in the original story in motion. Her name, 'Baptista' (3.2.234), is also identified with the Player Queen in some of the original speech headings, for example on page 268 of the First Folio. While this is a very unusual name for a woman, it actually corresponds with the second name of 'Emilia Baptist', as in the baptismal records on 27 January 1569. Furthermore, as if to confirm her identity, *The Mousetrap* is oddly surrounded by the canon's two explicit references to recorder playing, an 'inclusio' of two references to playing on a pipe (3.2.70–1 and 285–63), which imply her family name. The reader simply has to put both facts together.

What Lord Hunsdon Knew

Since Lord Hunsdon was establishing the Lord Chamberlain's Men in March 1594 specifically to perform the Shakespearean plays, and since there is now very good reason to suppose that they were written by his long-term mistress, we must suppose that Hunsdon himself helped place Mr Shakespeare in the company. In that way, Hunsdon could offer the mother of his (presumed) child both time to write the plays, and a safe mechanism for getting them performed. After all, Lord Hunsdon was nearly seventy years old, and well aware he would not live much longer. He needed a mechanism that would allow Amelia to write and to publish. It was also, of course, a way to assure his theatre company of an excellent supply of material. That does not mean, however, that he necessarily understood the allegories in the plays: indeed the likelihood is that he did not.

In July 1596, barely two years after the Lord Chamberlain's Men had been created, Lord Hunsdon died. One of the last plays he saw was *A Midsummer Night's Dream*, and there is a particular reason to suppose that Hunsdon was not aware of the allegories in this play. There are features of this play which are important to consider before we approach the poetry that Amelia wrote under her own name.

A Midsummer Night's Dream was commissioned to celebrate Hunsdon's granddaughter's wedding. Elizabeth Carey was to be married on 19 February 1596. The queen herself would be in attendance at the festivities. Hunsdon's son, Sir George Carey (Elizabeth's father), now returned from governing the Isle of Wight, would commission the music from John Dowland and others, to be performed by Dowland's own small musical troupe. The play itself would be performed at the new Blackfriars Theatre next to the Carey mansion. The workmen had to convert seven great rooms of what was formerly part of Blackfriars' Monastery into a performance space. It was going to be a gorgeous space, with a proper roof and even artificial lighting so there could be evening performances.

On 19 February there would be a conjunction of the first night of the new moon and Venus. Amelia therefore gave *A Midsummer Night's Dream* exactly the same chronology. In the first few lines of the play, Theseus and Hippolyta remark that it is four nights away from the new moon, namely Valentine's Day, which Theseus later explicitly confirms (4.1.138–9). They are looking forward to their marriage – 'our nuptial hour' – which is due to take place on exactly the same day as the Carey wedding. Lord Hunsdon's granddaughter Elizabeth, that 'excellent adored wonder of high wit', as her flatterers called her, was fascinated by the interpretation of dreams. Well, this would be a dream to interpret, for sure – but rather more like the *Terrors of the Night* which Nashe had dedicated to her than the dreams she was probably used to decoding.

This contemporary allegory was very obvious, and people probably wondered if Hippolyta represented Elizabeth Carey, and if Theseus represented her husband Sir Thomas Berkeley, and if one marriage was an allegory of the other. Hunsdon was no deep thinker – he was well known as a blunt man of action. This much, however, he would have immediately picked up on. There is yet another possibility, that the parallel lovers to young Thomas and Elizabeth were actually those in the famous mechanicals' play within the play, which was derived from two accounts of the character 'Sir Thopas', itself a name similar to Sir Thomas. As Patricia Parker notes, Thisbe's comical attempts to kiss Pyramus through the chink in the wall is communicated in rather tame language that punningly conceals a most vivid sexual description: 'Oh wall [buttocks] … my cherry lips [labia] have often kiss'd thy stones [testicles], thy stones with lime [slime] and [pubic] hair, knit [sexually] up in thee.' Worse still, Pyramus and Thisbe compare their love to that of Shafalus for Procris (5.1.197–8) as recounted by Ovid. As the audience, for whom Ovid was required reading, would surely recall, Shafalus (Cephalus) kills Procris. Lord Hunsdon probably would not have been amused by parodies of his granddaughter's nuptials, even in a play within a play, in which both bride and groom get killed. Therefore the playwright would only have created such a parody if it was fairly certain that nobody would be able to identify such an allusion from the performance, but only when the play was eventually published, which would not take place for another four years. One also might wonder why the playwright even cared to create a play about a dream that contained a hostile parody of Elizabeth Carey, Lord Hunsdon' granddaughter, known for her interest in interpreting dreams. For Amelia however, watching young Elizabeth, only seven years younger than herself, receiving such a wealthy and advantageous match might well have triggered such a resentment.

There are other allegories and allusions. It was understandable that nobody would recognise that Amelia had borrowed from Guarini's new pastoral play *Il Pastor Fido*, recently published in London in an Italian edition (1591). But some people would probably have appreciated that the theme of Duke Theseus coming home to Athens and encountering two young men who are rivals was borrowed from Chaucer's *The Knight's Tale*. Of course, whereas in Chaucer's story the singing birds in the forest are spoken of as the 'throstle' (or song thrush), the sparrowhawk, popinjay, and missel thrush, in *Dream* Bottom refers to the first of these birds that bears the unfortunate Latin name *Turdus musicus* (appropriate for a Bottom, of course). To emphasise the point, the playwright adds a second bird not in Chaucer, the ousel-cock or blackbird, whose Latin name is *Turdus merula*. The Host in Chaucer says the knight's tale is not worth one turd. Bottom's tale, hilariously, has two, though again this is a point of detail that would have only been clear to the careful reader of the play. All of this says nothing about the deeper meanings of the play. It is a pastoral comedy, which we know as a genre designed to conceal deeper meanings. Deeper than all these local allegories, if we may call them that, is another clear parody of the Jewish–Roman war.

One of the world's leading Shakespeare scholars, Professor Patricia Parker, has already uncovered the fact that the characters have parallel religious identities – Peter Quince for St Peter (Peter is derived from 'rock', as in Jesus' 'On this rock I build my church', and Quince is from 'quoin' or 'cornerstone'), Puck for a kind of devil, Bottom/Pyramus for Jesus, and Thisbe for the Church, and the Wall as the partition that separates heaven from Earth. The wall or partition supposedly comes down to mark the day of Apocalypse, but instead of Jesus and the Church being reunited, as in Christian doctrine, in the play both parties die. In this way, the play within the play parodies not only the apocalyptic return of Jesus in the Book of Revelation, but also the day of resurrection that takes place immediately after the Crucifixion.

If we extend the logic of Parker's work, we quickly see that the character Oberon is an invisible, jealous lord – Yahweh. This is indicated by the fact that a number of his lines clearly come from the solar Psalms, where the point of reference is the Hebrew God. Oberon welcomes Aurora, the harbinger of dawn (5.1.387), claiming to have made sport with the morning's love, and to tread the groves until sunset, until the sun sets fiery red in the 'eastern gate' in the sea, offering fair blessed beams (3.2.388–95). This language represents the sun god – which Yahweh was, according to various passages in the Psalms. The verse makes very specific references to an 'eastern gate', which is turned to 'yellow gold' and presents Oberon as having a full solar day, from playing with the dawn to the setting sun. This alludes to Psalm 19, which refers to Yahweh's solar journey, his 'rising place at one end of heaven and his circuit reaches the other'. Further, the passage in Psalm 24 'lift up ye heads oh ye gates' (verse 7) was interpreted by Jews and early Christians as referring to the eastern gate of the temple, known as the golden gate or sun gate – the gate to which Oberon is referring. The whole fairy portion of the play is set in motion because Oberon had a little Indian boy whose mother was a 'Virgin votress', and Titania had stolen him away, crowned him with thorny flowers, and turned him into a changeling. For this, Oberon is fighting a war against the fairy queen Titania.

The parallels are not far to seek. The 'Indian boy' easily becomes the 'Iudean' or 'Judean' boy, if the 'n' is recognised as an inverted 'u,' a common typesetter's error that probably occurred in *Othello,* too, where in the two different versions of the play, Othello describes himself as being like the Indian or Iudean who threw away a pearl 'worth more than all his tribe'. The Judean boy that Titania stole from Oberon therefore invokes the Judean boy, or the figure of the Messiah, which the 'Flavian hypothesis' in radical New Testament scholarship suggests the Emperor Titus did indeed steal away from the Jews, by changing it into the literary character we know as Christ (see Appendix 8). Further paralleling Oberon's war against Titania, the Jews, and so presumably their god, were at war with Titus, alluding to the Jewish–Roman War. It appears that Shakespeare is echoing a very specific kind of mystery play, that described by Stephen K. Wright in his book *The Vengeance of the Lord; Medieval Dramatizations of the Destruction of Jerusalem*, concerning Titus's victory in the first-century Jewish–Roman War. It was the subject of many European dramatisations: in France it was *La Vengeance Jhesucrist* and in Germany it was the 3,000-line *Ludus de Assumptione Beatea Mariae Virginis*. J. J. M. Tobin, in his essay 'A Touch of Greene, Much Nashe and All Shakespeare', has listed various examples in Shakespeare's plays. Shakespeare is parodying this material as well as passion plays like *Corpus Christi*.

As Parker notes, Jesus himself appears in *A Midsummer Night's Dream* as the character Bottom who, a 'changeling' himself, changes into Pyramus – an established medieval allegorical figure for Jesus. He promptly gets crowned with thorns (thorny musk-roses stuck in his ears to make him scratch, in his case), and dies as if being crucified in a comic parody of the Passion. We know this also because the sequence is framed between two mentions of the word 'passion'. In the text in-between, the light disappears, he is stabbed in the side, and people refer to dice-playing, just as the soldiers cast lots that are traditionally represented in paintings as dice at the foot of the cross. Then, as in the Gospel of Matthew, spirits come out of their graves and dance around. Once it is pointed out, the elaborate nature of the parallels really allows for no other interpretation. The play is very largely an anti-Christian parody, as described in more detail in my article '*A Midsummer Night's Dream*: A Religious Allegory' and in various articles by Patricia Parker.

As we will shortly see, understanding the Crucifixion allegories in *A Midsummer Night's Dream* is extremely important in interpreting the major piece of verse that Amelia would write under her own name.

A Tutor in a House of Adventurers (1604)

The next date at which we can we can locate Amelia is from spring to autumn 1604. Now aged around thirty-four, there was a possibility of escaping, at least temporarily, from her difficult marriage. By now her son Henry was away from home doing his apprenticeship. So Amelia was able to leave her house in the rural village of Hackney, and to stay at the country mansion at Cookham Dean, near

Windsor, where Margaret, Countess of Cumberland, employed her to assist in the education of her young daughter Anne Clifford, later Countess of Dorset.

Apart from alchemy, the Countess of Cumberland's interests lay mainly in overseas exploration and shipping. It had been one of the interests she had shared with her now separated husband, the Earl of Cumberland, who had equipped four ships for a voyage to the South Seas in August 1586. That was indeed, as the plays put it, a 'whole south sea of discovery' (*As You Like It*, 3.3.206). He followed it with nine other voyages that he made himself, most of them to the West Indies, capturing a town in the Azores in 1589, and capturing the fort of Puerto Rico in 1598. At least one of his voyages, in 1592, was with Sir Walter Raleigh. And when the new Armada had been threatened in 1599, he was the person charged with building a barrier across the Thames to create a defensive bridge, with 1,500 musketeers ready to shoot at any Spaniards who might sail into the river.

When he was away on his expeditions, the Countess of Cumberland would have followed his progress on maps, which is why she ensured that two atlases were incorporated in the family portrait. She took a personal interest in map-making and would write to Lord Burghley to advocate the map-maker Augustin Ryther. One can imagine her looking at Hakluyt's map of 1598, which showed 'the augmentation of the Indies' (*Twelfth Night*, 3.2.75–7), the rhumblines stretching across the page like the lines in her face as she described the earl's various voyages. Inside the family, her nickname (which she hated) was the 'Protestant Countess of the Royal Navy'. That the earl had been flag captain to the Earl of Essex at the Battle of Cadiz in 1596 is perhaps how Amelia learnt the story of how the Spanish ship *Andrew* had run aground in the harbour and was easily captured (*The Merchant of Venice*, 1.1.27). As for Antonio, the merchant of Venice himself, he is sometimes believed to have been based on the trustful Michael Lock, who ended up in Venice ruined by Frobisher's voyage – and who was the brother-in-law to Anne Lock, the sonnet-writing sister to Stephen Vaughan, the Bassanos' next-door neighbour.

The interest in navigation and exploration in the plays grows stronger from 1600 onwards. In *Macbeth*, the witches refer to the 'master of the Tyger', which has sailed to Aleppo. This was perhaps *The Tiger*, a 600-ton vessel that the Earl of Cumberland had hired in 1592. In *Twelfth Night*, the 'pension of thousands to be paid from the Sophie' alludes to Sir Antony Shurley, who had just returned to England on board the ship *The Sophie*, claiming to have been given a pension by the Shah of Persia, and recounted his adventures in *A True Report of Sir Antonie Shierlies Journey* (1600). In other cases, the plays refer to reports in books on exploration, such as the men 'whose heads / Do grow beneath their shoulders' (*Othello* 1.3.145–6), as in the woodcut in Sebastian Munster's *Cosmographia* (1572). Guyana, the mysterious world described by Sir Walter Raleigh after his explorations, reappears as the country in which Gonzago dies in the first quarto of *Hamlet*. In *The Tempest*, Sycorax's god Setebos probably comes from the reprint of Richard Eden's *Decades of the New World* (1577), and there are other allusions to Peter Martyr's *De Orbe Novo* (1516) in the play.

The Tempest also shows a particular interest in the settlement of Virginia. Thomas Harriot's *A Briefe and True Report of the New Found Land of Virginia* (1588) provided background on how the natives perceived the Bible: it contained 'such virtue' that they would touch it, kiss it, and rub it over their bodies, something that may be echoed in Stephano's 'kiss the book'. Finally, the shipwreck in *The Tempest* appears to derive in part from reports of the *Sea Venture*, the 300-ton flagship of the Virginia Company, wrecked off the coast of Bermuda, an event referred to in a letter by William Strachey of 15 July 1609. The shipwreck of the *Sea Venture* would have been of particular interest to the Countess of Cumberland, because she was one of the shareholders in the Virginia Company, as well as being the major figure to whom Amelia would dedicate *Salve Deus*. Furthermore, at the time, Amelia's cousin Albiano Lupo was also a subscriber to the Virginia Company, and was planning to emigrate, which he did on *The Swan* in 1610. He became one of the earliest settlers at Elizabeth City, and was joined by William Lupo and his brother Philip, as well as his wife and children, who came over on *The George* in 1616. He was awarded 350 acres of land, which today lie under the city of Hampton, Virginia. Forty years later they would be joined by John Lanier, the grandson of Amelia's cousin-in-law Nicolas Lanier the first and his wife Lucretia Bassano.

The Fit with her Poetry

So far we have demonstrated Amelia's biographical fit on the key areas of knowledge that the playwright possessed. Now we begin the literary task of addressing the one remaining factor: the characteristics of the verse that she wrote under her own name, and its similarities to and differences from the Shakespearean canon. Over the next two chapters we will be examining the verse in terms of many different factors, namely: use of religious parody, inventiveness, imagery, classical references, compositional style, use of rare words, word clusters, use of sources, use of apocalypse, use of metaphors, dramatic structure, disjunctive style and aesthetics.

The first of Amelia's poems to be considered, which will be examined in the remainder of this chapter, is the Cookham poem, a 210-line poem written after February 1609 but recalling a time around 1604 in which Amelia was serving the Countess of Cumberland. This is a piece of pastorale that bears a number of similarities to *A Midsummer Night's Dream* and is also the first country house poem to have been written since Roman times. The Countess of Cumberland is also the principal figure to whom the entire *Salve Deus* volume was dedicated in 1610–11).

Cookham Dean was near the village of Cookham. It would have been easy to walk to Maidenhead, only 2 miles away, or to visit the royal town of Windsor. Amelia would have occasionally visited the town when Lord Hunsdon had to attend court in the spring, when the queen was at Windsor. Across all the plays there are references to a dozen places in the narrow corridor between London and Windsor, and these represent about 10 per cent of all the place names in the plays. However, it was after Amelia's stay in Cookham that the quarto of *The Merry Wives of Windsor* (1602) was expanded to include more detailed Windsor references, such as the one to Datchet Mead, the name of an obscure meadow where women bleachers washed and starched the laundry of upper-class households.

After Margaret Russell, Amelia's employer, had 'parted houses' with her husband, the wealthy Earl of Cumberland, she stayed during the separation in a rented country house in Cookham. The countess was engaged in her constant struggles against the patriarchal legal system to reclaim her property from her husband, and evidently needed help in raising her young daughter Anne. Amelia looked after the girl, perhaps until Mrs Taylor arrived as her formal governess, or perhaps specifically to train her in Italian. Amelia would recall affectionately the exercise of participating in young Anne's 'sports'. The countryside at Cookham could be lovely, and offered opportunities for riding, hunting, angling, wildfowling, bird snaring, archery, and all the other sports Amelia had enjoyed at court in her youth:

> The walkes put on their summer Liveries
> And all things else did hold similies;
> The Trees with leaves, with fruits, with flowers clad
> Embrac'd each other seeming to be glad.
>
> *The Description of Cooke-ham*

It is hard, however, to separate Amelia's influence on her young charge from that of the thirty-eight-year-old poet Samuel Daniel. He was appointed Anne's tutor at about the same time that historians have deduced that Amelia joined the household. As the author of many sonnets, a history of England, a poem on the War of the Roses and a tragedy, *Cleopatra* (1594), they would have had much in common. Indeed, it was during this time that Daniel somehow became aware of some of the details in Amelia's own manuscript of *Antony and Cleopatra*, because he used them to revise his own play *Cleopatra*, which would be included in his collected works published in 1607, when Amelia's play was still unpublished. Daniel had also travelled in Italy before becoming a tutor, and had strong theatrical interests. (He later became Master of the Queen's Revels, responsible for royal masques). The poems and plays in Daniel's collected works show that he was strongly influenced by 'Shakespeare'.

The Earl of Cumberland would not permit Anne to be taught Latin or Greek, but, other than that, 'none was bred to greater perfection in all knowledge fit for her sex' as she herself put it. Later, as Countess of Dorset, she would become a powerful, self-assured and confident woman, a lover of Chaucer who had special interests in history and classics and in attending the theatre. Like Amelia, she 'made good books and virtuous thoughts my companions,' and fought against the unjust judgement of men. Intellectually Amelia fitted in with the little circle, the miniature court at Cookham. As the family portrait (illustration 26) taken a few years later indicates, it was a household in which books were important – to judge from the books in the painting, young Anne is reading Agrippa's *Vanity of Science*, *Don Quixote*, Castaglione's *Book of the Courtier*, Montaigne's *Essays*, Gerard's *Herbal*, Sidney's *Arcadia*, Chaucer, Spenser, Seneca, Ovid's *Metamorphoses*, the Bible and St Augustine's *City of God*.

Whereas the poetry of most of the other authorship contenders, such as Francis Bacon and the Earl of Oxford, is poor, the poetry in the *Salve Deus* collection has generally been positively received. In terms of style, A. L. Rowse declared Amelia 'a fair poet, far superior to the Queen for example'. Stephanie Hughes, the former editor of *The Oxfordian*, called it 'pretty darned good poetry'. Ilya Gililov went further and called her 'a gifted poet ... Many of the stanzas may justly be regarded as among the highest attainments of seventeenth century poetry in England.' Others have seen her as having significantly influenced Milton, especially in the conceptualisation of the fall and of Eve – which completely changes most twentieth-century judgements of her literary impact and significance.[2]

Matchinske called her poetry 'intractable as Shakespeare', thereby calling attention to one of the underlying areas of similarity. Indeed Gililov in *The Shakespeare Game*[3] was the first person to claim that the same person wrote both the *Salve Deus* collection and also the Shakespearean canon. Unfortunately he failed to appreciate Amelia's education at the hands of the Dowager Countess of Kent and the Duchess of Suffolk. Both moved in the highest court circles, since the countess had been handmaiden to Lady Jane Grey and her mother the duchess had previously married the elderly Charles Brandon, Duke of Suffolk, following the death of his wife Mary Rose, Henry VIII's sister (who was previously Queen of France). But Gililov ignored this and therefore fantasised that *Salve Deus* had to have been written by a countess – the Countess of Rutland, using Amelia as an allonym! At least he thought the quality of the poetry comparable to that expected from one of the country's leading noblewomen!

The *Salve Deus* collection shows that Amelia was a highly experimental and innovative poet, who intimately knew the Shakespearean works, and used a scholarly style of literary composition very like that used in composing the plays. We will address these points in the next chapter. Furthermore, Amelia wrote excellent court English, unlike the leading authorship contender the Earl of Oxford, whose English was dialectical and provincial, as shown in Alan Nelson's definitive biography *Monstrous Adversary*. Let us now prepare to consider the Cookham poem in detail, beginning with the methodological problems of making such comparisons.

The subject of her verse – parodies of Christianity and examinations of how women can get the better of men – match the Shakespearean plays very well. Yet Amelia's verse is not beautiful or honeyed, indeed in some places it seems almost deliberately clumsy. One then has to look further in order to consider the poetry in context. Firstly, as David Foster has argued, the quality of a literary work should not be a criterion in attribution studies at all since 'aesthetic impressions have scarcely any evidentiary value'.[4] Aesthetic impressions are indeed frequently erroneous. For example, when William Jaggard printed the *Passionate Pilgrim* (1599), he chose poems on aesthetic grounds that he thought were by Shakespeare but which later proved to be by Heywood, Barnfield, Griffin and Deloney. Similar mistakes were made by those who included *The Yorkshire Tragedy*, *The History of Thomas Cromwell* or *The London Prodigal* in the Third Folio (1664) as being by the canonical Shakespeare. So judgements on aesthetic grounds that a piece of verse is, or is not, by the author of Shakespeare are suspect and liable to be inaccurate.

Contrary to what most people think, the most significant characteristic of canonical Shakespearean verse is *not* the beauty of the surface verse – that characteristic is shared by several other Elizabethan writers, including those whose works Jaggard mistook for Shakespeare's. As leading Shakespearean scholar Sir Brian Vickers remarks in his book *Counterfeiting Shakespeare*, 'the key words for Shakespeare's stylistic individuality ... are variety, inventiveness and functionality'.[5] Inventiveness is certainly a characteristic of the Cookham poem, since it is the first country house poem to have been written since Roman times. Ben Jonson imitated it by writing his own version, *To Penshurst*, published in 1616. Quoting Vickers again, 'The chief characteristics of Shakespeare's verse are variety, flexibility and adaptation to the characterization of a huge number of speakers.' We might also add a degree of rebelliousness and creative thinking, since Shakespearean plays breach the conventions of Aristotle's unities by having not just one plot but many subplots, and far from being set purely on one day, some of the history plays are set over a period of forty years.

If continual variety and inventiveness are the chief characteristics of Shakespearean works, then a new Shakespearean work would necessarily be distinguished by its *dissimilarity* to previous work, at least on the surface! Arguably, it was this very flexibility and variety that enabled Amelia to write the *Salve Deus* collection differently from previous verse, most notably in pioneering the country house poem and integrating the epic form with dramatic episodic structure. This would imply that distinguishing other similarities to Shakespeare is only possible through detailed study of the underlying substructures.

Whereas the poetry of other authorship candidates such as the Earl of Oxford shows very little if any relationship to Shakespearean verse, the Cookham poem shows parallels to two different examples of Shakespeare's pastorale composed at around the same time. These similarities are not in verse structure, but rather philological similarities in clusters of words, the appearance of unique themes such as frost impacting plants, the appearance of rare and unusual objects (the palm tree), and the location of themes about the Crucifixion as a subtext beneath a pastoral surface. So although Amelia's informal poetry in the Cookham poem does not match the polished dramatic verse of *A Midsummer Night's Dream* or *As You Like It*, nonetheless the poem is using the same underlying motifs and imagery. This is stronger evidence, at corresponding dates, than exists for any other authorship candidate; we now need to consider the issues that arise in making comparisons in more detail.

In attempting to make a comparison between Amelia's verse and the Shakespearean works, account must be taken of a number of factors.

Situational Context. Firstly, Shakespeare's verse is highly dependent on the situation and context in which it was created. Crafting the mellifluous (honeyed) sweetness of the surface verse in Elizabethan literature was a rhetorical strategy designed to achieve a particular purpose. It was used in pastoral poetry for the purposes of deceiving the reader. 'Mellifluous Shakespeare', to use Heywood's phrase, used this strategy so that only the 'wiser sort' (as Gabriel Harvey remarked about *Hamlet*) would see beneath the surface. Therefore in comparing the poems in *Salve Deus* with the Shakespearean works it is important not to base decisions on the quality of the verse, because that is a rhetorical strategy which may be situation dependent. The meanings of the 'Salve Deus' poem are not disguised by a honeyed surface, but rather manifest a complex theological satire, resembling the one that appears in the plays once the surface is penetrated.

Intended Performance. Secondly, the *Salve Deus* collection was written for private reading, and not for stage performance and recitation. So there is absolutely no reason why it should resemble dramatic verse in any way whatsoever. It is written in a completely different context and for utterly different purposes. Dr Kate McLuskie and Dr C. W. R. D. Moseley both have objected to the regularity of the verse in the 'Salve Deus' poem as un-Shakespearean; however they both ignore the fact that this is simply a consequence of following the model of Fletcher's poem, and that Shakespeare's poems also had regular rhyming schemes – it should be compared to these, not to dramatic blank verse.

Genre of Writing. Thirdly, although *Salve Deus* is Jacobean patronage poetry, that does not make it possible to compare it directly to Shakespeare's Elizabethan patronage poetry, namely *The Rape of Lucrece* and *Venus and Adonis*. Both of those poems were written nearly twenty years before, were addressed to the Earl of Southampton and used a pseudonym. The *Salve Deus* collection employs no pseudonym. It is also directed at a very different patron, or rather a set of multiple patrons. This is why it is crafted throughout using the 'persona' of the seeker of patronage, and uses the 'humility topos' in which the seeker deliberately expresses his or her inferiority to the intended patron. Evidently Amelia could not afford to appear to be too skilled a poet, otherwise this could simply have alienated her second major dedicatee, the enormously wealthy but indifferent poet the Countess of Pembroke, Mary Sidney (sister of the well-loved poet Philip Sidney). She was listed by Francis Meres in *Palladias Tamia* (1598) as the only woman poet in the country (other than the queen), and was listed in *Bel-vedere* (1600) as a writer alongside Shakespeare, Spenser and Philip Sidney. So Amelia went out of the way to seemingly flatter her with a 224-line poem showing her as a 'faire earthly goddess' seated in 'Honour's chair', surrounded by classical nymphs, and crowned with eternal fame. Significantly, Amelia's flattering poem is of excessive length, almost as long as all of Sidney's original verse put together! Because *Salve Deus* was the first book of original poetry to be published by a woman, Sidney could very easily have viewed it both as competitive and extraordinarily arrogant, coming as it did from a mere commoner. These feelings would have only increased if in addition it had posed a poetic threat.

Intended Publication. Fourthly, the informality of the Cookham poem which we are about to discuss may be due to the fact that it does not appear to have been written with immediate publication in mind. As an informal poem composed to honour a country house, it does not have either the formality or the quality of verse found in, say, the epic *The Rape of Lucrece*, which was written for immediate publication. It might, however, seem similar to instances in the plays where the playwright was being especially informal, for instance the deliberately unsophisticated verse about singing in *A Midsummer Night's Dream*, or poems that were probably not intended for publication such as those that William Jaggard pirated and printed under the name 'Shakespeare' in *The Passionate Pilgrim*.

Time Period. Finally, the date and time period of writing are also relevant. Both the main 'Salve Deus' poem and the introductory prefaces were written in 1610. At this date, as we will see in the next chapter, the quality of the poetry in some of the plays degenerated as the playwright aged, attempted the new genre of the romance, and as the conventions of style changed in Jacobean London. This is clearly seen in certain plays of that period, notably in *Pericles* (1609) and *Cymbeline* (1610). So in addition to the factors above, the quality of the verse, for instance in the prefaces, may simply relate to the author's changing style, which degenerated in the late plays. Alternatively a possible explanation is that Amelia deliberately weakened her verse, both in her prefaces and in the 'Salve Deus' poem (see the next chapter) to prevent it being too obvious that the poems should be read intertextually with Shakespeare. If those meanings had been identified, this would have led to her death. It is well known that the author of the Shakespearean works shaped both verse and language according to extremely fine judgements of social contexts and situations.

Research into linguistic variation by Witmore and Hope, using a data-mining software tool, Docuscope, has examined 767 samples from the plays. At a macro level this work has shown that Shakespeare's syntax and vocabulary varies very significantly between the tragedies, the histories and the comedies. Witmore, who heads the Folger Shakespeare Library, rightly called this in a lecture 'the single most important fact linguistically about Shakespeare's writing'. However, major variations of language used also reflect much finer distinctions of social situation. Poetic verse is a 'dependent variable' depending on a host of detailed contextual and social factors. Brian Vickers gives two examples. In the plays the terms 'while', 'whilst' and 'whilest' occur two or three times more than 'whiles', whereas in the sonnets this is reversed. Equally, Latinate speech represents about 20 per cent of the language at the opening of *King Lear*, but this declines to almost 0 per cent when Lear is offering Cordelia in marriage. The language is finely and sensitively suited to the nuances of the situation. So, for example, as an ostensibly religious poem, 'Salve Deus' would not be expected to have the sexual undertones found in the plays, but that are not found, say, in 'The Phoenix and the Turtle'. Yet the overall situation that Amelia was facing was one for which there is no precedent in the Shakespearean canon, hence *any* comparison, whether to a comedy, a tragedy, a history or a sonnet, is significantly compromised.

For all these complex reasons, although the overall quality of the poetry in the *Salve Deus* collection is 'fair', as A. L. Rowse noted, it falls below the extraordinary achievements of the Shakespearean works before around 1608. The examination begun here in reference to the Cookham poem will be continued in the following chapter in relation to the main 'Salve Deus' poem (1611).

A meaningful comparison between two pieces of verse must always control for genre. For instance the 'Claremont Clinic', which studies poetry by claimants to the authorship, recognises that unless this is taken into account any attempt at comparison is invalidated. So we must compare the Cookham poem to other examples of the pastoral genre, and we must look extremely carefully into the detail of the poem, rather than be tricked into making aesthetic judgements.

> And in their beauties did you plain descrie,
> His beauty, wisdom, grace, love, majesty.
> In these sweet woods how often did you walk,
> With Christ and his Apostles there to talk;
> Placing his holy Writ in some faire tree
>
> *The Description of Cooke-ham*

The first comparison we might make is to *A Midsummer Night's Dream*, which, although it is high-quality dramatic verse for recital on stage, is still part of the pastoral genre. As Patricia Parker notes, the play features Christ (Bottom/ Pyramus), and Saint Peter (Quince) in the crazy wood, and a disaster in which the land experiences diseases and the plants are attacked by 'hoary-headed frosts'

(2.1.107) – a rare wording found in no other playwright of the period. In Amelia's Cookham poem, however, Christ is walking in the garden with all his apostles; later, the plants die, 'their frozen tops like Ages hoary hairs':

> Of your depart, their very leaves did wither,
> Changing their colours as they grew together.
> But when they saw this had no power to stay you,
> They often wept, though speechless, could not pray you;
> Letting their tears in your faire bosoms fall,
> As if they said, Why will ye leave us all?
> This being vain, they cast their leaves away,
> Hoping that pity would have made you stay:
> Their frozen tops, like Ages hoary hairs,
> Shows their disaster, languishing in fears
> A swarthy riveld ryne all over spread,
> Their dying bodies half alive, half dead.
>
> *The Description of Cooke-ham*

Another similarity, this time of word clusters, is the mentions in the Cookham poem of pretty/bird/sing/warble/Philomela/ditty.

> Those **pretty birds** that wonted were to sing,
> Now neither **sing**, nor chirp, nor use their wing,
> But with their tender feet on some bare spray,
> **Warble** forth sorrow, and their own dismay.
> Fair **Philomela** leaves her mournful **ditty**,
> Drowned in deep sleep, yet can procure no pity.
>
> *The Description of Cooke-ham*

This happens to neatly bridge the word clusters used in two Shakespearean works of about the same time, *A Midsummer Night's Dream* (1596) and the poem 'Loth to Depart' in the collection known as *The Passionate Pilgrim* (1599). The latter is especially helpful as a comparison since it is not dramatic verse, but designed for reading, although some scholars doubt that it was written entirely by Shakespeare:

> Lord, how mine eyes throw gazes to the east!
> My heart doth charge the watch; the morning rise
> Doth cite each moving sense from idle rest.
> Not daring trust the office of mine eyes,
> While **Philomela** sits and **sings**, I sit and mark,
> And wish her lays were tuned like the lark;

For she doth welcome daylight with her **ditty**,
And drives away dark dismal-dreaming night:
The night so pack'd, I post unto my **pretty**;
Heart hath his hope, and eyes their wished sight;
Sorrow changed to solace, solace mix'd with sorrow;
For why, she sigh'd and bade me come tomorrow.

The Passionate Pilgrim, XV

Oberon   Every elf and fairy sprite
                     Hop as light as **bird** from brier;
                     And this **ditty**, after me,
                     Sing, and dance it trippingly.

Titania   First, rehearse your song by rote
                     To each word a **warbling** note:
                     Hand in hand, with fairy grace,
                     Will we **sing,** and bless this place.

A Midsummer Night's Dream

These correspondences need to be seen within the broader context of similarities between the verse in *Salve Deus* and Shakespeare's pastorals. In addition to the similarities between *A Midsummer Night's Dream* and the Cookham poem, there are also resemblances between the play and the main 'Salve Deus' poem. In the play, Thisbe uses the words 'come blade, my breast imbrue'. The unusual word 'imbrue' (meaning to stain in blood) is used in *Salve Deus* to implore Pilate not to proceed with the Crucifixion: 'Do not in innocent blood imbrue thy hands' (line 750). This term is rare, used by at most 1 per cent of contemporary writers, but it could perhaps have been derived from one of them, or indeed from *A Midsummer Night's Dream*.

More significant is Thisbe's comment about Pyramus/Jesus: 'These lily lips, this cherry nose.' This reappears in 'Salve Deus' in the description of Jesus, 'His lips like lilies.' According to the EEBO database, these are the *only* two appearances of this peculiar metaphor until 1629, and since both are being applied to the Crucifixion they are surely connected. Evidently, Amelia knew that the death of Pyramus was a Crucifixion allegory – a fact scholarship has caught up with and rediscovered only in the twenty-first century. Since this was not referred to in any known contemporary document, she presumably knew this *because she wrote both works*.

In comparing the Cookham poem to a second example of Shakespeare's pastoralia, we will consider *As You Like It*. In *Cooke-ham*, the garden explicitly features Christ, an oak that is like a palm tree, and Holy Writ placed on trees ('placing his holy Writ in some faire tree'). The palm tree reference oddly imagines that someone 'would like a Palme tree spread his arms' (line 61), which is making a compound pun on the tree and its branches and on hands/palms. The spreading of arms could suggest a crucifixion, especially given that the author chose to precede it in the collection with 'Salve Deus', which is of course specifically about the Crucifixion. It is also interesting that the Cookham poem features a phoenix, a pun on the Greek word for palm tree, *phoinix*.

In the forest in *As You Like it*, we find 'Jove's tree' (God's tree), a palm tree, verse hung on trees, and Rosalind as one of the allegorical Christ figures. Rosalind's name is hung on trees including verses hung 'on a palm-tree' (3.2.171). The reference to the stretching of a span and being hung from east to west suggests the Crucifixion. Rosalind is clearly described as a 'god to shepherd turned', whose 'godhead' had been laid apart (4.3.39–45). Moreover, her name is hung up on thorny brambles and hawthorns, oddly 'deifying' her (3.2.349 F2). The body of the verse even has 'lame feet', presumably because they have been pierced with nails. At the end of the play Rosalind will faint and recover in a piece of verse that mocks the Passion story, like in *Midsummer Night's Dream*, and six times uses the word 'passion', bound up on each occasion with the critical word 'counterfeit'.

The appearance of palm trees in both works cannot be a coincidence, because palm trees were not at all common in English literature. The first palm tree was introduced to England in 1597. In 1600, *As You Like It* appeared in the Stationer's Register. Between 1600 and 1610 palm trees appeared only in three books, one by Chambers (1600), another by Hakluyt (1600), and Topsell's *History of Four-Footed Beasts.* (In emblem books like Paradin's *Devises Heroïques,* the palm tree is associated with Jerusalem.) So this establishes a number of parallels between the Cookham poem and two of the Shakespearean pastoral plays.

Another parallel is how both the plays and the *Salve Deus* collection employ the genre of the apocalyptic. 'The Phoenix and the Turtle' is not pastoralia, though the Greek term *phoinix* is the word for palm tree. Ovid's elegy on the death of Corina's parrot (which Marlowe translated) features a 'most friendly' turtle dove. The Flavian Emperors' favourite epic poet and propaganda writer, Statius, rewrote the poem so that the parrot became a phoenix. Sent to the shades in hot ashes scented with Assyrian perfume, she rises again, a happier and certainly better-smelling phoenix.

Using birds, in this case a phoenix and a turtle dove, as part of a funeral eulogy was traditional, but the writer has not merely copied Skelton's bird funeral (his *Phyllp Sparrow* had provided a mock funeral elegy for a sparrow). She turned it into her own commentary on scholastic philosophy by borrowing ideas from the *Dialoghi d'Amore* (1535) by the great Italian-Jewish philosopher Leone Ebreo (also known as Leo Judaeus and Judah Abarbanel), who had written his own poem about a female phoenix and a male turtle with neo-Platonic theories of love roughly a century earlier. In addition, rather in the manner of one of the French authorities on the same subject, *Le Phoenix de Jean Edouard du Monin* (1585), she fuses those neo-Platonic ideas with Christian theology and doctrine – and does so in order to provide a brilliant comic parody of Catholic ritual.

Firstly the poet draws on the writings of the Catholic theologian and Jesuit Robert Southwell, who had been hanged at Tyburn in 1595. In her seventh verse she uses one of his writings on Aquinas about the way the body and blood of Christ form a single unity in the Eucharist. She also draws on his poem 'Saint Peter's Complaint', which mentions *'threnes'* or lamentations. Similarly, Southwell's paragraph that referred to 'sole … Arabian Trees' provided the second line of her poem. Southwell's references to 'turtle twins' were also perhaps reflected, in her several mentions of their being 'twain'. Southwell had hated *Venus and Adonis*, and had written 'Saint Peter's Complaint' as a counter-attack in exactly the same poetic metre, describing the saint's anguish of having denied Jesus three times. 'The Phoenix and the Turtle' seems to have been Amelia's counter-counter-attack.

A key question to ask is why the writer employs scholastic theology to parody the relationship between the (turtle) dove and the phoenix as analogous to that between the characters of Jesus and the Holy Spirit – as multiple persons but of one substance within the Holy Trinity. As J. V. Cunningham pointed out in his article 'Essence and the Phoenix and the Turtle', many of the concepts that are used to describe their relationship, such as the terms 'essence', 'distincts', 'division', 'property', 'simple', and 'compounded', draw on medieval theology and the work of Tertullian. I suggest that this equation of the figures of the dove and the phoenix echoes the central religious allegories in the plays, by linking the true identity of the resurrected Christ (or phoenix) to the 'dove' (or in Latin, Titus), and hence links to the same heretical perspective on Christian origins as was advocated by Christopher Marlowe.

Furthermore, in order to craft the poem, Amelia draws on the Latin text of the Catholic liturgy, the Requiem Mass, and specifically the *Dies Irae*, the account of the Day of Wrath or Judgement. For instance, the phrase *fidelium defunctorum* gave her its peculiar English equivalent 'defunctive' in verse 4. Her line in verse 3, 'keep the obsequy so strict', was a translation of the Latin phrase *cuncta stricte discussurus*, which actually means 'to weigh everything strictly', and is a reference to the measuring or weighing that, in Hebrew tradition, takes place on Judgement Day. This is compatible with the reference to a 'session' or trial in verse 3, and to the use of the term 'interdict', meaning to place under legal or ecclesiastical sanction. In Roman Catholic theology the *Dies Irae* is the day on which the world will be consumed in fire, *solvet saeclum in favilla*, as the phoenix and her 'nest' will be burnt to ashes. Awaiting that day, the phoenix and the turtle dove in the poem lie 'enclosed in cinders' like the dusty seeds of the palm tree waiting to turn into new flame.

Even without going very deeply into the poem, it is clear that 'The Phoenix and the Turtle' is a neo-Platonic, apocalyptic, theological, allegorical poem that satirises and parodies Christian doctrine. It is therefore of *precisely* the same genre as the poem 'Salve Deus', written a decade later.

We can go further yet. We have just seen that Southwell's poem 'Saint Peter's Complaint' is used and parodied in 'The Phoenix and the Turtle'. In addition, it is treated this way in the 'Salve Deus' poem as well. I will address this specific point by drawing on Susanne Woods' essay 'Lanyer and Southwell: A Protestant Woman's Re-vision of St Peter'. 'Salve Deus' seems almost deliberately to take an opposite standpoint to the Jesuit poet. Most notably, whereas Southwell's poem praises Christ's beauty, Lanier's poem, as we shall see, uses the same trope, but makes it into a catalogue of grotesque deformity. Whereas Southwell's poem is a long and anguished confession by Saint Peter in his own voice as a penitent saint, in which he blames the wicked women who identified him as a follower of Christ, 'Salve Deus' depicts him as weak, foolish and obstinate, and not as penitent at all. Peter is not presented as saintly; he violently cuts off the guard's ear at Gethsemane, and does not even try to heed the prophecy that he would betray his master three times. Far from blaming the women, 'Salve Deus' places the blame entirely upon Peter himself, who arrogantly thinks his faith so pure that it would never fall, and would allow him to climb. Although he is a key character in the Gospel narrative, 'Salve Deus' restricts Peter's speech. Instead, new speech is given to women characters and Peter's actions are covered in part by dramatic anticipation.

Finally, and of course unlike Southwell's poem, 'Salve Deus' not only has strong female characters but has a heroine, Amelia herself, who echoes Shakespearean heroines such as Perdita, Marina, Imogen and Helena. She even proposes dressing as a man – namely a priest – like a cross-dressing Shakepearean heroine!

By around 1609, give or take a few years, Amelia would have been experiencing menopause, which normally took place around the age of forty. This fits with the common belief that the playwright became preoccupied with the darker themes of the tragedies around the year 1606 – oddly around the time that the plays were receiving their greatest success at the court of King James. Furthermore, as Colleen Kennedy has noted, this was about the time when the playwright showed an unusual interest in the consequences of menopause *Macbeth* and *King Lear*. When Lear curses Goneril, he imagines stopping up her menstrual blood, so that the organ of increase in her womb should dry up (1.4.74–7). In a similar fashion Lady Macbeth unsexes herself and, according to Elizabethan psychology, the lack of her menstrual flow drives her mad: 'Come, you spirits / That tend on mortal thoughts, unsex me here' (1.5.40–1).

Relationship with the Earl of Southampton: 1607

Any authorship theory has to explain the loving dedications of the two early long poems to the Earl of Southampton, including the frankly pornographic *Venus and Adonis*, which, with its detailed sexual descriptions, is not the most conventional subject for patronage poetry, and could never have been printed under the name of a female author. *The Rape of Lucrece* also seems to go beyond the normal conventions of patronage dedications when it declares, 'The love I dedicate to your lordship is without end,' and 'What I have done is yours; what I have to do is yours; being part in all I have, devoted yours.' It is also generally thought that some of the sonnets are rather affectionately addressed to the earl: 'For nothing this wide universe I call, Save thou, my rose; in it thou art my all.' (Sonnet 109). As Martin Green emphasises in his book *Wriothesley's Roses*, Southampton's family name Wriothesley was pronounced Rosely, and his coat of arms included roses. The problem, however, is that neither of the leading authorship cases has been able to show any personal connection between their candidate and the Earl of Southampton. (Sir William Davenant, whom Schoenbaum describes as a 'self-promoting embellisher of the Shakespeare mythos', invented an undocumented, imaginary, and improbably large monetary gift by Southampton to Mr Shakespeare in an unsuccessful attempt to fill this gap.) However, if we take into account the analysis of *Love's Labour's Lost* which shows that the earl wanted to marry the 'Brown Lady', the lovesick H. W. in *Willobie His Avisa*, and the fact that in *Venus and Adonis* it is the woman, older than the youth, who advises him to marry and have children, then in combination with the sexualised nature of the pseudonym we can infer the nature of Amelia's relationship to Southampton.

Amelia, growing up from the age of thirteen at Old Somerset House, actually lived next door to the earl, who as a youngster was living as a ward in Burghley House. However, there is at least one surviving piece of unquestionable documentary evidence which inexplicably shows the Earl of Southampton being supportive of Amelia's family in 1607. This is a letter from Bishop Bancroft to Robert Cecil, which notes that the Earl of Southampton supported Amelia's husband's application for a hay patent. While not conclusive, this evidence of caring for Amelia's family is better evidence of an association to the Earl of Southampton than exists for any other leading authorship candidate.

The Dark Lady Sonnets: 1608–9?

And so we come to the so-called 'Dark Lady' sonnets (see Appendix 3). The author of the canon acknowledged a relationship with Southampton by dedicating the two long narrative poems to him, both under the name 'Shakespeare'. Yet in Sonnet 36 the writer declares:

> I may not evermore acknowledge thee,
> Lest my bewailed guilt should do thee shame
> Nor thou with public kindness honour me,
> Unless thou take that honour from thy name.

The only way of resolving this inconsistency is if, in addressing the narrative poems, the writer had not used their own true name but was instead using 'Shakespeare' as a pseudonym. In Sonnet 111 the writer even says 'my name receives a brand' and in 112 that vulgar scandal stamped 'an impression' upon their brow. In *The Comedy of Errors* Adriana imagines having the stained skin of a 'harlot brow', and in *Hamlet* Laertes refers to a cause that 'brands the harlot' on the brow. It is not clear to what extent this punishment was actually inflicted in Elizabethan England, but the point is that the writer of the sonnets is identifying with a woman punished for harlotry by branding, and thence permanently stigmatised. While there is no evidence that Amelia was so treated, she was indeed exiled from court guilty of being a pregnant harlot.

It was A. L. Rowse in 1973 who first identified Amelia as the so-called 'dark lady' of the Shakespearean sonnets (1609), and the identification has been supported both by Martin Green and Stephanie Hopkins Hughes (see Appendix 3). In the same way that several plays mock or parody the work of Edmund Spenser, the chief apologist for the queen and Christianity, the Shakespearean sonnets parody Spenser's sonnets. Spenser's *Amoretti and Epithalamion* begins with his eighty-nine sonnets, the *Amoretti*, or 'little cupids' – love sonnets. The middle section has four anacreontic (using the metre of the Greek poet Anacreon) epigrams about Cupid, who stings his hand, which has to be bathed in a dainty well. Finally the sequence ends with the 430-line poem *Epithalamion*, meaning a wedding song (from the Greek *thalamos* or bridal chamber). Precisely the same structural design is followed in the Shakespearean sonnets, beginning with the love sonnets to the fair boy (1–126), followed by the Dark Lady sonnets (127–52), followed by a pair of anacrenotic sonnets (153–4) and concluding with *The Lover's Complaint*, a long poem about a romance that, parodying Spenser, did *not* lead to the wedding chamber.

Spenser's innovation – in Sonnet 75 – had been to feature not only the voice of the poet but also the voice of the mistress. In the Shakespearean sonnets this innovation is outdone to an extraordinary degree. These sonnets contain several different voices, which have to be sorted out like a puzzle. It seems that the main voices are Amelia herself, the imaginary 'Shakespeare' who is the fair boy who has supposedly written all these works, and the imaginary words of the real Mr William Shakespeare, the play broker. In Spenser's sonnets it is the voice of the male lover that is 'real': in the Shakespearean sonnets it is the voice of the Dark Lady.

In terms of content, Sonnet 130, to the mistress' eyes which are nothing like the sun, parodies Spenser's 'I sought to what I might compare those powerful eyes ... Not to the sun' (Sonnet 9). Amelia's 'if snow be white why then her breasts are dun' parodies Spencer's 'her breasts are like lilies' (Sonnet 64). The honest admission that there is more delight in some perfumes than in the mistress's breath parodies Spenser's hyperbolic claim that the 'sweet odour of his mistress excels that of fragrant flowers' (Sonnet 64).

Amelia's sonnets also echo Spenser in other ways. Spenser's 'fair you are to be sure but cruel and unkind' (Sonnet 56) and 'more than fair' (Sonnet 8) were answered in the sonnets to the fair youth. Whereas Spenser compared himself to a 'silly barque' tossed sore on the sea (Sonnet 63) Amelia has 'my saucy barque' (Sonnet 63). Whereas Spenser's Sonnet 61 described the beloved as 'the Idol of my thought', Amelia's begins 'Let not my love be called to idolatry' (Sonnet 105). Borrowing a common motif of devouring time from Jocelin du Bellay's *Les Antiquités de Rome* (1557), Spenser wrote in Sonnet 69 that 'even this verse vowed to eternity shall be thereof eternal monument and tell her praise to all posterity'. Amelia's equivalent Sonnet 55 states, 'Not marble nor the gilded monuments / of princes shall outlive this powerful rhyme ... your praise shall still find room / Even in the eyes of all posterity.' The odd phrase 'all posterity' emphasises the borrowing.

However, to understand the deepest meaning of the sonnets, it is as always necessary to probe the allegory. Spenser had explicitly acknowledged that his sonnets contained hidden meanings and were merely 'wanton shows of better hidden matters'. Helen Vendler, in *The Art of Shakespeare's Sonnets*, rightly noted that the sonnets represent 'something cryptographic' and that the author is trying to work out positions without the assistance of any 'systematic doctrine' and scorns the 'consolations of Christianity'.

Spenser made theological claims for his beloved. He claimed that his beloved was derived from the Holy Spirit: 'That is true beauty; that doth argue you to be divine and born of heavenly seed; derived from that fair spirit, from whom all true and perfect beauty did at first proceed' (Sonnet 79). The Shakespearean Sonnet 106 argues that the Hebrew prophets who looked with 'divining eyes' wrote their prophecies and praises not as prefigurings of Jesus but of Will. Similarly, whereas Spenser's Sonnet 68 talked of the dear Lord whose 'dear blood clean washt from Sin', in the universe in which Amelia's beloved existed there was no need for such washing, since it is 'preposterous' to think that such a staining could have ever occurred (68, 10). This is the same point about the nonexistence of original sin that is made in the central section of 'Salve Deus'. On the same theme, in Sonnet 108 it is not the name of God the Father that should be hallowed daily in the Lord's Prayer, but the fair name of the beloved. This shows that the sonnets seem to have an implicit theological subtext, and may even anticipate the Jesus satire in *Salve Deus*.

Shakespeare scholars have generally been willing to regard the sonnets as autobiographical, so we should also consider what they reveal of the Dark Lady and her concerns. The way that Amelia was given to Lord Hunsdon could indeed be described as having her 'maiden virtue rudely strumpeted' (Sonnet 66). By the early 1600s Amelia was indeed 'poor' and 'despised' (Sonnet 37), and indeed correctly predicted, as it turned out, that 'the earth can yield me but a common grave' (Sonnet 81). Indeed it was the experience of the sonnets that led Dr Maya

Angelou to announce famously that Shakespeare had been a young black girl, so well did the sonnets reflect her experience of isolation, discrimination and sexual abuse.[6] What is unquestionable is that unlike the other leading candidates for the authorship, who were mostly wealthy, had public success, and had titles, Amelia lacked all this:

> Let those who are in favour with their stars
> Of public honour and proud titles boast,
> Whilst I whom fortune of such triumph bars ...
>
> Sonnet 25

It was in this sorrowful state – 'in sorrow's cell', as she put it – that, as the literary climate gradually changed, she would finally be able to publish a book of poetry under her own name: 'Written by Mistress Aemilia Lanyer, Wife to Captain Alfonso Lanyer, Servant to the Kings Majestie.'

8

A Poet in Her Own Right:
1611–1617

We now come to late 1610, when the initial presentation copies of *Salve Deus* appeared. The first volume of original poetry ever to be published by a woman, it was released to the public the following year. The main poem, also called 'Salve Deus', is modelled on Giles Fletcher's poem 'Christ's Victory', and on the surface, the volume seems to be an un-Shakespearean collection of religious patronage poetry. It also seems un-Shakespearean in its lack of commercial success – a success that not only many of the plays, but also the long narrative poems notably enjoyed.

But if we look very carefully beneath the surface, then, as an apocalyptic, neo-Platonic poem, the central 1,840-line poem has strong resemblances to *The Rape of Lucrece*, and as a crucifixion is actually linked to the requiem for two persons in the Trinity found in 'The Phoenix and the Turtle'. Like the Shakepearean plays, it is a rewriting of a source text – and one written by a member of the Fletcher family recalling that John Fletcher co-authored *Two Noble Kinsmen* and *Henry VIII*. Furthermore, as several scholars have pointed out, Lanier's work encompasses social relationships, freedom, equality and democracy, and unruly women trying to get the upper hand of men – the same kind of content that appears in the Shakespearean plays, with the religious materials employed merely as the overall framing device. Overall, 'Salve Deus' shows closer resemblances to the late Shakespearean works than the poetry of any other candidate. It is, after all, a Crucifixion poem, and as Sean Benson shows in *Shakespearean Resurrection*, this overall theme appears in about a third of the plays in the canon. Moreover, the fundamental technique of elaborating on the words of Jesus while transforming them into a multi-plot structure comes from the mystery plays, which are so critical to the history plays. It is probably significant that 'Salve Deus' focuses on a theophany, the appearance of a god, and it is the late plays especially that also show the appearance of gods, namely Diana in *Pericles*, Jupiter in *Cymbeline* and Iris, Ceres, and Juno in *The Tempest*.

Addressed to the God of the Jews, the main epic poem only pretends to be pious, mystical verse like John Donne's or Richard Crashaw's, but is rather an adaptation of the Gospels, focusing on the Passion. Beneath the superficially pious language, Boyd Berry notes that the main poem opens and closes with 'a sense of mischief, perhaps of satire'. There are several reasons for reading this work as a satirical burlesque or parody – and not a reverential exercise in Christian mysticism. Firstly, the writer is using the account for her own commercial ends in seeking patronage, and is mixing up the Gospel with her own purposes. Secondly, the poem modifies Christian theology in critical ways, such as putting Amelia herself in the role of priest and most critically by not accepting original sin. If original sin did not exist, then a crucifixion to ransom or redeem the world from it, let alone an apocalypse in which the saviour returns, all becomes a mere farce. Thirdly, the poem uses the tropes of *The Rape of Lucrece*, implicitly and heretically constructing the poem as a grotesque rape of Jesus.[1] Fourthly, this poem is being written by a woman and therefore, like the Katherina character in *The Taming of the Shrew*, by claiming a right to speak it is challenging male authority, and therefore the Pauline texts upon which that authority rests[2] and is thus undoing the Bible! It is also prefaced by numerous letters recalling how critical women's letter-writing is to many of the Shakespearean plays.

There are plausible grounds for supposing that Amelia Lanier did not intend *Salve Deus* as an exercise in pious Christian apologetic, as critics have largely assumed. For one thing, quite apart from her status as a Marrano, we have documentary evidence that she had interests incompatible with that of a believing Christian. Her physician, the astrologer Dr Simon Forman, clearly records that she told him 'tales of invoking spirits' with which she had intended some kind of 'villainy.' (An interest in summoning spirits was demonstrated in *Henry VI* in 1592 where devils appear on stage, reminiscent of *Dr Faustus*, and Joan of Arc offers them her body and soul.) This suggests that when she wrote the 'Salve Deus' poem it was by no means written as a piece of reverential and pious New Testament Christian poetry, as it appears on the surface, but something entirely different. While it is true that all of the dedicatees of her poetry were Christian noblewomen, and indeed her social networks can be mapped – as Kim McLean-Fiander has done – within the radical Puritan community, this should not be surprising. In Elizabethan London, radical Puritans such as Henry Finch could be almost as dismissive of the New Testament and as committed to the Old Testament as Jews.[3]

Quite apart from its use of epic, a different genre, and its being written as patronage poetry and not dramatic verse, even a quick glance will reveal that some, perhaps most, of the verse in the *Salve Deus* collection is not very good. A. L. Rowse was perhaps right in calling it 'fair', but Gililov surely exaggerated in calling it 'among the highest attainments of seventeenth-century poetry'. Certainly the verse in the main 'Salve Deus' poem is inferior to that in the Cookham poem, and seems almost deliberately bad. Apart from the major factor that the 'Salve Deus' poem was written as a *parody of another text*, and then necessarily follows its style, there are two different possible explanations for this.

Firstly, it has long been recognised that short passages of deliberately bad Shakespearean verse appear in many of the plays, and are used in very specific ways. Hardin Craig in his article 'Shakespeare's Bad Poetry' in the first volume of

Shakespeare Survey has examined in detail how the playwright deliberately uses doggerel for prophecies and oracles and the like. Theophanies and parodies of the Crucifixion, in particular, are subjects that the Shakespearean plays typically parody with deliberately wooden verse, as we will see shortly. These are *precisely* the subject matter of the *Salve Deus* collection – with the critical difference that instead of being small pieces in a longer brilliant verse about something else, they constitute the entire work.

Secondly and more recently, some Shakespeare critics are beginning to suspect that much longer passages of verse which, because of their inferior quality, have been generally assumed to have been written by a collaborator, are actually by the Shakespearean author. Take, for instance, the first two acts of *Pericles* (*c.* 1608), which Sidney Thomas calls 'verse and prose of an almost unrelieved pedestrian dullness'. They are often thought to be by Wilkins or Heywood, yet in his article 'Gower and Shakespeare in Pericles', Professor David Hoeniger challenged this consensus and argued that Acts 1 and 2 'are the authentic work of Shakespeare, here deliberately lowering his style to achieve a congruity of effect with the Medieval mode of his narrator, Gower'.[4] Parodying Gower generates inferior verse in *Pericles* much as parodying *Christ's Victory* does in 'Salve Deus'. Hoeniger seems to be at least partially right. The transformation of the scene at Tarsus in Act 1, Scene 4 into something that alludes to the famines in the Jewish–Roman war as described by Josephus is certainly compatible with the use of Josephus in other plays, such as *Coriolanus* and *Measure for Measure*. The figure of Simonides in Act 2, Scene 1 also seems to be by the Shakespearean author because it is integral to the allegorical system in Act 3, which is of undisputed authorship (Simonides comes from the five town Pentapolis, of which the largest town is Cyrene, and parallels the figure of Simon of Cyrene in the Gospels). Yet the verse is unremarkable:

> Alas, the sea hath cast me on the rocks,
> Wash'd me from shore to shore, and left me breath
> Nothing to think on but ensuing death:
> Let it suffice the greatness of your powers
> To have bereft a prince of all his fortunes;
> And having thrown him from your watery grave,
> Here to have death in peace is all he'll crave.
>
> *Pericles*, 2.1.5–11

If the playwright could deliberately adopt a lower register for *Pericles*, then there is no reason why the author's style might not have been similarly lowered in writing *Salve Deus*. At the minimum, both these factors emphasise that verse quality is a very unreliable basis for making judgements about the authorship.

The writings of St Teresa of the Cross in the 1570s capture the grotesqueness of Christian encounters with the cross, and were later depicted in Bernini's famous sculpture of Teresa in orgasmic ecstacy after having been repeatedly stabbed with an arrow. However Lanier's verse is much more extreme and more sadomasochistic in how she describes the Crucifixion in all its revolting detail. She ironically insists that it is beautiful, as it evidently appeared to some Christians. In her very extremity Lanier is offering us a burlesque which perhaps recalls the mocking of Jesus. The term for mocking in Spanish is *burlarse*, which shares the same root as burlesque in the sense of being a grotesque parody. That she certainly depicts. Indeed she exploits Catholic theological tropes such as Mary swooning and kneeling at the Crucifixion specifically in order to parody them.

In some respects, the 'Salve Deus' poem anticipates the work of later baroque metaphysical poets such as Crashaw. Using the conventions of that style, which was at the time barely emerging in English verse, it is marred by its bad taste. Whereas Donne acknowledged he was using a poetic metaphor when he spoke of God ravishing him, in this poem there is a lack of metaphor in its account of the poet and the countess ravishing Jesus while he lies helpless on the cross. Lanier inserts comments about pressing financial concerns among what might appear to be spiritual reflections. The deliberate and offensive vulgarity is also akin to that in Crashaw's epigram 'On Our Crucified Lord, Naked and Bloody':

> They have left thee naked, LORD, O that they had!
> This Garment too, I would they had deny'd.
> Thee with thy selfe they have too richly clad,
> Opening the purple wardrobe in thy side:
> O never could there be garment too good
> For thee to weare but this of thine own blood.

To take another example, it also resembles the grotesque excesses of Crashaw's 'On the Wounds of Our Crucified Lord':

> O these wakeful wounds of thine!
> Are they Mouthes? or are they eyes?
> Be they mouthes, or be they eyne,
> Each bleeding part some one supplies.

However, despite this superficial similarity to baroque metaphysical poetry, 'Salve Deus' is actually something rather different. It is more like Shakespearean grotesque, in the same vein as the comedy of the grotesque that Wilson Knight identified in *King Lear*. In *Henry IV, Part 1* Falstaff 'sweats to death', like roasted beef, larding the earth with his sweat, as his precursor Oldcastle did when he was both hung and roasted on a spit. In 'Salve Deus' the 'sweet Lamb' also is seemingly being cooked: 'In midst of bloody sweat and dying breath ... his precious sweat came trickling to the ground.'

As Professor Piero Boitani notes in his new book *The Gospel According to Shakespeare*, 'from the second section of *Hamlet* onwards, Shakespeare is engaged in developing his own Gospel'. Boitani claims that these plays are Shakespeare's gospel. I agree of course that Shakespeare has appropriated the Gospels, but more importantly has also reinvented them. This unusual interest is paralleled in Lanier's work, as Guibbory recognises in her article which was significantly titled 'The Gospel According to Aemelia'. Lanier thus parallels one of the key interests of the writer of the Shakespearean plays in the Bible, which is referred to about 3,000 times.

The first thing to be said about the *Salve Deus* collection is that the central poem is also focused on the Bible, specifically the Gospel of Matthew. Oddly, around half a dozen Old Testament women figures – Deborah, Sheba, Susanna, Jael, Judith and Hester – appear both in *Salve Deus* and in the Shakespearean plays. Deborah surfaces in *Henry VI* when the King of France praises Joan, 'thou art an Amazon / And fightest with the sword of Deborah' (*Henry VI, Part 1*, 1.2.83–4), providing a positive view of the courageous heroine derived from the feminist writer de Pizan's *Le Ditié de Jehanne d'Arc* (Tale of Joan of Arc).

The Ethiopian Queen of Sheba appears as a judge in *Salve Deus* and also appears around the same time in *Henry VIII* as 'Saba', which is a Spanish variant of her name. Joachim's wife Susannah appears explicitly in *Salve Deus* as a 'fair and constant dame', and in the plays is alluded to in the song 'The Constancy of Susannah', whose first line 'There Dwelt a Man in Babylon' is mentioned in *Twelfth Night* and *The Merry Wives of Windsor*. Jael, who hammered a nail into the head of the sleeping Sisera, appears in *Salve Deus* in the preface, 'To the Virtuous Reader', and is then oddly echoed by Caliban, who wants to hammer a nail into the head of Prospero. From the *Book of Judith* 'Judeth' appears in *Salve Deus* as bearing away a head, and in *Love's Labour's Lost* Holofernes appears, understandably 'out of countenance' and lacking a face (5.2.599–601) for the very good reason that Judith has decapitated him. Finally, although the 'virtuous Hester' appears specifically in *Salve Deus* but does not appear by name in Shakespeare, elements of the *Book of Esther* have been identified in *Henry VIII*.

In a previous chapter we considered some of the ways in which the main 'Salve Deus' poem relates to the parody of the Crucifixion in *A Midsummer Night's Dream*. Written in her poverty, from 'Sorrow's cell' as she put it, in an attempt to get patronage, *Salve Deus* is the first original book of poetry published by an English woman under her own name, and is also the first work in English to use and acknowledge *Hallellu-iah* as a Hebrew word. Its very length of 1,840 lines makes it excessive compared to, say, Crashaw's 200-line 'Hymn to Saint Teresa' (1646), and the verse form it is using makes it clear that the author was writing an epic poem. Unlike other Jacobean religious verse, such as that of John Donne, or Mary Sidney's 'To the Angel Spirit', instead of the poet's own spiritual experience it substitutes a literary account taken from the biblical text. Finally, of course, it is a parody, and some of its strange features come from the long poem that it is parodying, *Christ's Victory* by Giles Fletcher (a cousin of the dramatist John Fletcher who co-authored some of the later Shakespearean plays). *Salve Deus* presents no victory of Christ but glories in the bloody and broken death of Jesus in a grotesque way that parodies literary convention. Would any woman, let alone the Countess of Cumberland as the bride of Christ really want to embrace a groom like this?

> Sometime imprison'd, naked, poore, and bare,
> Full of diseases, impotent, and lame,
> Blind, deafe, and dumbe, he comes unto his faire
>
> 'Salve Deus', lines 1,352–5

The curiosities in Amelia's poem begin with the very title. The greeting 'Salve' is found in Livy: 'Salute him as a god, address him as a god with *salve deus*.' But it is curious. One normally would not address a man on a cross with the word *salve*, since it comes from the word *salveo*, meaning to be in good health, and was a common morning greeting used to mean 'Are you well?'

Unlike any other religious writer of the period – other than the author of Shakespeare – Amelia sees these fundamental Christian texts as literary fictions that she is free to alter and rewrite, in the way she would any other literature. Her blasphemous and heretical view implies that the Gospels have no divine authority, but were simply written by men, for their own worldly ends. Significantly, therefore, she does not even treat these texts as sacred, because she exploits them for *her* own worldly ends in pursuit of patronage, thus producing a peculiar combination of religious verse and personal claims to status and earthly entitlement that is unique in seventeenth-century verse. Indeed, she not only rewrites the New Testament books, she mocks and undermines them, and audaciously rewrites them. For instance, she incorporates the key passages of the Gospel of Matthew into a narrative of women, adding in her own imaginary passages about Pilate's wife – again a completely heretical thing to do. She also claims that the apocalypse is actually happening – by casting one of her patrons as the woman clothed with the sun from the *Book of Revelation*. The poet also undermines the social position of the noble ladies of England by comparing them to a long series of powerful Hebrew women, one of whom – the Queen of Sheba – will come to sit in judgement on them.

Amelia's position in writing *Salve Deus* was theologically unlike any other in seventeenth-century England, except Shakespeare. *Salve Deus* presupposes that the core documents of Christianity are a literary fiction and attempts to write a new parodic gospel, to remake Christian doctrine, to bypass the Church, and to describe and create a post-Apocalyptic – and thus post-Christian – literary reality. It is significant that she makes no favourable references to the Church or its sacraments but instead refers to herself, in a spirit of utter heresy, as the host who – instead of a male priest – will present the body of Jesus as manifested in her book. As Micheline White, in her article 'A Woman with Saint Peter's Keys?', and other commentators would observe, this is antithetical to Christian doctrine. Her work is, as Schnell puts it, 'radically at odds with … the institution of the church' and as Guibbory notes, 'independent of church tradition', putting her in a position that is utterly heretical.[5] Since the author was a Marrano Jew this is hardly surprising.

The language also makes heavy use of the Psalms. For instance Lanier's lines 'With Majestie and Honour is He clad, And deck'd with light, as with a garment faire' echo Psalm 104; 1–2 in the Coverdale translation: 'Prayse the Lord O my soul: O Lord my God, thou art become exceeding gloryous; thou art clothed with majesty and honoure.' Verse 4 of the same Psalm would be alluded to in both *Hamlet* and *Othello*.

The turn of the sixteenth century saw various feminist publications, including *Jane Anger, Her Protection for Woman* (1589) by an unknown author, which ends with an odd poem, 'A sovraigne Salve'. In Venice, two important publications addressed the role of women, Moderata Fonte's dialogue *Il Merito delle Donne* (1600) and Lucrezia Marinella's *La Nobilta et l'Eccellenza delle Donne* (1600), which was a theme she revisited in her epic poetry many years later.

While the writings of Cornelius Agrippa on hunting and other themes influenced the Shakespearean plays in ways that are not fully documented, his book *Of the Nobilitie and Excellence of Womankinde* (1542) was one of the most prominent feminist texts of the period, and specifically influenced Lanier's criticisms of Pauline thinking. About the same time in Geneva, Marie Dentiere, who wrote under the pseudonym of a Geneva merchant – wrote her *Very Useful Epistle to Margaret of Navarre* (1539). It contained a section with the subheading 'On Defence of Women', which began by referring to Old Testament heroines like Sarah, Deborah, Ruth and the Queen of Sheba, and then gave several examples of how women were specially treated in the Gospels. For instance, Jesus had appeared first to a woman and then declared himself to other women rather than men. Marie Dentière claimed to be writing for other women and argued that there should not be two Gospels but one Gospel, and that women should be able to preach and have a ministerial role.

Dentière in particular influenced *Salve Deus*. Right at the centre of the poem is the passage about Eve and Pilate's wife. This includes 'Eve's Apology', in which Amelia argues that there was no original sin, and that if there was it was Adam's fault and not Eve's. Eve was simply trying to do good and had been deceived, and even though she offered Adam the apple, having greater strength he could have refused it. How absurd it is to think that God, having created Adam, the perfect man, would then allow him to lose that perfection all over an apple. If Eve did err it was for the sake of knowledge; her only fault was too much love. (Granted my remarks about the poem *Willobie His Avisa*, it is worth noting that this is also a feminist text, which in its final segment blames Adam's fall on his aspiring pride, and Eve, far from being the protagonist, merely 'gave consent'.) As Esther Gilman Richey remarks in her article 'To Undo the Booke', if women were to find a place for themselves as writers they had to call into question Paul's interpretation of Genesis, and 'no woman did so with more art, authority or skill' than Amelia Lanier, who revised the fundamental Christian myths of Eden, the Passion of Christ and the Communion of Saints.

Curiously, one place where we find a theological reflection that is comparable to 'Eve's Apology' is in *Love's Labour's Lost*. In this preposterous, back-to-front play we find the character Jaqenetta, 'a child of our grandmother Eve', and a man whose name is Costard, meaning the costard apple. In a reversal of the Bible the apple essentially picks Eve, rather than the other way around, and the apple gets punished, not the girl. This play also contains a little exposition of the meanings of *salve*, which Amelia would use in the title of her book *Salve Deus Rex Judaeorum* (1611). Costard is a herald or envoy, and *l'envoi* is the term for the conclusion of a letter, and therefore the opposite of the Latin *salve*, meaning 'greeting'. Thus the inconsiderate people who take *salve* for *l'envoi* (3.1.75) are getting things back to front.

By the time that *Salve Deus* appeared, the late Shakespearean plays had developed certain unusual stylistic characteristics. Written between 1608 and 11, the late plays are very different from those written earlier, which is why they are sometimes called the romances. While these plays were not specifically identified as a cluster in the First Folio, which distinguished between comedies, tragedies and histories, they nonetheless have distinct features. As Michael Witmore and Jonathan Hope noted in their article 'Shakespeare by the Numbers', these plays have unique linguistic features including their references to the past, and the fact that the characters make more asides, speaking to the audience or referring to external events. These techniques create a dream-like ambience which is also true of Lanier's poetry.

According to Russ McDonald's book *Shakespeare's Late Style*, the late plays are characterised by a disjunctive style of varying sentence length, disjointedness, obscure reasoning, and digression. Lanier's use of varying sentence length is shown in her two-page letter to Ladie Margaret, which consists of five sentences of decreasing length, namely 145, 141, 76, 43 and 22 words. Disjointedness is literally a key theme of *Salve Deus*, in which Christ has 'His joints dis-joynted'. In the line 'His holy name prophan'd, He made a scorn' ('Salve Deus', line 1,133), the omission of the verb is an instance of the effect that Macdonald describes as causing the syntax to become convoluted. Lanier's verse also constructs extremely complicated and obscure chains of reasoning. For instance, by conflating the unworthiness of her presentation of Christ with her unworthy hand she is 'establishing her primary relationship as one who approaches equality with the

Son of God ... Thus the conventionally humble declaration of unworthiness becomes paradoxically, a claim to spiritual and epistemological superiority over the woman she would have as her patron.'[6] In terms of digression, in one of the few examinations of the rhetorical textures of the poem, Boyd Berry's article '"Pardon ... though I have digressed": Digression as Style in *Salve Deus Rex Judaeorum*' argues that digression is the 'most obvious, frequent and fundamental rhetorical strategy of the poem'. It is used as a subversive tactic, for instance in the way that the narrator's voice is interrupted by 'Eve's Apology', and the constant oscillation between the Countess of Cumberland and Jesus. Berry notes that in the final 'Cooke-ham' poem, in some places 'so many rhetorical moves are made so quickly it is difficult to explain them briefly'.

The late plays are also focused on theophanies and on dreams. For instance in *Cymbeline*, Posthumus in a dream sees the descent of Jupiter on an eagle, and in *The Winter's Tale* Hermione appears in a dream to Antigonus (3.3.15–17). Similarly the postscript of *Salve Deus* emphasises that the poem came to the author in a dream. Moreover, in the address to the Countess of Pembroke titled 'The Author's Dream to the Lady Marie' (a dream within a dream), which is a re-writing of Chaucer's 'House of Fame' and Sidney's 'To the Angel Spirit', there is a long account of how the author saw the countess in a dream. The landscape is also populated by various classical deities such as Dictina, Bellona, Aurora, Minerva, Apollo and Pallas. This is also similar to the late plays.

Additionally, the way that *Salve Deus* draws attention to itself as an artifact is a literary characteristic similar to that of *The Winter's Tale*. This title is a term that means a 'fairy story', and the plot drives from a story told to Frolic and Fantastic in Peele's *Old Wives Tale*. It repeatedly refers to itself as an 'old tale', and similarly in *Pericles* what is dramatised is the process of storytelling itself. *Pericles* is blatantly based, in part, on the fifteenth-century mystery play *Mary Magdalene*. Further, as Peggy Muñoz Simonds has shown, the play is a parody of Petrach's triumphs in which the pilgrim wearing the armour of Christ is successively defeated by Love, by Chastity, by Death and so on. Indeed, all the Shakespearean romances foreground the Christian material, including the theophanies, in a way that is much more blatant than in the earlier plays, and in this respect *Salve Deus* can be seen as a kind of culmination of the romances.

Michael Baird Saenger, in his essay 'Pericles and the Burlesque of Romance', was very on target in seeing *Pericles* as a kind of parody. Indeed, the genre of knightly romances was commonly burlesqued onstage. Stephen Gosson for instance referred around 1580 to such depictions of the amorous knight 'encountering a terrible monster made of brown paper'. This insight can be extended to see *Salve Deus* as a burlesque of the greatest romance, and the most fantastic tale of them all – namely the Passion Story. Similar to the way that the supposed 'author' Gower, the learned poet, interrupts the telling of *Pericles* seven times, so another poet, Amelia herself, interrupts the unfolding of the 'Salve Deus' poem by constantly addressing the Countess of Cumberland (at lines 145, 250, 265, 1.321, 1.673, and in prefatory and concluding poems). Indeed, similar to the Petrarchian parodies in *Romeo and Juliet*, 'Salve Deus' can be seen as a kind of grotesque Petrarchian parody of the world's greatest love story. Replacing Petrarch's Laura, the body of Christ is substituted as the beloved feminised object, with which people are 'inflamed' in love in a typically Shakespearean parody of Petrarchian conventions. Specific parallels with individual romances will be addressed in detail below.

In terms of literary composition, *Salve Deus* is similar to the Shakespearean works in its incorporating of fictional passages and characters into the source material. For instance, the key passages of the Gospel of Matthew are incorporated into a narrative of women, and new imaginary passages about Pilate's wife and an angel are added in. Like the Shakespearean works, *Salve Deus* uses biblical typology. The scholarly compositional process is similar to that of the plays and is so complex and layered that it has been described as being as 'intractable as Shakespeare'.[7]

In terms of sources, the *Salve Deus* prefaces assume a community of noblewomen and use the humility topos in a manner similar to the writings of Christine de Pizan, whose work does not seem to have been alluded to by any other writer during the English Renaissance except Shakespeare. In addition, *Salve Deus* also draws upon other Shakespearean sources including Chaucer, Gower, Ovid, Boccaccio, Petrarch and the Gospel of Matthew.

'Salve Deus' explicitly recalls *The Rape of Lucrece*, which Lanier refers to in the words 'T'was Beautie made chas(t)e Lucrece loose her life' ('Salve Deus', 211). It has been suggested that the entire Crucifixion account in 'Salve Deus' was actually modelled on *The Rape of Lucrece*, which it quotes directly in the odd expression, such as 'no excuse nor end' ('Salve Deus', line 832/*Rape of Lucrece*, line 238). Barbara Bowen, in her article 'The Rape of Jesus: Aemilia Lanyer's *Lucrece*', notes that Lanier's stanzas 'simultaneously veer away from and recall Shakespeare's seven-line rhyme royal in *Lucrece*'. 'Salve Deus' also uses similar imagery to *Lucrece*, when it refers in anticipation to blood being used to 'wash' (*Rape of Lucrece*, 1,258) before a reference to a 'purple fountain' (*Lucrece*, 1,785) and crimson blood bubbling 'in two slow rivers' (*Lucrece*, 1,789), which resembles the grotesque imagery of souls bathing their wings in the blood of Jesus as a fountain of life in 'Salve Deus' ('Salve Deus', 1,730–5):

> For by his glorious death he us enrolls
> In deep Characters, writ with blood and teares,
> Upon those blessed Everlasting scroules;
> His hands, his feet, his body, and his face,
> Whence freely flow'd the rivers of his grace.
>
> Sweet holy rivers, pure celestial springs,
> Proceeding from the fountain of our life;

Swift sugared currents that salvation brings,
Clear christall streams, purging all sin and strife,
Faire floods, where souls do bathe their snow-white wings,
Before they fly to true eternal life...

'Salve Deus', lines 1,724–34

Furthermore, in his book *Early Responses to Renaissance Drama*, Charles Whitney shows that Lanier (like the author of Shakespeare) systematically drew on plays as sources. Her account of Cleopatra demonstrates knowledge of four different plays: Daniel's *Tragedie of Cleopatra* published 1594, the translation by Mary Pembroke of Garnier's play *The Tragedy of Antoine* of 1592, Daniel's revised play about Cleopatra of 1607, and the unpublished *Antony and Cleopatra* composed around 1606–7, which was either read in manuscript or known through an undocumented stage performance.

While the *Salve Deus* collection refers to the plays of Lyly and Daniel, the greatest number of allusions are to Shakespeare. The volume features the Nine Worthies and Holofernes which appear in *Love's Labour's Lost*. There are also close associations to other plays. The letter to Mary Pembroke makes a unique reference to 'faire Dictina', as the moon goddess who appears also as 'Dictima' in *Love's Labour's Lost* (4.2.37). Each is an absolute *hapax legomenon*, used only once in English literature. The name is normally spelt Dictynna, originally a hunting goddess of Mount Dicte in Minoan Crete, and later identified with the goddess Diana. *Salve Deus* even uses the same imagery for Jews, referring to 'Jewish wolves' found elsewhere only in *The Merchant of Venice*, where Shylock's desires are 'wolvish'. *Salve Deus* refers to the blood of Christ as a 'river' or a 'spring' proceeding from a 'fountain', in which winged souls will 'bathe' their wings. In the standard edition, Susanne Woods comments that this 'extended transformation of Christ's blood is not characteristic of Jacobean poetics'. Indeed it is not. It is characteristic of Shakespearean satirical depictions of Christ figures, for instance in *Julius Caesar*, where at Caesar's death people drink the 'reviving blood' from his wounds, so that his body is compared to a fountain 'like a fountain with an hundred spouts / Did run pure blood; and many lusty Romans / Came smiling and did bathe their hands in it' (2.2.77–9). Indeed they are invited to 'bathe our hands in Caesar's blood / up to the elbows' (3.1.106). The fountain of blood reappears in *Salve Deus*, where the winged souls bathe their wings rather than their arms (the word 'bathe' is used in both instances). The fountain imagery is also used in *Titus Andronicus* and in *Macbeth*. However, in *Julius Caesar*, immediately thereafter Caesar actually is stabbed and Brutus invites us to count the number of the wounds, which are not a hundred, but thirty-three, one for every year in the life of Christ.

More generally, the religious theme of *Salve Deus* is also comparable to the contemporary Shakespearean romances, which Northrop Frye perceptively described as 'secular scriptures' paralleling the central myths of Christianity. We will shortly examine each romance in turn, after reviewing some overall structural features.

One similarity between the author of *Salve Deus* and Shakespeare is that both are highly innovative and make use of multiple verse forms. Both also make puns, for example, on the word 'grace'. The Three Graces in the letter 'To Mary Sidney' allude to the correct address to a countess as 'your grace', then the letter refers to 'grace' as the theological category, 'grace' as a granting of patronage, and 'grace' as in elegance. A similar triple pun is made by Falstaff in *Henry IV, Part 1* referring to 'grace' as the correct address for a king, 'grace' as a prayer before a meal, and 'grace' as in elegance. (1.2.16–21). Similarly in *Measure for Measure*, Lucio puns on the senses of 'grace' as a prayer over a meal, a theological category of mercy towards sinners, and a kind of elegance or propriety (1.2.4–6). Stefani Brusberg-Kiermeier also calls Lanier a 'musical writer, because she often uses musical metaphors'. In the Cookham poem, for instance, the line 'made their sad consort sorrow's harmony' puns on the meanings of consort as a companion and also as a musical ensemble. A similar musical pun appears in *As You Like It*, a 'broken consort' refers to an ensemble that played broken music featuring mixed instruments, and to Eve as the consort of Adam, whose side is broken.

The letters 'To Lady Susan' and 'To Lady Katherine' are written in a verse form (ababcc), like *Venus and Adonis*. 'To Ladie Lucie' is in seven-line rhyme royal (ababbcc), like *The Rape of Lucrece*. To respond to Giles Fletcher's *Christ's Victory*, which is in nine-line irregular Spenserians (ababbcbcc), the main 'Salve Deus' poem was written as an epic, in ottava rima (abababcc) – a form not used in the Shakespearean canon but which recalls Shakespeare's seven-line rhyme royal in *Lucrece*. The Cookham poem is written in heroic couplets like *A Midsummer Night's Dream*, or like the end of Act 3, Scene 2 of *Measure for Measure*.

To those who would claim that it is unlikely that a covert primary co-author of the plays would end their career by publishing under their own name a volume of *poetry*, two things must be said. Firstly, as Patrick Cheney has observed, to contemporaries Shakespeare was primarily seen as a poet and not as a playwright. Secondly, even by 1611 it would not have been possible for any woman – let alone a mere gentlewoman – to publish an original play. Even Countess Mary Sidney, with her illustrious connections, had merely published a translation.

The unusual and distinctive qualities of the *Salve Deus* volume become most evident in contrasting it with Fletcher's four-part epic poem, 'Christ's Victory', which it is satirising. This comparison clearly shows that unlike Fletcher's poem, *Salve Deus* has dramatic qualities and that these structural qualities resemble what Jean Howard calls the 'art of orchestration' deployed in the Shakespearean plays. Although Shakespearean poetry does not necessarily demonstrate dramatic quality – 'The Phoenix and the Turtle' does not – one indication that Lanier conceived her poetry in theatrical terms as a kind of performance, akin to a 'closet drama' designed to be read aloud, is that she writes that she was appointed to *perform* this work. The term 'perform' had begun to be used in a theatrical context perhaps a decade previously. Her poem was an exercise in theatrical performance – not only is the queen 'acting her part upon a stage' but everything, including her poetry, is a stage: 'this *world* is but a *Stage*. Where *all* doe play their parts, and must be gone'. The poem she is parodying is by Fletcher, which leads directly to the family of the dramatist who collaborated on the late plays. Furthermore, *Salve Deus* specifically refers to the Countess of Cumberland, one of the characters in the poem, as 'a glorious Actor' (line 87), implying the theatrical status of all the characters and the entire work which takes place in a variety of private enclosed spaces or 'closets'. This implies the status of the work as a kind of closet Passion play (obviously this subject matter could not have been treated in a more direct dramatic form). While the collection shows some degree of characterisation, it is fairly limited. However, in the late plays characterisation is not significant either, most notably in *The Tempest* and in *Timon*, where the characters have been called 'two-dimensional'.[8]

The forty or so short 'scenes' of *Salve Deus* begin in the contemporary world of the court, with a community of many noble ladies and incorporating a kind of pastoral classical dream masque. The book then moves into the first century and concludes once more in contemporary times with a pastoral set in a garden at Cookham. This movement from court to country resembles many plays such as *As You Like It*, *A Midsummer Night's Dream*, *The Tempest* and even *King Lear*. (See Fig. 3)

When considered as a whole, like many of the plays, the *Salve Deus* volume provides a series of alternations between poetry and prose. The book also creates tension by alternating between engaging the audience's attention and being more detached, notably in the alternating passages of first-century visualisation and addresses to the Patron, which is a structural feature not found in Fletcher's original. This counterpoint or juxtaposition of two kinds of speech is also characteristic of Shakespeare's compositional techniques. The direct address to the countess provides relief from the tedium of the religious description, and creates bizarre juxtapositions of mood and tone between the public and the private spheres. For instance, an ornate, hyperbolic description of how the King of Heaven will rain down fire and brimstone upon the 'wicked monsters in their berth' together with 'snares, storms and tempests' is followed in the address to the elderly Patron by a domestic reflection on her complexion, her virtue, and retirement from court. That, in turn, is followed by an account, in a completely different tone, describing the seizure of Helen of Troy, the beauty of Cleopatra and of chaste Lucrece. These devices enable the poem to progress through a series of emotional peaks and troughs, at times rejoicing in the Christ's physical beauty, yet at other times commenting grotesquely on his broken and bloody body.

Furthermore, like many of the plays, the main poem is arranged in two parts, one before and one following 'Eve's Apology'. Not only are these arranged

Fig. 3: **FRAME STRUCTURE OF THE *SALVE DEUS* VOLUME**

To the Queen
To Lady Elizabeth
To Virtuous Ladies in General
To Lady Arabella
To Lady Susan
To Lady Pembroke PASTORAL DREAM (*c.* 200 lines)
To Lady Lucy
PROSE TO PATRON LADY MARGARET
To Lady Katherine
To Lady Anne

PROSE TO THE VIRTUOUS READER
Prologue to Salve Deus
Address to Patron 8–56
Theological reflection/Theophany 57–144
Address to Patron 145–200
Historical reflection on CLEOPATRA 201–264
Individual address to Muse 265–329
        Sorrow of Jesus 330–354
DREAM Followers of Jesus
        Caiphas/Pilate 633–760
EVE'S APOLOGY 761–832
        Pontius Pilate 834–968
DREAM Women of Jerusalem
        Sorrow of Mary 1010–1168
Address to Patron 1170–1176
Theological reflection 1177–1264
Address to Patron 1265–1272
Theological Reflection 1273–1320
Address to Patron 1321–1345
Theological reflection 1346–1360
Address to Patron 1361–1408
Comparison of Patron to CLEOPATRA 1409–1464
Historical Reflection/Theophany 1465–1672
Address to Patron 1673–1696
Theological Reflection 1696–1824
Address to Patron 1825–1840

Cookham Poem, PASTORAL RECOLLECTION (*c.* 200 lines)

PROSE TO THE DOUBTFUL READER

symmetrically, inside an overall frame-story structure, but they alternate between presenting groups and individuals, a dramatic technique used by Shakespeare to orchestrate the numbers of bodies in scene composition. These contrasts also help close up discrete sections of the poem.

In addition, Jean Howard also notes the unusual diversity of voices in the Shakespearean plays. Similar diversity can also be found in the volume which combines Lanier's own heroic voice as an impoverished gentlewoman exiled from the court with representations of various members of the nobility, classical and biblical figures. In the process it combines at least four time frames: seventeenth-century London, first-century Judea, the Garden of Eden in 4,004 BCE, and Cleopatra's Egypt, in a way that resembles both *Cymbeline* and *Pericles*. Variety is also an appropriate term to describe the disparate kinds of texts that make up the *Salve Deus* volume, which continually jump between contrasting situations: at one moment a courtly address, then a pastoral, then a grotesque apocalyptic and back again.

How Does Salve Deus *Match Shakespeare?*

LITERARY CRITERIA	MATCH
FORMAL/STRUCTURAL MATCH	
Must be structured symmetrically end to end resembling a circle narrative	STRONG
Must be an explicit, detailed re-writing of a source text(s)	STRONG
Must merge present time with other historical periods	STRONG
Must employ a complex frame narrative, of texts boxed within texts	STRONG
Must alternate between poetry/prose, and in presenting groups/individuals	STRONG
Must be a multiple layered text	STRONG
CONTENT MATCH	
Must be highly inventive and innovative	STRONG
Must make use of biblical materials especially Revelation	STRONG
Must support a feminist perspective	STRONG
Must offer a heretical critique of Christian doctrine	STRONG
Must demonstrate contrasting variety	STRONG
Must use unusual Shakespearean sources e.g. Tasso, Chaucer, de Pizan	STRONG
Must use biblical and classical characters found in the plays	STRONG
Must reuse neologisms invented by Shakespeare	SOME
Must allude to multiple Shakespearean works	STRONG
STYLISTIC MATCH TO SHAKESPEAREAN PLAYS WRITTEN THAT YEAR	
Must match quality of the Romances written that year	SOME
Must use literary devices like the Romances e.g.digression	STRONG
Must use literary devices like the Romances e.g. interruption	STRONG
Must use literary devices like the Romances e.g. disjointedness	STRONG

Must use rare Shakespearean metaphors and unique words	STRONG
Must incorporate dreams and masques	STRONG
Must tailor its verse to different situations	STRONG

We might finally also note Lanier's obsession with the audience and the reception of her work, and whether it will bring her any income, evidenced by the dedications not only to many individual noble ladies, but also to all virtuous ladies in general, the virtuous reader and concluding with a kind of talkback to the doubtful reader. This concern about audience reception is not something that appears in Fletcher's original, but is implicit in the Shakespearean plays.

The above diagram summarises the main areas of literary similarity between the poems contained in the *Salve Deus* collection and the Shakespearean works, showing overall a remarkable number of matches. These become even more decisive if a detailed comparison is made to the contemporaneous plays. The 'Salve Deus' poem can be tied specifically to the romances, which were written at about the same period, each in different ways. We will now examine, play by play, specifically how 'Salve Deus' compares to *Pericles*, *Cymbeline* and *The Tempest*.

Specific Parallels

Pericles *(1609), A Christian Knight Parody*

The play *Pericles* ends, very oddly with the triumph of the divine feminine, the pre-Christian goddess Diana. Although the source texts refer to her only twice, this is vastly expanded in the play, where she is referred to at least a dozen times. Pericles swears by her (3.3.28), as does Mariana (4.2.140). Thaisa calls her 'dear Diana'. Pericles promises to offer her oblations (5.3.69–71) and the play concludes at the Temple of Diana in Ephesus. Significantly perhaps, this is the very same Temple of Diana that in *The Comedy of Errors* is presided over by an abbess called Aemilia.

There are several different time frames in the play. There are the contemporary Christian clowns and a contemporary sixteenth-century Spanish admiral. There is also Gower, the medieval poet, as a ghost narrator. However, the main time frame, contemporaneous with Apolonius of Tyre, who is the model for Pericles, is during the reign of one of the kings called Antiochus, in the second or third century BCE. The travels of Pericles to and from Antioch, Tyre, Tarsus and Ephesus are also flavoured with a different kind of romance narrative – the first-century travels of St Paul in the *Book of Acts*. There, upon his visit to Ephesus, the shouts 'Great is Diana of the Ephesians' (Acts 28:17) rejected the Pauline story of Christ. Similarly, in the play, the worship of Diana triumphs over Gower's Christian god, and over the model of the Christian pilgrim knight.

Around the time *Pericles* was being written, complex dramatic forms were being used in meta-theatrical burlesques like Munday's *The Downfall of Robert*

Earl of Huntingdon (1598). Similarly Barnabe Barnes' *The Devil's Charter* (1607), a parody about a pope, is based on a book by Francesco Guicciardini – who is presented on stage to open and close the play, introduce each act and introduce the dumbshows. For our purposes, the most significant was *The Knight of the Burning Pestle* (1606) by Francis Beaumont. This is a burlesque romance about a serving boy who is encouraged by his master and mistress in the audience to go on stage and become a comic knight errant, and to create a new play to replace the one that the audience had become bored with. In the seventeenth century, like today, a successful new theatre production spurred imitators. *The Knight of the Burning Pestle* seems to have been the inspiration for Shakespeare to take the Spenserian image of the chivalric Christian knight and burlesque it.

In the original sources the Pericles character encounters only one fisherman, who gives him some clothing, and he subsequently finds a suit of armour. Echoing the Gospel passage where Jesus meets fishermen and calls them up to be fishers of men instead, Pericles meets three Christian fishermen who make anachronistic references to churches, and who then fish his suit of rusty armour from the sea. The rust on the armour alludes to Sidney and his account of a knightly tournament in *Arcadia*, as does his *impressa* of a withered stick with a green tip, an allusion to the rod of Jesse. That this is all a parody is indicated by the *impressa* carried by another knight, a pestle burning upside down – which would of course extinguish itself – and which is a direct allusion to Beaumont's play. The rusty armour is no protection against the darts of love and is abandoned. As Peggy Muñoz Simonds has noted, Pericles is defeated by the triumphs of Love, Chastity, Death, Fame, Time and Divinity, all based on Petrarch's *Trionfi*.

Finally, as Claire Preston remarks in her article 'The Emblematic Structure of Pericles' '*Pericles* appears to follow no conventional Shakespearean dramatic pattern: its abiding qualities are statis, formality and inaction.' The play consists of various highly visual scenes, almost tableaux, such as Gower's dumbshows and the miracles, on which there are reports and commentary to reveal the morals in the actions presented. Gower indeed interrupts the action a total of seven times. It is this peculiar metatheatrical form that is perhaps the most obvious parallel to *Salve Deus*, where Lanier's addresses and comments to the Countess of Cumberland keep interrupting the poem in which Jesus is hanging as if in a tableau. Like *Pericles*, the volume *Salve Deus* is also a burlesque or parody of Christian tradition. While the 'Salve Deus' poem does not embrace a feminine conception of God, such as Diana, it is nonetheless a feminist theological poem. As the central section 'Eve's Apology' makes clear, it advocates that the author as a woman is able to replace the priests of the Church, and that her telling of the Gospel story is able to replace those told by men. In all these ways *Pericles* anticipates and is compatible with the *Salve Deus* collection.

Cymbeline *(1609–10), A Theophany*

Salve Deus also has particular resemblances to *Cymbeline*. An examination, for instance, of the introductory poem of dedication to Queen Anne shows that *Salve Deus* used a number of uncommon words that also appeared in *Cymbeline*, but that appeared only in a tiny percentage of the other texts published in that year. These include: 'dispossessed', 'distempered', 'unlearned', and 'affliction'.

That *Salve Deus* and *Cymbeline* both feature theophanies is significant, but the resemblances go deeper than this. Sleep and dreams are used prominently in both works. Both are set at the time of Christ – one at his birth, the other at his death – and both are extremely unusual in mixing up first-century Romans with modern contemporaries, as well as combining noble characters with those of low birth. Both works also draw on Tasso, in the case of *Salve Deus* for the use of *ottava rima* and rules of composition, and in *Cymbeline* where Book VII of *Jerusalem Delivered* provides the story of the princess who is taken in by a father and his shepherd sons.

The works draw on a similar repertoire of imagery, even when they differ in how they use it. Cloten's headless corpse comes from Book VIII of Tasso, whereas the headless corpse that oddly concludes *Salve Deus* is that of John the Baptist and comes from the Gospel. The 'stately cedar' in *Cymbeline* appears in prophecy and will have its branches lopped. The 'comely Cedar' in the Cookham poem is only a metaphor, used to describe an oak tree. The flowers in *Cymbeline* are 'never-withering' (5.4.98), whereas at Cookham by contrast the 'very leaves did wither', both of the flowers and fruit.

According to Peggy Muñoz Simonds, *Cymbeline* is 'primarily concerned with marriage', which is a theological allegory for the 'marriage between Christ and His Church'. So is *Salve Deus*. Imogen (whose alternate name 'Fidele' means 'Faith') embraces the headless trunk of Cloten thinking that it is her husband, and carefully naming his various body parts; his leg, his hand, his foot, his thigh, his brawns, his face. Afterwards her husband reappears as Posthumus (born after death) in a kind of resurrection, 'like a descended god' (1.7.169), which suggests his allegorical identity as Jesus. Imogen/Fidele has her own resurrection as a 'dead thing alive' (5.5.123). *Salve Deus* is also a theological allegory for the 'marriage between Christ and His Church'. The Countess of Cumberland, as the allegorical Church or bride, is oddly invited to embrace the dead and mutilated Jesus: 'His bleeding body there you may embrace.' She also lists his body parts: his joints disjointed, his legs hanging, his bloody side, his members torn, his eyes dimmed and his pierced feet.

The poem 'To Mary Pembroke' uses four-line stanzas like those in 'The Phoenix and the Turtle', or the descent of Jove in *Cymbeline* given below:

> No more, you petty spirits of region low,
> Offend our hearing; hush! How dare you ghosts

Accuse the thunderer, whose bolt, you know,
Sky-planted batters all rebelling coasts?

Poor shadows of Elysium, hence, and rest
Upon your never-withering banks of flowers:
Be not with mortal accidents opprest;
No care of yours it is; you know 'tis ours.

Whom best I love I cross; to make my gift,
The more delay'd, delighted. Be content;
Your low-laid son our godhead will uplift:
His comforts thrive, his trials well are spent.

Our Jovial star reign'd at his birth, and in
Our temple was he married. Rise, and fade.
He shall be lord of lady Imogen,
And happier much by his affliction made.

Cymbeline, 5.4.93–108

The verse quality of the descent of Jupiter in *Cymbeline* was described by Dowden as 'made of wood that has no resonance', and Bloom notes, 'It is certainly an outrageous parody of the descent of any god from a machine, and we are expected to sustain it as travesty.'[9] Like Gower's interruptions in *Pericles*, it is a deliberate metatheatrical attempt to draw attention to the play's own artificiality with 'the artificial mode and incantatory verbal style of this episode, with its archaic diction and its old-fashioned verse forms'.[10] It is also the case that the other theophanies (in which a god appears) in the Shakespearean plays are characterised by rather pedestrian verse. This applies to the appearance of the god Hymen in *As You Like It*, or the appearance of Diana in *Pericles*. This is a clue that the verse in 'Salve Deus', which can be viewed as one long theophany, also seems to be a parody. It is simply a very long parody of 1,840 lines.

The Tempest *(1610), Compositional Structure*
In terms of verse structure and aesthetics, *The Tempest* is very possibly the finest Shakespearean play. None of the verse resembles *Salve Deus* at all. Yet there are other connections and similarities. Robert Johnson, who was probably Amelia's maternal cousin, has long been known to have written several of the songs in *The Tempest*, but the involvement may have been even deeper. In 2011 Dr Jonathan Holmes argued that the play was actually a collaboration between the playwright and Robert Johnson.

Among the similarities of content between *Salve Deus* and *The Tempest* are the parallel references to the unusual story of Jael and Sisera. One of those is in *The*

Tempest, where Caliban (as Jael) offers to knock a nail into Prospero's (Sisera's) head (3.2.60). Another is in *Salve Deus*, in the preface 'To the Virtuous Reader', 'As was cruel Caerus by the resolution ... of Jael wife of Heber.' Such references are very rare in contemporary literature. Other than in translations of the Bible, Jael was mentioned only twelve times in the 4,500 publications that appeared between 1600–11.

Even more interesting are the detailed structural similarities. Keir Elam, in his book *Shakespeare's Universe of Discourse*, notes how the comedies typically include one or more embedded texts, like the reading of a letter or poem placed in a 'boxed' position in the main text, and accompanied by metadiscursive commentary, jokes, and misinterpretation. *Salve Deus* and its many prefaces has precisely this kind of literary structure, one that features different kinds of audience address. Like many of the plays, it uses the conventions of a multiple-frame narrative, and resembles an ongoing commentary to the audience about a play performance, addressed to various concentric circles of audience. The central 'performance' 'onstage' is a historical religious play within a play, featuring Jesus, Pilate's Wife, the Virgin Mary, an angel and so on. These characters occasionally speak directly, but are mostly dumb, their actions being narrated in the third person. Then there is the main two-person contemporary play into which they are set, comprising the narrator and writer (Lanier herself), and the Countess of Cumberland, who does not speak, but who the narrator sometimes addresses, suggesting the relevance to her life of what has been happening. The next concentric circle of the audience includes noble ladies like the queen and Mary Sidney, who would perhaps at the Globe Theatre have been seated in a special room for nobility above the stage. Beyond them is the audience of virtuous readers in general. The narrator addresses each of these audiences separately. Finally, to complicate the matter further, inside the address to Mary Sidney there is the unusual theatrical device of a masque within the play, in which Mary Sidney and classical characters are actors. This is not a typical poetical structure: it is a *theatrical* structure. The peculiar overall structural design appears to be the direct result of the author using a theatrical model which features the inset dramatic devices that are so distinctive in Shakespeare.

Although none of *Salve Deus* is written explicitly as a drama, one 160-line section of the volume has dramatic qualities very similar to a Jacobean masque. It not only includes nymphs, Juno, Flora, flowers and singing of praises, but most unusually Juno's chariot descends to Earth. This inset masque and also the inset dreams (like the vision of Mary Sidney) resemble the inset dramas in the plays. They especially resemble how the masque has been inset into the otherwise underlying symmetrical play structure of *The Tempest*. Indeed *The Tempest*'s seventy-nine-line masque sequence has similar content, since it includes nymphs, Juno, Ceres, plants and the singing of blessings. Both versions seem to be rewritings of Daniel's *The Vision of the Twelve Goddesses* (1604):

Yet studying, if I were awake, or no,
God *Morphy* came and took me by the hand,
And willed me not from Slumbers bower to go,
Till I the sum of all did understand.
When presently the Welkin that before
Look'd bright and clear, me thought, was overcast,
And dusky clouds, with boistrous winds great store,
Foretold of violent storms which could not last,
And gazing up into the troubled sky,
Me thought a Chariot did from thence descend,
Where one did sit repleat with Majesty,
Drawn by four fiery Dragons, which did bend
Their course where this most noble Lady sate,
Whom all these virgins with due reverence
Did entertain, according to that state
Which did belong unto her Excellence.

From 'To Mary Sidney', one of the Prefaces to *Salve Deus*

Finally, there is another structural resemblance to *The Tempest*. Earlier in this book, where I outlined some of the requirements an authorship candidate must meet, an examination was made of how *The Tempest*'s symmetry is composed not through the physical space, but by the grouping of the characters. The centre is the pair of lovers, flanked by the grouping Caliban/Stephano/Trinculo, which in turn is flanked by Alonso/Sebastian/Antonio, and the outlying grouping is Prospero/Ferdinand/Miranda. The whole is enclosed in-between the 'bookends' of the ship, which appears initially in lieu of a prologue, and reappears at the end of the play (see Fig. 4).

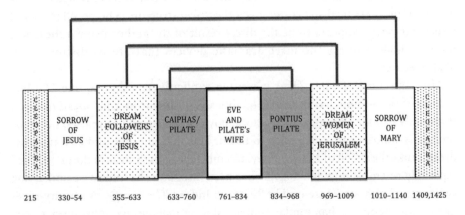

Fig. 4: The internal symmetrical structure of the 'Salve Deus' poem.

A very similar approach to literary composition is found in *Salve Deus*, in which the symmetry is also created by the pairings of characters. There is a distinct centre of Eve and Pilate's wife, flanked by outliers of Pontius Pilate/Caiphas, flanked in turn by the Women of Jerusalem/Followers of Jesus, who in turn are flanked by the Sorrow of Mary/ Sorrow of Jesus. As bookends, the whole of the poem is ultimately framed by two outlier passages about Cleopatra. For a further discussion of the similarities between *The Tempest* and *Salve Deus*, see the discussion of the genre of apocalyptic below.

Shakespeare's Plays Are Religious Plays

Unlike the world today, Elizabethans had a very good knowledge of the Bible, and the sense of living in the end time was very common, since various religious and political figures predicted the end of the world as around the year 1600. In Elizabethan society this was a mainstream belief. This was the context in which Shakespeare's works were created, and why they are to be understood as religious plays. They were written using fourteen different translations of the Bible. As Sean Benson notes in *Shakespearean Resurrection*, there are fourteen near resurrections in the plays and, as Peter Milward showed in *Shakespeare's Apocalypse*, roughly the same number of the plays concern the apocalypse. None of the authorship candidates – the Earl of Oxford, Sir Francis Bacon, Christopher Marlowe, Sir Henry Neville, Queen Elizabeth or any of the other seventy-odd – wrote poetry about the apocalypse. But Amelia Lanier certainly did. Unlike other Elizabethan plays, Shakespeare's plays are parodies of the Gospel and Book of Revelation: but so is *Salve Deus*. As an apocalyptic, neo-Platonic poem, it also resembles the explicit content of 'The Phoenix and the Turtle' (and has other similarities to *The Rape of Lucrece*).

Salve Deus is set on doomsday from the Book of Revelation, which is why God is raining down fire and brimstone. 'Storms and tempests he will rain', consuming fire will go before him, fiery flames will be his ministers, and when the scroll is unrolled:

> The Heav'ns shall perish as a garment old
> Or as a vesture by the maker changed.
>
> 'Salve Deus', lines 57–8

Salve Deus continues to follow the account in the Book of Revelation. The moon and stars are hidden in darkness, the earth trembles, monuments open and saints rise out of their graves, and the temple veil is torn. Surrounded by a rainbow, the Lord will sit on a jasper throne in heaven, and thunder and lighting will proceed from his throne and he will undo the Book of Judgement. The way that Lanier interweaves her remarks to the Countess of Cumberland makes it appear that Jesus' Crucifixion is taking place in current time, as is his return in glory. Doomsday is actually happening, and the countess is being set up as his bride, the woman clothed with the sun. The entire account is entirely satirical, for instance, in its use of the Elizabethan grotesque, though it pretends to be extremely serious. Right in the centre, however, and destabilising the entire structure is 'Eve's Apology', which invites the reader to contemplate that original sin is an entire man-made fiction, and if so there was no need for Jesus, for the Crucifixion, nor for restitution in the form of apocalypse.

Of the dozen or so Shakespearean apocalypses, one of the most important actually appears in *The Tempest*. The Book of Revelation is about the idealised utopian coming of a new heaven and a new world, when the old world shall melt away, and a new city appears, the heavenly city of Jerusalem. As Christopher Hodgkins notes in his article 'Prospero's Apocalypse', the Book of Revelation is set on a small island, the home of a powerful spiritual figure, where there is a representation of the city of Jerusalem, together with spirits, monsters, and a highly theatrical judgement. All of those features reappear on Prospero's island. However this is no 'utopia' (the Greek word means no place, and was used by Sir Thomas More as the title of his book). Punning on this, in the play Alonso says 'no more. Thou dost talk nothing' (2.1.146).

The play uses several sets of overlapping imagery to present this theme of a new world – notably the metaphor of colonising the Americas, including allusions to Peter Martyr's significantly titled book, *De Orbe Novo*. This is overlain with imagery from the Bible – the creation of the Earth as a new world, and the formation of Adam and later Joseph who prospered in Egypt. The play also incorporates the theme of Aeneas being called to create a new city from Virgil's *Aeneid*. All of these themes are integrated with images from the Book of Revelation. The play begins with the tempest and with the messenger in flames of fire whose name is Ariel, a name for Jerusalem. This echoes the translation in the newly published King James Bible of Isaiah 29:1–6, which had influenced the account in Revelation:

> Woe to Ariel, to Ariel, the city where David dwelt! ... Yet I will distress Ariel, and there shall be heaviness and sorrow ... Thou shalt be visited of the Lord of hosts with thunder, and with earthquake, and great noise, with storm and tempest, and the flame of devouring fire.
>
> Isaiah 29:1–6

While Steven Marx pushes these parallels too far in 'The Tempest as Apocalypse' in his book *Shakespeare and the Bible*, one of Prospero's roles is indeed that of the irascible god who issues thunder and lightning. He is Christ who creates illusions of storms, becomes invisible, animates urchins and cramps, and provides illusory disappearing banquets. This echoes Marlowe's Dr Faustus, who was in part based on Christ and Simon Magus, who used the Latin name Faustus, the favoured one. In Italian this can be translated as Prospero. Caliban momentarily represents Adam, because he is first addressed as 'earth' (1.2.314), drawing upon the original Hebrew term for Adam who was the 'earth creature'. The same allusion appears in *Salve Deus*, when Eve, being made from Adam, is made from 'the ground of all'. But Caliban is also a 'puppy headed monster', like his predecessor in the romance *The Primaleon,* and he soon becomes the monstrous, many-headed beast of Apocalypse. Like that beast he is consigned to a noxious, filthy lake. Towards the end of the play people put on glistening raiment, then as in the apocalypse, the 'sea gave up her dead' (Revelation, 20:13), and mention is made of how the globe dissolves into the air. The old city of Jerusalem, namely Ariel, is set free from captivity, and according to the Book of Revelation we then await the coming of the new city – or a version of it – knowing that Shakespearean cities have ranged from the name of Fortinbrass in *Hamlet* to the globular Luce who was shaped like a square, and contained whole countries in *The Comedy of Errors*.

Oddly, in *The Tempest,* the new city, which echoes the 'brave new world' that Miranda mentions, appears in the form of the chess game. Chess was a common aristocratic game, and the Shakespearean plays refer to it several times – Kent compares himself to a pawn in *King Lear; Henry VI, Part 2* refers to checkmate; and *King John* refers to the ability of a queen to put a piece in check. With a name deriving from *miraculum,* the Latin for 'wonder', Miranda is the wonder in heaven (Revelation, 12:1), the woman clothed with the sun from Book of Revelation. She considers whether she is 'any god of power' (1.2.10), is greeted as a 'goddess' (1.2.424 and 5.1.187), and oddly her eyes are covered with fringed curtains like those covering the Holy of Holies in the Temple of Jerusalem. Ferdinand is heralded as a 'temple' (1.2.457) and 'a thing divine' (1.2.418). So evidently the couple are an allegory for both God and Temple, which have been kept under the control of the Christian divinity and are now finally being reunited. Ferdinand thinks himself King of Naples (Neapolis meaning new city), but instead of descending from heaven with the new city of Jerusalem, the young people are 'discovered' playing chess – 'discovered' is a term in chess which refers to the previous regime, i.e. that of Prospero, having been overtaken.

In his widely circulated *Book of Chess* (1474), Iacopo de Cessolis regarded the chessboard as a city, claiming that it originally represented the city of Babylon. In the Book of Revelation, the old Jerusalem (equated with Babylon) has fallen and a new Jerusalem appears, which is very oddly the shape of a cube. The equivalent of this in *The Tempest* is the square chessboard. As described in W. Poole's article 'False Play; Shakespeare and Chess', this is a scene of sixty-four words, the same number as the squares on a chessboard, which can be arranged, as the Oxford edition shows, in eight lines of verse representing the eight rows of the chessboard – a technique known as a 'calligram' (5.1.172–81). Miranda and Ferdinand, the future king and queen, are indeed contained 'inside' this representation of the Christian new city. In other words, in *The Tempest*, the traditional story of Apocalypse is destabilised, since the Jesus/God figure gives up his powers. He does *not* marry the Virgin Bride, who is instead (re)united with the Temple in the New Jerusalem, and who shortly departs for the literal new city of Naples.

The romances are unusual in employing independent narrators who are extraneous to the action, such as Gower in *Pericles* and Time who provides a chorus in *The Winter's Tale*. They have masque-like figures, like the goddesses who descend in the chariot of Juno in *The Tempest* or Jupiter in *Cymbeline*. There is a mixture of the pastoral and the courtly. Courtly figures are in exile, such as Prospero in *The Tempest*, Pericles who is in exile from Tyre and shipwrecked in *Pericles*, the king's sons who are exiled to a cave in *Cymbeline*, and in *The Winter's Tale* Perdita, who is brought up by shepherds, and King Polixines, who is in exile, both in Bohemia.

In *Salve Deus* the masque-like figures include the god Morpheus, who guides Amelia around her dream, and Juno descending in her chariot. The first part of the volume is set in contemporary London and comprises letters to courtly ladies, but includes an inset pastoral scene of Mary Sidney in a wood. The second half goes back in time to the year 33 CE and the Crucifixion; and the volume ends with a pastoral. The author herself acts as an independent narrator, and the focus on the noble ladies at court creates a contrast which emphasises her own position of exile in 'sorrow's cell', paralleling Prospero's 'poor cell' or the 'cell of ignorance' in *Cymbeline*. She hopes that patronage might enable her to return to a better state.

There are just too many coincidences here. By reworking the *Aeneid*'s epic, Shakespeare writes *The Tempest*, a play about alchemy, which is a kind of parody of the Book of Revelation and based on the wrecking of a ship belonging to the Virginia Company. It contains the same rare biblical imagery as *Salve Deus*, has a similar underlying literary structure, and its masque uses the same source. *Salve Deus* was written the same year, as the work of a poet who satirises the Crucifixion and Book of Revelation, and whose cousin wrote music for *The Tempest*. It is dedicated to an alchemist who was one of the Virginia Company shareholders, in a collection which ends with a pastoral poem echoing Virgil's *Eclogues*. Furthermore, *Salve Deus* mixes Roman characters (the wife of Pilate), classical gods (Juno and Morpheus) and contemporary figures (the Countess of Cumberland). This resembles the extraordinary way that Roman characters, classical gods (Jove), and contemporary Italians are mixed together in *Cymbeline*, shattering the unities of space and time. Altogether, *Salve Deus* structurally bridges *both* of these Shakespearean plays in a way that is inexplicable unless they were created by the same writer.

9

The Final Years, School Teacher, Litigant and More: 1617–1645

We now return to pick up Amelia's biography again. It would appear that *Salve Deus* was not successful in creating any patronage income: indeed, very few copies of it exist and it was barely known until the 1970s. Lanier is still little known as a poet, despite being the first Englishwoman to publish a book of original poetry. The next time we hear of her, the other Bassanos and Laniers are having successful careers working as members of the consort of musicians for the King's Men, and working on masques at court for Ben Jonson and others. Jonson worked with Lanier's cousin Robert Johnson, the lute player who directed the music for *The Masque of Oberon* – whose extensive wind music required thirteen shawms and two cornetts as well as flageolets (recorders). Jonson also worked with Lanier's sister-in-law's second husband, his 'excellent friend' Alfonso Ferrabosco II. Most of all, he worked with her brother-in-law, Alphonso Lanier's younger brother, Nicholas Lanier II, who was something of a virtuoso both for his taste in paintings, and as a composer. Indeed, Ben Jonson described one of his masques as having 'the musique composed by that excellent pair of kinsmen, Mr Alphonso Ferrabosco and Mr Nicholas Lanier'.

However by around 1609, because Alfonso had wasted their money on unsuccessful real-estate speculations and on supporting Lord Essex as a gentleman volunteer, unpaid and without expenses, Amelia was now in a difficult financial position, almost a pauper. She describes herself as being in 'great misery'. For many years Alphonso had been trying to get legal rights to a hay patent that he thought would make their fortune – he was going to get sixpence for every load of hay brought in to the city and three pence for every load of straw. Yet for various bureaucratic reasons it still hadn't happened – even though he got Bishop Bancroft to write a letter stating that he was his old friend and a fine fellow. So by 1609 they had moved out of Central London to the small suburban village of Hackney, best known for its turnip fields. They were not happy there either; the last we see of Alphonso is him getting into a street fight in which he abused the 'headborough', or constable of the parish, kicking him and pulling him on the nose, for which he was bound over to keep the peace.

By 1617 Amelia's brother-in-law, the virtuoso Nicholas Lanier, had extended his collaboration with Ben Jonson so that he composed the music, painted the scenery, and even performed in Jonson's masque *Lovers Made Men* (1617), for which he had written what was later claimed to be England's very first operatic *recitativo*. This masque would show him to be a virtuoso not only of art but of music. Although the new *recitativo* would not be well accepted, because it did not affect the native manner of speaking as well as it might, it made a great impression. As the *New Grove Dictionary of Music* puts it, Nicholas Lanier was 'one of the most important English songwriters of his time, particularly as an innovator'. For instance, he helped develop declamatory airs with chordal accompaniment like 'Hero and Leander'. However, it must have seemed enormously unfair that young Nicholas Lanier had a position at court for which he was paid £200 a year, and was off travelling in Italy, drinking wine, having a good time and buying pictures by Van Dyck for His Majesty, while Amelia had to look after her grandchildren Mary and Henry, and was unable to get the £20 that she needed to live on from the hay patent.

Unfortunately Amelia's relationship with Alphonso's other brothers Clement and Innocent had worsened. She was still embroiled in her series of legal actions to try and get the money she was owed for her share of her husband's hay patent – which had finally been granted only a year before his death. She filed the lawsuit as a pauper *in forma pauperis* in the Court of Requests so she didn't have to pay costs. She would even petition the Privy Council twice. The lawsuit would go on for over ten years, and must have been very difficult and complex. Her ability to pursue and manage these major lawsuits suggests that she had the legal knowledge that is found in the Shakespearean plays, although the law references in *Salve Deus* – seven mentions of 'law', six mentions of 'case', five mentions of 'justice' and so on – are limited.

So in 1617, at the age of forty-eight, when Nicholas Lanier was enjoying the fame of his *recitativo* at court, Amelia moved from the turnip fields of Hackney closer to Central London, to rent a farmhouse in St Giles-in-the-Fields, just east of Charing Cross. It was a sluttish part of town, with Drury Lane running through the middle of it, but was located midway between the court and the City. The farmhouse cost £22 a year, and Amelia wanted to open a school. She would indeed be one of the first women in England to found, own and teach in a school, but almost immediately she ran into new legal problems:

> Emelia Lanier … by the death of [her] husband being left in very poor estate (he having spent a great part of his estate in serving of the late Queen in her wars in Ireland and other places) for her maintenance and relief she was compelled to teach and educate the children of divers worth and understanding …
>
> Records of Chancery Case, November 1620

Amelia kept falling behind with the rent. Edward Smith, the owner of the farmhouse she was using as a school, wanted to break the lease, and quarrelled with her over repairs. This resulted in yet another lawsuit in which Amelia sought to recover the £10 she had spent in repairs. The school closed down after only two years.

However, over all these years it would appear that Amelia continued to modify and revise the plays, including writing a brand-new scene for *The Merry Wives of Windsor*, which could conceivably draw on her experience of school teaching in the 1620s. It features a schoolboy, William Page, who is being taught Latin in a language lesson. William's teacher is a Welshman who makes fritters of English, and has a poor knowledge of Latin, merely repeating William's errors in a Welsh accent (4.1.42). Evidently, such a young man with such a poor education at the hands of a Welshman would be able to make a very poor 'page' (of writing). Indeed, his language lesson is quite obscene. Asked for a genitive case William amusingly quotes from his textbook 'harum, horum', making the conventional pun that a vagina, or in slang, a 'case', would be the correct case for a *gens* (the Latin term referring to a people). Mistress Quickly (Quick-Lay) is naturally shocked that he should know such a word, since she thinks that 'horum' is the plural of whore.

But when asked for the vocative case he does no better. The case in the 'focative' (4.1.45) is another obscene 'case' (or container), the 'O' or 'no-thing' (as it is called in *Hamlet*) is once more the vagina, which he addresses literally, 'O, vocative – O.' Most comically, Amelia is parodying young Will and his activities as whoring; he engages in the pretence of love, but it is merely a financial transaction. Whereas Touchstone wanted to kill the clown William, *The Merry Wives of Windsor* merely shows William being tested on 'some questions in his accidence' (4.1.15), this being William Lily's *Accidence* or *Latin Grammar*, a standard third-form text which Amelia had probably used on the students in her own schoolroom. The question that he is asked, 'how many numbers is in nouns?', can be found at page one of the *Accidence*, so Amelia is clearly depicting William as needing the most basic kind of grammatical education.

Ben Jonson had assembled his own collection of plays, or 'works', as he called them – the first of his to be printed as a collection. Since he was a friend of Lanier's family, and one of England's leading writers, he was the logical person to edit the First Folio, and to write the introduction (even though it would be credited to the actors Heminge and Condell). Jonson's involvement would endorse the project's legitimacy, although prevailing opinion would still have regarded a volume composed entirely of plays as trivial and not possibly worth the cost. Yet Amelia had eighteen manuscripts of plays that had never been printed. Moreover, of her manuscripts that included a specific Amelia/Emily type character, several had not been printed: *Antony and Cleopatra*, *Julius Caesar*, *The Comedy of Errors*, *Two Noble Kinsmen* and *The Winter's Tale*. She had evidently resisted having them printed, possibly in case it made it easy to identify her, and she had been working for years on the revisions. But since she was now around fifty years old it was important that there should be a collected edition of all her works. Apart from anything else, this would make it more likely that in future people would be able to study all the plays and comprehend their allegories.

Although the brothers Christopher and Edward Blount were distant relatives of the Willoughby family, Peregrine Bertie, the Lord Willoughby, specifically called them 'cousin' and 'kin', and Christopher had served under him in the Low Countries. Around 1594 Edward Blount had set up his own business, and since then had gradually become one of the best stationers/publishers in London. There had been some problems with the printing of *Love's Martyr*, which had several slightly differing editions, but his books were generally of a high quality. By 1620, cousin Edward had been in business on his own for over fifteen years, and his bookshop, The Black Bear, was well established. For two decades he had been a 'good and kind friend' of fellow bookseller Thomas Thorpe, who had brought out *The Passionate Pilgrim* (1609) as well as the proper registered collection of *Shakespeare's Sonnets* (1609). Blount's other friends included the Oxford don he called 'my good friend Mr Mabb', who in his spare time was acting on behalf of Spain as a 'perpetual spy' on the Church of England, and Digges, whose book on *The Rape of Prosperine* (1617) he had already published.

In Digges' poem the title is dedicated to the memory of Shakespeare, whereas the following twenty-two-line poem refers three times to the name with a hyphen, implying that these refer to two different individuals, the author and the actor. Digges' praise is deliberately and obviously misleading. He praises the plays for never plagiarising, when whole plots were lifted from Holinshed and the Gospels. He praises them for never imitating Latin or Greek writers, when whole speeches are taken from Plutarch. He praises them for not borrowing scenes from others when the early plays for instance borrow heavily from Marlowe. Digges is giving false praise as a deliberate rhetorical device, in order to indicate to the reader that the subject of that praise, Mr Shake-speare, is equally false.

In view of his literary reputation, it was easy for Jonson to act as the overall public editor of the First Folio, which was grandly conceived as an equivalent to the works of Plato. The title page of the First Folio lists the contents of thirty-five plays, but the actual volume contains thirty-six, including *Troilus and Cressida* – which is not listed on the title page. When *Troilus and Cressida* is added, the thirty-six plays divide into three tables, each of twelve plays, representing the histories, comedies and tragedies. It would appear that they were arranged in this fashion in order to suggest that they should be regarded as an equivalent to the works of Plato, who also wrote thirty-six Dialogues, of which one is lost, so only thirty-five remain.

Edward Blount himself would help Jonson draft something appropriate for the noble lords to sign as the 'Epistle Dedicatorie'. There was a standard protocol for these things which Blount had used elsewhere, for instance in his publication of *Hero and Lysander*. The protocol should regret that the author was not there to personally see the book through to publication, and should take action as an executor on behalf of his literary children 'to procure his orphans guardians' and as a kind of funeral rite 'an office to the dead'.

As June Schlueter's article 'Martin Droeshout Redivivus' has shown, the well-known portrait in the First Folio was made by Martin Droeshout the Younger. His uncle Michael, who was a coppersmith, may have helped with the copper etching. The First Folio itself was an expensive book, so buyers would have expected that it would have a high-quality engraving. Most oddly, unlike, say, Jonson's collected works or other contemporary publications, the title page contains merely the engraving, without any border or frame, and without the mythological emblems that this printer conventionally used. The portrait is set like an icon against a barren page. In fact, all of the apparatus that was normally used by a printer to situate an author into a context, such as depictions of Mr Shakespeare's land holdings, his properties in Stratford, even any play quartos, or literary characters from the plays, is all entirely missing.

Moreover, although the engraving appears blank and wooden, this is not due to a lack of the engraver's skill, but is due to the original design and the fact that it was presumably intended as a satire: the younger Droeshout's expertise was in creating satirical engravings. There would have been no reason to choose this particular engraver unless the editors wanted to create a *satire* of the man from Stratford.

The engraving is a visual reflection of the satires in the plays. The engraving is unusually large and takes up 400 per cent more of the space on the title page than any other portrait of the period. So it is being given unusual prominence. Most inexplicably, his coat of arms is also missing, strongly suggesting that the man from Stratford was not to be identified as the author. In a Shakespeare-like pun, instead of a heraldic coat of arms the figure itself wears a *literal* coat of arms. His doublet is back to front, as an article in a tailoring magazine hundreds of years later would point out, making him look like a harlequin or a clown. And he has two left arms – or to be precise, the correct left arm in its normal place, but instead of a right arm the engraving has the back of another left arm. In the words of the title of an article by John Rollett, this is 'Shakespeare's Impossible Doublet', and was evidently intended as a satire. The words that Jonson wrote to accompany the engraving, 'To The Reader', may also be suggestive. One of the clues in the engraving is in its 'brasse' (significantly in French this means 'arms'), a word that is mentioned twice even though engravers actually did not work in brass; they worked in copper. Apart from meaning the metal, in Elizabethan English it also meant impudence, brazenness or effrontery. In *Love's Labour's Lost* a character asks, 'Can any face of brass hold longer out?' (5.2.395)

> ... but these wayes
> Were not the paths I meant unto thy praise;
> For seeliest Ignorance on these may light,
> Which, when it sounds at best, but eccho's right;
> Or blinde Affection, which doth ne're advance
> The truth, but gropes, and urgeth all by chance;
> Or crafty Malice, might pretend this praise,
> And thine to ruine, where it seem'd to raise.
> These are, as some infamous Bawd, or Whore,
> Should praise a Matron. What could hurt her more?
>
> Ben Jonson, *To the Memory*

Jonson had been unable to say what he wanted directly in his prefaces. Here in his poem 'To the Memory of My Beloved' Jonson discusses the precise nature of the praise that he wishes to give to Shakespeare, and draws attention to the difficulty that the task is causing him. The praise may sound 'best' and 'right', but is instead governed by the sort of artificial blindness, referred to as 'seeliest', which is the blindness of a hawk when its eyelids are sewn shut during training. Such words might seem to praise, but by seeming to raise Shakespeare's reputation, might actually 'ruin' the reputation of the true author. Jonson also most oddly compares the author to a 'Matron' – an elderly lady, which Amelia now certainly was since she was aged fifty-three – about whom the praise of an 'infamous Bawd or Whore' could only be harmful. He doesn't want to hurt Amelia, the 'Matron', by falsely praising Mr Shakespeare, but cannot praise her directly without breaching her pseudonym. Jonson is clearly stating that he cannot praise the author in the way he would wish, and therefore has to praise that 'infamous Bawd or Whore'.

It was common for classical authors to leave a concealed signature in their works: it was known as a *sphragis*, or signet. In *Titus Andronicus*, she had left her signature in a simple and straightforward way. The signature was obvious, you simply had to look at the beginning and end of the play where two characters appear who don't really have very much to do. They have equivalent roles, in the crowning of the new emperor at the end and the beginning of the play, and should therefore be considered as linked by this rhetorical parallelism. While the figure of Bassianus appears in *Christ's Tears over Jerusalem*, and also appears in a rewriting of Herodian by Antonio de Guevara, the life of the historical Bassianus, better known as the Emperor Caracalla, was one of bloodcurdling cruelty. By contrast the Bassianus character in the play is moral and upright, speaks of freedom, justice and nobility, and reproaches Titus for his lack of piety. To understand these characters as a literary signature, simply turn them around so that the last is first and there you have her name, in the masculine tense.

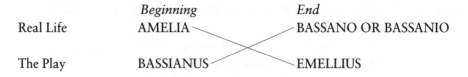

	Beginning	*End*
Real Life	AMELIA	BASSANO OR BASSANIO
The Play	BASSIANUS	EMELLIUS

However, by making an amendment to the text of the 1622 quarto of *Othello* (and possibly another to *King John*), Amelia left behind an even more complex signature crossing multiple plays. The standard image of the great poet was the swan dying to music. It had been applied to Ovid not only by himself in the *Tristia*, the book he wrote in exile, but also by the poet Arion, who dies in the *Fasti* making a noise like the plucking of a harp.

It was also an image commonly used in the English Renaissance. In his last work, *Groats-Worth*, playwright Robert Greene noted, 'The swan sings melodious before death that in all his life useth but a jarring sound' thus 'Greene sends you his swanne like song.' Poet Sir Philip Sidney is praised by Matthew Roydon as a dying swan in *The Phoenix Nest* (1593). Even John Weever is praised as a dying swan in an introduction to his writings. The metaphor is also used by Sir Thomas Wyatt, Thomas Lodge, Thomas

Watson, Phineas Fletcher and by Erasmus in a reference to John Skelton. The literary allusions in English literature go back to Chaucer, and were used in a madrigal by Orlando Gibbons in 1612. So it is a well-established literary symbol. And it contrasts with the reference to Mr Shakespeare from Stratford-upon-Avon as a 'sweet swan', since English swans were mute! When the extra 163 lines were added to *Othello*, strengthening the part of the character Emelia, she is made to repeat the willow song, and says:

> I will play the swan
> And die in music, Willow, willow, willow
>
> *Othello*, 5.2.245–6

Another character who is contemplated as dying a similar dramatised swan-like death appears in *The Merchant of Venice*, and his name is Bassanio, the alternative spelling of her own family name found in the London burial records:

> Let music sound while he doth make his choice;
> Then, if he lose, he makes a swan-like end,
> Fading in music
>
> *The Merchant of Venice*, 3.2.43–5

The third example is in *King John* in which John's son Henry says:

> I am the cygnet to this pale faint swan
> Who chants a doeful hymn to his own death
>
> *King John*, 5.7.21–2

In this manner the standard image of the great poet is associated with these four names, including her mother's name of Johnson (she was not married to Baptista), her father's name, her first name, and the name of her adopted family:

EMILIA from *Othello*
WILLOW(BY) from *Othello*
JOHN's SON from *King John*
BASSANIO from *The Merchant of Venice*

We can also assume that it was in this later period that Amelia added the scene in *The Merry Wives of Windsor* in which a William Page has problems with page one of the Latin grammar, and also his depiction as the drunken tinker in the induction of *The Taming of the Shrew*.

It is conventionally thought that *Two Noble Kinsmen* was written around 1614 because Ben Jonson is believed to refer to it, in which case it would be the last Shakespearean play to have been composed. It was definitely the last to appear in print, since the quarto did not appear until 1634. The story from Chaucer's *Canterbury Tales* had been dramatised before in *Palamon and Arcyte* (1566), and *The Knight's Tale* had also been used in *A Midsummer Night's Dream*, where Chaucer's character Emeyle is divided into two, although the male characters retain their names. She revisited Chaucer for *Two Noble Kinsmen* and created a fiendishly complicated allegorical story; we can only wonder if it was a coincidence that a central figure in this last play, Princess Emilia, is the sister of the Amazon queen Hippolyta.

We know almost nothing of Amelia's final years, although now that we know which lens to look through, there are certain matters that deserve investigation. There is the strange matter of someone who took a copy of the Second Folio (1632) and made thousands of corrections to it. Some of them were undoubtably made by Collier the forger – but all of them? The copy still exists, today, in the Huntingdon Library, where it is known as the Perkins Folio. It includes, for instance, a correction of an error in *Titus Andronicus* that had appeared in the First Folio – one that restored the reading that had appeared in the 1594 quarto. This was either done by an extremely zealous and scholarly corrector who had a copy of the quarto published nearly thirty years previously, or was done by someone who knew what was really meant.

As for Stratford-upon-Avon, Leonard Digges's poem in the First Folio foresees that at some point in the future the stonework of Mr Shakespeare's monument would be 'rent' (broken open). At that point, when 'time dissolves thy Stratford moniment', those who are alive will at last view the author through the words of the plays and not through that *moniment* – a pun on monument and a Scottish word meaning 'a laughing stock'. After 400 years, that process of dissolution is now clearly taking place, though it has been a long and difficult journey.

There has been previous recognition, since the 1960s, by Hirschorn, Basch and others, that the main author of the plays was a Marrano Jew and the Marrano community in London was dominated by a single family, the Bassanos. Stephanie Hopkins Hughes had suggested in an article that the Earl of Oxford worked on the plays with Amelia Bassano among others, and Joseph Atwill had speculated (in a personal communication) that several members of the Bassano family collaborated on the plays – for which there is no evidence at all. Ilya Gililov, in his book *The Great Phoenix*, published originally in Russian in 1997, was correct – before revising his opinion – in identifying the author of *Salve Deus*, which she wrote under her own name, with the primary co-author of the Shakespearean canon. In keeping with the scriptwriting conventions of the period, and varying from play to play, she worked as designer (or plotter), coadjutor, contributor and collaborator (together with Kyd, Peele, Marlowe, Fletcher and others).

But all that is for future investigators to examine. New documents will undoubtedly turn up in the future as scholars finally begin to pay Amelia Bassano Lanier the attention she deserves. As for today, in marked contrast to the elaborate 'Shakespeare Shrine' of Stratford-upon-Avon, she still lies quietly where she has remained ever since April 1645, at St James's, Clerkenwell, London EC1, in her unmarked grave, without even a plaque.

10

Conclusion

This book has aimed not merely to provide a new approach to the question of who wrote the poems and the plays, but also to address the related questions of why they were written and how the plays should be performed to reveal the playwright's underlying meanings. Although this work is just a beginning, Professor Kelly Morgan, founder of the Mint Theatre in New York City, and formerly Chair of Theatre at Case Western Reserve University, concludes that the present research opens up 'new and breathtaking performance avenues for professional companies and a multitude of possibilities for academic researchers'.

In 2016 the world will stage massive celebrations for the 400th anniversary of the death of Shakespeare. Yet this book has shown that Mr William Shakespeare cannot have written the plays that are published under his name. It also eliminates all the other leading contenders for primary authorship. A *new* candidate was needed. So now, 150 years since the first female author was proposed in 1857, this book has proposed Amelia Bassano Lanier. The case for her is not complete – that would hardly be feasible since she has only been known to modern scholars since the 1970s, and she has been the subject of very little research. There are a couple of hundred publications on Amelia, compared to over 2 million for Mr Shakespeare. Whereas there has been about a century of investigation on Marlowe, Bacon and Oxford as authorship candidates, the case for Amelia is only a few years old. Whereas cumulatively millions of years' work by tens of thousands of scholars have gone into investigating Mr Shakespeare, this book is just one small step in making the case for Lanier's involvement.

Attempts to resolve the problem that Mr Shakespeare could not have written the plays have led some people to go to extreme lengths. Popular Internet discussion groups speculate that the Shakespearean plays were written by an alien, or a 1,000-year-old vampire, by a time traveller who took the collected works back to the sixteenth century and had Mr Shakespeare copy them out, or by a very sophisticated future computer program that sent the plays to him through a time warp. Leaving aside such fantastic explanations, it is clear that at the minimum, the author had to have been a poet who lived in London in the late sixteenth and early seventeenth centuries. Out of London's total population of perhaps 200,000, only a very limited number of such individuals existed. The Claremont Clinic, for instance, has considered and excluded all the following writers: William Alexander, Francis Bacon, Richard Barnfield, Barnabe Barnes, Robert Burton, Henry Chettle, Samuel Daniel, Edward de Vere (Earl of Oxford), Thomas Dekker, Robert Devereux (Earl of Essex), John Donne, Sir Edward Dyer, John Fletcher, Thomas Kyd, Thomas Lodge, John Lyly, Christopher Marlowe, Thomas Middleton, Anthony Munday, Thomas Nashe, George Peele, Henry Porter, Sir Walter Raleigh, Mary Sidney, Sir Philip Sidney, Edmund Spenser, Queen Elizabeth, Robert Greene, Bartholomew Griffin, Thomas Heywood, Ben Jonson, William Warner, John Webster, and Robert Wilson. If you exclude all of these as impossible, then really there is only *one* possible candidate left. She is the subject of this book. The 'negative' argument by elimination shows that she is the only candidate. The 'positive' argument, showing how and why she wrote these plays, as outlined in these last few chapters, has only just begun.

After 400 years there are at last signs of change, which may mean that the present work will help to bring about a reorientation of the field. If the plays had been written by, say, the Earl of Oxford, the discovery would have made little difference and nothing would have to change. It would have carried no implications about what the plays actually are, why they were written, or what meanings an audience is supposed to gather from them. That is why the case for Amelia Bassano Lanier is very different, because unlike these others, it changes the meaning of the plays in a way that has profound implications for performance, and which will be the subject of a separate book.

Today, as theatres go out of business and audiences become increasingly elderly, there is much discussion of new 'immersive' and participative kinds of theatre to attract new audiences. In these, the consumer helps select the narrative, and the audience are no longer passive spectators, but people who are more actively engaged with the actors and the world they are manufacturing. To me, this is a welcome return to a theatre model that seems more akin to that of the Elizabethan theatre. There the stage was always a venue for the actors to engage in 'direct address' with the audience – indeed, audience members could sit on chairs on the stage itself. Moreover, the playhouse as a venue was consciously situated within an entire cityscape of immersive performances, the hub of which was the court of Gloriana herself. In the absence of both newspapers and theatre critics, deciphering the play was the job of any intelligent observer.

So it is a hopeful sign that one of the most successful Shakespeare adaptations of the twenty-first century took the text of *Macbeth*, severely cut it, and added layers of complex intertextual meanings, ranging from the movies of Hitchcock to classical references, in order to create the immersive production *Sleep No More*, produced by the wildly popular UK company Punchdrunk. The resulting meanings were conveyed through choreography and elaborate sets in scores of darkened rooms, spread over several warehouses, through which the audience wandered around in masks. I spent a day with the company in 2011 being shown how to place bundles of hair into little boxes and how to build real walls in their maze-like garden. The result has been frustrating to those expecting a linear narrative, but has been compared to a video game in which the participant has to uncover and engage with successive layers of meaning. Such theatre is part of our postmodern and Internet-enabled world, which has led immersive moviemakers like James Cameron to attempt to create a universe into which the viewer can immerse him or herself deeper and deeper. However, as is finally being appreciated, that is precisely what the designer of these plays did over 400 years ago.[1]

Sleep No More is very much in the tradition of the complex allegorical games that shaped Shakespeare's plays. It has also successfully attracted audiences, and a cult following devoted to solving the meanings of the production.[2] Somewhat similarly, the genre known as armchair treasure hunts was sparked by a children's book, *Masquerade*, which sold hundreds of thousands of copies and generated nationwide treasure hunts to understand the inner meanings of the book, and identify the UK location at which a gold pendant had been buried. The present book is a small first step towards repositioning the Shakespearean canon as the precursor of such literary games. An understanding of how and why they were written may, I hope, stimulate people to crowdsource the multiple layers of meanings in the plays in order to reveal the treasures that they contain.

Although the Shakespearean works present deep clues to the identity of the author – such as the Aemelius and Bassianus in *Titus Andronicus*, the 'swan signatures' across *The Merchant of Venice* and *Othello*, and Touchstone as the *basanos* in *As You Like It* – all of these are only apparent if one investigates beneath the surface of the text. At the level of a superficial reading, the Shakespearean works go out of their way to conceal the author's biography and identity.

Patrick Cheney, in his book *Shakespeare's Literary Authorship*, has commented that the author is not foregrounded in writing the plays, but stands back in order to foreground the characters. He refers to this as 'Shakespeare's strategy of self-concealment', and concludes that this 'self-concealing authorship may indeed be unique'. Today, it would seem that there were very good reasons for this. The playwright needed to conceal her authorship because, if the wrong people had solved the amazing anti-Christian allegories in the plays, she would certainly have been executed.

Another side of this argument was discussed by E. A. J. Honigmann in an article in *Connotations*.[3] Having previously referred to the dramatist as 'unknowable', he followed it up by remarking on Mr Shakespeare's secretiveness in his everyday life. He frequently changed his lodgings and 'throughout his life he seems to have been a far less visible presence than other, less admired writers. He neither offered nor requested complimentary verses ... he did not proof-read or write dedications for his plays. Why?' The answer, it now appears, is that since Mr Shakespeare was simply the play broker, he would not have been able to engage in deep conversations about them and therefore needed to minimise his social involvement: this is why, very remarkably, only one literary figure, Ben Jonson, claimed to know him – and satirised him unmercifully.

Richmond Crinkley was on track in his article 'New Perspectives on the Authorship Question' when he asked, 'Is it possible that both Stratfordians and anti-Stratfordians have asked the authorship question in the wrong way?' Indeed, it not only possible, it is, I believe, exactly what happened, so that people did not see what was right in front of their eyes.

It appears that the only person who has included Amelia Lanier in a stylistic analysis of authorship candidates was Hugh Craig, who co-edited *Shakespeare, Computers, and the Mystery of Authorship*. For his article 'Common-words frequencies, Shakespeare's style, and the Elegy by W. S.', he took 2,000-word samples from all the poets born between 1560 and 1600 contained in the *Norton Anthology*. This meant he included the central 'Eve's Apology' section of the 'Salve Deus' poem, and the Cookham poem. However, the tests Craig applied were statistical counts of the appearance of common words such as 'and', 'but', 'not', 'so' and 'that'. Unfortunately there are no good grounds to suppose that the distribution of such common words is a valid way of identifying a Shakespearean poem.

As Brian Vickers emphasised, the chief characteristic of the Shakespearean works is their variety and adaptability, not a distinctive usage of the word 'and', or other common words. Indeed, Craig himself admits that there are problems in comparing dramatic verse with non-dramatic verse, he acknowledges that even when comparing known Shakespearean texts one to the other, either because the 'works have unusually high internal variation, or because they show few stylistic quirks, they do not ... form strong clusters when tested with established multivariate methods'. Granted this, it is not strange that Craig's research, with such a small sample of text and no matching by date or genre, failed to notice the characteristics which identify Lanier as the author of the Shakespearean works. Let me take another example, a recent article 'Language Individuation and Marker Words: Shakespeare and His Maxwell's Demon' by John Marsden, Budden, Craig and Moscato. It examined over 55,000 unique words in 168 plays, and claims to have identified a unique Shakespearean vocabulary. Unfortunately the study does not take genre into account, nor does it distinguish the language in the extensive prose passages from the language in the dramatic verse. More critically, this is a study only of plays and thus includes neither the sonnets, *The Rape of Lucrece*, *Venus and Adonis*, nor any other poems. It is of no use in interrogating the Shakespearean dimensions of Lanier's poetry.

Sadly, the entire search for Shakespeare is full of people who have chosen inappropriate search methodologies, and have as a result got nowhere. The search probably reached its nadir in December 2009 when the Shakespearean Birthplace Trust in Stratford-upon-Avon began a fantastic archaeological investigation of the ruins of the house in which Shakespeare had lived. As a member of the Trust commented, they were dreaming of finding 'a first draft of

The Tempest', but appropriately enough all they actually managed to find was (perhaps) Mr Shakespeare's cesspit or latrine. Similarly, in 1938 the UK Bacon Society endeavoured to dig up the tomb of poet Edmund Spenser in Westminster Abbey in search of proof that he collaborated with Sir Francis Bacon on writing the plays. However, because they did not know which tomb was Spenser's they ended up excavating the tomb of the eighteenth-century poet Matthew Prior. One of them then proposed displaying his body to the public for six shillings a head, presumably to recover their expenses. All these pieces of 'research' and many, many, others ended up going nowhere. Researchers simply need to do what any intelligent person would have done and as the First Folio advises us to do – to look deeply into the plays themselves, and use not complex databases and big data mining tools, but much more simply the elements of an Elizabethan mindset.

In a critical review 'The State of Authorship Attribution Studies' Joseph Rudman concluded that computer-based word analysis studies of Shakespeare had 'serious problems', noted that there is no consensus in the field about methodologies or key findings, and that the approach promises nothing but a 'spate of flawed articles'. That was more than a decade ago, however, and there are promising developments in the area of Shakespeare and big data, including the Stanford Literary Lab, the data-mining work led by Michael Witmore at the Folger, and a range of interesting student projects.[4] Such initiatives may eventually allow computer-based studies to answer sophisticated questions. That, however, lies some years in the future. In the recent article 'Shakepeare and Authorship Studies in the Twenty-First Century', Sir Brian Vickers summarises the research in the words of its critics as being 'in a state of confusion' and 'in disarray'. He concludes that 'the discipline remains in flux' and in 'turmoil', fundamentally because it wrongly assumes that language can be usefully fragmented into isolated words for analytical purposes. It gives, as he puts it 'the illusion of scientific procedure,' but 'generates no useful results'.

This book brings together a number of well-known problems in the case for the man from Stratford. Having his name on the cover can no longer be considered to be sufficient evidence that he actually wrote the plays: it is purely circumstantial. Nobody claims that they saw him writing the plays, and there is no evidence anyone ever wrote with him collaboratively face to face in the same room. The fact that he handed the plays to the acting company, even if these fair copies were in his own handwriting, does not mean that he actually *composed and authored* these texts. To demonstrate that requires more specific evidence. The proper way of testing the hypothesis that Mr Shakespeare wrote the plays would be to see if it can be falsified and if there is data that the hypothesis cannot explain. Indeed there is. The hypothesis cannot explain a long list of anomalies.

In any normal process of scientific inquiry, such anomalies would be quite definitive in getting the hypothesis rejected. Unfortunately the Shakespeare industry is self-regulating, and the consumer has no protection from those who make unsubstantiated claims, motivated by bias and self-interest. The following table provides a systematic presentation of the knowledge bases known to have been possessed by the author of the plays, and compares Mr Shakespeare against the other candidates. It is easy to see that he has a very poor fit against these criteria.

Knowledge Map of Candidates for the Shakespearean Authorship

Key: Oxf. = The Earl of Oxford, Bac. = Francis Bacon, Mar. = Christopher Marlowe, Lan. = Amelia Lanier, Sh. = William Shakespeare.

Key Knowledge Criteria	Oxf.	Bac.	Mar.	Lan.	Sh.
Known friendly association with Earl of Southampton	0	1	0	5	0
Alive to make changes to 1622 quarto of Othello	0	10	0	10	0
Match to the sonnets as lacking a proud title	0	0	10	10	10
Match to the sonnets as to be buried in a common grave	0	0	0	10	0
Known to Ben Jonson, who comments on the author	0	10	0	10	10
Documented to have used a library of books	9	10	10	9	0
Took an anti-Christian stance	10	0	10	10	0
Was documented as an innovative experimental poet	2	2	9	9	0
Known links to The Lord Chamberlain's Men	0	0	0	10	10
Substantial known contact with falconers	2	2	0	10	0
Known association with feminists	0	0	0	10	0
Known associations with Jews	3	0	0	10	0
Access to resources to learn Hebrew	0	10	0	10	0
Knowledge of Italian	10	10	10	10	0
Proven to have visited Italy	10	10	0	3	3
Known deep associations with musicians	4	4	0	10	0
Known visits to northern England	3	3	3	8	0
Known relationship with generals	3	3	0	10	0
Known association with visitors to Denmark	0	0	0	8	1
Experience at court	10	10	2	10	2
Known association with judges and lawyers	7	10	2	8	2
Known association with silk weavers	0	0	0	10	0
Known association with leading medical doctors	3	3	3	3	1
Known sea/river journeys to learn seamanship	10	10	10	10	0
Known associates involved in Danish astronomy	0	0	0	10	0
Known association with collectors of rare plants	0	0	0	10	0
Known association with navigators/explorers	3	3	0	6	0
Wrote poetry in standard English	4	10	10	10	4
Wrote poetry on biblical, apocalyptic themes	0	0	0	10	0
Had span of free time to research/write plays	2	0	0	10	0
Known association with the public theatre playhouses	9	0	10	7	10
Known access to diplomats to Scotland and Navarre	0	7	0	10	0

Note: The evidence in this book was assessed by a small panel, and scores given to show how each candidate rated on each factor, 10 indicates a perfect fit and 0 indicates no fit at all. The criteria are inferred from the knowledge capacities shown in the plays and poems.

Perhaps because they do not come from a background familiar with scientific inquiry, 'Stratfordians' usually dismiss all such analyses. Instead they resort to fantastic and unsubstantiated claims that the playwright picked up fluent Italian in a local Italian restaurant, or that all the music in the plays could have been learnt in only six music lessons. The prominent Stratfordian Professor Stanley Wells oddly insisted in a letter in *The Stage* that the 'proper reaction' to the plays is to be full of wonder that Shakespeare wrote them, and *not* to ask how he could have done so. In other words, Professor Wells wants to suppress critical inquiry and instead recommends that people should engage in romantic wonder. This is paralleled by the suppression of the actual meanings of the plays. Studies of these religious aspects account for a tiny fraction of a percent of the Shakespearean literature. As Peggy Muñoz Simonds observed in her essay on *Pericles*, the religious frame of reference for understanding the meanings of the plays has been 'systematically suppressed by scholars who should know better'.

As mentioned in the introduction, the leading biographer Samuel Schoenbaum even wanted us to wonder at Mr Shakespeare as a superman. He states, 'There is something incomprehensible about genius. Shakespeare was superhuman.' In this circular argument, by admiring Mr Shakespeare as a superman, his incomprehensible achievements become explained by his superhuman identity. It is a variation of the romantic explanation that Mr Shakespeare was possessed by a 'divine afflatus', as *Chambers's Edinburgh Journal* put it in 1852. It was this that led Thomas Carlyle to identify Shakespeare as a kind of 'saint' of poetry, and Herman Melville, writing in *The Confidence Man*, to call him 'a kind of deity'. He was the 'god of our idolatry', as the eighteenth-century actor David Garrick called him. We need a better explanation than that.

The New Paradigm

This book has falsified the proposition that Mr Shakespeare wrote the plays; it has shown that the arguments supporting this proposition are erroneous and that the theory does not adequately explain a long list of problems. The lack of any explanation of these anomalies means that the hypothesis is falsified. Consequently an entirely different paradigm is needed.

The case for Amelia Bassano Lanier provides precisely such a new paradigm. It not only explains the literary signatures and the unusual number of Emilia characters, it is an exact biographical fit. Like the Shakespearean plays, her verse is religious in nature, both in the final 200-line poem that describes the consequences of Christ and his Apostles walking in the garden at Cookham, and also in the grotesque 1,840-line poem which depicts the Crucifixion and the apocalypse. Her verse also matches the Shakespearean canon in many detailed characteristics, including her use of parody, inventiveness, imagery, classical references, compositional style, rare words, word clusters, use of sources, apocalyptic imagery, rare metaphors, dramatic structure, symmetrical design, and use of disjunctive style.

As mentioned above, the only examination in print of Amelia Bassano Lanier as the primary author of Shakespeare's works was by Gililov in 1997, which he did not pursue, and incidentally in Hugh Craig's computer-based survey of all the poets born between 1560 and 1600 contained in the *Norton Anthology*. Not only are there problems with computer-based vocabulary analyses in general, but there were sampling problems in this study related to matching date and genre, and problems with the common words that were used in order to discriminate a pattern. Apart from these limited investigations it seems that Lanier has not been considered as a possible co-author of the plays because people have been deceived by the surface level of the verse. Very obviously, *Salve Deus* does not resemble the 'mellifluous & honytongued Shakespeare', as Francis Meres called it in 1598. How can this be explained? Firstly, it is critical to remember that in Elizabethan literary theory the surface verse was regarded as a deception, especially in pastorals where the entire genre was deliberately designed to deceive. It is therefore important for what Gabriel Harvey called 'the wiser sort' *not* to focus emotionally on the beautiful honeyed surface of Shakespearean verse and how it sounds, but to look analytically at what lies underneath.

Secondly, Stratfordians tend to make disingenuous claims that the 'Salve Deus' poem does not 'sound the same' as the generality of Shakespeare's verse – implying thereby that it should. Of course it doesn't, and there is absolutely no reason at all why it should. To insist that to be demonstrably Shakespearean, a poem written in 1610–11 as a parody of a poem by Giles Fletcher must demonstrate stylistic similarities to plays written years earlier is methodologically absurd. *Cymbeline* (written after March 1610) doesn't sound much like the rest of Shakespeare either. One popular commentary, SparkNotes, says the verse in *Cymbeline* is 'often clumsy', refers to the 'mediocrity' of some scenes, and states that overall it feels like 'a pastiche'. Granville-Barker in his *Prefaces to Shakespeare* refers to its 'sophisticated artlessness' and 'clumsiness', which is a deliberate device to counteract dramatic illusion and create a kind of realism. Yet it is *unquestionably* a late Shakespearean play. The vast majority of the Shakespearean works were written before 1610 when styles and circumstances were different. Since that material was all written earlier, and mostly for public performance, it has little if any relevance as a stylistic comparator to the 'Salve Deus' poem, which was written, like *Cymbeline*, in 1610.

Thirdly, we also need to recall that, like Chaucer, the author of the plays deliberately wrote bad poetry from time to time – and especially did so in verse, like the poems in *Salve Deus*, which concerned a theophany (as in *Cymbeline*) or a parody of the Crucifixion (as in *A Midsummer Night's Dream*). So if treated in context, Lanier's verse is actually a very precise fit indeed. Controlling *by both date and by genre*, as a matched sample to the theophany in *Cymbeline*, the fit of Lanier's poem becomes apparent – despite differences due to one text having been composed to be recited on stage by male actors and the other to be quietly read in private by noblewomen.

Finally, in any case, the aesthetics and sound of the verse is only one sub-factor out of many. Judgements about verse have to be made very carefully looking at multiple factors, listed above, all of which are equally important. The other authorship candidates do not match Shakespearean verse characteristics in any significant fashion at all. While it would have been easier to see if Lanier's verse had been representative of the majority of the Shakespearean canon, such representativeness is not a necessary criterion. At least Lanier's verse matches *some* of the Shakespearean canon – and there is a match with the time it was written.

In an article titled 'What's in a Name?' in the now defunct journal *Réalités*, the well-known historian Hugh Trevor-Roper concluded,

> Of all the immortal geniuses of literature, none is personally so elusive as William Shakespeare. It is *exasperating, and almost incredible*, that he should be so. After all, he lived in the full daylight of the English Renaissance, in the well-documented reigns of Queen Elizabeth and King James 1st. He wrote thirty-five plays and 150 highly personal sonnets. He was connected with some of the best-known public figures in the most conspicuous court in English history. Since his death, and particularly in the last century, he has been subjected to *the greatest battery of organized research that has ever been directed upon a single person*. And yet the greatest of all Englishmen, after this tremendous inquisition, still remains so close a mystery that even his identity can still be doubted. [Emphasis added]

For those unwilling to contemplate that 'the greatest of all Englishmen' was actually a dark-skinned Jewish woman poet who wrote these plays as anti-Christian allegories, then there is only one alternative. It is, frankly, even *more* fantastic, almost on par with the theories about aliens, superheroes and time travellers.

Firstly, if the plays were created by someone else, it becomes necessary to explain why Amelia Bassano has all these areas of fit, including the existence of her literary signatures on the plays, which can be statistically demonstrated to be no coincidence. Secondly, it supposes that after this amazing 'battery of organized research' which has taken place over three centuries, and after *excluding every known poet or writer* in Elizabethan and Jacobean London, there must still somewhere be hiding yet *another* major poet, with musical and Jewish associations, knowledge of the court, the town of Bassano, falconry, Italian, Hebrew, silk weaving, Gospel satire, and so on, and this person must be so far *completely unknown* to historians of the period, but has nonetheless written these plays. That seems to me utterly impossible.

Yet creating support for this new story, and showing that it matters, will not be easy. Too many people have too much invested, in terms of careers, reputations and finances, to allow rational evidence to get in the way of old models from which they have benefited so much. Without the support of major universities or foundations and the funding and endorsement they provide, it is very hard to achieve institutional change and transformation. It is especially hard for invisible problems that do not impact people's lives in some obviously adverse way. We cannot point to starving children, or those ravaged by disease: the consequences of the old Shakespeare model are much less visible and the chains of causation are much longer. Unlike, say, the extinction of the bees, world hunger or global warming, this issue does not naturally generate constant and insistent visual images clamouring for our attention with global, life-threatening consequences. Visual symbols have to be crafted through a careful dramaturgy and remain esoteric even so. If this is framed as an issue in 'the arts', and in the increasingly marginal field of theatre, then the societal benefits of creating and promoting a new model of Shakespeare may seem remote. It may seem to simply offer a questionable improvement in the aesthetic experience of a tiny urban elite. That perception, however, ignores how Shakespeare functions globally as a cultural symbol. Furthermore, the conventional model of Shakespeare does cause society-wide problems, and invidious ones, by upholding forms of control that discriminate against women, those of colour, and those not persuaded by the charms of Christianity. Moreover, while some modern productions of Shakespeare are absolutely dazzling, to focus on the surface presentation of the plays and ignore their underlying systems of meaning is to reject a major opportunity from which we might learn how to deconstruct the theatrical stagecraft that poisons much of our modern political systems.

A New Story at Last

For 400 years the world has been enthralled by a romantic and fantastic story – the story of a real-life superman who came not from Planet Krypton but from Stratford-upon-Avon. It is the improbable fantasy of how a poor glove-maker's son, without even a documented grammar school education, suddenly and inexplicably transformed into a literary genius who wrote the world's most important plays, and then inexplicably returned to his mansion where he died leaving a will that showed he had no intellectual interests of any kind.

Now, however, we have a new story which is even more fascinating. It tells how a dark-skinned girl, from a family of Venetian musicians living as secret Jews in the London of Queen Elizabeth I, acquired an education normally only given to countesses. It enabled her to live for ten years at court as mistress to the queen's half-brother, the man in charge of the English theatre. It enabled her to have an affair with Christopher Marlowe, and to acquire the knowledge necessary to write these plays. More importantly, as we have seen in the example of A *Midsummer*

Night's Dream, she used literary techniques to hide underneath the surface of these plays a heretical Jewish story about Christianity – waiting for a time in the future when 'eyes not yet created shall o'er-read it' (Sonnet 81). As a protection mechanism, in case the true meanings of the plays were discovered during her lifetime, she used the man from Stratford as a play broker to conceal her identity. Mr Shakespeare's rags-to-riches story turns out to be not that of a genius at all but that of the clownish William from *As You Like It* who was filled up with rhetorical knowledge by the great poet Touchstone (the *basanos*). Mr Shakespeare brokered the plays, ignorant of the dangerous heresies they really contained, and even claiming that his fair copies were his original drafts. Despite Ben Jonson's scathing satire, he was never exposed and retired to his mansion in Stratford with his fraudulent reputation intact. But no more.

Our traditional 'map' of the territory 'Shakespeare' has been shown to be inconsistent, faulty, and very out of date. It is time for a new and better map that will highlight new and overlooked features and take us in a new, more intelligent, direction. Those in Britain can still be proud of their 'Shakespeare', but this is a very different, and more relevant Shakespeare, who stands as a symbol for different qualities. It will be a 'Shakespeare nation' that is not glorifying the inequalities and injustices of the past, but one that tries to create a more egalitarian and multi-racial society. Amelia's story shows how in the fullness of time – an amazing 400 years – the truth will out. As our world slowly becomes less racist, less sexist, and less religiously dogmatic, perhaps the time has come at last for her story to get a hearing.

Appendices

Appendix 1: Recognition at Last

The tenth-century German nun Hrovist, or Roswitha, was probably the first woman dramatist in Europe. Her plays were first published in Latin in 1510, and may have influenced the Shakespearean works in their daring to breach Aristotle's unities. The first Englishwoman to compose a non-commercial play was Abbess Katherine of Sutton who produced a liturgical drama in which the three Marys were acted by nuns, around 1376. During the English Renaissance it was thought that women could not write plays, and so the first Renaissance woman to do so was Elizabeth Cary, the Lady Falkland (1585–1639), who composed a 'closet drama' that was only read aloud. Aphra Behn (1640–89) has been thought of as the first English Renaissance woman who was a commercial playwright. This history now needs to be revisited.

In the years since Rowse published *The Poems of Shakespeare's Dark Lady* in 1978, there has been a small wave of scholarship and the beginnings of public awareness. In 2009, Robert Brustein's play *The English Channel* at the Abingdon Theatre in New York misleadingly imagined an affair between Shakespeare and Lanier. On the other hand, in 2013, Dr Andrew Harris premiered at the University of North Texas his play *The Lady Revealed*, which is a rather good account of A. L. Rowse's discovery of the identity of the Dark Lady. Currently Bella Poynton, a playwright at the University of Iowa, is writing a play that presents Amelia as the major playwright responsible for the Shakespearean works. A different recognition of her as a writer is Sally O'Reilly's novel *Dark Aemilia*, which, while sticking to the old model of her as Shakespeare's mistress, imagines in a fanciful way that she wrote the precursor to *Macbeth*. There has also been a musical setting of *Salve Deus*, 'Symphony for Amelia' was composed by Jaron Lanier. So very slowly public awareness and representation in the media has been building, including an artwork for *Reform Judaism* magazine in 2010, which had a cover story 'Unmasking Shakespeare' by Michael Posner, and a cover showing a woman at a theatre holding the mask of Mr Shakespeare over her face.

Appendix 2: Spelling

No standardised spelling existed in Elizabethan England, so Lanyer was also spelt Lanier, and Aemelia had various spellings. Rowse for instance calls her 'Emilia Lanier'. Here I have used a modernised spelling, 'Amelia Lanier'.

Appendix 3: Other Dark Lady Theories

Other candidates have been put forward. Dr Duncan Salkfield in *Shakespeare Among the Courtesans* argued for the prostitute Lucy Negro, who had actually been suggested as a joke by Harold Bloom many years ago. Dr Aubrey Burl in his book *Shakespeare's Mistress* suggests it was Aline Florio, wife to the Italian translator John Florio. In the 1880s Thomas Tyler identified her as Mary Fitton – which became untenable after a portrait of her was discovered and she was found to be blonde. There have also been other candidates. However they are not nearly as satisfactory as A. L. Rowse's identification of Amelia Bassano Lanier, even though the original claim was in part based on a misreading of Simon Forman's handwriting, which Rowse claimed stated that she was very 'brown' in her youth. This is irrelevant since the skin colour of the Bassano family, as stated in their police arrest records, was actually perceived by Elizabethans as 'black'. Martin Green, in his article 'Emilia Lanier IS the Dark Lady of the Sonnets',[1] sets out the case most fully.

Appendix 4: The Portrait

The main problems with the currently proposed portrait of Amelia is that the face in the portrait is white rather than 'dark', and that it is dated at a time when Amelia had left court, and being heavily pregnant, would not have been sitting for a Hilliard portrait. Dr David Lasocki, in a 2013 supplement to his definitive biography of the Bassano family, provides the following discussion of the proposed Hilliard portrait of Lanier, and the alternative that I have suggested should be investigated. It is kindly used with his permission.

> The well-known British actor and playwright Tony Haygarth has written an article arguing that he had identified a portrait of Emilia. (Simon Tait, 'Revealed? The Identity of Shakespeare's Dark Lady,' *The Independent on Sunday* [London, England], 7 December 2003, section Home, 13). He reports that a miniature by Nicholas Hilliard now in the Victoria & Albert Museum, London, painted on the back of a playing card (five of spades) depicts a pale young woman with black hair and dark eyes, wearing a black dress with a white ruff and a white

bodice decorated with stags, winged insects, and trees. It is dated 'Ano Dm. 159' and also includes the Latin phrase 'Etatis Suae 26' (in the [year] of her age 26, or in her 26th year). There is a *fleur-de-lis* (stylised lily) to the right.

Haygarth notes that in the eighteenth century, the sitter was thought to be a Mistress Holland. He remembered that Emilia's older sister Angela married a Joseph Holland, gent., but she had died by 1584. Then Haygarth calculated that Emilia herself, baptised on 27 January 1569, would have been (probably, depending on her date of birth) in her 26th year in '1593' for at least two months, between 1 January and 25 March 1593, Old Style (1594, New Style). He wonders whether the portrait was painted for her birthday. Furthermore, he says, the winged insects on the sitter's bodice are 'identical' with the silkworm moths in the Bassano family coat of arms. He relates the *fleur-de-lis* to the arms of Rouen, the city where the father of Emilia's husband, Alphonso Lanier, was born, and perhaps Alphonso himself.

The most telling objection to his theory is that Emilia would have been heavily pregnant in January 1593, therefore away from Court and not a suitable candidate for a portrait. John Hudson has proposed a different Hilliard miniature portrait for Emilia: Victoria & Albert Museum P.8–1945. The woman has dark brown hair, grey or black eyes, and a skin color significantly darker than any of Hilliard's other portraits. She is wearing Court costume. The handling of the paint suggests it was painted in 1590 although the costume might be a couple of years earlier. In conjunction with his theory that Emilia wrote Shakespeare's plays and poems Hudson cites the evidence in Sonnet 16, 'Much liker than your painted counterfeit,' that the poet was painted, presumably by Hilliard. See: Erna Auerbach, *Nicholas Hilliard* (Boston: Boston Book & Art Shop; London: Routledge & Kegan Paul, 1961); Leslie Hotson, *Mr. W. H.* (London: Rupert Hart-Davis; New York: Alfred A Knopf, 1964); Roy C. Strong, *Artists of the Tudor Court; The Portrait Miniature Rediscovered, 1520–1620; 9 July–6 November 1983, the Victoria & Albert Museum* (London: the Museum, 1983); Marjorie Weeden Champlin, *Changing the Face of Shakespeare* (privately printed, 1996).

Appendix 5: The Bassanos

The most useful source of information on the Bassano family is the book by David Lasocki and Roger Prior, *The Bassanos*, which was reissued by Dr Lasocki as an ebook in 2013, available at http://www.instantharmony.net/Music/ebooks.php with a new thirty-seven-page update. In addition to works cited, other sources that provide background on specific aspects of Amelia's life include the following:

Florence Amit, 'Apples of Gold Encased in Silver' in Dr Norman Simms (ed.) *Mentalities/Mentalities* vol. 17 (New Zealand: Waikato University, Hamilton,

2002); David Basch, *The Hidden Shakespeare: A Rosetta Stone* (Revelatory Press CT, 2000); David Basch, *Shakespeare's Judaica and Devices* (Revelatory Press CT, 1996); Peter Bassano, 'Was Shakespeare's Dark Lady Byrd's Librettist?', *Early Music Review* 114 (August 2006), 11–17; Peter Bassano, 'Dark Theories', Letters to the Editor, *The Daily Telegraph* (11 October 1997); Georgina A. E. K. Bertie, *Five Generations of a Loyal House: Part I Containing the Lives of Richard Bertie and His Son Peregrine Lord Willoughby* (London: Rivingtons, 1845); Peregrine Bertie Correspondence, in Historical Manuscripts Commission, *Report on the Manuscripts of the Earl of Lancaster Preserved at Grimsthorpe* (Dublin: HMSO John Falconer, 1907), cmnd. 3429, Historical Manuscripts Commission, *13th Report App VI* (1893); Barbara Bowen, 'Amelia Lanyer and the Invention of White Womanhood' in Susan Frye and Karen Robertson (eds), *Maids and Mistresses, Cousins and Queens: Women's Alliances in Early Modern England* (Oxford: Oxford University Press, 1999), 274–303; Barbara Bowen, 'Beyond Shakespearean Exceptionalism' in Lloyd Davis (ed.), *Shakespeare Matters: History Teaching Performance* (Newark: University of Delaware Press, 2003); Pamela A. Brown and Peter Parolin, *Women Players in England 1500–1600: Beyond the All-Male Stage*, (Aldershot: Ashgate, 2005); D. J. H. Clifford (ed.), *The Diaries of Lady Anne Clifford* (Wolfeboro Falls, NH: Alan Sutton, 1991); John P. Cutts, 'Robert Johnson and the Court Masque', *Music and Letters* vol. 41, no. 2 (April 1960), 111–26; John P. Cutts, 'Robert Johnson: King's Musician in His Majesty's Public Entertainment', *Music and Letters* 36:2 (1955), 110–25; Jack D'Amico, *Shakespeare and Italy: The City and the Stage* (Gainesville: University Press of Florida, 2001); Susan M. Felch, '"Noble Gentlewomen famous for their learning": The Public Roles of Women in Elizabethan England', unpublished paper, University of Calgary (28 October 2003); Gary Goldstein, 'Shakespeare's Little Hebrew', *Elizabethan Review* 7:1 (1999), 70–7; Cecilie Goff, *A Woman of the Tudor Age* (London: John Murray, 1930); Andrew Gurr, 'Henry Carey's Peculiar Letter', *Shakespeare Quarterly* vol. 56:1 (2005), 51–75; Neil Hirschorn, 'Shakespeare and the Marrano World', *Midstream* 39:9 (1993), 6–11; Neil Hirschorn, 'Shakespeare Shylock and the Marrano Factor', *Midstream* 31:9 (1985), 51–4; Eldred Jones, *Othello's Countrymen* (London: Oxford University Press, 1965); Edna Krane, 'The Marrano of Stratford', *Midstream* (May 1985), 43; Mary Ellen Lamb, 'Towards a Heterosexual Erotics of Service in Twelfth Night and the Autobiographical Writings of... Anne Clifford', *Criticism* 40 (1998), 1–25; Barbara K. Lewalski, 'Rewriting Patriarchy and Patronage: Margaret Clifford, Anne Clifford and Aemelia Lanyer', *The Yearbook of English Studies* volume 21 (1991), 87–106; Barbara Lewalski, 'Of God and Good Women: The Poems of Aemilia Lanyer' in Margaret Patterson Hannay (ed.), *Silent but for the Word* (Kent University Press: Kent OH 1985); Cristina Malcolmson, 'Early Modern Women Writers and the Gender Debate: Did Aemilia Lanyer Read Christine de Pisan?', unpublished conference paper presented at the Centre for English Studies, University of London (1998); Michele

Marrapodi (ed.), *Shakespeare's Italy: Functions of Italian locations in Renaissance Drama* (New York: Manchester University Press, 1993); Nicholas McDowell, 'The Stigmatizing of Puritans as Jews in Jacobean England: Ben Jonson, Francis Bacon and the Book of Sports Controversy', *Renaissance Studies* 19:3 (2005), 348–63; Lynette McGrath, 'The Feminist Subject: Idealization and Subversive Metaphor in *Salve Deus Rex Judaeorum*' in *Subjectivity and Women's Poetry in Early Modern England* (Aldershot: Ashgate 2002), 209–49; David C. McPherson, *Shakespeare, Jonson, and the Myth of Venice* (Newark: University of Delaware Press, 1990); Giulio M. Ongaro, 'New Documents on the Bassano Family', *Early Music* 20, np.3 (August 1992) 409–13; Roger Prior, 'More (Moor? Moro): Light on the Dark Lady, *Financial Times* (10 October 1987); Benjamin C. Ravid, *Studies on the Jews of Venice 1382–1797* (Ashgate: Variorum, 2003); Evelyn Read, *Catherine Duchess of Suffolk: A Portrait* (London: Jonathan Cape, 1962); Cecil Roth, *History of the Marranos* (New York: Hermon Press, 1974), A. L. Rowse, *Simon Forman: Sex and Society in Shakespeare's Age* (London: Weidenfeld & Nicolson, 1974); David B. Ruderman and Giuseppe Veltri (eds) *Cultural Intermediaries: Jewish Intellectuals in Early Modern Italy* (Philadelphia: University of Pennsylvania Press, 2004); Naseeb Shaheen, 'Shakespeare's Knowledge of Italian', *Shakespeare Survey* 47 (1994), 161–9; Steve Sohmer, 'Another Time: The Venetian Calendar in Shakespeare's Plays', *Shakespeare Yearbook* (1999), 141–61; Lawrence Stone, 'Office under Queen Elizabeth: The Case of Lord Hunsdon and the Lord Chamberlainship in 1585', *The Historical Journal* vol. 10:2 (1967), 279–85; Jane West, *The Brave Lord Willoughby: An Elizabethan Soldier* (Edinburgh: Pentland Press, 1998); Michael Wilson, *Nicholas Lanier: Master of the King's Music* (Brookfield Vermont: Ashgate Press, 1994); Michael Wyatt, *The Italian Encounter with Tudor England: A Cultural Politics of Translation* (Cambridge: Cambridge University Press, 2005).

Appendix 6: State Theatre and Popular Theatre

In Elizabethan London, on the one hand there was state theatre – the formal state theatrical apparatus of ceremonies, pageants, processions, performances by the Queen's Men, and for a time performances of mystery plays under Church supervision. On the other hand, popular theatre was comprised of carnivals and informal dramatics. Somewhere in-between was playhouse theatre, comprising plays in the playhouses which were created at a local level, but to some extent were controlled from the top down through the apparatus of censorship.

Anticipating twentieth-century dramaturgical sociology, as Jaques says in *As You Like It*, all the world is a stage, in which all are players and have their parts. The same is reflected in Lanier's letter to the Lady Anne, 'For well you knowe, this world is but a Stage, Where doe play their parts and must be done' (*Salve Deus*,

'To the Ladie Anne' 121–2). Even the queen herself freely admitted 'we princes are set on stages in sight of all the world', whereas Sir Walter Raleigh noted all the 'potentates' were 'acting each other's actions' and tailoring every move to create the best political advantage. Elizabeth's court was a massive social stage on which all the actors had to control every sentence they said and every glance they gave. They constantly managed their costumes, the settings, and their appearances for theatrical effect, not just when they were in a pageant or entertainment. They would also retreat to backstage spaces, to break character, reflect on their actions and to plot their next steps, as Richard does for instance in his asides to the audience in *Richard III*. It was at court that the author derived the experience of the calculated dramaturgy of social roles that sociologist Erving Goffman called 'impression management', which was required to enact the daily performance of an artificial self. *Richard II* for instance can be seen entirely as an account of this split between the social role and the true person underneath.

As John Hayward wrote in his *Certain Yeres of Queen Elizabeth's Raigne* (1636), 'In pompous ceremonies a secret of government doth much consist, for that the people are naturally both taken and held with exterior show.' Everyday life at court was governed by political power games which undergirded the frequently allegorical court entertainments. The play *Gorbudoc*, for instance, provided an allegory of the marriage suit of the King of Sweden. Even giving up a major office could require staging a theatrical drama, which Lord Burghley did twice at his country house Theobalds, in 1591 and 1594, featuring an actor dressed as a hermit asking that he be allowed to retire, which the queen refused both times. In addition to participating in formal dramatics, every day courtiers had to informally enact their offices, and lay claims to better ones, which took considerable political calculation.

This use of stagecraft as a managerial technique is continued in the modern state. David Boje has shown how the American Presidency, like many corporate institutions, uses showmanship, staging, and the creation of imagery as a deliberate theatrical enterprise designed to create illusion and as a tool for manipulation. Boje has also made the distinction between state theatre and popular theatre, which he sees engaged in a continual power struggle. That is very much compatible with the suggestion in this book that the plays in the Elizabethan playhouses were in some cases – notably in the works of Shakespeare – engaged in an attempt to remake, redefine and to parody state theatrical works. This is most obvious in the well-known way that the Shakespearean plays parody the plays of the state theatre company the Queen's Men.

See also: Philip Edwards 'Person and Office in Shakespeare's Plays', *Proceedings of the British Academy* 56 (1972), 93–109; Waldo F. McNeir, 'The Masks of Richard the Third', *Studies in English Literature 1500–1900*, 11 (1971), 1667–86; David M. Boje, John T. Luhman, and Ann L. Cunliffe, 'A Dialectic Perspective on the Organization Theatre Metaphor', *American Communication Journal* 6:2

(2003), 1–16; David M. Boje, 'Deconstructing Visual Theatric Imagery of the Bush Presidency', Paper presented to August 2003 meeting of the Academy of Management in Seattle.

Appendix 7: Anti-Semitism

It is sometimes argued that *The Merchant of Venice* is anti-Semitic, which would make it improbable for Amelia Lanier to have written it. However in 1998, an international survey of 1,000 teachers carried out by the education arm of the Globe Theatre found 61 per cent did not find *The Merchant of Venice* to be anti-Semitic. Some 20 per cent were unsure: they felt anti-Semitism in *Merchant* resulted from directors presenting the play in a certain fashion, not from what is inherent in the text. Just 17 per cent found the play inherently anti-Semitic, and that is by considering the surface of the text, not the underlying meanings.

It is important not to judge *Merchant* by the anachronistic standards of the twenty-first-century theatre. Rather, it is important to consider the play by the standards and the context of the time in which it was written. In Elizabethan England, Jews were routinely referred to as dogs or worse. On the Elizabethan stage, the traditional depiction of the Jew was as a stage-devil; the presentation in *The Jew of Malta* was very much in that vein. *Merchant*, however, goes a step beyond this. In a culture that considered Jews to be dogs or devils, the central character's demand that he be accorded basic rights as a human being, and that Jews be seen as subject to the same passions, diseases, organs, dimensions and affections as Christians (3.1.49–61), represents an extraordinary, amazing plea for equality.

As for the pound of flesh, the playwright borrowed much of the plot, including the man who goes to a Jewish moneylender to help a friend and is asked for a pound of flesh should the money not be repaid on time. The source material is Ser Giovanni Florentino's *The Big Sheep*, a collection of stories available only in Italian as *Il Pecorone* (1558). To understand the real meaning of *Merchant*, as with all sophisticated Elizabethan literature, one must look beyond the honeyed sweetness of the verse and solve the underlying allegories of the play. The name Shylock resembles Shiloh, which is mentioned in the Talmud as one of the names of the Messiah. It is derived from Jacob's blessing in Genesis (49:10), which is why Caleb, a contemporary European messianic candidate, was called Caleb Shilocke.

As Anthony Brennan notes in his chapter 'The Three Trials in Merchant of Venice' in his book *Shakespeare's Dramatic Structures* that unlike the simple trial in *Il Pecorone*, the author of *Merchant* puts Shylock through three of them. The first is before the duke (4.1.16–118). The second is before Portia, ending with Shylock's declaration to leave (4.1.164–344). The third is the judgement (4.1.345–98). We do not have to look far for a parallel example of a Jewish Messiah who undergoes three trials: one among Jewish leaders, a second by Pontius Pilate, a third by Herod. This is just part of rethinking the play as an anti-Christian satirical allegory – which completely changes the significance of the pound of flesh. Thanks to the Clyde Fitch Report for reuse of my article 'Is *Merchant of Venice* a Cannibal Satire?', which provides a fuller discussion.

Appendix 8: Marlowe's Atheism

Simon Aldrich told Henry Oxinden that 'Marlo(we) ... was an atheist and had writ a book against Scripture; how it was all one man's making',[2] and comprised stories about the 'deceiver' Jesus that had been created as a matter of 'policy'. Other records claim that Marlowe had 'better reasons' for his atheism than any clergyman in the country had for his beliefs and that Christianity was not 'thought upon' until after Titus and Vespasian conquered Jerusalem in 70 CE, as Barabas puts it in *The Jew of Malta*.

Marlowe had apparently determined that the New Testament, the Gospels in particular, were written at the instigation of Vespasian and Titus Caesar as Roman satires against the Jews. In this view, known today in New Testament scholarship as the 'Flavian Hypothesis', the Gospels are not accounts of the ministry of a historical Jewish Jesus compiled by his followers forty years after his death. Rather they are texts – war propaganda – deliberately created to deceive Messianic Jews into worshipping the Roman Emperor 'in disguise'. The majority of the key events in the life of Jesus are in fact satirical: each is an elegant literary play on a military battle in which the Jewish armies had been defeated in the Jewish–Roman War.

Marlowe strongly influenced the writing of *Titus Andronicus* on the same model. The Shakespearean plays begin with a crude system of Gospel parallels in *Sir Thomas More*, reuse the typology from the mystery plays, cover the theology of the Pauline letters and then create very sophisticated Gospel parodies. Marlowe's conclusions were rediscovered in modern times and are set out by Dr Rod Blackhirst, a lecturer in Religious Studies at La Trobe University, Australia, in his YouTube video 'The Flavian Thesis: the Origin of Christianity'; by Cliff Carrington in *The Flavian Testament* (*c.* 2002, web document); and most exhaustively by Joseph Atwill in *Caesar's Messiah*.

Appendix 9: The Allegories in the Plays

Several scholars have previously noted the oddity of Shakespeare's imagery. Battenhouse points out there is a pattern of 'consistently disparaging allusions to Caesar throughout Shakespeare's works.' In 1939, R. W. Chambers detected another remarkable parallelism that appeared across a variety of Shakespearean plays. The images he detected included: violations of order, images of a river overflowing its banks, the killing of the aged and very young, and images of monsters, especially 'self-devouring monsters and cannibals'. John Velz has more recently noted that this pattern appears in *Titus Andronicus, Troilus and Cressida*, and in *King Lear*, and that some of these aspects also appear in Ovid's imagery of the Iron Age. In the 1970s Wentsdorf applied the same approach to a selection of thirteen Shakespearean plays, and identified two additional elements, namely cruel pagans/savages, and supplicants who make their knees their feet. Chambers had indeed noted the oddity of this last motif in discussing the passage when More asks the rebels to make their 'unreverent knees their feet'. See also: Roy Battenhouse (ed.), *Shakespeare's Christian Dimension: An Anthology of Commentary* (Bloomington, Indiana: Indiana University Press, 1994), p. 326; R. W. Chambers, *Man's Unconquerable Mind* (London: Jonathan Cape, 1939); John W. Velz, 'Sir Thomas More and the Shakespeare Canon' in T. H. Howard-Hill (ed.), *Shakespeare and Sir Thomas More: Essays on the Play and Its Shakespearean Intent* (Cambridge: CUP, 1989), pp. 171–95; Karl P. Wentsdorf, 'Linkages of Thought and Imagery in Shakespeare and More', *Modern Language Quarterly* 34, 4, December (1973), 384–405.

Unfortunately it is easy to create inaccurate readings of this imagery, as Clare Asquith does in her book *Shadowplay: The Hidden Beliefs and Coded Politics of William Shakespeare*. She gets credit for appreciating that these allegorical codes exist and for attempting to solve them: unfortunately she does not manage to do so, and instead creates an arbitrary, simplistic, and one-dimensional interpretation. For example, she is convinced that the plays were written by a conventional Catholic when she turns to *The Taming of the Shrew*. She believes Bianca (White), the younger, represents Catholicism, and that Katherina, the small, low, elder sister, who is 'brown in hue as a hazelnut', represents the Church of England (low church). Now surely this identification does not fit. Since Catholicism is the older religion surely it should be Katherina? I would therefore reject this hypothesis and look for a new one. Moreover, this hypothesis has weak explanatory power since it certainly does not cover 'every detail of the plot material' which Asquith stated as the objective of her research. Indeed, it explains very little of the detail of the multiple layers in the play. Similarly, in *Othello* Asquith assumes a one-dimensional contemporary allegory only, and argues that the character of Othello represents King James I, and that the stories Othello tells Desdemona 'echo the anecdotes that James liked to tell about his past'. As evidence, she suggests that the deserts travelled by Othello resemble the locations travelled by the king, who was 'taken by the insolent foe' (1.3.139) as a teenager. There may be some contemporary allegory to James, but King James's experience surely did not include being made a slave, nor experiencing cannibals and sieges. Nor for that matter was King James either a Moor or a general in league with the Italians, nor a 'base Judean'. Underneath any contemporary allegory to James is the deeper level of the first-century allegory, in which Othello represents Josephus, and also two other Joseph figures, to which he is a perfect fit.

Most scholars claim that the man from Stratford had to have written the plays, even though nobody has been able to demonstrate how he could have done so. This is completely unsatisfactory as a *literary* explanation. Why would he have used these particular kinds of imagery? Why would he have had an interest in the situation of Marrano Jews? What in his background led him to integrate musical material so closely into the plays? Why would he have been so hostile to Christianity? If he was going to write plays, why would he write these particular plays in this particular way? These are the questions a literary critic is bound to address, and nobody has yet done so. Instead the literature on Shakespeare consists of historical-biographical materials masquerading as literary explanations. It is only by creating performances of the multiple allegorical layers, and showing in practice how these all work together before an audience, that their overall significance can be appreciated.

Appendix 10: Operating a School

Amelia's school in Drury Lane operated from 1618 to November 1620, when according to court records, 'for her maintenance and relief she was compelled to teach and educate the children of divers worth and understanding'. This makes her one of the very first women in England to create, own, and teach in a school. The records of other women who also established schools have been compiled by K. Charlton from letters and memoirs of the period. The histories of all these pioneering women who broke from the Elizabethan tradition of an all-male teaching profession deserve to be better known. See: Kenneth Charlton, *Women, Religion and Education in Early Modern England* (Routledge; New York, 1999), A. Monroe Stowe, *English Grammar Schools in the Reign of Queen Elizabeth* (New York: The Teachers College, 1908).

Appendix 11: Learning by Reading Plays

It is sometimes supposed that the author of the Shakespearean plays learnt their skills by watching and performing in the plays in the public playhouses. However, of all the plays that are alluded to, the majority are not recorded as having appeared on the public stage within the previous five years, and a good number never could have done so since they weren't in English. Evidently the author learnt most of their playcraft not by acting in plays, nor even watching them, but by reading them. Indeed, of the roughly 2,000 plays that were produced in the three playhouses throughout the 1590s, the Shakespearean plays refer to under 1 per cent, which would have required the author to go to the theatre on average only once every six months.

Taken from G. Bullough, *Narrative and Dramatic Sources of Shakespeare* and Stuart Gillespie *Shakespeare's Books*, the English plays used by the author of the Shakespearean works up to the year 1600 are as follows, listed by their decade of publication:

1560s and Earlier

Mary Magdalene (fifteenth-century mystery play)

Worms of Conscience (mystery play)

Everyman (mystery play, used in reference to character Five Wits, possibly performed in the 1580s, and used in *Twelfth Night*)

The Nature of the Four Elements, John Rastell (?), 1519 (used in *Henry IV, Part 2*)

The World and the Child, Anon, 1522 (used in *Henry IV, Part 2*)

King Johan, John Bale (1548) (used in *King John*, maybe 1596)

Frederyke of Jennen, Anon, 1560 (used in *Cymbeline*, 1610)

A New Enterlude called Thersytes, (1562, used in *Henry IV, Part 1*)

1570s

Promos and Cassandra, George Whetstone, 1578 (used in *Measure for Measure*, 1603)

Richardus Tertius, Thomas Legge, 1579 (acted in Latin in Cambridge)

1580s

Zelauto or The Fountaine of Fame, Anthony Munday, 1580 (used in *The Merchant of Venice*, 1596)

The Three Ladies of London, Robert Wilson, 1584 (used in *The Merchant of Venice*, 1596)

Campaspe, John Lyly, Court 1584, later at Blackfriars after 1596 (used in *Timon of Athens*, 1608)

The Rare Triumphes of Love and Fortune, Anon, 1589 (used in *Cymbeline*, 1610)

1590s

The Chronicle History of King Leir, public performance, 1594 (influenced *King Lear*, 1608)

Endimion, John Lyly, 1591 (used in *Henry IV, Part 1*)

Mother Bombie, Lyly, 1594 (performed before 1591, used in *The Taming of the Shrew*, 1632)

Gallathea, Lyly, 1585 (performed 1588, used in *A Midsummer Night's Dream*, 1596)

The Troublesome Raigne of King John, 1591 (performed 159, used in *King John*, 1596)

Jew of Malta, performed 1592–3 (influenced *The Merchant of Venice*, 1596)

The Life and Death of Jack Straw, Anon, 1593/4 (used in *Henry VI, Part 2*)

The Tragedie of Dido Queene of Carthage, Marlowe and Nashe, 1594 (used in *Hamlet*, 1603)

The Tragedy of Antonie, Robert Garnier, tr. Mary Herbert, 1595 (not performed, used in *A Midsummer Night's Dream*, 1596)

The True Tragedy of Richard III, 1594 and performed 1594 (used in *Richard III*, printed 1597)

John a Kent and John a Cumber, Anthony Munday, 1594 (used in *Tempest* 1610)

Mucedorus, 1598 and others, performance in 1610 (used in *The Tempest*, 1610)

The Famous Victories of Henry the Fifth, 1598 (used in *Henry IV, Part 2*)

A Warning of Faire Women, 1599 (used in *Hamlet*, 1603)

The Tragey of Cleopatra, Samuel Daniel, 1599, not performed? (used in Antony and Cleopatra)

Syr Clyomon and Clamydes, 1599, acted in 1599 (used in *As You Like It*, 1600)

Foreign Plays

Gl'Ingannati (*The Deceived*, 1537), performed in Latin in 1595 in Cambridge, used in *Twelfth Night*; *Epitia* by Cinthio; *Aminta by* Tasso; *Hecatommithi* by Cinthio; *La Celestina* by Rojas; *Of Two Lovers* by Pierre Boaistuau; *Menaechmi* by Plautus, tr. 1595 by William Warner (used in *The Comedy of Errors*); *Amphitryon* by Plautus (*The Comedy of Errors*); *Mostellaria* by Plautus, Italian 1530 translation; *Captiv,* by Plautus; *Miles Gloriosus* by Plautus; *Caduiana* by Plautus; *Rudens* by Plautus; *Hippolytus* by Seneca; *Medea* by Seneca; *Oedipus* by Seneca; *Hercules Ontaeus* by Seneca; *Alcestis* by Euripides; *Hecuba* by Euripides; *Iphigenia* by Euripides; *Andria* by Terence.

Appendix 12: Use of Dialect

Words from the Northern dialect represent over 80 per cent of the dialect uses in the plays, and there very few are definitively from Warwickshire. In *A Shakespeare Glossary* (2010), C. T. Onions listed thirteen Shakespearean dialect words as being used in Warwickshire, seven of them exclusively. However, Nordling cross-tabulated these with the six-volume standard work *The English Dialect Dictionary* (1898) by Joseph Wright, which lists only eight of the words as being used in Warwickshire at all. Only one of these, 'honey-stalk' – which appears in *Titus Andronicus* – was used exclusively in Warwickshire and does not appear in print elsewhere. In 1916 Bradley had suggested his own possible six words of Warwickshire dialect, and only one of these, the expression 'in his lines' (used in *The Merry Wives of Windsor* for being in a rage), turns out to be exclusively a Warwickshire term. So this means that there are only *two* words that are exclusively Warwickshire dialect which could not have been borrowed from a printed source and must derive from contact with a Warwickshire speaker.

Some of the examples I have rejected are as follows: 'Urchin' (meaning a hedgehog), which appears first in *Titus Andronicus*, is a Warwickshire usage but it is also found in other regions, and was used by Caxton, Palsgrave (1530) and in Heywood's *Spider and Fly* (1556). 'Quat', meaning a pimple, found in *Othello* (published in 1622) was used in Warwickshire, but also in Leicestershire, It could also have been borrowed from Dekker *Gul's Hornbook* (1609), William Langham's *Garden of Health* (1597) or other printed sources. 'Basimecu' (*Henry VI, Part 2*, 4.4) is derived from the French 'baise mon cul' meaning 'kiss my arse', and versions of the term were widespread, so a usage found in the Midlands in the 1850s means nothing.

Another popular claim regarding plant names is that the 'golden-lads' mentioned in the song 'Fear No More' in *Cymbeline* is a Warwickshire reference to the dandelion. The song claims that the most golden life will come to dust – as in the phrase 'dust unto dust' in the funeral service – in the same way that golden dandelion flowers turn into a brush of seeds that looks a bit like the brush used to sweep chimneys of soot, and hence is referred to in the poem as a chimney sweeper. Jonathan Bate, in his paper in *Shakespeare's Face*, claims as evidence a reported use in the mid-twentieth century – based on third-hand hearsay – which was noted by Hugh Kenner in *The Pound Era*. The Early English Books Online database records no other usage in the sixteenth or seventeenth century, so there is no contemporary record in print. The twentieth-century usage could be borrowed from the song in *Cymbeline*, rather than representing a prior tradition, and in neither case is it indicated that this usage is or was exclusive to Warwickshire. My conclusion is that the 'golden-lads' reference does indeed refer to the dandelion, but probably derives from a more widespread regional use. Indeed, the second part of the verse, the reference to chimney sweepers, is revealing because the black heads of another plant – the ribwort, *plantago lanceolata* – were indeed referred to in English dialect as chimney sweepers, but as *The English Dialect Dictionary* shows, these are found not in Warwickshire but in the more northern dialects of Lancashire and Cheshire.

Finally, the only sustained passage of dialect in the plays is Edgar's speech in *King Lear* (4.6.231–42), which the Arden editor claims is standard stage West Country dialect, although both Gilbert Slater and Bradley claim it is Kentish – in which case it may reflect Amelia's early life after the age of seven, spent with the Countess of Kent.

Appendix 13: Did the Man from Stratford Write the Apocryphal Plays?

In her challenging book *The Apocryphal William Shakespeare* (2011), Sabrina Feldman argues that the man from Stratford was indeed a successful playwright and had quite a number of his plays published under his name – namely, the so called 'apocryphal' plays, such as *The London Prodigal, Thomas Lord Cromwell, The Puritan, Locrine, The Birth of Merlin* and *The Yorkshire Tragedy*. She sees the apocryphal plays as having a coherent common style, which she describes as 'bombast, a breezy style, clumsy blank verse, a salty sense of humor, food jokes, crude physical slapstick ... very funny clown scenes'. She might have added that it is also noteworthy what this group of plays do not have – deep theological meanings, multidimensional allegories, parodies of Christianity, use of Hebrew, Italian, and Jewish literature, musical puns, letters, books, plots from Boccaccio or women disguising themselves as men.

Feldman's first argument is the standard one normally used by Stratfordians, the physical evidence that these plays were published in quarto with his name, or initials, on the cover. Furthermore, some of them were incorporated into the third and fourth editions of the First Folio. Secondly, Feldman also argues that some other plays, without his name on the cover, were also by the man from Stratford, notably *Mucedorus*, a romance for eight actors featuring a talking mouse. Here the evidence is circumstantial. Estimated to have been written around 1590, in an old-fashioned alliterative style, *Mucedorus* was the best-selling play of the time, according to the title page was later performed by the King's Men (like the other Shakespearean plays), and was first attributed to Shakespeare in 1656, and bound with two other apocryphal plays in a volume titled 'Shakespeare volume 1' in the library of King Charles II. The play also features a bear, which has a major role and is 'killed' offstage, suggesting a possible production at the Bear Gardens with which Mr Shakespeare has been associated. Finally it would appear that for the King's Men performance at court in 1610, a number of additions were made to the play, and some alterations. The king's melancholy response to music for instance seems to be based on the canonical Shakespearean bear play *Twelfth Night*. Also the Mouse's meta-theatrical comment that the bear is surely not a real bear but an actor in a costume reflects a new courtly production context (see Pavel Drabek's paper, 'Shakespeare's Influence on Mucedorus' (2008)).

This argument that the man from Stratford was the author of the plays is supported by the fact that various passages from *Mucedorus* are incorporated into the romance play *Guy, Earl of Warwick*. Dated probably to the early 1590s, and printed under the initials B. J., this is possibly a very early work by Ben Jonson who was parodied for writing it as the 'villainous Guy' in Dekker's *Satiromastix*. It has another animal clown character called Sparrow (pronounced Spear-o), who comes from Stratford-upon-Avon! He has left his pregnant girlfriend at home in order to chase wenches, be a high-minded sparrow and make a religious pilgrimage to Rome. There is even a comic reconstruction of his conversation with his father when he tells him he is leaving home. However, he has violent tendencies and when he meets an old hermit his first reaction is to want to kill him. He also talks about his competence in slaughtering calves (an allusion to the story about Shakespeare later told by John Aubrey). All of these characteristics echo aspects associated with the man from Stratford.

Taken together, this is the core of a new explanation for the famous 'Lost Years', namely that Mr Shakespeare was indeed an actor/writer with a theatre company in the period before 1594 when the Chamberlain's Men were formed. But is there any direct evidence? Such a depiction indeed appears in the text of the anonymous morality play *Histriomastix*, which was (perhaps incorrectly) credited to John Marston during the late nineteenth century. Printed in 1610, it was written around 1598 and probably reworked an original dating some years earlier. This is a play designed for a non-professional cast of over 100, and is about the adventures of a boastful actor/writer – and tax avoider – called Master Posthaste the Poet. He leads a troupe called Sir Oliver Owlet's Men. They perform a play which starts off being called *The Prodigal Child* (alluding to *The London Prodigal*), but turns into a version of *Troilus and Cressida* (1609) in which the knight 'shakes his furious Spear', suggesting a revision was made shortly before the time it was printed in 1610. That the company are performing these particular plays suggests that Master Posthaste is a parody of Shakespeare and not Antony Munday as argued in David Mann's article 'Sir Oliver Owlet's Men: Fact or Fiction' (1991).

This suggests a new understanding of the role of William Shakespeare, who initially probably worked at the Bear Gardens, where he produced *Mucedorus* and comic private performances (parodied as Oliver Owlet's Men). After he joined the Lord Chamberlain's Men, and had a higher calibre permanent acting troupe, he added the works of others into his repertoire, especially those high-minded plays for which he was not the writer but what today would be called the 'show-runner'. It is that which Ben Jonson describes in his famous reference to the 'Poet-Ape' who would be thought the chief (among London's playwrights). He has become a bold thief by play brokering, and buying up the reversion of old plays made by others which he claims as his own, but which the sluggish audience members do not even notice:

> Poor Poet-Ape, that would be thought our chief,
> Whose works are e'en the frippery of wit,
> From brokage is become so bold a thief,
> As we, the robb'd, leave rage, and pity it.
> At first he made low shifts, would pick and glean,
> Buy the reversion of old plays; now grown
> To a little wealth, and credit in the scene,

He takes up all, makes each man's wit his own:
And, told of this, he slights it. Tut, such crimes
The sluggish gaping auditor devours;
He marks not whose 'twas first: and after-times
May judge it to be his, as well as ours.
Fool! as if half eyes will not know a fleece
From locks of wool, or shreds from the whole piece?

Ben Jonson, 'On Poet Ape', Epigrams 56

Appendix 14: More Satires of Mr Shakespeare: The Parnassus Plays

Various satires, such as those found in *As You Like It* and in *Every Man out of His Humour* support the depiction of Mr Shakespeare as a boastful actor who fronted the writings of others. However, the most systematic parody is in the three Parnassus plays written for Christmas performance at St John's College, Cambridge. Little known today except to specialists, these are examples of Tudor academic theatre that mock the world outside 'Parnassus', where academic work is held in little regard. Each parodies Mr Shakespeare in a different way.

The most revealing is the last of the plays. Written between 1599 and 1601, Richard Burbage and William Kempe are depicted as illiterate actors auditioning students seeking to join their theatre company at the Globe. In Act 4, Scene 2, Burbage wants to get them cheap at a 'low rate' and hopes they may be able to assist writing plays 'it may be besides they will be able to pen a part'. Kempe however, does not like the idea of hiring students because they cannot walk and talk at the same time, and replies:

> Few of the university (men) pen plays well, they smell too much of that writer *Ovid*, and that writer *Metamorphosis*, and talk too much of *Prosperina & Juppiter*. Why heres our fellow *Shakespeare* puts them all downe, ay, and *Ben Jonson* too. Oh that *Ben Jonson* is a pestilent fellow, he brought up *Horace* giving the Poets a pill, but our fellow *Shakespeare* hath given him a purge that made him beray his credit.

Once the students appear, Kempe sells them on the career they can have in the theatre:

> Be merry my lads, you have happened upon the most excellent vocation in the world for money: they come North and South to bring it to our playhouse, and for honours, who of more report than *Dick Burbage & Will: Kempe*. He is not counted a Gentleman, that knows not *Dick Burbage* and *Will Kemp* ...

Burbage then says that he would like to audition one of the students for a Shakespearean play, *Richard III*, and asks him to act a little of it, so the student recites the famous opening words:

> Now is the winter of our discontent
> Made glorious summer by the sonne of York.

Yet once the actors are out of the room, the student complains to his fellow (named Studioso) about the prospect of having to relieve their poverty by such base means:

> And must the basest trade yield us relief?
> Must we be practices to those leaden spouts,
> That nought (do) vent but what they do receive?

Nonetheless, Studioso concludes that it is better, as in *Henry VI, Part 3*, to be:

> ... king of a mole hill, than a Caesar's slave
> Better it is 'mongst fiddlers to be chief
> Than at a player's trencher beg relief
> But is't not strange (that) mimic apes should prize
> Unhappy Scholars at a hireling rate?
> Vile world, that lifts them up to high degree,
> And treads us down in groveling misery.
> England affords those glorious vagabonds,
> Coursers to ride on through the gazing streets,
> Sooping it in their glaring Sattin suits,
> And Pages to attend their masterships:
> With mouthing words that better wits have framed
> They purchase lands, and now Esquires are (named).

The writer of this Parnassus play began by depicting Mr Shakespeare as one of these 'mimic apes' who is specifically praised for his ignorance of Ovid. This is highly revealing, since all the works in the canon are so obviously Ovidian that in 1598 Francis Meres imagined that Ovid's sweet witty soul had taken up residence in Shakespeare's breast. Ovid, the Roman poet of metamorphosis, had been himself metamorphosed into Shakespeare. Jonathan Bate has even written an excellent book documenting how entirely Ovid pervades Shakespeare's work, so for anyone to depict the actor Mr Shakespeare as not 'smelling' of Ovid is highly significant.

Furthermore, this specific reference, to an actor who had been created an esquire and who had purchased lands, can only refer to Mr Shakespeare. He had acquired the right to display a coat of arms as a gentleman in October 1596 and had bought 107 acres of land in May 1601. Yet instead of being depicted as a poet in his own right, here like the other 'leaden spouts' he 'mouths the words' written by 'better wits'. These are comically imagined as university students like Studioso, hired by the Globe Theatre as cheap scriptwriters. This explains why in the first Parnassus play Studioso employs distinctive imagery of Boreas and the winter freezing the flowers in a garden, in a literary style which parodies that of the early Shakespeare.[3]

Shakespeare's poetry is parodied somewhat differently in the second Parnassus play. Early on, the figure of Judicio criticises Shakespeare's works as dealing with love and sex, instead of more serious matters:

> Who loves not Adons love, or Lucrece rape?
> His sweeter verse contains heart-throbbing line,
> Could but a graver subject him content
> Without love's foolish lazy languishment.

The dramatist then depicts a vain and foolish courtier, Gullio, who is such a fan that he wants Shakespeare's picture hung up in his study at the court. Gullio hires a writer, Ingenioso, to write verses in Mr Shakespeare's 'vayne', modelled upon the opening lines of *Venus and Adonis*, which he can send to his mistress. On receiving them he is so happy that he responds, 'Ey marry, sir, these have some life in them! Let this duncified world esteem of Spencer and Chaucer, I'll worship sweet Mr Shakespeare and to honour him will lay his *Venus and Adonis* under my pillow.'

Eric Sams has convincingly argued that Ingenioso is a satire of Thomas Nashe,[4] a graduate of St John's, who was referred to (using Greene's nickname for him) as 'Juvenal' the 'ingenious' Moth in *Love's Labour's Lost*. In the Parnassus play he appears holding a copy of Juvenal and quotes from it in Latin. Sams recognises Gullio as a portrait of the Earl of Southampton, another graduate of St John's, to whom Shakespeare's long poems were of course dedicated as patronage poetry. Gullio quotes extensively from *Venus and Adonis,* and in one place from *Romeo and Juliet*. He alludes to *As You Like It* in having Ingenioso pretend to be his mistress, so he can practise a parody of a Shakespearean speech which claims that in comparison to her beauty the moon is a slut and Cleopatra a black-browed milkmaid. This is a demonstration that a man who recites Shakespearean verse, and even claims it as his own, may actually be a 'post put into a satin suit' who is merely reciting words that were actually written by someone else.

Notes

Introduction

1. Explorandum, 2008.
2. Campbell, 1966.
3. Demos, 2011.
4. Aspden, 2013.
5. Strong, 1969.
6. Erne, 2003.
7. Gurr, 2000.
8. Rushkoff, 2013.
9. Velz, 1985.
10. Michell, 1999.
11. Niederkorn, 2007.
12. Masters, 2013.
13. Fox, 2013.
14. Ephraim, 2013.
15. Smith, 1979.

1 Elizabethan London: City, Court and Theatre

1. Puttenham, *The Art of English Poesie*, 1589.
2. From *The Passage of our Most Dread Sovereign Lady*, 1558, in Arber, 1895–6.
3. Wilkinson, 2009. See also John Wagner's *Encyclopedia of Tudor England* and Alan Palmer's *Who's Who in Shakespeare's England*.
4. Hibbert, 1991.
5. James, 1999.

2 Shakespeare's Remarkable Mind: A Shopping List

1. Shapiro, correspondence with Stephen Greenblatt in the *New York Review of Books*.
2. Tricomi, 2001.
3. Weiss, 1971.
4. Duffin, 2004.
5. Scott-Warren, 2003.
6. Dickey, 1991.
7. Erne, 2003.
8. Andrew Gurr, 'Maximal and Minimal Texts: Shakespeare *v*. the Globe' (1999) in C. M. S. Alexander (ed.) Cambridge Shakespeare Library vol. 1, *Shakespeare's Times, Texts and Stages* (Cambridge: CUP, 2003), pp. 147–165.
9. Rackin, 2000.

10. Morgann, 1777.
11. Rose, M., 1972.
12. Boika Sokolova, 1992.
13. Prior, 'Was *The Raigne of King Edward III* a Compliment to Lord Hunsdon?' (1993/4).
14. Guthrie, 1964, 201–11.
15. Olson, Strasser Olson and Doescher, 1998.
16. Peter Usher, *Hamlet's Universe* (San Diego: Aventine, 2006).

3 The Man From Stratford: A Bad Buy

1. Reisz, 2013.
2. Feldman, 2010.
3. Feldman, 2011.
4. Peachman, 2006.
5. Feldman, 2011.
6. Gaenor Cimio, 1963.
7. Aelwyn Edwards, 2008.
8. Frampton, 2013.
9. See Walker, 1952.
10. Halbig, 2007.
11. Velz, 1985.

4 Some Rotten Alternatives

1. TopTenz, 2011.
2. Thomas Nashe, *Strange News*, 1592.
3. Editor of the Penguin edition of *Cymbeline*.
4. Masters, 2013.
5. Farey, 2010.
6. Brenda James and William Rubinstein, 2006.

5 Amelia's Early Life: 1569–1582

1. Brown, 2003.

6 Amelia at Court: 1582–1593

1. Winstanley, 1921,
2. Harold Bloom, 1992.
3. Tacitus, *Histories*, 1.10.
4. Christina Valhouli, *Salon* magazine.
5. Hopkins, 1998.

7 Amelia, a Poet in Exile: 1594–1610

1. I have used the edition by De Luna, 1970.
2. Chedgzoy, 2010.
3. Published originally in Russian in 1997.
4. Quoted by Brian Vickers in *Counterfeiting Shakespeare*, p. 426.
5. Vickers, 2002.
6. Prior, 2013.

8 A Poet in Her Own Right: 1611–1617

1. Bowen, 2001.
2. Richey, 1997.
3. Clark, 2007.
4. Summarised by Sidney Thomas, 1983.
5. Keohane, 1997.
6. Schnell, 1997.
7. Matchinske, 1966.
8. Tiffany, 2011.
9. Bloom, 1998.
10. Wells, 1997.

10 Conclusion

1. Rose, 2011.
2. Kozusko, 2012.
3. E. A. J. Honigmann, 2002–3.
4. Thiel, 2010.

Appendices

1. Martin Green, 'Emilia Lanier IS the Dark Lady of the Sonnets', *English Studies* 87, 5 (2006) 544–76.
2. Paul Kocher, *Christopher Marlowe*, 1962, p. 30.
3. Sams, 1995.
4. Sams, 1995.

Bibliography

Film

The Dark Lady Players, www.darkladyplayers.com.

Riggs, M., *The Dark Lady: The Woman Who Wrote Shakespeare* (2008) http://www. youtube.com/watch?v=tyn-3GNOd7w.

Print

Alger, J., 'Aemelia Lanyer's Threads in the Tapestry of Dialectical Devotion' (Masters Thesis: University of Central Oklahoma, 2010).

Altimont, A. J., 'The Meaning of Nedar in *A Midsummer Night's Dream*', *Notes and Queries* 54 (2007), 275–7.

Amini, D., 'Kosher Bard: Could Shakespeare's Plays Have Been Written by the "Dark Lady", a Jewish Woman of Venetian-Moroccan Ancestry? John Hudson Thinks So', *New Jersey Jewish News*, 28 February (2008), pp. 32–3.

Anderson, M. K., *'Shakespeare' by Another Name: A Biography of Edward de Vere, Earl of Oxford, the Man Who Was Shakespeare* (New York: Penguin, 2005).

Angell, P. K., 'Light on the Dark Lady: A Study of Some Elizabethan Libels', *Publications of Modern Language Association* 52:3, Sept. (1937) 652–74.

Arber, E., *English Garner: Ingatherings from our History and Literature* (Westminster: Constable, 1895–6).

Aspden, P., 'Breakfast with the FT: Mark Rylance', *Financial Times* (13 September 2013). Downloaded on 17 September 2013 from: http://www.ft.com/intl/cms/s/2/6179aa70-1a10-11e3-93e8-00144feab7de.html#axzz2fHJDmMiF.

Astington, J. H., *English Court Theatre 1558–1642* (Cambridge: Cambridge University Press, 1999).

Astley, R., 'The Structure of Shakespeare's Second Tetralogy' (PhD Thesis: Temple University, 1982).

Ayres, R., 'Evidence that Marlowe was Gregorio', *The Marlowe Society Research Journal* 7 (2010). Downloaded on 20 June 2013 from: http://www.marlowe-society.org/pubs/ journal/downloads/rj07articles/jl07_03_ayres_gregorio.pdf.

Baker, T., *Coffee, Tea or Me?* (New York: Bartholomew House, 1968).

Baldwin, T. W., *The Organization and Personnel of the Shakespearean Company* (Princeton: Princeton University Press, 1927).

Baldwin, T. W., 'Light on the Dark Lady', *Publications of Modern Language Association* 55:2, June (1940) 598–602.

Baldwin, T. W., *William Shakespeare's Small Latin and Lesse Greeke* (Urbana: University of Illinois Press, 1944).

Baldwin, T. W., *On the Literary Genetics of Shakespeare's Plays 1592–1594* (Urbana: University of Illinois Press, 1959).

Bancroft, R., Letter to Robert Cecil saying that the Earl of Southampton supports Lanier's application for a hay patent. (London: Public Records Office, 24 August 1604).

Banes, D., *Shakespeare, Shylock and Kabbalah* (Silver Spring: Malcolm House Publishing, 1978).

Barton, A., *Shakespeare and the Idea of the Play* (Baltimore: Penguin, 1967).

Basch, D., *Shakespeare's Judaica and Devices: Judaic Influences in Shakespeare's Work* (West Hartford: Revelatory Press, 1996).

Bate, J., *Shakespeare and Ovid* (New York: Oxford University Press, 1993).

Bate, J., *The Genius of Shakespeare* (London: Picador, 1997).

Bate, J. and E. Rasmussen (eds) William Shakespeare's *Twelfth Night* (Royal Shakespeare Company: Palgrave Macmillan, 2010).

Battenhouse, R. W., *Shakespearean Tragedy: Its Art and Its Christian Premises* (Bloomington: Indiana University Press, 1969).

Battenhouse, R. W. (ed.), *Shakespeare's Christian Dimension: An Anthology of Commentary* (Bloomington: Indiana University Press, 1994).

Bawcutt, P., 'A Note on Sonnet 38', *Shakespeare Quarterly* 35:1, Spring (1984),77–9.

Bednarz, J., *Shakespeare and the Truth of Love: The Mystery of the 'Phoenix and the Turtle'* (New York: Palgrave Macmillan, 2012).

Belkin, A. (ed.), *Leone de' Sommi and the Performing Arts* (Tel Aviv: Tel Aviv University, 1997).

Benson, S., *Shakespearean Resurrection: The Art of almost Raising the Dead* (Pittsburgh: Duqesne University Press, 2009).

Berry, B., '"Pardon though I have digrest": Digression as a style in *Salve Deus Rex Judaeorum*', in M. Grossman (ed.), *Aemilia Lanyer: Gender, Genre and the Canon* (Lexington: University of Kentucky Press, 1998).

Berry, E. I., *Shakespeare and the Hunt: A Cultural and Social Study* (Cambridge: Cambridge University Press, 2001).

Berry, H., 'The View of London from the North and the Playhouses in Holywell' *Shakespeare Survey* (2000), 196–212.

Blits, J. H., *Deadly Thought; Hamlet and the Human Soul* (New York: Lexington Books, 2001).

Bloom, H., 'Introduction' in M. Meyer, *Gospel of Thomas: The Hidden Sayings of Jesus* (San Francisco: HarperSanFrancisco, 1992).

Bloom, H., *Shakespeare; the Invention of the Human* (New York: Riverhead Books, 1998).

Boitani, P., *The Gospel According to Shakespeare* (Notre Dame: University of Indiana, 2013).

Bono, B. J., *Literary Transvaluation: From Virgilian Epic to Shakespearean Tragic Comedy* (Berkeley: University of California Press, 1984).

Booth, S., *Shakespeare's Sonnets* (New Haven: Yale University Press, 1977).

Bowen, B., 'Amelia Lanyer and the Invention of White Womanhood', in S. Frye and K. Robertson (ed.) *Maids and Mistresses,Cousins and Queens: Women's Alliances in Early Modern England* (Oxford: Oxford University Press, 1999).

Bowen, B., 'The Rape of Jesus: Aemilia Lanyer's *Lucrece*' in J. E. Howard and S. C. Shershaw (eds), *Marxist Shakespeares* (London: Routledge, 2001).

Bowen, B., 'Beyond Shakespearean Exceptionalism' in L. Davis (ed.), *Shakespeare Matters: History, Teaching, Performance* (Newark: University of Delaware Press, 2003).

Boynton, L., *The Elizabethan Militia 1558–1638* (London: Routledge, 1967).

Bradbrook, M. C., *The School of Night; A Study in the Literary Relationships of Sir Walter Raleigh* (Cambridge: Cambridge University Press, 1936).

Brandes, G., *William Shakespeare: A Critical Study* (New York: Macmillan, 1935).

Brown, P. A., *Better a Shrew than a Sheep: Women, Drama and the Culture of Jest in Early Modern England* (Ithaca: Cornell University Press, 2003).

Brusberg-Kiermeier, S., "'Never shall my sad eies againe behold these pleasures": Aemilia Lanyer and her Idealization of Tudor Court Life' in T. Betteridge and A. Riehl (eds), *Tudor Court Culture* (Selinsgrove: Susquehanna University Press, 2010).

Bryant, J. A., *Hippolyta's View: Some Christian Aspects of Shakespeare's Plays* (Lexington: University of Kentucky Press, 1981).

Bullough, G., *Narrative and Dramatic Sources of Shakespeare* (New York: Columbia University Press, 1964).

Burton, J. A., 'An Unrecognized Theme in *Hamlet*', *The Shakespeare Newsletter* (2000–2001) 71–82.

Campbell, O. J., *The Reader's Encyclopedia of Shakespeare* (New York: Crowell, 1966).

Cervo, N. A., 'Shakespeare's *Coriolanus*', *Explicator* 57:1 (1998), 7–8.

Chambers, E. K., *William Shakespeare: A Study of Facts and Problems* (Oxford: Clarendon Press, 1930).

Chambers, E. K., *The Elizabethan Stage* (Oxford: Clarendon Press, 1965).

Chambers, R. W., *Man's Unconquerable Mind* (London: Jonathan Cape, 1939).

Chedgzoy, K., 'Remembering Aemilia Lanyer', *Journal of the Northern Renaissance* (2010). Downloaded on 20 July 2013 from http://www.northernrenaissance.org/remembering-aemilia-lanyer/.

Cheney, P., *Shakespeare's Literary Authorship* (Cambridge: Cambridge University Press, 2008).

Chiljan, K., *Shakespeare Suppressed* (San Francisco: Faire Editions, 2011).

Cho, K. S., *Emblems in Shakespeare's Last Plays* (Lanham: University Press of America, 1988).

Clark, V., *Allies for Armageddon: The Rise of Christian Zionism* (New Haven: Yale University Press, 2007).

Clarkson P. S. and C. T. Warren, *The Law of Property in Shakespeare and the Elizabethan Drama* (New York: Gordian Press, 1968). Conan Doyle, A., *The Sign of Four* (London: Spencer Blackett, 1890).

Conan Doyle, A., *The Sign of Four* (London: Spencer Blackett, 1890).

Cooper, A. D., *Sergeant Shakespeare* (London: Hart-Davis, 1949).

Cooper, T., 'Queen Elizabeth's Public Face', *History Today* 53, (May 2003) 38–41.

Cox, J. D., *Shakespeare and the Dramaturgy of Power* (Princeton: Princeton University Press, 1989).

Cox, V., *Women's Writing in Italy, 1400–1650* (Baltimore: John Hopkins University Press, 2008).

Craig, D. H., 'Common-Words Frequencies, Shakespeare's Style, and the Elegy by W.S', *Early Modern Literary Studies* 8.1 (2002) 31–42.

Craig, D. H., *Shakespeare, Computers and the Mystery of Authorship* (New York: Cambridge University Press, 2009).

Craig, H., 'Shakespeare's Bad Poetry' *Shakespeare Survey* (1966) 51–6.

Crinkley, R., 'New Perspectives on the Authorship Question', *Shakespeare Quarterly* 36:4 (1985), 515–22.

Cunningham, A. J. V., 'Essence and the Phoenix and the Turtle', *English Literary History* 19:4 (1952) 265–76.

Cutting, B., 'Shakespeare's Will … Considered Too Curiously', *Brief Chronicles* 1 (2009) 205–36.

D'Amico, J., *Shakespeare and Italy: The City and the Stage* (Gainesville: University Press of Florida, 2001).

Dawkins, P., *The Shakespeare Enigma* (London: Polair Publishing, 2004).

De Luna, B. N., *The Queen Declined: An Interpretation of Willobie His Avisa* (Oxford: Clarendon Press, 1970).

Demary, J. G., *Shakespeare and the Spectacle of Strangeness: The Tempest and the*

Transformation of Renaissance Theatrical Forms (Pittsburgh: Duquesne University Press, 1998).

Demos, 'Britons More Proud of the National Trust than the Royal Family', (20 November 2011). Downloaded on 28 June 2013 from: http://www.demos.co.uk/press_releases/britonsmoreproudofthenationaltrustthantheroyalfamily.

Dickey, S., 'Shakespeare's Mastiff Comedy', *Shakespeare Quarterly* 42:3 (1991) 255–75.

Dobson, M., *The Making of the National Poet: Shakespeare, Adaptation and Authorship 1660–1769* (New York: Oxford University Press, 1992).

Doebler, J., *Shakespeare's Speaking Pictures: Studies in Iconic Imagery* (Albuquerque: University of New Mexico Press, 1974).

Dollimore, J. and A. Sinfield (eds), *Political Shakespeare: Essays in Cultural Materialism* (Manchester: Manchester University Press, 1994).

Donker, M., *Shakespeare's Proverbial Themes: A Rhetorical Context for the Sententia as Res* (Westport: Greenwood Press, 1992).

Doran, S. and T. S. Freeman (eds), *The Myth of Elizabeth* (New York: Palgrave Macmillan, 2003).

Duff, M., 'Marlowe and the Dark Lady', *The Marlowe-Shakespeare Connection Blog*. Downloaded on 22 June 2013 from: http://marlowe-shakespeare.blogspot.com/2011/09/marlowe-and-dark-lady-by-maureen-duff.html.

Duffin, R. W., *Shakespeare's Songbook* (New York: W.Norton, 2004).

Dureau, Y., *The Christian Cabbalah Movement in Renaissance England and Its Influence on William Shakespeare* (Lewiston: Edward Mellon Press, 2009).

Edmondson, P. and S. Wells, *Shakespeare Bites Back* (Stratford-upon-Avon: Shakespeare Birthplace Trust (28 October 2011).

Edmondson, P. and S. Wells, *Shakespeare Beyond Doubt: Evidence, Argument, Controversy* (Cambridge: Cambridge University Press, 2013).

Edwards, A., *Shakespeare in Italy* (2007). Downloaded on 20 June 2013 from: http://robedwards.typepad.com/shakespeare_in_italy/.

Egan, M., 'Are There Any Clear Links to Be Made Between Shakespeare's Plays and the Area around Stratford Upon Avon?', in J. M. Shahan and others (eds), 'An Historic Document: Shakespeare Authorship Coalition Answers the Shakespeare Birthplace Trust', *The Oxfordian* 14 (2012), 4–103. Downloaded on 20 June 2013 from: http://shakespeare-oxford.com/wp-content/oxfordian/Shahan_Historic_Document.pdf.

Einstein, L., *The Italian Renaissance in England* (New York: Columbia University Press, 1935).

Elam, K., *Shakespeare's Universe of Discourse: Language Games in the Comedies* (Cambridge: Cambridge University Press, 1984).

Ellis, D., *The Truth about William Shakespeare: Fact, Fiction, and Modern Biographies* (Edinburgh: Edinburgh University Press, 2012).

Elliott, W. and R. Valenza, 'Was the Earl of Oxford the True Shakespeare? A Computer-Aided Analysis', *Notes and Queries* 236 (1991), 501–6.

Elliott, W. and R. Valenza, 'And Then There Were None: Winnowing the Shakespeare Claimants', *Computers and the Humanities* 30 (1996), 191–245.

Elliott, W. and R. Valenza, 'Oxford by the Numbers: What are the Odds that the Earl of Oxford Could Have Written Shakespeare's Poems and Plays?', *Tennessee Law Review* 72:1 (2004), 323–453.

Ephraim, M. K., *Deborah's Kin: Playing the Jewish Woman on the English Renaissance Stage* (PhD Thesis: University of Wisconsin-Madison, 1999).

Ephraim, M., 'Screwing the Bardbody: *Kill Shakespeare* and North American Popular Culture', *Upstart: A Journal of English Renaissance Studies* (2013). Downloaded on 30 August 2013 from: http://www.clemson.edu/upstart/Essays/bardbody/bardbody.xhtml.

Erne, L., 'Shakespeare and the Publication of His Plays', *Shakespeare Quarterly* 53:1, (2002) 1–20.

Erne, L., *Shakespeare as Literary Dramatist* (Cambridge: Cambridge University Press, 2003).

Everitt, E. B. and Armstrong, R. L., *Six Early Plays Related to the Shakespeare Canon* (Copenhagen: Rosenkilde and Bagger, 1965).

Explorandum, *Shakespeare Survey* (2008). Downloaded on 20 July 2013 from: http://getrealnews.blogspot.com/2008/08/43-of-uk-population-say-shakespeare-did.html?m=1.

Faherty, T., 'Othello dell'Arte: The Presence of "Commedia" in Shakespeare's Tragedy', *Theater Journal* 43:2 (1991), 179–94.

Faith, M., *The Epic Structure and Subversive Messages of Aemilia Lanyer's* Salve Deus Rex Judaeorum', (MA Thesis: Virginia Polytechnic Institute, 1998).

Falconer, A., *Shakespeare and the Sea* (London: Constable, 1964).

Farey, P., 'John Matthew alias Christopher Marlowe', *The Marlowe–Shakespeare Connection* (24 July 2010). Downloaded on 23 June 2013 from: http://marlowe-shakespeare.blogspot.com/2010/07/john-matthew-alias-christopher-marlowe.html.

Feldman, S., 'The Swallow and the Crow: The Case for Sackville as Shakespeare', *The Oxfordian* 12 (2010), 119–37.

Feldman, S., *The Apocryphal William Shakespeare* (Indianapolis: Dog Ear Publishing, 2011).

Fergusson, F., *Trope and Allegory: Themes Common to Dante and Shakespeare* (Athens: University of Georgia Press, 1977).

Fletcher, E., '*Noble Virtues*' and '*Rich Chaines*': *Patronage in the Poetry of Aemilia Lanier*, (MA Thesis: University of Missouri-Columbia, 2009).

Forse, J., *Art Imitates Business: Commercial and Political Influences on the Elizabethan Theatre* (Bowling Green: Bowling Green State University Popular Press, 1993).

Fox, B-L., 'Xpress Reviews: Fiction/First Look at New Books', *Library Journal* (26 September 2013). Downloaded on 28 September 2013 from: http://reviews.libraryjournal.com/2013/09/books/fiction/xpress-reviews-fiction-first-look-at-new-books-september-27-2013/.

Frampton, S., 'Who Edited Shakespeare?', *The Guardian* (12 July 2013). Downloaded on 13 July 2013 from: http://www.guardian.co.uk/books/2013/jul/12/who-edited-shakespeare-john-florio.

Frey, D. L., *The First Tetralogy, Shakespeare's Scrutiny of the Tudor Myth: A Dramatic Exploration of Divine Providence* (The Hague: Mouton, 1976).

Gaw, A., *The Origin and Development of 1 Henry VI* (Los Angeles: University of Southern California, 1926).

Gililov, I., *The Shakespeare Game: The Mystery of the Great Phoenix* (New York: Algora Press, 2003).

Gillespie, S., *Shakespeare's Books: A Dictionary of Shakespeare's Sources* (Continuum: New York, 2004).

Goldberg, J., *James I and the Politics of Literature: Jonson, Shakespeare, Donne, and Their Contemporaries* (Baltimore: Johns Hopkins University Press, 1983).

Goldberg, J., 'Canonizing Aemilia Lanyer,' in J. Goldberg (ed.), *Desiring Women Writing: English Renaissance Examples* (Stanford: Stanford University Press, 1997).

Goldstein, G. B., 'Did Shakespeare Read Dante in Italian?', *Elizabethan Review* 1:1 (1993), 61–2.

Gray, A. K., 'The Secret of *Love's Labour's Lost*', *PMLA* 39:3, (September 1924) 581–611.

Gray, H. D., 'Shakespeare, Southampton and Avisa', in H. Craig (ed.), *Stanford Studies in Language and Literature. 1941: Fiftieth anniversary of the founding of Stanford University* (Stanford: The University, 1941).

Green, M., *Wriothesley's Roses: In Shakespeare's Sonnets, Poems and Plays* (Baltimore: Clevedon Books, 1993).

Greenblatt, S., *Shakespearean Negotiations: The Circulation of Social Energy in Renaissance England* (Berkeley: University of California Press, 1988).

Greenblatt, S., *Will in the World: How Shakespeare Became Shakespeare* (New York: W. W. Norton, 2004).

Greenblatt, S., 'The Death of Hamnet and the Making of *Hamlet*', *The New York Review of Books* (21 October 2004). Downloaded on 23 June 2013 from: http://www.nybooks.com/articles/archives/2004/oct/21/the-death-of-hamnet-and-the-making-of-hamlet/?pagination=false.

Greenblatt, S., 'Reply to James Shapiro', *New York Review of Books* LVII (October 14 2010), 81.

Greg, W. W., *The Shakespeare First Folio: Its Bibliographic and Textual History* (Oxford: Clarendon Press, 1955).

Greg, W. W., *The Editorial Problem in Shakespeare* (Oxford: Clarendon Press, 1967).

Grossman, M. (ed.), *Aemilia Lanyer: Gender, Genre and the Canon* (Lexington: University Press of Kentucky, 1998).

Groves, B., *Texts and Traditions; Religion in Shakespeare 1592–1604* (Oxford: Oxford University Press, 2007).

Guibbory, A., 'The Gospel According to Aemilia: Women and the Sacred' in Marshall Grossman (ed.), *Aemelia Lanyer: Gender, Genre and the Canon* (Lexington: University of Kentucky Press, 1998).

Gulick, S. L., 'Was "Shakespeare" a Woman?', *College English* 15:8 (May 1954), 445–9.

Gurr, A., *The Shakespearean Stage 1574–1642* (Cambridge: Cambridge University Press, 1980).

Gurr, A., *Playgoing in Shakespeare's London* (Cambridge: Cambridge University Press, 1987).

Gurr, A., *Rebuilding Shakespeare's Globe* (London: Weidenfeld and Nicolson, 1989).

Gurr, A., *The Shakespearian Playing Companies* (Oxford: Clarendon Press, 1996).

Gurr, A., 'Metatheatre and the Fear of Playing' in R. H. Wells (ed.), *Neo-Historicism: Studies in Renaissance Literature, History, and Politics* (Rochester: D. S. Brewer, 2000).

Gurr, A., *The Shakespeare Company 1594–1642* (Cambridge: Cambridge University Press, 2004).

Guthrie, W. G., 'The Astronomy of Shakespeare', *Irish Astronomical Journal* 6:6 (1964) 201–11. Downloaded on 20 June 2013 from: http://articles.adsabs.harvard.edu//full/1964IrAJ....6..201G/0000211.000.html.

Hadfield, A., *Shakespeare and Republicanism* (Cambridge: Cambridge University Press, 2008).

Halbig, C., 'Shakespeare's *Othello* and the Insidious Creation of an Unwilling Villain', *Amalgam* 2 (2007), 25–30.

Hassel, R. C., *Renaissance Drama and the English Church Year* (Lincoln: University of Nebraska Press, 1979).

Hassel, R. C., *Faith and Folly in Shakespeare's Romantic Comedies* (Athens: University of Georgia Press, 1980).

Hassel, R. C., 'Last Words and Last Things: St John, Apocalypse and Eschatology in *Richard III*', *Shakespeare Studies* 18 (1986), 25–40.

Hassel, R. C., 'Painted Women: Annunciation Motifs in *Hamlet*', *Comparative Drama* 32 (1998), 47–84.

Hawkins, S., 'Structural Pattern in Shakespeare's Histories', *Studies in Philology* 88:1 (1991) 16–45.

Hibbert, C., *The Virgin Queen: Elizabeth I, Genius of the Golden Age* (Reading: Perseus Books, 1991).

Hill, J., *Stages and Playgoers: From Guild Plays to Shakespeare* (Montreal: McGill-Queen's University Press, 2002).

Hirschfeld, H., *Joint Enterprises; Collaborative Drama and the Institutionalization of the English Renaissance Theater* (Amherst: University of Massachusetts Press, 2004).

Hirschorn, N., 'The Jewish Key to Shakespeare's Most Enigmatic Creation', *Midstream* (February/March 1989).

Hodgkins, C., 'Prospero's Apocalypse' in B. Batson (ed.), *Word and Rite: The Bible and Ceremony in Selected Shakespearean Works* (Newcastle: Cambridge Scholars, 2010).

Hoeniger, D., 'Gower and Shakespeare in *Pericles* '*Shakespeare Quarterly* 33:4 (1982) 461–79.

Hoenselaars, A. J., 'Italy Staged in English Renaissance Drama' in M. Marrapodi and others (eds), *Shakespeare's Italy: Functions of Italian Locations in Renaissance Drama* (Manchester: Manchester University Press, 1997).

Hoff, L. K., *Hamlet's Choice: Hamlet A Reformation Allegory* (Lewiston: E. Mellon Press, 1988).

Holland, P. (ed.), *Shakespeare Survey*, Volume 54, *Shakespeare and Religions* (Cambridge: Cambridge University Press, 2001).

Holsti, O., *Content Analysis for the Social Sciences and Humanities* (Reading: Addison-Wesley, 1969).

Honigmann, E. A. J., and S. Brock, *Playhouse Wills 1558–1642* (Manchester: Manchester University Press, 1993).

Honigmann, E. A. J., *Shakespeare: The Lost Years* (Manchester: Manchester University Press, 1998).

Honigmann, E. A. J., 'Catholic Shakespeare? A Response to Hildegard Hammerschmidt-Hummel', *Connotations* 12:1 (2002–3), 52–60. Downloaded on 27 June from: http://www.uni-tuebingen.de/uni/nec/honigmann121.htm.

Hooks, A. G., 'Shakespeare at the White Greyhound', *Shakespeare Survey* (2011), 260–75.

Hope, W., and K. J. Holston, *The Shakespeare Controversy: An Analysis of the Authorship Theories* (Jefferson: McFarland & Company, 2009).

Hopkins, L., *The Shakespearean Marriage: Merry Wives and Heavy Husbands* (London: Macmillan, 1998).

Howard, J. E., *Shakespeare's Art of Orchestration: Stage Technique and Audience Response* (Urbana: University of Illinois Press, 1984).

Howard, J. E., *Engendering a Nation: A Feminist Account of Shakespeare's English Histories* (New York: Routledge, 1997).

Howard, J. E., *Marxist Shakespeares* (London: Routledge, 2001).

Hudson, J., Review of Shakespeare's *The Taming of the Shrew* (directed by Rebecca Patterson for the Queen's Company at the Walkerspace Theatre, New York, November 2005), *Shakespeare* 2:2 (2006) 222–4. Available for download from: www.ReviewingShakespeare.com.

Hudson, J., 'Amelia Bassano Lanier: A New Paradigm', *The Oxfordian* 11 (2008), 65–82. Downloaded on 20 June 2013 from: http://shakespeare-oxford.com/wp-content/oxfordian/Hudson_Bassano.pdf.

Hudson, J., 'A Meta-Theatrical Staging in New York City: Shakespeare's Virgin Mary Allegories', *The Birmingham Journal of Literature and Language* 2 (2009), 75–8. Downloaded 23 June 2013 from: http://ejournals.org.uk/bjll/%5Bz73-79%5D_NOTES_1_2_3.pdf.

Hudson, J., interviewed by S.Condusta, 'Does the Elizabethan Understanding of the Actor as Puppet Unlock the Meaning of Shakespeare's Plays?', *New York Puppet Forum* (2009). Downloaded on 20 June 2013 from: http://www.nypuppets.org/elizabethan.htm.

Hudson, J., '*A Midsummer Night's Dream*: A Religious Allegory', *The Birmingham Journal* of *Literature and Language* 3 (2010), 44–58. Downloaded on 20 June 2013 from: http://ejournals.org.uk/bjll/vIII%5Bz44-58%5D_Hudson.pdf.

Hughes, S., 'New Light on the Dark Lady', *Shakespeare Oxford Newsletter* 36:3 (2000), 1–15.

Hunt, M., *Shakespeare's Religious Allusiveness: Its Play and Tolerance* (Aldershot: Ashgate Publishing, 2004).

Huston, C., *The Shakespeare Authorship Question: Evidence for Edward Vere 17th Earl of Oxford* (Philadelphia: Dorrance, 1971).

Ingram, W., *A London Life in the Brazen Age: Francis Langley 1548–1602* (Cambridge: Harvard University Press, 1978).

Iyasere, S., 'The Liberation of Emilia', *Shakespeare in Southern Africa* 21:1 (2009), 69–72.

James, B. and W. Rubinstein, *The Truth Will Out: Unmasking the Real Shakespeare* (New York: Regan, 2006).

James, S. L., 'A New Source for Shakespeare's *Taming of the Shrew*', *Bulletin of John Rylands University Library of Manchester* 81:1 (1999), 49–62.

Jimenez, R., 'The Case for Oxford Revisited', *The Oxfordian* 11 (2009), 45–64.

Johnson, J., *Timber or Discoveries Made upon Men and Matter*, ed. F. E. Schelling (Boston: Ginn, 1892).

Jolly, E., 'Shakespeare and Burghley's Library Bibliotheca Illustris: Sive Catelogus Variorum Librorum', *The Oxfordian: The Annual Journal of the Shakespeare Oxford Society* 3 (2000). 3–18.

Jones, E., *The Origins of Shakespeare* (Oxford: Clarendon Press, 1977).

Jones, G. L., *The Discovery of Hebrew in Tudor England: A Third Language* (Manchester: Manchester University Press, 1983).

Jones, T. P., *The Second Coming of the Second Tetralogy* (PhD thesis: North Carolina State University, 2006).

Joseph, B. L., *Elizabethan Acting* (Oxford: Oxford University Press, 1964).

Kathman, D., 'Oxford's Bible: Critically Examining Oxfordian Claims', The Shakespeare Authorship Page (n. d.). Downloaded on 30 June 2013 from: http://shakespeareauthorship.com/ox5.html.

Kehler, D., 'Shakespeare's Emilias and the Politics of Celibacy' in D. Kehler and S. Baker (ed.), *Another Country: Feminist Perspectives on Renaissance Drama* (Metuchen: Scarecrow, 1991).

Kennedy, C., 'Deodorizing King Lear', *Appositions: Studies in Renaissance/Early Modern Literature and Culture* 6 (2013). Downloaded on 20 June 2013 from http://appositions.blogspot.com/2010/05/colleen-kennedy-deodorizing-king-lear.html.

Keohane, C., '"That Blindest Weaknesse Be Not Over-Bold": Aemilia Lanyer's Radical Unfolding of the Passion', *English Literary History* 64:2 (1997), 359–89.

Kiefer, F., *Shakespeare's Visual Theatre: Staging the Personified Characters* (Cambridge: Cambridge University Press, 2003).

Kiernan, P., *Shakespeare's Theory of Drama* (Cambridge: Cambridge University Press, 1996).

Kiernan, P., *Filthy Shakespeare: Shakespeare's Most Outrageous Sexual Puns* (New York: Gotham Books, 2007).

Knapp, J., 'What is a Co-author?', *Representations* 89 (2005), 1–29.

Knapp, J., 'Shakespeare as Co-author', *Shakespeare Studies* 36 (2008), 49–59.

Knight, G. W., '*King Lear* and the Comedy of the Grotesque' in J. Adelman (ed.), *Twentieth Century Interpretations of King Lear* (Englewood Cliffs: Prentice Hall, 1972).

Kolve, V. A., *The Play Called Corpus Christi* (Stanford: Stanford University Press, 1996).

Kozusko, M., 'Site, Space and Intimacy: *Sleep No More*'s Immersive Intertext', *Borrowers and Lenders: The Journal of Shakespeare and Appropriation*, Fall (2012), 2. Downloaded on 1 October from: http://www.borrowers.uga.edu/461/display.

Kuriyama, C. B., *Christopher Marlowe: A Renaissance Life* (Ithaca: Cornell University Press, 2000).

Lasocki, D., and R. Prior, *The Bassanos: Venetian Musicians and Instrument Makers in England 1531–1665* (Aldershot: Scolar Press, 1995). Revised edition (2013) downloaded on 20 July 2013 from: http://www.instantharmony.net/Music/ebooks.php.

Law, R. L., 'Shakespeare in the Garden of Eden', *Studies in English* 21 (1941), 24–38.

Leahy, W., *Elizabethan Triumphal Processions* (Burlington: Ashgate, 2005).

LeJacq, S. S., 'The Bounds of Domestic Healing: Medical Recipes, Storytelling and Surgery in Early Modern England', *Social History of Medicine* (2013). Downloaded on 22 June 2013 from: http://shm.oxfordjournals.org/content/early/2013/04/16/shm.hkt006.abstract.

Levin, R., 'On Fluellen's Figures, Christ Figures, and James Figures', *PMLA* 89 (1974), 302–11.

Logan, R., *Shakespeare's Marlowe: The Influence of Christopher Marlowe on Shakespeare's Artistry* (Burlington: Ashgate, 2007).

Looney, J. T., *Shakespeare Identified in De Vere, the Seventeenth Earl of Oxford* (New York: Frederick A. Stokes, 1920).

Loughlin, M. H., '"Fast ti'd unto Them in a Golden Chaine": Typology, Apocalypse, and Woman's Genealogy in Aemilia Lanyer's *Salve Deus Rex Judaeorum*', *Renaissance Quarterly* 53:1 (2000), 133–79.

Luppi, A. and E. Roche, 'The Role of Music in Francis Bacon's Thought: A Survey', *International Review of the Aesthetics and Sociology of Music* 24:2 (1993), 99–111.

Macht, D. I., 'Biblical Allusions in Shakespeare's *The Tempest* in the Light of Hebrew Exegesis' in H. Bloom (ed.), *Major Literary Characters: Caliban* (New York: Chelsea House Publishers, 1992).

Maisano, S., 'Shakespeare's Last Act: The Starry Messenger and the Galilean Book in *Cymbeline*', *Configurations* 12:3 (2004), 401–34.

Mallin, E. S., *Godless Shakespeare* (London: Continuum, 2007).

Marche, S., 'Wouldn't It Be Cool if Shakespeare Wasn't Shakespeare', *New York Times* (21 October 2011).

Marino, J. J., 'The Anachronistic Shrews', *Shakespeare Quarterly* 60:1 (2009), 25–46.

Markiewicz, A., Salve Deus Rex Judaeorum: *A New Gospel for Women by Women* (Undergraduate Thesis: Pace University, 2005). Downloaded on 20 July 2013 from: http://digitalcommons.pace.edu/honorscollege theses/21.

Marsden, J., D. Budden, H. Craig and P. Moscato, 'Language Individuation and Marker Words: Shakespeare and His Maxwell's Demon'. *PLoS ONE* 8:6 (2013). Downloaded on 28 September 2013 from: http://www.plosone.org/article/info%3Adoi%2F10.1371%2Fjournal.pone.0066813.

Marshall, C., *Last Things and Last Plays: Shakespearean Eschatology* (Carbondale: South Illinois University Press, 1991).

Marx, S., *Shakespeare and the Bible* (Oxford: Oxford University Press, 2000).

Masters, T., 'Ros Barber Faced Hostility over *The Marlowe Papers*', *BBC News* (28 June 2013). Downloaded on 29 June 2013 from: http://www.bbc.co.uk/news/entertainment-arts-23100252.

Matchinske, M., 'Credible Consorts: What Happens when Shakespeare's Sisters Enter the Syllabus?', *Shakespeare Quarterly* 47:4, (1996) 433–50.

McDonald, R., *Shakespeare and the Arts of Language* (Oxford: Oxford University Press, 2001).

McDonald, R., *Shakespeare's Late Style* (Cambridge: Cambridge University Press, 2006).

McCrea, S., *The Case for Shakespeare: The End of the Authorship Question* (Westport: Praeger, 2005).

McGrath, L., '"Let us have our Libertie Againe": Amelia Lanier's 17th Century Feminism',

Women's Studies 20 (1992), 331–48.

McLean-Fiander, K., 'Textual Geographies: The Literary and Social Networks of Aemilia Lanyer (1569–1645)', paper delivered at the Conference in Intellectual Geography: Comparative Studies, 1550–1700, (6 September 2011). Downloaded on 20 July 2013 from: http://intellectualgeography.history.ox.ac.uk/?page_id=481#fiander.

McMillin, S., *The Queen's Men and Their Plays* (Cambridge: Cambridge University Press, 1998).

Melchiori, G., 'The Rhetoric of Character Construction: *Othello*', *Shakespeare Survey* (1981), 61–72.

Melchiori , G. (ed.), *King Edward III* (Cambridge: Cambridge University Press, 1990).

Melchiori, G., *Shakespeare's Garter Plays: 'Edward III' to 'Merry Wives of Windsor'* (Newark: University of Delaware Press, 1994).

Michell, J., *Who Wrote Shakespeare?* (London: Thames and Hudson, 1999).

Miller, A., *Roman Triumphs and Early Modern English Culture* (New York: Palgrave, 2001).

Milward, P., *Shakespeare's Apocalypse* (London: St Austin Press, 1999).

Milward, P., *Shakespeare's Religious Background* (Bloomington: Indiana University Press, 1973).

Moffet, R., '*Cymbeline* and the Nativity', *Shakespeare Quarterly* 13:2 (1962), 207–18.

Molà, L., *The Silk Industry of Renaissance Venice* (Baltimore: Johns Hopkins University Press, 2000).

Molekamp, F., 'Reading Christ the Book in Aemilia Lanyer's *Salve Deus Rex Judaeorum* (1611): Iconography and the Culture of Reading', *Studies in Philology* 109:3 (2012), 311–32.

Morrison, G., *Shakespeare's Lancastrian Tetralogy* (PhD thesis: Stony Brook University, 1977).

Muir, K., 'Shakespeare and Dante', *Notes and Queries* vol. CXXIX (1949), 333.

Muir, K., 'Pyramus and Thisbe: A Study in Shakespeare's Method', *Shakespeare Quarterly* 5:2 (1954), 14–53.

Muller, G., *Was Shakespeare a Jew? Uncovering the Marrano Influences in His Life and Writing* (Lampeter: Edwin Mellen Press, 2011).

Neely, C. T., *Broken Nuptials in Shakespeare's Plays* (New Haven: Yale University Press, 1985).

Nelson, A., *Monstrous Adversary: The Life of Edward de Vere, 17th Earl of Oxford* (Liverpool: Liverpool University Press, 2003).

Ng, S. F., 'Aemilia Lanyer and the Politics of Praise', *English Literary History* 67:2 (2000), 433–51.

Nicholl, C., *The Reckoning: The Murder of Christopher Marlowe* (Chicago: University of Chicago Press, 1992).

Nicholl, C., *The Lodger Shakespeare: His Life on Silver Street* (New York: Penguin Group, 2007).

Nicoll, A., *The Development of the Theatre* (New York: Harcourt, Brace, 1967).

Niederkorn, W., 'Shakespeare Reaffirmed', *New York Times* (22 April 2007). Downloaded on 30 August 2013 from: http://www.nytimes.com/2007/04/22/education/edlife/shakespeare.html?_r=1&.

Noble, R. S. H., *Shakespeare's Biblical Knowledge and Use of Book of Common Prayer as Exemplified in the Plays of the First Folio* (Octagon Books: New York, 1970).

North, M. L., *The Anonymous Renaissance: Cultures of Discretion in Tudor-Stuart England* (Chicago: University of Chicago Press, 2003).

Olson, D. and others, 'The Stars of *Hamlet*', *Sky and Telescope* (November 1998), 68–73.

Parfaitt, T., *Black Jews in Africa and the Americas* (Cambridge: Harvard University Press, 2013).

Parker, P., 'Teaching and Wordplay: The 'Wall' of *A Midsummer Night's Dream*' in B. McIver and R. Stevenson (eds), *Teaching with Shakespeare: Critics in the Classroom* (Newark: University of Delaware Press, 1994).

Parker, P., *Shakespeare from the Margins* (Chicago: University of Chicago Press, 1996).

Parker, P., 'Murals and Morals: *A Midsummer Night's Dream*' in G. W. Most (ed.), *Editing Texts*, APOREMATA, Kritische Studien zur Philologiegeschichte (Gottingen: Vanenhoeck & Ruprech, 1998).

Parker, P., 'The Name of Nick Bottom' in C. Gheeraert-Graffeuille and N. Vienne-Guerrin (eds), *Autour du Songe d'une Nuit d'Été de William Shakespeare* (Rouen: University of Rouen, 2003).

Partridge, E., *Shakespeare's Bawdy* (New York: Routledge, 1968).

Patrides, C. A. & J. Wittreich (eds), *The Apocalypse in English Renaissance Thought and Literature* (Manchester: Manchester University Press, 1984).

Patterson, A., *Censorship and Interpretation: The Conditions of Writing and Reading in Early Modern England* (Madison: University of Wisconsin Press, 1986).

Patterson, T. H., 'On the Role of Christianity in the Political Philosophy of Francis Bacon'. *Polity* 19:3 (1987), 419–42.

Patricca, N., '"Shakespeare in Love" – The Supressed Italian Connection' (n. d.). Downloaded on 30 August 2013 from http://www.dramaticpublishing.com/ AuthorsCornerDet.php?titlelink=9731&sortorder=1.

Peachman, J., 'Links between *Mucedorus* and *The Tragical History, Admirable Achievments and Various Events of Guy Earl of Warwick*', *Notes and Queries* 53:4 (2006), 464–7. Downloaded on 20 July 2013 from: http://guyofwarwick.blogspot.com/p/links-between-mucedorus-and-tragical.html?m=1.

Pinksen, D., 'Was Robert Greene's "upstart crowe" the Actor Edward Alleyn?' *The Marlowe Society Research Journal* 6 (2009). Downloaded on 20 June 2013 from: http://www.marlowe-society.org/pubs/journal/downloads/rj06articles/jl06_03_pinksen_ upstartcrowalleyn.pdf.

Pointon, A. J., *The Man Who Was never Shakespeare: The Theft of William Shakspere's Identity* (Tunbridge Wells: Parapress, 2011).

Poole, W., 'False Play: Shakespeare and Chess', *Shakespeare Quarterly* 55:1 (2004), 50–70.

Posner, M., 'Rethinking Shakespeare', *Queen's Quarterly* 115:2 (2008), 3–15.

Posner, M., 'Unmasking Shakespeare', *Reform Judaism* (2010) 34–9, 46. Downloaded on 23 June 2013 from: http://reformjudaismmag.org/Articles/index.cfm?id=1584.

Preston, C., 'The Emblematic Structure of *Pericles*', *Word and Image: A Journal of Verbal/ Visual Enquiry* 8:1 (1992) 21–38.

Price, D., *Shakespeare's Unorthodox Biography: New Evidence of an Authorship Problem* (Westport: Greenwood Press, 2001).

Prior, K. S., 'What Maya Angelou Means when She Says "Shakespeare Must be a Black Girl"', *The Atlantic Magazine* (30 January 2013). Downloaded on 20 July 2013 from http://www.theatlantic.com/sexes/archive/2013/01/what-maya-angelou-means-when-she-says-shakespeare-must-be-a-black-girl/272667/.

Prior, R., 'The Bassanos of Tudor England', *Jewish Chronicle* (Literary Supplement) (1 June 1979), 1, 11.

Prior, R., 'Jewish Musicians at the Tudor Court', *The Musical Quarterly* 69:2 (1983), 253–265.

Prior, R., 'Was *The Raigne of King Edward III* a Compliment to Lord Hunsdon?', *Connotations* 3.3 (1993/4), 243–64. Downloaded 20 June from: http://www. connotations.uni-tuebingen.de/prior00303.htm.

Prior, R., 'Aemilia Lanyer and Queen Elizabeth at Cookham', *Cahiers Elisabéthains* 63 (2003), 17–32.

Prior, R., 'Shakespeare's Visit to Italy', *Journal of Anglo-Italian Studies* 9 (2008), 1–31.

Rabkin, N., *Shakespeare and the Problem of Meaning* (Chicago: University of Chicago Press, 1981).

Rackin, P., 'Misogyny is Everywhere' in D. Callaghan (ed.), *A Feminist Companion to Shakespeare* (Oxford: Blackwell, 2000).

Rakoczy, K., 'Was Shakespeare Sicilian? Crollalanza?' (n. d.). Downloaded on 20 June 2013 from: http://www.timesofsicily.com/shakespeare-sicilian-crollalanza/.

Reaves, J., 'Why I Don't Love the New Yorker Festival Any More' (4 October 2011). Downloaded on 20 July 2013 from: http://jotandquill.com/why-i-don%E2%80%99t-love-the-new-yorker-festival-anymore/.

Regnier, T., 'Could Shakespeare Think like a Lawyer? How Inheritance Law Issues in *Hamlet* May Shed Light on the Authorship Question', *The University of Miami Law Review* 57 (2003), 377–428. Downloaded on 20 June 2013 from: http://www.shakespearefellowship.org/virtualclassroom/Law/regnier.htm.

Reisz, M., 'Labouring for Invention', *Times Higher Education* (26 September 2013). Downloaded on 27 September 2013 from: http://www.timeshighereducation.co.uk/infinite-in-faculties/2007606.article.

Rhodes, N., *Elizabethan Grotesque* (London: Routledge and Kegan Paul, 1980).

Richey, E. G., '"To Undoe the Booke": Cornelius Agrippa, Aemilia Lanyer and the Subversion of Pauline Authority', *English Literary Renaissance* 27:1 (1997), 106–28.

Roberts, W. M., 'Gnosis in Aemilia Lanyer's "Salve Deus Rex Judaeorum"', *Rocky Mountain Review of Language and Literature* 59:2 (2005), 11–28.

Robertson, V., *Images in an Antique Book: An Investigation into Shakespeare's Knowledge and Use of Dante's Divinia Commedia in His Plays* (PhD thesis: University of New South Wales, 2002).

Roe, R. P., *The Shakespeare Guide to Italy: Retracing the Bard's Unknown Travels* (Harper: New York 2011).

Rollett, J. M., 'Shakespeare's Impossible Doublet: Droeshout's Engraving Anatomized', *Brief Chronicles* 2 (2010), 9–24.

Rose, F., *The Art of Immersion* (New York: W. W. Norton, 2011).

Rose, M., *Shakespearean Design* (Cambridge: Harvard University Press, 1972).

Rosenbaum, R., 'Glove Me Tender: Shakespeare in the Skin Trade', *The New York Observer* (27 July 1998). Downloaded on 29 July 2013 from: http://observer.com/1998/07/glove-me-tender-shakespeare-in-the-skin-trade/.

Rowse, A. L., *The Poems of Shakespeare's Dark Lady* (London: Jonathan Cape, 1978).

Rowse, A. L., *Eminent Elizabethans* (Athens: University of Georgia Press, 1983).

Rubinstein, F., *A Dictionary of Shakespeare's Sexual Puns and Their Significance* (New York; St Martin's Press, 1995).

Rudman, J., 'The State of Authorship Attribution Studies; Some Problems and Solutions', *Computers and the Humanities* 31:4 (1997–8), 351–65.

Rushkoff, D., *Present Shock: When Everything Happens Now* (New York: New York, 2013).

Rutter, C. C. (ed.), *Documents of the Rose Playhouse* (Manchester: Manchester University Press, 1984).

Sadie, S. (ed.), *The New Grove Dictionary of Music and Musicians* (London: Macmillan, 2001).

Salgado, G., *The Elizabethan Underworld* (London: J. M. Dent and Sons, 1977).

Sams, E., 'The Influence of Marlowe on Shakespeare' (1990). Downloaded on 20 June from: http://www.ericsams.org/index.php/shakespeare-archive/essays-and-reviews-unpubl/276-the-influence-of-marlowe-on-shakespeare.

Sams, E., *The Real Shakespeare: Retrieving the Early Years 1564–1594* (New Haven: Yale University Press, 1995).

Sams, E., 'Hamnet or Hamlet, that is the Question', *Hamlet Studies* 17 (1995), 94–8.

Downloaded on 20 June 2013 from: http://ericsams.org/index.php/on-shakespeare/essays-and-reviews/178-hamnet-or-hamlet-that-is-the-question.

Saner, R. A., 'Gemless Rings in Purgatorio XXIII and Lear', *Romance Notes* 10:1 (1968) 163–7.

Satin, J., '*Macbeth* and the Inferno of Dante', *Forum* 9:1 (1971), 18–23.

Schlueter, J., 'Martin Droeshout Redivivus: Reassessing the Folio Engraving of Shakespeare', *Shakespeare Survey* (2007), 237–51.

Schnell, L., 'Breaking "the Rule of *Cortezia*": Aemilia Lanyer's Dedications to *Salve Deus Rex Judaeorum*', *Journal of Medieval and Early Modern Studies* 27 (1997), 77–101.

Schoenbaum, S., 'Shakespeare's Dark Lady: A Question of Identity' in P. Edwards and others (eds), *Shakespeare's Styles: Essays in Honour of Kenneth Muir* (Cambridge: Cambridge University Press, 1980).

Schoenbaum, S., in A. Austin, 'Who Wrote Shakespeare?', PBS Frontline 'The Shakespeare Mystery' (1989). Downloaded on 22 June 2013 from: http://www.pbs.org/wgbh/pages/frontline/shakespeare/debates/austinarticle.html.

Schöenfeld, S. J., 'A Hebrew Source for "The Merchant of Venice"', *Shakespeare Survey* (1979), 115–28.

Schuler, R. M., 'Magic Mirrors in *Richard II*', *Comparative Drama* 38:2/3 (2004), 151–81.

Schuler, R. M., 'De-coronation and Demonic Meta-ritual in *Richard II*', *Exemplaria* 17:1 (2005), 169–214.

Schuler, R. M., 'Holy Dying in *Richard II*', *Renaissance and Reformation*, 30:3 (2006/7) 51–87.

Scott-Warren, J., 'When Theaters Were Bear Gardens or What's at Stake in the Comedy of Humors', *Shakespeare Quarterly* 54:1 (2003), 63–82.

Scoufos, A. *Shakespeare's Typological Satire: A Study of the Falstaff-Oldcastle Problem* (Athens: Ohio University Press, 1979).

Shaheen, N., *Biblical References in Shakespeare's Plays* (Newark: University of Delaware Press, 1999).

Shapiro, J., *Shakespeare and the Jews* (New York: Columbia University Press, 1996).

Shapiro, J., *1599: A Year in the Life of William Shakespeare* (London: Faber and Faber, 2005).

Shapiro, J., *Contested Will; Who Wrote Shakespeare?* (New York: Simon and Schuster, 2010).

Shapiro, J., 'Shylock in Red', *New York Review of Books* LVII:15 (October 14, 2010), 81.

Shea, C., 'Literary Authority as Cultural Criticism in Aemilia Lanyer's *The Authors Dreame*', *English Literary Renaissance* 32 (2002), 386–407.

Shea, C., '*Author of Prodigies*': *Representing the Female Letter-Writer in English Renaissance Literature* (PhD thesis: Queen's University, 2009).

Simonds, P. M., *Myth, Emblem and Music in Shakespeare's Cymbeline* (London: Associated University Press, 1992).

Simonds, P. M., '"My charms cracked not": The Alchemical Structure of *The Tempest*', *Comparative Drama*, 31:4 (1997/98), 538–70.

Simpson, R. R., *Shakespeare and Medicine* (Edinburgh E. & S. Livingstone, 1959).

Slater, E., *The Problem of 'The Reign of King Edward III': A Statistical Approach* (Cambridge: Cambridge University Press, 1988).

Slater, G., *Seven Shakespeares: A Discussion of the Evidence for Various Theories with regard to Shakespeare's Identity* (London: C. Palmer, 1931).

Smith, J. C., 'The Denial of the Shepherd' in R. Battenhouse (ed.), *Shakespeare's Christian Dimension: An Anthology of Commentary* (Indiana University Press: Bloomington, 1994).

Smith, J. S., '*A Midsummer Night's Dream* and the Allegory of the Theologians', *Christianity and Literature* 28 (1979), 15–23.

Sohmer, S., *Shakespeare's Mystery Play: The Opening of the Globe Theater 1599* (Manchester: Manchester University Press, 1999).

Sohmer, S., 'Shakespeare's Time Riddles in *Romeo and Juliet* Solved', *English Literary Renaissance* 35 (2005), 407–28.

Sohmer, S., 'Posting to the SHAKPER bulletin board concerning Twelfth Night' (20 October 2009). Downloaded 20 June 2013 from: http://shaksper.net/archive/2009/278-october/27247-anagrams.

Sokol, B. J. and M. Sokol, *Shakespeare's Legal Language: A Dictionary* (New Brunswick: Athlone Press, 2000).

Sokolova, B., *Shakespeare's Romances as Interrogative Texts: Their Alienation Strategies and Ideology* (Lampeter: Edwin Mellen Press, 1992).

Sousa, G. U. de, *Shakespeare's Cross-Cultural Encounters* (London: Macmillan, 1999).

Spurgeon, C., *Shakespeare's Imagery and What It Tells Us* (Cambridge: Cambridge University Press, 1971).

Stapfer, P., *Shakespeare and Classical Antiquity* (Burt Franklin: New York, 1970).

Stevens, A., 'First Catch your Satyrs', *Didaskalia* 9 (2012). 64–83. Downloaded on 20 July 2013 from: http://www.didaskalia.net/issues/9/13/DidaskaliaVol9.13.pdf.

Stow, K. R., *Jewish Dogs: An Image and Its Interpreters: Continuity in the Catholic–Jewish Encounter* (Stanford: Stanford University Press, 2006).

Strong, R., *The English Icon: Elizabethan and Jacobean Portraiture* (London: Routledge and Kegan Paul, 1969).

Sturrock, P. A., *AKA Shakespeare: A Scientific Approach to the Authorship Question* (California: Exoscience, 2013).

Sweet, G. E., *Shake-speare the Mystery* (Stanford: California, 1956).

Symposium, 'Who Wrote Shakespeare? An Evidentiary Puzzle', *Tennessee Law Review* 72:1 (2004), 1–453.

Tabeaux, E. and M. M. Lay, 'The Emergence of the Feminine Voice, 1526–1640: The Earliest Published Books by English Renaissance Women', *JAC: A Journal of Composition Theory* 15:1 (1995), 53–81.

Tassinari, L., *John Florio: The Man Who Was Shakespeare* (Montreal: Giano Books, 2009).

Taylor, A. and F. Mosher, *The Bibliographical History of Anonyma and Pseudonyma* (Chicago: University of Chicago Press, 1951).

Taylor, D. and D. N. Beauregard, *Shakespeare and the Culture of Christianity in Early Modern England* (New York: Fordham University Press, 2003).

Taylor, G. and J. Jowett, *Shakespeare Reshaped 1606–1623* (Oxford: Clarendon, 1993).

Taylor, M. A., *'Bottom, Thou Art Translated': Political Allegory in* A Midsummer Night's Dream (Rodopi: Amsterdam, 1973).

Tempera, M., *Feasting with Centaurs: Titus Andronicus from Stage to Text* (Bologna: Cooperativita Libraria Universiaria Editrice Bologna, 1999).

Thiel, S., *Understanding Shakespeare* (Thesis: University of Applied Science Potsdam, 2010). Downloaded on 20 August 2013 from: http://www.understanding-shakespeare.com/about.html.

Thomas, D. L. and N. Evans, 'John Shakespeare in the Exchequer', *Shakespeare Quarterly* 35:3 (1984), 315–18.

Thomas, S., 'The Problem of *Pericles*', *Shakespeare Quarterly* 34:4 (1983), 448–50.

Thomas, T., *Shakespeare's Shrine: The Bard's Birthplace and the Invention of Stratford-Upon-Avon* (Philadelphia: University of Pennsylvania Press, 2012).

Tiffany, G., 'Shakespeare's Parables', *Reformation* 16 (2011), 145–160.

Tobin, J. M. M., *Shakespeare's Favorite Novel: A Study of The Golden Ass as Prime Source* (New York: University Press of America, 1984).

Tobin, J. M. M., 'A Touch of Greene, Much Nashe and All Shakespeare' in T. A. Pendleton (ed.), *Henry VI: Critical Essays* (New York: Routledge, 2001).

TopTenz, 'Top Possible Authors for the Works of Shakespeare' (2011). Downloaded on

20 July 2013 from: http://www.toptenz.net/top-10-possible-authors-for-the-works-of-shakespeare.php.

Trevor-Roper, H., 'What's in a Name?', *Brief Chronicles* 2 (2010), 1–8.

Trill, S., 'Feminism versus Religion: Towards a Re-reading of Aemelia Lanyer's *Salve Deus Rex Judaeorum*', *Renaissance and the Reformation* 25:4 (2001), 67–80.

Tyson, E. S., 'Shakespeare's *Macbeth* and Dante's *Inferno*: A Comparison of the Images of Hell, Damnation and Corruption', *Iowa State Journal of Research* 54:4 (1980), 461–8.

Valhouli, C., 'Courtesan Power', *Salon* (15 November 2000). Downloaded on 27 June 2013 from: http://www.salon.com/2000/11/15/courtesan_1/.

van Es., B., *Shakespeare in Company* (Oxford: Oxford University Press, 2013).

Velz, J. W., 'From Jerusalem to Damascus: Bilocal Dramaturgy in Medieval and Shakespearian Conversion Plays', *Comparative Drama* 15 (1981–2), 4, 311–26.

Velz, J. W., '*Topoi* in Edward Ravenscroft's Indictment of Shakespeare's *Titus Andronicus*', *Modern Philology* 83:1 (1985), 45–50.

Vendler, H., *The Art of Shakespeare's Sonnets* (Cambridge: Harvard University Press, 1999).

Vickers, B., *Counterfeiting Shakespeare: Evidence, Authorship, and John Ford's Funerall Elegye* (Cambridge: Cambridge University Press, 2002).

Vickers, B., *Shakespeare, Co-Author: A Historical Study of Five Collaborative Plays* (Oxford: Oxford University Press, 2002).

Vickers, B., 'Shakespeare and Authorship Studies in the Twenty-First Century', *Shakespeare Quarterly* 62:1 (2011), 106–42.

Waldo, T. R. and T. W. Herbert, 'Musical terms in *The Taming of The Shrew*', *Shakespeare Quarterly* 10:2 (1959), 186–99.

Waldo, T. R., *Musical Terms and Rhetoric: The Complexity of Shakespeare's Dramatic Style* (Salzburg : Universitat Salzburg, 1974).

Walker, A., 'The 1622 Quarto and the First Folio *Othello*', *Shakespeare Survey* (1952), 16–24.

Walker, J. M., *Dissing Elizabeth: Negative Representations of Gloriana* (Durham: Duke University Press 1998).

Webster, A., 'Was Marlowe the Man?', *The National Review* (September, 1923). Downloaded on 20 June 2013 from: http://www.themarlowestudies.org/author-webster.html.

Weir, A., 'Reflections of Emelia' in A. Weir, *Marlowe: Being in the Life of the Mind* (1994), privately printed.

Weis, R., *Shakespeare Unbound: Decoding a Hidden Life* (New York: Henry Holt and Company, 2007).

Weiss, T., *The Breath of Clowns and Kings: Shakespeare's Early Comedies and Histories* (Chicago: University of Chicago, 1971).

Welch, C., *Six Lectures on the Recorder and Other Flutes in Relation to Literature* (London: H. Frowde, 1911).

Wells, R. H., *Elizabethan Mythologies: Studies in Poetry, Drama, and Music* (Cambridge: Cambridge University Press, 1994).

Wells, S., and Taylor, G., *William Shakespeare: A Textual Companion* (Oxford: Clarendon Press, 1987).

Wells, S., *Shakespeare: A Life in Drama* (New York: Norton, 1997).

Wells, S., Letter in *The Stage* magazine (27 September 2007). Downloaded on 28 June 2013 from: http://doubtaboutwill.org/debate.

Wember, H., 'Illuminating Eclipses: Astronomy and Chronology in *King Lear*', *Brief Chronicles* 2 (2010), 31–42.

Wentersdorf, K., 'The Date of *Edward III*', *Shakespeare Quarterly* 16:3 (1965), 227–31.

Whalen, R., '*Commedia dell'arte* in *Othello*: A Satiric Comedy Ending in Tragedy', *Brief Chronicles* 3 (2011), 71–85. Downloaded on 20 July 2013 from: http://www.theshakespeareunderground.com/wp-content/uploads/2012/09/BC-Commedia.pdf.

White, M., 'A Woman with Saint Peter's Keys?: Aemilia Lanyer's *Salve Deus Rex Judaeorum* and the Priestly Gifts of Women', *Criticism* 45:3 (2003), 323–41.

Whitney, C., *Early Responses to Renaissance Drama* (Cambridge: Cambridge University Press, 2006).

Wickham, G., '*Love's Labor's Lost* and *The Four Foster Children of Desire*, 1581', *Shakespeare Quarterly* 36 (1985), 49–55.

Wilkinson, J., *Mary Boleyn: The True Story of Henry VIII's Favourite Mistress* (Stroud: Amberley, 2009).

Williams, N., *All the Queen's Men: Elizabeth and Her Courtiers* (Weidenfeld and Nicolson: London, 1972).

Williams, R., *Sweet Swan of Avon: Did a Woman Write Shakespeare?* (Sante Fe: Wilton Circle Press, 2012).

Wilson, R., *Secret Shakespeare: Studies in Theatre; Religion and Resistance* (Manchester: Manchester University Press, 2004).

Winstanley, L., *Hamlet and the Scottish Succession* (Cambridge: Cambridge University Press, 1921).

Witmore, M. and J. Hope, 'Shakespeare by the Numbers: On the Linguistic Texture of the Late Plays' in R. Lyne and S. Mukherjee (eds), *Early Modern Tragicomedy* (Cambridge: Boydel and Brewer, 2007).

Woods, S., 'Aemilia Lanyer and Ben Jonson: Patronage, Authority, and Gender', *Ben Jonson Journal* 1 (1994), 15–30.

Woods, S., *Lanyer: A Renaissance Woman Poet* (New York: Oxford University Press, 1999).

Woods, S., 'Anne Lock and Aemilia Lanyer: A Tradition of Protestant Women Speaking', in A. Boesky and M. T. Crane (eds), *Form and Reform in Renaissance England: Essays in Honor of Barbara Kiefer Lewalski* (Newark: University of Delaware Press, 2000).

Woods, S., 'Women at the Margins in Spenser and Lanyer' in P. Cheney and L. Silberman (eds), *Worldmaking Spenser: Explorations in the Early Modern Age* (Lexington: University Press of Kentucky, 2000).

Woods, S., 'Aemilia Lanyer, *Salve Deus Rex Judaeorum*' in A. Pacheco (ed.), *A Companion to Early Modern Women's Writing* (Oxford: Blackwell, 2002).

Woods, S., 'Lanyer and Southwell: A Protestant Woman's Re-Vision of St. Peter' in D. W. Doerksen and C. Hodgkins (eds), *Centered on the Word: Literature, Scripture, and the Tudor-Stuart Middle Way* (Newark: University of Delaware Press, 2004).

Woolfson, J., *Padua and the Tudors: English Students in Italy 1485–1603* (Toronto: University of Toronto Press, 1988).

Worthen, W. B., *Drama: Between Poetry and Performance* (Chichester: Wiley-Blackwell, 2010).

Wraight, A. D., *Christopher Marlowe and Edward Alleyn* (Chichester: Adam Hart, 1993).

Wraight, A. D., *Shakespeare: New Evidence* (London: A. Hart, 1996).

Wright, H. G., 'How Did Shakespeare Come to Know the *Decameron*?', *Modern Language Review* XLIX (1955), 45–8.

Wright, H. G., *Boccaccio in England: From Chaucer to Tennyson* (London: Athlone Press, 1957).

Wright, S. K., *The Vengeance of the Lord: Medieval Dramatizations of the Destruction of Jerusalem* (Toronto: Pontifical Institute of Medieval Studies, 1989).

Yates, F. A., *A Study of Love's Labour's Lost* (Cambridge: Cambridge University Press, 1936).

Yates, F. A., 'Queen Elizabeth as Astraea', *Journal of the Warburg and Courtauld Institutes* 10 (1947), 27–82.

Zacha, R. B., 'Iago and the Commedia dell'Arte', *Arlington Quarterly* 2 (1969), 98–116.

Zbierski, H., 'Possible Echoes of Boccaccio's *Decameron* in the Balcony Scene of *Romeo and Juliet*', *Studia Anglia Posnaniensia* 3:1–2 (1971), 131–38.

Acknowledgements

Special thanks to Dr Catherine Alexander, Dr William Green, Dr Saul Rosenberg, Dr Andrew B. Harris, Dr Robin Hirsch, Dr C. W. R. D. Moseley, and Dr David Lasocki for their comments on the manuscript, to Michael Posner for writing the Foreword, and to Joseph Atwill for suggesting the topic a decade ago. Thanks to Megan Abell, Florence Amit, Melisa Annis, David Basch, Ted Berger, Nicky Bishop, Ellen Brodie, Jen Browne, Andrée Aelion Brooks, Melody Brooks, Amanda Bruton, Alex Carney, Alexandra Cohen-Spiegler, Meaghan Cross, Bernardo Cubria, Ashley Diane Currie, Dajiela Dakic, Morganne Davies, Peter Dawkins, Stephen Day, Petra Denison, Christian Duck, Lila Dupree, Dr Michael Egan, Shykia Fields, Jonah Friedman, Dr Jane Gabin, Alicia Giangrisostomi, Alaina Hammond, Juliet Hanlon, Mimi Hirt, Aron Hirt-Manheimer, Linda Kay Hoff, Rebecca Honig Friedman, Dr Jean Howard, Leonard Jacobs, Dr Alan Jacobson, Morgan Jenness, Rafael Jordan, Mahayana Landowne, Donna Lazar, Michael Khan, Tatanya Kot, Sam Kahler, Dr Katherine Kurs, Sarah Lasley, Megan McGrath, Vicky McMahon, Edward Malin, Ana Martiny, Nicholas Martin-Smith, Hamilton Meadows, Edith Meeks, Michael Merriam, Laurie Mittelman, Kelly Morgan, Kate Murray, Rebecca Patterson, Kirsta Peterson, Kathleen Potts, Danielle Quisenberry, David Reck, Andrea Reese, Mitchell Riggs, Mark Rylance, Mark Sameth, Gary Schatsky, Isaac Scranton, Jonathan Slaff, Shana Solomon, M. George Stevenson, Stephen Squibb, Peggy Suzuki, Lindsay Tanner, Diane Tucker, Carey Urban, Ludovica Villar-Hauser, Dr Jack Wann, Elizabeth Weitzen, Cheri Wicks, Stephen Wisker, John Wyver and the librarians at Columbia University, the New York Public Library Schwartzman Reading Room, the British Library, the Shakespeare Institute Library at the University of Birmingham, and New York University Library. The curators at the Museum of London, the Folger Library and the Metropolitan Museum of Art have kindly answered my questions. The Halbreich Foundation and Dr Robert Brashear have generously supported the Dark Lady Players' demonstration productions, recognising their importance for social change. Jenny Greeman has worked with me as a director or assistant director for the last six years, finding ways to dramatise the underlying meanings of the plays. Bella Poynton has helped me understand the perspective of a young woman playwright and Monserrat Mendez has taught me how modern TV scriptwriting resembles the process of writing for the Renaissance theatre.

Thanks also to the Columbia University Shakespeare Seminar and to the institutions and venues where I have presented this material, including: the Smithsonian Institution, the Shakespearean Authorship Trust, Eastern Connecticut State University, Pace University,

State University of New York, City University of New York, New York University, the Shakespeare Oxford Society, the Kennedy Center American College Theatre Festival, the Lotos Club, Cornelia Street Café, Pleasantvillle Community Synagogue, West Park Church, the Manhattan JCC, Hudson Warehouse, Manhattan Theatre Source and H. B. Studios. Finally I am grateful for the illustrations to the Yale Center for British Art, to Edward Whitley at Bridgeman Art Library New York, to Eleanor Taylor at Berkeley Castle, to the Victoria & Albert Museum for permission to reproduce the Hilliard portrait, and acknowledge Boika Sokolova's book *Shakespeare's Romances as Interrogative Texts* (1992) for my modified diagram on the literary composition of *The Tempest*.

List of Illustrations

Art, Paul Mellon fund.

16   Amelia's lover, the Earl of Southampton (1594). *Henry Wriothesley, 3rd Earl of Southampton*, in the collection of the Fitzwilliam Museum, Bridgeman Art Library.

17   Amelia's lover, Christopher Marlowe. Portrait believed to be of Marlowe, Master and Fellows of Corpus Christi College, Bridgeman Art Library.

18   Venetian Recorder Players: woodcut from *Opera Intitulata Fontegara* by Silvestro Ganassi (1535), courtesy of *American Recorder Magazine*.

19   The Shoreditch Theatres (pre-1599). Detail of *The View of the Cittye of London from the North Towards the South*. For permission to reproduce this detail from the original in their collection (Ms. 1198 fol. 83), thanks to Utrecht University Library; for supplying the photograph, thanks to the Billy Rose Theatre Division, the New York Public Library for the Performing Arts, Lenox and Tilden Foundations.

20   The Globe Theatre and the Bear Garden, Bankside. Engraving by Edward John Roberts (1825) after unknown artist (the Bear Garden is the smaller building to the left), courtesy of the Yale Center for British Art.

21   Theatre Interior Bankside (*c.* 1595): Arendt van Buchell, after original now lost; *Interior of the Swan Theatre on Bankside*. Courtesy of Jonathan Reeve JR1080b3p299 16001650.

22   Shakespeare satirical cartoon in the First Folio. Engraving by cartoonist Martin Droeshout in the First Folio (1623). Courtesy of Stephen Porter and the Amberley Archives.

23   Idealised Shakespeare portrait. Engraving by George Vertue (1719), courtesy of the Yale Center for British Art.

24   *Willobie His Avisa*. Woodcut, frontispiece of *Willobie His AVISA OR The True Picture of a Modest and a Chast and Constant Wife* (1594), private collection.

25   Amelia's successful brother-in-law, Nicholas Lanier (1588–1666). Courtesy of the Yale Center for British Art.

26   Household of the Countess of Cumberland. Jan van Belcamp, *The Great Picture* (1646), Bridgeman Art Library.

27   Amelia remains buried in the parish church of St James, Clerkenwell, where she has lain since 1645. Licenced by Canstockphoto.com.

Index